Approaches to Teaching Pound's Poetry and Prose

Approaches to Teaching Pound's Poetry and Prose

Edited by

Demetres P. Tryphonopoulos

and

Ira B. Nadel

The Modern Language Association of America

New York 2021

Library of Congress Cataloging-in-Publication Data

Names: Tryphonopoulos, Demetres P., 1956– editor. | Nadel, Ira Bruce, editor.
Title: Approaches to teaching Pound's poetry and prose / edited by Demetres P. Tryphonopoulos and Ira B. Nadel.
Description: New York : The Modern Language Association of America, 2021. | Series: Approaches to teaching world literature, 1059-1133 ; 165 | Includes bibliographical references. | Summary: "Offers pedagogical techniques for teaching works by Ezra Pound, including his prosody, his references to classical and Asian traditions, and his role in modernism, as well as his fascism, anti-Semitism, and other problematic beliefs. Gives syllabus suggestions for undergraduate and graduate literature courses, including many online resources"— Provided by publisher.
Identifiers: LCCN 2020048460 (print) | LCCN 2020048461 (ebook) | ISBN 9781603294706 (hardcover) | ISBN 9781603294492 (paperback) | ISBN 9781603294508 (EPUB) | ISBN 9781603294515 (Kindle edition)

Subjects: LCSH: Pound, Ezra, 1885–1972—Study and teaching (Higher) | Authors, American—20th century—Study and teaching (Higher) | American literature—20th century—Study and teaching (Higher)
Classification: LCC PS3531.O82 Z5419 2021 (print) | LCC PS3531.O82 (ebook) | DDC 811/.52—dc23

LC record available at https://lccn.loc.gov/2020048460
LC ebook record available at https://lccn.loc.gov/2020048461

Approaches to Teaching World Literature 165
ISSN 1059-1133

Cover illustration: Lawrence Atkinson, *Abstract Composition*, c. 1914–18. Private collection, Mayor Gallery, London/Bridgeman Images.

Published by The Modern Language Association of America
85 Broad Street, Suite 500, New York, New York 10004-2434

www.mla.org

To Mary de Rachewiltz, who
"saw the splendour and wreckage
in that clarity
Gods moving in crystal
ichor amor"
—Ezra Pound, *The Cantos*

Σην μητέρα μου Παναγιώτα (1925–2018),
που χωρίς η ίδια να έχει πολλές γνώσεις πίστευε ακράδαντα πως η
"Παιδεία μόνη των κτημάτων αναφαίρετον και ζώντι και
τελευτήσαντι παραμένουσα."
—DPT

For Levi and Gideon, new readers of poetry and prose
—IBN

CONTENTS

ACKNOWLEDGMENTS

For a project this large and wide-ranging we must begin with thanks to Poundians worldwide who over the years have spearheaded the scholarship, criticism, textual study, and readings of Pound that have contributed to his sustained reputation as a major modernist. Our eighteen contributors reflect the diversity of research conducted today and the experience of Pound in the classroom. We are grateful to our fellow scholars and contributors for their brilliance but also for their patience and perseverance. One such scholar and mentor who deserves above all others our gratitude is Mary de Rachewiltz. We have dedicated this volume (the first of its kind) to her, since she has taught those of us who have had the good fortune to meet her, to read her work, to learn from attending the Ezuversity she, like her father, has run for decades at Brunnenberg—but also to learn from her graceful way in entertaining all readers and critics of Pound, even when she does not share their opinions or approaches.

The editors also wish to thank the editorial and production team at the MLA, in particular James Hatch, Jaime Cleland, and Zahra Brown. Their assistance has been vital in seeing this project develop from conception to completion. Declan Spring of New Directions has also been instrumental in responding to repeated requests for permissions. The Ezra Pound Society has also been supportive, not only through the valuable scholarship appearing in its online journal *Make It New* and in their continuing digital commentary on *The Cantos* but also in the overall support of the volume by society members.

Demetres thanks Litsa for her perseverance and support, and Panayiota and Panayiotes for their encouragement and faith in his work as a scholar. He would also like to thank the research officers and the library staff of the three institutions where he worked during the preparation of this volume (University of New Brunswick; Brandon University; and Augustana Faculty, University of Alberta) for their support. While working on this book, Demetres held (Canadian) Social Sciences and Humanities Research Council grants, and he would like to acknowledge the council's important contribution to this and other projects. Finally, he wishes to thank Ira B. Nadel, who stole time from his other projects so that he could do some of the heavy editorial lifting.

Ira gives constant thanks for the encouragement and love of Anne Mackenzie; Ryan Nadel; and Dara, Jon, Levi, and Gideon Pavlich; and commends his indefatigable coeditor Demetres Tryphonopoulos, clearly the most energetic Poundian on the planet.

Final acknowledgment must be to the teachers and readers of Pound, whether in Tokyo, London, Rome, or Brunnenberg. Without their active curiosity, Pound would likely not be discussed, challenged, or even read.

PREFACE

Poet, editor, essayist, translator, anthologist, and literary kingpin, Ezra Pound is unquestionably one of the most important, most fascinating, and most problematic writers of the twentieth century. Writing in the 1970s, his bibliographer Donald Gallup observed that Pound "attempted to give the [modernist] 'movement' more of a focus, perhaps, than it ever actually had, but by sheer force of personality and conviction he effected a revolution which still, a half century later, seems miraculous" (qtd. in Rossa 1).

No serious discussion of twentieth-century literature can overlook Pound's contributions to the body of modernist work as poet, translator, and literary critic, or his principal role in shaping the modernist movement. Both were acknowledged in his time; for instance, T. S. Eliot paid him the ultimate compliment in the dedication of his paradigmatic modernist poem *The Waste Land* (which Pound had edited heavily and championed as "the justification of the 'movement,' of our modern experiment, since 1900" [*Selected Letters* 180]). The dedication acknowledged Pound as "il miglior fabbro" ("the better craftsman"). Later Eliot praised Pound as "the inventor of China for the west," declaring that "Chinese poetry, as we know it to-day, is something invented by Ezra Pound" (Introduction [*Selected Prose*] 14, 15).

During Pound's long confinement at St. Elizabeths Hospital in Washington, D.C., following his indictment for treason, his influence did not wane, nor was his literary production suspended; in fact, many young but also established writers and critics (along with several sycophants, acolytes, and eccentrics) made pilgrimages to visit him—from Marianne Moore, Robert Lowell, Allen Ginsberg, Marshall McLuhan, Hugh Kenner, Charles Olson, Elizabeth Bishop, and H. L. Mencken to Harry M. Meacham, John Kasper, and Thomas T. Horton. Even the irascible Robert Frost was willing to join with Pound's advocates to advance his cause, arguably winning for him his release. If nothing else, Frost's action indicates that the New England poet had not forgotten the service Pound had provided him some forty years earlier by authoring a few influential reviews of his two first volumes of poetry, or the job Pound had done early on in drumming up his work. Indeed, Pound discovered, encouraged, promoted, and fed many artists, and helped them get published, without asking for anything in return. As Ernest Hemingway put it in *A Moveable Feast*, "Ezra was the most generous writer I have ever known and the most disinterested. He helped poets, painters, sculptors and prose writers that he believed in . . ." (98–99).

Through such advocacy and through his own work, Pound is largely responsible for making possible the innovations of successive generations of American poets, and it may be argued that he influenced the development of twentieth-century poetry and poetics more than any other individual. *The Cantos* is the poem most responsible for the unprecedented blossoming in American literature of formally innovative, open, and open-ended poetry. Pound's poetry questions received notions of poetic form through its radically modernist, abrupt, paratactic techniques of disconnectedness and discontinuity, visual experimentation, textual heteroglossia and heterogeneity, and undigested reality. "Any work of art," he said in 1913, "that is not a beginning, an invention, a discovery, is of little worth" ("How I Began" [*Early Writings*]).

Pound's poetry, and *The Cantos* specifically, may also be viewed as a summing up of the most abhorrent twentieth-century ideologies and prejudices. The author's misogyny, anti-Semitism, radical and often absurd economics, sexual politics, Fascism, and support of Mussolini ensure that teaching Pound is of necessity teaching conflict and controversy. One of the goals of this volume is to teach the troubling and difficult Pound by providing pedagogically sound examples of teaching the conflicts in his work. His politics and his personal history are rife with conflict but also ripe for class discussion, debate, and the sharpening of attentiveness to pivotal twentieth-century ideas and perspectives.

Another goal of this volume is to suggest ways of overcoming resistance to the elitism, fragmentation, indeterminacy, and obliqueness of avant-garde, experimental, complex modernist poems like the ones Pound and his high modernist fellow poets wrote. This is achieved by considering the ways in which, over the past hundred years, Pound's modernist experiments and literary and cultural criticism have influenced the reading, writing, and teaching of poetry and literature in the English-speaking world and beyond. Succeeding generations of poets have imitated, censured, contested, analyzed, praised, or spurned his experiments, aesthetics, criticism, ideas, and writerly example—but they have never dared to ignore his work.

Pound's writing has long been included in anthologies of English, American, and British literature, and his poetry, translations, and essays have appeared on syllabi from high school to the graduate level. The nearly one hundred responses we received to the MLA's survey of instructors who teach Pound's work offered generous, imaginative, expert, and pedagogically interesting information; they also suggested that Pound is taught across North America and overseas at all levels. This volume grapples with the pedagogical issues of teaching Pound and with his role as a radical experimentalist and a controversial figure whose aesthetics and problematical presence within modernism remain central to the study of literature of the twentieth century and beyond.

Basil Bunting's poem "On the Fly-Leaf of Pound's Cantos" may be read in various ways, including as a statement on the inescapability of Pound's epic poem "including history" (*ABC of Reading* 46). When it comes to delving Pound's work, one could wait until, like the Alps, it crumbles—or simply deal with the fact of its reality and sense, whatever that might be:

> There are the Alps. What is there to say about them?
> They don't make sense. Fatal glaciers, crags cranks climb,
> jumbled boulder and weed, pasture and boulder, scree,

et l'on entend, maybe, *le refrain joyeux et leger.*
Who knows what the ice will have scraped on the rock it is smoothing?
There they are, you will have to go a long way round
if you want to avoid them.
It takes some getting used to. There are the Alps,
fools! Sit down and wait for them to crumble!

This volume challenges readers and students to begin to delve into Pound's (and modernism's) aesthetics but also addresses those controversies which, however repugnant, make teaching Pound a perplexing, often frustrating, but always thought-provoking challenge and opportunity.

Part One

MATERIALS

Editions

When Ezra Pound published his first book of poems (*A Lume Spento*, privately printed in Venice in 1908) he was still very much a late-nineteenth-century poet, steeped in the archaisms of the Pre-Raphaelites. For *Ripostes*, however, published four years later, he reinvented himself as a modernist proponent of imagism before moving on, in rapid succession, to the avant-garde aesthetics of vorticism and translations from the Chinese (*Cathay*; 1915), Japanese (*"Noh"; or, Accomplishment*; 1916), Provençal ("Arnaut Daniel Poems"; 1920), and Latin (*Homage to Sextus Propertius*; 1934). Each of these forays into new identities and new languages constituted, as Pound explained, a "search for oneself" that entailed "casting off, as it were, complete masks of the self in each poem" (*Gaudier-Brzeska* 85). The poet's long career spanned a diversity of publishers as well as selves and genres, beginning with periodicals and newspapers and moving on to little magazines, like *Poetry*, *Blast*, and *The New Age*, and limited edition presses such as those of Elkin Mathews and John Rodker in London and the Hours Press in Paris. In the 1930s, Pound moved to university and literary trade presses like Faber and Faber, Farrar and Rinehart, and, finally, New Directions. For his economic or political materials, which James Laughlin at New Directions would not touch, he turned to Stanley Nott in the United Kingdom and Henry Regnery in the United States.

Different editions of Pound's poetry and prose employ diverse principles of selection and organization and tend to focus on some manageable number of Pound's many selves. For example, two early collections of his prose, *The Literary Essays of Ezra Pound* (1954) and *Selected Prose, 1909–1956* (1973), present drastically different, mutually exclusive Pounds. The first, edited by T. S. Eliot, presents Pound as strictly a paradigmatic modernist literary critic, craftsman, and translator, while the second, edited by William Cookson, allows some space for Pound's less vociferous essays on economics and politics. In Eliot's collection, readers encounter the representative great poet and cultural critic who founded modernism; in Cookson's, the crank who insisted that history, politics, and culture must be judged in racial terms.

The interested reader arrives at a similar impression in comparing D. D. Paige's early, largely sanitized *Selected Letters of Ezra Pound, 1907–1941* (1950) with *"I Cease Not to Yowl"* (1998), the collection of his letters to Olivia Rossetti Agresti in an edition by Demetres P. Tryphonopoulos and Leon Surette; of these, the latter volume does not shy away from honestly presenting Pound's pro-Axis and anti-Semitic sentiments. Such observations may also be made about "competing" collections of poetry and even the various Pound documentaries made over the years. For instance, a neophyte watching Lawrence Pitkethly's otherwise excellent and informative *Ezra Pound, American Odyssey* (1988) would learn about Pound's longtime companion, Olga Rudge, and Mary de Rachewiltz, their daughter, but would come away with no notion of the existence of Dorothy Shakespear Pound, the poet's wife, or Omar Pound, his son.

The ways in which Pound has been represented in the major anthologies are of much interest since instructors frequently use these works—for instance, *The Norton Anthology of American Literature*—for teaching Pound. Though not always choosing the same poems (and rarely choosing any of Pound's major prose statements), many anthologies do represent Pound's major phases, from the imagistic "In a Station of the Metro" to the translations of *Cathay*, the poet's farewell to London in *Hugh Selwyn Mauberley* (Pound's last single poem before becoming consumed entirely with *The Cantos*, his long "poem including history" [*ABC of Reading* 46]), and perhaps selections from *The Cantos* (often the first, "Homeric," canto and the forty-fifth, the famous usura canto).

Increasingly, teachers are also turning to digital versions of Pound's early imagist poems. The National Poetry Foundation's Web site, for example, offers a substantial selection of poetry and prose by Pound as well as a brief but accurate biography, an extensive bibliography of work by and about Pound, articles about Pound, and an "Audio and Podcasts" section (www.poetryfoundation.org/poets/ezra-pound). In addition, the Modernist Journals Project (MJP) offers access to *Poetry* magazine and other journals from the modernist period; on its Web site, teachers and students may read Pound's poems and other works in the context in which they first appeared and in the company of many of the very poets and writers encouraged, supported, and published by Pound himself ("Periodical Database").

Six print editions of Pound's early poetry (and, in one case, of his early poetry and prose) have been used over the last several decades. *Selected Poems* (1949), commissioned by Laughlin for New Directions and selected by the American poet and critic John Berryman, showcases, as Pound himself wished, the poetry written before 1922, and also includes forty-three percent of the already published portions of *The Cantos*. This volume, as Hugh Witemeyer has noted, "has probably introduced more American readers to Pound's verse than any other book" ("*Selected Poems*").

An increasing number of those who in the past had chosen the still available *Selected Poems of Ezra Pound* (1928; 1957) or other early collections now prefer Richard Sieburth's New Directions paperback entitled *New Selected Poems and Translations* (2010), which offers 281 pages of poems and 70 pages of notes. The text presents the poems in the chronological order of their original publication in little magazines, including the *English Review*, *Poetry*, *The Little Review*, *Blast*, and *The Dial*.

Essential for tracing Pound's early poetic development is the *Collected Early Poems of Ezra Pound* (1976), edited by Michael John King, with an introduction by Louis Martz. The volume includes ninety-nine poems from the early collections—*A Lume Spento*, *A Quinzaine for This Yule* (1908), *Personae* (1909), *Exultations* (1909), *Canzoni* (1911), and *Ripostes* (1912)—that Pound omitted in preparing his *Personae* (1926).

A substantial number of instructors wishing their students to become familiar with Pound's pre-*Cantos* poetic record choose *Personae: The Shorter Poems of Ezra Pound* (1990). This revised edition, arranged by Lea Baechler and A. Walton Litz, is based on the *Personae* of 1926, about which Pound had written to his father on September 12, 1925, "Have long wanted collected edtn." (*Ezra Pound to His Parents* 575). For *Personae*, Pound selected poetry from *Ripostes* and from his imagist and vorticist phases but also from his early major poetic sequences, *Cathay*, *Homage to Sextus Propertius*, and *Hugh Selwyn Mauberley* (1920). In an appendix, the editors add "Three Cantos" (1917).

Several teachers looking for a representative, accessible, and affordable introduction of both poetry and prose recommend Pound's *Early Writings: Poems and Prose* (2005), edited by Ira B. Nadel. Besides presenting useful introductory material, a valuable chronology, and finely tuned notes, it also offers a generous collection of early poetry, including "The Seafarer," *Homage to Sextus Propertius*, *Hugh Selwyn Mauberley*, "Three Cantos," several of the early cantos, and a number of Pound's essays on imagism and vorticism, as well as *The Chinese Written Character as a Medium for Poetry*, Pound's edited version of the essay by Ernest Fenollosa that is undeniably one of the most influential essays on modern poetry.

One of the factors informing the choice of poems to teach is the availability of companions, guides, and monographs dealing with certain poems or phases of Pound's poetic career, such as K. K. Ruthven's *A Guide to Ezra Pound's* Personae *(1926)* (1969); Peter Brooker's *A Student's Guide to the* Selected Poems of Ezra Pound (1979); Christine Froula's *A Guide to Ezra Pound's* Selected Poems (1983); and Akiko Miyake and colleagues' *A Guide to Ezra Pound and Ernest Fenollosa's* Classic Noh Theatre of Japan (1994).

Of course, also frequently taught is Pound's "endless poem of no known category," the 824-page-long *The Cantos*, published in nine volumes over a fifty-two-year period, its first periodical publication dating from 1917 (*Pound/Joyce* 102). To be more precise, instructors choose to teach individual cantos found in the anthologies or in other sources. The most favored are cantos 1–4, 8–11, 13, 17, 23, 45, 53, 74, 67, 81, and 116.

Most teachers note their preference for the first readable, affordable paperback edition of *The Cantos*, published by New Directions in 1996. It contains the entire poem in the order that it appeared beginning in 1917, but, as so many instructors note, it is not annotated and can appear daunting and dense. For guidance, readers may turn to works such as George Kearns's *Guide to Ezra Pound's Selected Cantos* (1980); William Cookson's *A Guide to* The Cantos *of Ezra Pound* (1985; revised and expanded 2001); Peter Makin's *Pound's* Cantos (1985); Richard Parker's *Readings in the* Cantos, *Vol. I* (2018), the first of a projected three-volume sequence of essays written by leading Poundian modernists and dealing with either informed approaches and analyses of a single canto or a small number of related cantos; and, most importantly, Carroll F. Terrell's two-volume *A Companion to the* Cantos *of Ezra Pound* (1980, 1984; combined edition 1993).

A few instructors in graduate courses use the 1996 New Directions edition of the poem to teach either individual sections or, more rarely, the entire poem. When time is short, *The Pisan Cantos* (particularly the 2003 New Directions paperback with annotations by Richard Sieburth) is often preferred as a representative section of the poem that is easier to analyze, its personal voice and relative informality establishing valuable clarity for the work.

Many instructors reported that they found it useful, and indeed necessary, to supplement the teaching of Pound's poetry with a number of his critical and cultural works, especially those he wrote in London in the 1910s and published in little magazines on both sides of the Atlantic. Depending on the nature and range of the course, instructors chose to include several of the following Poundian texts: "A Retrospect," "How to Read," "The Serious Artist," "The Teacher's Mission," and "Irony, Laforgue, and Some Satire"; excerpts from (and sometimes the entire texts of) *ABC of Reading*, *The Chinese Written Character as a Medium for Poetry*, "Vorticism" (as chapter 11 of *Gaudier-Brzeska* [81–94]), and *"Ezra Pound Speaking": Radio Speeches of World War II*; and essays from *Selected Prose*, including "I Gather the Limbs of Osiris," *Patria Mia*, "The Jefferson-Adams Letters as a Shrine and a Monument," "What Is Money For?," "A Visiting Card," "Gold and Work 1944," "Affirmations—As for Imagisme," and "Marianne Moore and Mina Loy."

Other Primary Sources

This section offers a glimpse at what has survived of Pound's enormous literary production and at the connections between the archive and the published history of literary politics. Given the importance of textual studies and the interest in recent decades in assessing Pound in broader literary and social contexts, including his central role in modernism, two kinds of resources are worth pointing to here: archival materials, and published collections of Pound's correspondence and periodical production.

There are extensive unpublished materials by and related to Pound available in manuscript libraries, including the Beinecke Rare Book and Manuscript Library at Yale; the Manuscript Division of the New York Public Library; the Harry Ransom Humanities Research Center, University of Texas, Austin; the Lilly Library at Indiana University; the Library of Congress; the University of Delaware Library; and the Rosenbach Museum and Library in Philadelphia. Canada's major Pound holdings include, among others, the National Public Archives, Ottawa, Ontario; and the University of Victoria Archives and Special Collections, McPherson Library, Victoria, British Columbia. Several libraries in the United Kingdom, including the British Library's Archives and Manuscripts Department, have extensive Pound collections. Though much of what used to be held at what is now the Ezra Pound Research Center in Brunnenburg and Merano in Italy has been sold (primarily to the libraries in the United States mentioned above), there are still many miscellaneous manuscripts by or related to Pound in various Italian collections, including, for instance, the Vivaldi collection in the Biblioteca Nazionale in Turin. These repository libraries have been mined over the years and continue to be explored for unpublished work, especially for letters written by and to the poet. For example, the Rosenbach Museum in Philadelphia houses the Marianne Moore papers, including the extensive Pound-Moore correspondence.

Reading Pound's correspondence is a valuable way to familiarize oneself with his career, the development of his aesthetics and thought in general, and his role in the genesis of modernism. During his lifetime Pound had well over six hundred correspondents and wrote approximately a quarter of a million letters. More than thirty volumes of single-author correspondences have appeared so far, several of them by New Directions and Norton.

Published correspondences may be organized in terms of recipients, although the first edition of Pound's letters, the *Selected Letters, 1907–1941* (1950), edited by D. D. Paige, comprises letters to eighty-seven correspondents; Roxana Preda's *Ezra Pound's Economic Correspondence 1933–1940* (2006) and Zhaoming Qian's *Ezra Pound's Chinese Friends* (2008) also include letters to diverse recipients. Many collections, such as *Pound/Williams: Selected Letters of Ezra Pound and William Carlos Williams* (1996), edited by Witemeyer, or *Pound/Cummings: The Correspondence of Era Pound and E. E. Cummings*, edited by Barry Ahearn, document Pound's correspondence with fellow writers. Others collections contain letters to his family and friends, such as *Ezra Pound and Dorothy Shakespear: Their Letters, 1909–1914* (1985), edited by Omar Pound and A. Walton Litz; *The Selected Letters of Ezra Pound to John Quinn, 1915–1924* (1991), edited by Timothy Materer; *Ezra and Dorothy Pound: Letters in Captivity, 1945–1946* (1999), edited by Omar Pound and Robert Spoo; and *Ezra Pound to His Parents: Letters 1895–1929* (2010), edited by de Rachewiltz and others. Several collections bring together letters to and from editors of little magazines and publishers, including *Pound, Thayer, Watson and* The Dial*: A Story in Letters* (1994), edited by Walter Sutton, and *Ezra Pound and James Laughlin: Selected Letters* (1994), edited by David M. Gordon. A few, such as *Ezra Pound and Senator Bronson Cutting: A Political Correspondence 1930–1935* (1995), edited by E. P. Walkiewicz and Witemeyer, document Pound's various communications with politicians in the United States.

Several instructors report assigning series of letters or excerpts from published correspondences such as Paige's *Selected Letters*, especially Pound's 1916 letters to Iris Barry on poetics (86–97), the 8 July 1922 letter to Felix E. Schelling on his early poetry and Eliot's *The Waste Land* (178–182), and the 11 April 1927 letter to his father on the structure of *The Cantos* (210–11).

Finally, the key (and certainly most complete and reliable) published resource for the reader who wishes to follow the development of Pound's thought is the eleven-volume *Ezra Pound's Poetry and Prose: Contributions to Periodicals* (1991), now out of print but available in digital form to members of the Ezra Pound Society (www.ezrapoundsociety.org/index.php/english-language-scholarship-on-ezra-pound/poetry-and-prose).

Modern Critical Reception

The controversy generated by Pound's Rome Radio broadcasts, his indictment for treason, his six-month imprisonment in Pisa, and his sentencing to confinement in St. Elizabeths Hospital in 1945 contributed to the neglect of his work at a time when the New Critics were already unsympathetic to his poetic project and his readership had fallen. But his thirteen years at St. Elizabeths after his long exile in Europe (Venice, 1908; London, 1908–21; Paris, 1921–25; and Rapallo, 1925–45) also seemed to revitalize him and his reputation: a constant stream of important writers and critics made the pilgrimage to visit him, particularly after the publication of the widely admired but controversial *Pisan Cantos* (1948), which won a newly established award, the Library of Congress's first Bollingen Prize "for the highest achievement in American poetry" (qtd. in Cole); and he continued to write copiously, borrowing books from the Library of Congress and the Catholic University of America.

It was primarily thanks to the work of a Canadian scholar working on a Ph.D. at Yale that Pound's work then began to receive serious critical attention. Hugh Kenner, who in early June 1948 had been driven by Marshall McLuhan from Toronto to Washington, D.C., to visit Pound at St. Elizabeths, published the groundbreaking *The Poetry of Ezra Pound* in 1951. Initiating the discussion and annotation of Pound's work was John Hamilton Edwards, the editor of the *Pound Newsletter* (1954–1956) and author, with William W. Vasse, of the *Annotated Index to the* Cantos *of Ezra Pound* (1957). Also heralding the serious study of Pound in the 1950s was the publication or reissuing of editions of his prose work and essays, beginning with Paige's *Selected Letters of Ezra Pound, 1907–1941*, which focused especially on Pound's aesthetics and his contributions to the founding of modernism. *The Translations* (1953), introduced by Kenner, demonstrated Pound's impact on translation studies and comparative literature; and *Literary Essays* (1954), edited and introduced by Eliot, signaled Pound's influence, as Eliot argued, as the most important literary critic of modernism.[1] John Espey's *Ezra Pound's* Mauberley (1955), a New Critical study of Pound's "farewell" to London that is part explication and part justification of Pound's aesthetics circa 1920, remains important to this day.

Additional recommended early works include Clark Emery's *Ideas into Action: A Study of Pound's* Cantos (1958), Donald Davie's *Ezra Pound, Poet as Sculptor* (1964), Noel Stock's *Reading the* Cantos (1966), Daniel S. Pearlman's

The Barb of Time: On the Unity of Pound's Cantos (1969), Herbert Schneidau's *Ezra Pound: The Image and the Real* (1969), and Witemeyer's *The Poetry of Ezra Pound, Forms and Renewal, 1908–1920* (1969). Kenner's *The Pound Era* (1971) is the fullest and certainly the most influential early account of Pound and modernism. Two later works that advanced Pound studies are Ronald Bush's *The Genesis of Ezra Pound's* Cantos (1976) and Michael André Bernstein's *The Tale of the Tribe: Ezra Pound and the Modern Verse Epic* (1980).

In 1971, Terrell established the National Poetry Foundation (NPF) at the University of Maine at Orono as a center for Pound scholarship and begun publishing *Paideuma: A Journal Devoted to Ezra Pound Scholarship.* Under Terrell's editorship (1972–1998), this journal remained the primary venue for Pound studies, explicating and annotating Pound's work, especially *The Cantos.* It was also during this period that Terrell compiled and published his two-volume companion to *The Cantos*; hosted a series of conferences for poets and Pound scholars;[2] and published more than a dozen important Pound-related books in a new series under the NPF imprint.[3] Once the job of glossing Pound's work had been largely accomplished, the journal was retitled twice, most recently as *Paideuma: Modernist and Contemporary Poetry and Poetics.* The Ezra Pound Society, under the direction of Preda, its president, responded to the ongoing need for a Pound-focused journal by founding the online *Make It New* in 2013.

It was not until after Pound's death in 1972 that his reputation as a major poet and the preeminent literary figure of the modernist era took final shape. A number of critics began to respond to *The Pound Era,* arguing for or against Kenner's presentation of Pound as the key figure of international literary modernism. In the 1970s, critics as different as Davie (*Ezra Pound*), Brooker, Stock (*Life*), William M. Chase, Christine Brooke-Rose, Leon Surette (*Light*), Timothy Materer, Max Nänny, Sieburth (*Instigations*), and James Wilhelm (*Dante and Pound*) produced critical studies that took for granted Pound's status as a major figure but often investigated and questioned his ambition and achievement, especially in *The Cantos.*

In the 1980s, Pound scholarship deepened substantially, placing *The Cantos* at the very center of efforts to evaluate Pound's status and influence. The explicatory work done in dissertations and articles in the 1970s made possible the work of scholars such as Michael Alexander (*The Poetic Achievement of Ezra Pound* [1980]) and Guy Davenport (*Cities on Hills: A Study of I–XXX of Ezra Pound's Cantos* [1983]. A number of other books published in the 1980s follow this kind of approach, applying it primarily to *The Cantos,* but with different emphasis in each case. These include Massimo Bacigalupo's bold *The Forméd Trace: The Later Poetry of Ezra Pound* (1980); Forrest Read's quirky *'76, One World, and the* Cantos *of Ezra Pound* (1981); and Wendy Stallard Flory's informed *Ezra Pound and* The Cantos*: A Record of Struggle* (1980). A parallel series of important studies began with Ronald Bush's *The Genesis of Ezra Pound's* Cantos (1976) and Richard Taylor's ambitious—as can be gathered from his *Variorum Edition of "Three Cantos" by Ezra Pound: A Prototype* (1991)—but still incomplete efforts to construct a variorum edition. Taylor's project examined the history of the text and tracked the aesthetic and political choices made in textual transmission. Attention to textual matters is also central to *Ezra Pound's* Cantos*: The Story of the Text, 1948–1975*, by Barbara Eastman (1979); *To Write Paradise: Style and Error in Pound's* Cantos, by Christine Froula (1984); *The Hall of Mirrors:* Drafts and Fragments *and the End of Pound's* Cantos, by Peter Stoicheff (1995); and *A Poem Containing History: Textual Studies in* The Cantos, an edited collection by Lawrence S. Rainey (1997).

While explication remains the main impetus and methodology for the study of *The Cantos*, poststructuralist readings of Pound's poetics, politics, and economics also began to emerge in the '80s. Such early studies continue to be divided along these lines and also between two opposing arguments: on one side, that Pound is aware of the arbitrariness of the sign, and that his poetic praxis is one of liberating and redemptive indeterminacy; and, on the other, that he is innocent of such understandings and that he practices the totalitarian poetics of logocentricity. This kind of divide can be seen in work by Ian F. A. Bell (*Critic as Scientist* [1981] and *Ezra Pound: Tactics for Reading* [1982]) and Paul Smith (1983), and in the essays collected by Marianne Korn in *Ezra Pound and History* (1985). Jean-Michel Rabaté's nuanced *Language, Sexuality, and Ideology in Ezra Pound's* Cantos (1986) and John Steven Childs's *Modernist Form: Pound's Style in the Early* Cantos (1986) further advance this critical division.

Writing in 1998, D. Britton Gildersleeve describes Pound publishing during the 1980s as "fast and furious" and in the 1990s as "a virtual explosion" (229, 232). As books designed to annotate, explicate, and summarize various readings of *The Cantos* continued to appear (George Kearns's *Ezra Pound:* The Cantos [1989] is one such example), many scholars were now producing general studies that questioned Pound's cultural views and aesthetics. While Tim Redman in *Ezra Pound and Italian Fascism* (1991) and Paul Morrison in *The Poetics of Fascism: Ezra Pound, T. S. Eliot, Paul de Man* (1996) offer even-handed narratives of Pound's Italian allegiances, Robert Casillo, in his earlier, aptly titled *The Genealogy of Demons: Anti-Semitism, Fascism, and the Myths of Ezra Pound* (1988), castigates Poundians who conveniently refuse to consider the gravity of Pound's troubling fascism and anti-Semitism. More recently, Matthew Feldman, in *Ezra Pound's Fascist Propaganda, 1935–45* (2013), uses the archive effectively to show that Pound was a staunch and vocal Fascist.

Other monographs focused on a variety of topics (from Pound's obsession with Fascism and his radical economic theories to his symbolist inheritances and his appropriations of Chinese poetry) not thoroughly or authoritatively confronted until this time. These included *The Futurist Moment*, by Marjorie Perloff (1986); *Shapes of Power*, by Bruce Fogelman (1988); *The American Ezra Pound*, by Flory (1989); *Ezra Pound as Literary Critic*, by K. K. Ruthven (1990); *Imitating the Italians*, by Reed Way Dasenbrock (1991); *The Final Sculpture*, by Michael North (1991); *ABC of Influence*, by Christopher Beach (1992); *Ezra Pound and the Symbolist Inheritance*, by Scott Hamilton (1992); *A Calculus of*

Ezra Pound, by Philip Kuberski (1992); *Learning to Be Modern*, by Gail McDonald (1993); *Ezra Pound, Wyndham Lewis, and Radical Modernism*, by Vincent Sherry (1993); *Changing Voices: The Modern Quoting Poem*, by Leonard Diepeveen (1993); *The Origins of Modernism: Eliot, Pound, Yeats and the Rhetorics of Renewal*, by Stan Smith (1994); *Ezra Pound, Popular Genres, and the Discourse of Culture*, by Michael Coyle (1995); *Orientalism, Modernism, and the American Poem*, by Robert Kern (1996); and *Ezra Pound and the Appropriation of Chinese Poetry*, by Ming Xie (1999). Several of these studies focus on Pound's poetics but also place his work in a broader literary and cultural context; others are reassessments of modernism in which Pound continues to hold a key role.

Throughout his life Pound remained interested in metaphysics and especially the occult and Neoplatonism. Introduced by Surette in *A Light from Eleusis* (1979), this interest was also explored by Kevin Oderman in *Ezra Pound and the Erotic Medium* (1987), James Longenbach in *Stone Cottage: Pound, Yeats, and Modernism* (1988), and Miyake in *Ezra Pound and the Mysteries of Love: A Plan for* The Cantos (1991); it was further developed in Tryphonopoulos's *The Celestial Tradition: A Study of Ezra Pound's* The Cantos (1992) and was addressed definitively by Surette himself in *The Birth of Modernism: Ezra Pound, Eliot, W. B. Yeats, and the Occult* (1993). More recently, in *Ezra Pound and Neoplatonism* (2004), Peter Liebregts has extended this important thread in Pound's thought by arguing that Pound was attracted to Neoplatonism because the movement was not dogmatic and was not part of an organized religion (*Ezra Pound and Neoplatonism*). Mark Byron has taken this topic in another fruitful direction in *Ezra Pound's Eriugena* (2014), presenting the Carolingian thinker as a fulcrum in Pound's work for both Neoplatonism and Confucianism.

Another important angle pursued in the 1990s is a reconsideration of Pound's economics, often in terms of its relation to his Fascist ideology and fixation with banking conspiracies. Peter Wilson's *A Preface to Ezra Pound* (1997) explains how Pound's interest in Fascism informs his economics. Alec Marsh's *Money and Modernity: Pound, Williams, and the Spirit of Jefferson* (1998) and Surette's *Pound in Purgatory: From Economic Radicalism to Anti-Semitism* (1999) demonstrate Pound's deep commitment to economic theory but also the troubled provenance and consequences of his ideology. In *Mosaic Modernism: Anarchism, Pragmatism, Culture* (2000), David Kadlec positions modernist literature within an anarchist discourse, arguing as well that Pound began his economic and political education not within Orage's *The New Age* but in the feminist circles of Dora Mardsen and Harriet Shaw Weaver's *New Freewoman* and the *Egoist*. Rainey offers further materialist criticism in *Ezra Pound and the Monument of Culture: Text, History and the Malatesta Cantos* (1991) and in his important edited collection *A Poem Containing History: Textual Studies in* The Cantos (1997) as well as his own *Institutions of Modernism* (1998), this last an outstanding model of cultural criticism in which the writer interrogates his own ideological commitments.

In the first decade of the twenty-first century, a number of key texts emerged dealing with Pound's involvement in the literary, visual, and performing arts (for seminal earlier scholarship on Pound and visual art, see Harriet Zinnes [1980] and Richard Humphreys and Allen Bowness [1985]). Steven Yao's superb *Translation and the Language of Modernism: Gender, Politics* (2002) offers an absorbing study of translation as a mode of literary production in Anglo-American modernism. Zhaoming Qian's *The Modernist Response to Chinese Art: Pound, Moore, Stevens* (2003), in which he points out that literary scholars, preoccupied with hunting for marks of literary influence, have missed the prevailing impact of Chinese art (painting in particular) on both the modernists mentioned in his title and others, fulfills the promises of his *Orientalism and Modernism: The Legacy of China in Pound and Williams* (1995)—promises that also eventuate in his edited collection *Ezra Pound and China* (2003). In *Ezra Pound and the Visual Culture of Modernism* (2007), Rebecca Beasley argues convincingly that Pound's intense focus on the visual arts coincides with those early periods of aesthetic crisis in his work, which *The Edinburgh Companion to Ezra Pound and the Visual Arts* (2019), edited by Preda, explores. Margaret Fisher and Robert Hughes continue the important work on Pound and music first undertaken in *Ezra Pound and Music: The Complete Criticism*, by R. Murray Schaffer (1977). A number of publications have ensued, including Margaret Fisher's *Ezra Pound's Radio Operas: The BBC Experiments, 1931–1933* (2002)—arguably the best study of Pound and music written to date—but also *Cavalcanti: A Perspective on the Music of Ezra Pound*, edited by Hughes and Fisher (2003), and performance and facsimile editions of Pound's 1923 opera *Le Testament*, also edited by Hughes and Fisher (2008).

There is a dearth of studies of Pound's masculinity and sexuality and his personal and professional relationships with women. To quote Michael André Bernstein, in Pound's poetry and prose, representations of sexuality (and women) are useful so long as they are "bounded and made serviceable by the shaping, linear, and phallic male order" (358). And yet, with the exception of a couple of critics (Oderman and Tryphonopoulos come to mind), in the 1980s and 1990s, mainstream critics seem to continue the tradition started in *The Pound Era*, Kenner's magnum opus, in which even the names of modernist women poets are largely ignored, with H.D. receiving half a dozen references and "Miss Lowell" mentioned along "with Miss Sitwell, the Amy Lowell of poetry" (553). It's fortunate therefore that a number of critics, mostly women, have addressed the topic in nonexclusionary narratives. Best among them may be Shari Benstock, who, in *Women of the Left Bank: Paris, 1900–1940*, expands our perception of the vibrant Parisian modernist community of American, British, and French writers, editors, and publishers working in the first half of the twentieth century. Other works by scholars of feminism, gender, and sexuality that have helped rescue modernist literary scholarship from one-sidedness include Susan Stanford Friedman's groundbreaking *Psyche Reborn: The Emergence of H.D.* (1987); Jane Marcus's *Virginia Woolf and the Languages of Patriarchy* (1987); Rachel Blau

DuPlessis's *Writing beyond the Ending: Narrative Strategies of Twentieth-Century Women Writers* (1985) and *The Pink Guitar: Writing as Feminist Practice* (1990); Wayne Koestenbaum's "The Waste Land: T. S. Eliot's and Ezra Pound's Collaboration on Hysteria" (1989); Bonnie Kime Scott's edited *The Gender of Modernism: A Critical Anthology* (1990); Andrew Hewitt's *Political Inversions: Homosexuality, Fascism, and the Modernist Imaginary* (1996); and Janet Lyon's *Manifestoes: Provocations of the Modern* (1999).

New collections of essays, letters, and editions of Pound's work, both previously published and archival, have appeared recently, namely *Ezra Pound's* Cantos*: A Casebook* (2006), edited by Makin. A wonderful resource for both teachers and first-time readers of Pound, the *Casebook* reprints key essays, formerly difficult to obtain, on the poet and his work, and two important critical interviews, including Donald Hall's *Paris Review* interview from 1962. Nadel's edited collection *Ezra Pound in Context* (2010) contains forty-two densely argued new essays on a broad range of topics of vital interest to specialists, teachers, and students of Pound. Moreover, *Ezra Pound and* Globe *Magazine: The Complete Correspondence* (2015), edited by Michael T. Davis and Cameron McWhirter, along with textual editions such as *Posthumous Cantos* (2015), edited by Bacigalupo, offer good examples of the kind of archival work that continues to be the focus of new and seasoned Pound scholars.

Critical studies in the 2000s continue with such work as Vincent Sherry's *The Great War and the Language of Modernism* (2003), which includes a substantial chapter on Pound that works to restore a key understanding of modernism's historicity; Feng Lan's *Ezra Pound and Confucianism: Remaking Humanism in the Face of Modernity* (2005); Miranda Hickman's *The Geometry of Modernism: The Vorticist Idiom in Lewis, Pound, H.D., and Yeats* (2005); Sean Pryor's *W. B. Yeats, Ezra Pound, and the Poetry of Paradise* (2011), Surette's *Dreams of a Totalitarian Utopia: Literary Modernism and Politics* (2011), David Ten Eyck's *Ezra Pound's Adams Cantos* (2012); Robert Stark's *Ezra Pound's Early Verse and Lyric Tradition: A Jargoner's Apprenticeship* (2012), and Paul Stasi and Josephine Park's *Ezra Pound in the Present: Essays on Pound's Contemporaneity* (2016). In 2019, Mark Byron and Sophie Barnes published an edition of *The Blue Spill*, an unfinished detective novel collaboratively written by Pound and Olga Rudge during the winter of 1930. Finally, in late 2019, Peter Liebgrets's superb *Translations of Greek Tragedy in the Work of Ezra Pound* breaks new ground but also acts as a corrective. While scholars have made much of Pound's translations from Latin, Chinese, and Provençal, they have paid little attention to his translations of Greek tragedy (including those of Aeschylus's *Agamemnon* and Sophocles's *Women of Trachis* and *Elektra*). Liebgrets proves wrong the misconception that Pound's Greek was inadequate and shows the importance of his translations of Greek to his later work.

Investigation of Pound's literary career is not only continuing but expanding. Instructors and students may follow the trends of Pound criticism and experience its volume by reading *American Literary Scholarship: An Annual*, published by

Duke University Press. The annual devotes a long chapter in each volume to "Pound and Eliot": Pound is, thenceforth, discussed in sections entitled "Text, Biography, and Bibliography"; "General Studies"; "Relation to Other Writers"; "The Shorter Poems and Translations"; and "*The Cantos*." The amount of space devoted to Pound in each volume indeed suggests that there is no American poet or novelist who attracts more critical interest.[4]

Biographical Backgrounds

This section contains brief critical discussions of all book-length biographies of Pound. The earliest of the principal biographies of Pound, Charles Norman's *Ezra Pound* (1960, rev. 1969) and Eustace Mullins's *This Difficult Individual, Ezra Pound* (1961), are both difficult to evaluate today because of their biases. Mullins, an anti-Semite and Pound acolyte, sees Pound as a polemicist; for context, readers should consult *The Secrets of the Federal Reserve* (1952), a controversial book (its publication caused Mullins to lose his job at the Federal Reserve) written at Pound's request and with his intellectual and material support. Norman's account presents Pound as an accessible poet and teacher but offers an impressionistic, occasionally exaggerated profile.

Other early lives include Patricia Hutchins's *Ezra Pound's Kensington* (1965), offering helpful details about Pound's early London life, and *The Trial of Ezra Pound* (1966), by Julien Cornell, the lawyer whom Laughlin selected to represent Pound in 1945. This book offers an accurate account of Pound's early Washington, D.C., days following his arrival from Italy on 18 November 1945 and documents his brief period in and out of District Court before being committed, on 21 December, to St. Elisabeths Hospital.

Stock's *The Life of Ezra Pound* (1970) is a helpful account of the poet's life that was written with the support of Pound and his immediate family. Stock also had full access to Pound's collection of books and papers at Brunnenburg Castle, Tirolo di Merano, Italy. Much of this material was later sold to the Beinecke Library at Yale; Stock's own papers are at the University of Toledo in Ohio.

C. David Heymann, in *Ezra Pound: The Last Rower* (1976), the first biography after Pound's death, emphasized the political rather than the literary Pound, using newly released FBI files to provide a documentary record of Pound's Fascist activity. In *The Roots of Treason: Ezra Pound and the Secrets of Saint Elizabeth* (1984), an animated account of Pound's St. Elizabeths years (1945–1958), the psychiatrist E. Fuller Torrey argued that Pound was psychotic but not mentally unstable. Torrey, who worked for nine years as a ward physician at St. Elizabeths, had full access to Pound's psychiatric records.

John Tytell, in *Ezra Pound: The Solitary Volcano* (1987), provides a more literary account. He argues that Pound's influence as an American bohemian in

London and Paris, who led the march toward modernism through his writing, his promotion of Eliot and Joyce, and his general literary rabble-rousing, should outweigh the author's political prejudices in the evaluation of his legacy. Humphrey Carpenter's *A Serious Character: The Life of Ezra Pound* (1988) is a 1,005-page narrative, the first since Noel Stock's to offer a complete life, but contains little literary criticism. Carpenter's Pound is agile and slippery, by turns an editor, translator, librettist, poet, economist, Sinologist, and expert on foreign affairs. The volume of material included ensured the book's prominence among Pound biographies for nearly two decades.

James J. Wilhelm, in *Ezra Pound in London and Paris, 1908–1925* (1990) and *Ezra Pound, The Tragic Years, 1925–1972* (1994), offers a chronological rather than thematic narrative that rarely attempts to define or present Pound's personality, reflecting a deep knowledge of the work but perhaps not of the man. The two volumes stand as an examination rather than an analysis but are useful for their documentation and incorporation of other figures, such as Nancy Cunard and Wyndham Lewis, into the story.

Anne Conover draws on the extensive correspondence between Pound and Rudge, his lover and the mother of his daughter, to deliver the first account of their relationship in *Olga Rudge and Ezra Pound* (2001). Even though Pound and his wife, Dorothy Shakespear Pound, lived with Rudge (and later with de Rachewiltz) for a time, Conover says little about that difficult and persistent triangle or Rudge's view of Pound's other romantic involvements over the course of their fifty-year relationship.

David Moody's three-volume *Ezra Pound: Poet: A Portrait of the Man and His Work* is the most recent and comprehensive reading of Pound as a writer. *The Young Genius, 1885–1920* (2007), *The Epic Years, 1921–1939* (2014), and *The Tragic Years, 1939–1972* (2015) are accurate and detailed and work toward the reconceptualization of Pound as a modernist poet par excellence rather than simply a polemicist and promoter of modernism. This is a thoughtful reading of Pound's full life, using his publications to tell the story. Instead of offering drama or hagiography, Moody works to link texts and life, repeatedly showing their interrelation. Pound the editor becomes as important as Pound the writer.

Three additional and useful texts that highlight Laughlin's role in Pound studies as the founder and longtime publisher of New Directions begin with Laughlin's *Pound as Wuz: Essays and Lectures on Ezra Pound* (1987). Gregory Barnhisel's *James Laughlin, New Directions, and the Remaking of Ezra Pound* (2005), is a study that may be viewed as a sequel to Laughlin's stories about his experiences at Pound's Ezuversity in Rapallo, Italy, during the early 1930s. The term *remaking* in Barnhisel's title alludes to Laughlin's struggle, largely effective, to sanitize Pound by ignoring and containing his repugnant politics and economic views, privileging instead his literary achievement. Ian S. MacNiven's *"Literchoor Is My Beat": A Life of James Laughlin, Publisher of New Directions* (2014) complements Barnhisel's narrative and reveals important personal details about Laughlin and Pound.

Helen Carr's "group biography" aptly entitled *The Verse Revolutionaries: Ezra Pound, H.D., and the Imagists* (2009) is another key, thoroughly researched text. An authoritative, 982-page history of the imagist movement, part intellectual history and part social history of early-twentieth-century London, it provides a detailed account of the lives of the imagists, that famous, avant-garde group of American and British poets who changed poetic form for ever.

For brief lives of Pound, see Nadel's *Ezra Pound, A Literary Life* (2004) and Marsh's *Ezra Pound* (2011). Nadel attempts a concise narrative of the literary career, while Marsh stresses the poet's final period and his economic and political ideas.

Finally, a recent biographical profile of Pound at St. Elizabeths by Daniel Swift, *The Bughouse: The Poetry, Politics, and Madness of Ezra Pound* (2017), mixes biography with memoir and intellectual, social, and publishing history, concentrating on the psychodrama of Pound's stay at St. Elizabeths, where he and his visitors created, in Swift's words, "the world's most unorthodox literary salon" (99).

Reference Materials

The most comprehensive bibliography of Pound's primary works is Donald Gallup's *A Bibliography of Ezra Pound*, first published in 1963; reissued in a second, corrected edition in 1969; and revised and reissued as the "definitive," 548-page edition in 1983. The Yale bibliographer and curator's expert bibliography is especially useful for providing the original context, often in the little periodicals and modernist magazines of the period, of Pound's poetry and prose; its publication made possible the systematic study of Pound.

Gallup's successor, Archie Henderson, has continued to revise and correct the bibliography, and in 1983 he published "Additions and Corrections to the Revised Edition of the Ezra Pound Bibliography" (Gallup and Henderson). Henderson's "Updating the Pound Bibliography" (2008) describes and lists materials produced by the Pound industry since the 1980s; another result is the "Bibliography of English Language Scholarship on Ezra Pound," assembled and edited by Henderson and Preda.

Much of Pound's early poetry and prose (along with the work of the modernist poets and prose writers he supported) is now available through the Modernist Journals Project (modjourn.org/journal), which reproduces electronically entire series of such little magazines as *Blast*, *The Little Review*, *The New Age*, and *Poetry*. As of this writing, MJP has digitized little magazines that appeared in Boston, Chicago, Dublin, Florence, Garden City (New York), London, and New York from 1896 to 1928. The MJP also offers "Teaching and Research Pages," including lesson plans and ideas for classroom and research projects using MJP resources (modjourn.org/teaching-and-research), as well as an interactive wiki on the theme "Towards a Theory for Periodical Studies."

Other online resources of particular interest to teachers and students include, first, the Ezra Pound Society Web site (ezrapoundsociety.org), which publishes the online journal *Make It New* and offers a wide variety of information and links, including biographical and bibliographical information, an extensive number of which are interactive, and digital versions of most of Pound's works (as of this writing, sixteen of his poetry collections and sixteen prose texts). The New Directions site (www.ndbooks.com/author/ezra-pound) lists all the books published and kept in print since the mid-1930s by New Directions (including bibliographical information and brief, precise descriptions of each). Project Gutenberg (www.gutenberg.org) offers ten Pound texts that have been digitized and may be downloaded or read online without charge. The Internet Archive (archive .org), a nonprofit that was founded to build an Internet library, contains—as of January 4, 2020—825 Ezra Pound "results," not only from searchable texts by and about Pound but also including numerous audio files, movies, and documentaries. An instructor could create a syllabus on Pound using this resource alone. Letters, reports, and transcriptions of Pound's Rome Radio broadcasts are available from the Web site of the United States Department of Justice at www.justice .gov/criminal/frequently-requested-records-0. MAPS, the Modern American Poetry site (www.modernamericanpoetry.org), contains, among other resources, a brief biographical note on Pound by Clive Wilmer, excerpts from Pound's essays, and abridged critical commentary on early poems and several cantos.

For criticism of secondary sources and further bibliographic information besides the important, ongoing work by Henderson, the most useful resources are *Ezra Pound, The Critical Heritage* (1972), edited by Eric Homberger, and *Ezra Pound Criticism 1905–1985: A Chronological Listing of Publications in English* (1991), by Volker Bischoff. The Gale *Literature Resource Center* offers useful background information as well as an *MLA International Bibliography* module with citations for books, articles, and dissertations from 1926 to the present, with links, when available, to the full texts (www.gale.com/c/literature-resource-center).

Multimedia Resources

Increasingly, teachers consult and point their students to a plethora of multimedia and Internet resources. We provide here a few secure and easily accessible examples from this ever-changing and growing landscape and refer readers to Anderson Araujo's essay in this volume for additional resources.

Recommended multimedia resources include the documentary *Ezra Pound: American Odyssey* (1988), directed by Lawrence Pitkethly; Bernard Dew's two dramatizations of Pound (*Canto 116, Cathay*); and the 2011 album and digital download *Ego Scriptor Cantilenae: The Music of Ezra Pound*. Additionally, there is the indispensable online exhibition by the University of Delaware Library Special Collections Division entitled *Ezra Pound in His Time and Beyond: The Influence of Ezra Pound on Twentieth-Century Poetry* (www.lib.udel.edu/ud/spec/exhibits/pound/index.htm [2006]). There is no shortage of recordings of the poet reading his own work, though instructors may find all they need by turning to the wonderful Pound page on the *PennSound* Web site, edited by Richard Sieburth (writing.upenn.edu/pennsound/x/Pound.html). The site includes a useful essay by Sieburth, "The Sound of Pound: A Listener's Guide," which offers an instructive account of Pound's lifelong endeavor to leave a record of his reading of his own poetry as well as his prose. Equally important and easily accessible are the Pound recordings made available by the Woodberry Poetry Room, Harvard University (library.harvard.edu/poetry/listeningbooth/poets/pound.html).

Pound and Pedagogy

Though Pound criticism has repeatedly (almost obsessively) addressed the periphrastic and allusive nature of his work, as well as his didacticism and obsession with the pedagogical import of poetry, the topos of pedagogy as it is related to the teaching of Pound's work has not received sufficient attention. Given modernism's difficulties in general, and Pound's "celebrated" opaqueness in particular, it is surprising to discover that there are no books dealing solely with the teaching of his poetry and prose other than *Ezra Pound and Education* (2012), published by the National Poetry Foundation. This valuable collection of essays approaches the topic from the perspective of Pound as teacher rather than addressing the difficulties and challenges of teaching Pound, the latter being the goal of the current volume. More recently, *Modernist Cultures* published an essay on Pound and antipedagogy, entitled "The Cantos and Pedagogy" (2017). Its authors, Michael Kindellan and Joshua I. Kotin, contend that *The Cantos* is not compatible with any model of education; Perloff, Yao, Charles Altieri, Alan Golding, and Michael Coyle respond to this contention, and Kotin and Kindellan offer a counter-response.

Work addressing the teaching of modernist and contemporary poetry includes *Poetry and Pedagogy: The Challenge of the Contemporary* (2006), edited by Joan Retallack and Juliana Spahr, which deals with ways whereby students in the classroom may experience and make meaning of the poetics of contemporary poetry, especially poetry written since the 1960s. There is also a collection of essays that grew from a 2008 MSA Pedagogy Roundtable Teaching Forum Cluster and is introduced and edited by Helen Sword in *Modernism/Modernity* (2009).

Sword's introduction, "Making It New: Innovative Approaches to Teaching Modernism," along with three of the six essays (Golding's "Faking It New," Marsha Bryant's "Counter-Intuitive Innovation," and Suzanne W. Churchill's "Modernism in Black and White") are likely to be of special interest to teachers and students of Pound. And *Teaching Modernist Poetry* (2010), edited by Nicky Marsh and Peter Middleton, offers interesting insights and pedagogical ideas regarding modernism's complex history, its intellectual scope, its aesthetic and linguistic intricacies, its radical politics, and its endurance in later traditions.

NOTES

[1] "I hope," Eliot writes in his introduction to *Literary Essays*, "that this volume will demonstrate that Pound's criticism is the most important contemporary criticism of its kind" (x).

[2] See "NPF Conferences 1980 to Present" at npfconferences.wordpress.com.

[3] When one considers as well NPF's publication of the Man and Poet / Woman and Poet Series, with sixteen large volumes comprising important essays as well as bibliographical information on the poets Pound was affiliated with or influenced substantially (including Eliot, Williams, H.D., and Moore but also Mina Loy, Lorine Niedecker, Basil Bunting, George Oppen, Carl Rakosi, and Louis Zukofsky), one begins to grasp the immense contribution made to the reception history of modernist poetry generally and Pound's work specifically by NPF and Terrell.

[4] For the past twenty years, Alec Marsh has performed the onerous task of writing the Pound section; he is about to be succeeded by Archie Henderson.

Part Two

APPROACHES

Introduction

Demetres P. Tryphonopoulos and Ira B. Nadel

Every reader of Pound participates in the ongoing debate over his status as poet or polemicist, critic or reactionary. This dilemma remains at the center of Pound's vitality as a modernist who formulated many of the critical ideas and concepts that have propelled the modernist project. His undeniable literary influence has ensured the inclusion of his poetry in all major anthologies of twentieth-century American literature as well as those anthologies devoted exclusively to poetry, and he is taught widely in high school, undergraduate, and graduate classrooms not only in the United States, Britain, Canada, and Australia, but also in Europe, especially in Italy (Italian universities, academic publishers, and journals continue to produce considerable scholarship on Pound), as well as in China, Korea, Japan (where Pound societies and Pound studies have had a long tradition), South America, and elsewhere. Although his poetry and prose are widely available in volumes kept in print by New Directions, new collections and selections continue to appear.

The paradox of Pound is that he is a major force in the development of European modernism whose virulent political and economic views at times dominated his aesthetic energies. From his creative use of Provençal poetry to his celebration of the sculptor Henri Gaudier-Brzeska, his introduction of imagism, his contribution to vorticism, and his literary reviews, essays, translations, letters, and other forms of prose, Pound dominated the literary and cultural landscape in Europe, the United States, and beyond for most of the twentieth century. His poetic methods and concepts were adopted by writers as diverse as H.D., Marianne Moore, Eugenio Montale, Charles Olson, Robert Lowell, George Seferis, Alan Ginsberg, Louis Zukofsky, Basil Bunting, and Robert Creeley. In his engagement with economics and politics, he reasserted the classical role of the poet as a participant in the world, in which endeavor he was preceded by figures like Pindar, Virgil, Ovid, Horace, and Milton. Yet Pound's participation was malignant in ways that cannot be ignored.

In middle age, Pound, believing that a conspiracy of bankers, Communists, Jews, and speculators would destroy the world, made countless radio broadcasts from Rome, aimed at America and American soldiers fighting in Europe. These attacks, in which he criticized the United States, Jews, and Franklin D. Roosevelt, led to his indictment for treason by a grand jury in 1943. Claiming mental instability to avoid a trial after his arrest in May 1945 meant incarceration at St. Elizabeths Hospital for the Criminally Insane in Washington, D.C., from 1945 to 1958. During this time Pound was awarded the 1948 Bollingen Prize for Poetry, a decision that rocked the literary world with debates over the aesthetics and ethics of the panel, Pound, and his contemporaries.

Many of the essays in this volume subscribe to the view that teaching Pound is also teaching conflict. His misogyny and anti-Semitism, his controversial politics and radical economics, his enduring enthusiasm for Fascism and support of Mussolini, the contested bestowal of the Bollingen award upon a poet whose radicalization and agitation were only amplified during his twelve and a half years in an institution, are all conflictual. Pound never avoided engagement, and neither should teachers of Pound. There is value, as Gerald Graff emphasized in *Professing Literature* and later in *Beyond the Culture Wars*, in addressing and teaching conflict, rather than avoiding it. While students and even teachers may be uncomfortable addressing these matters, one should not—indeed, cannot—avoid them in the study of Pound's time, his work, and his overall thought and aesthetics.

Those aesthetics as realized throughout Pound's oeuvre present plentiful technical and linguistic challenges. A page of Pound from any recent anthology will demonstrate why readers find his poetry difficult; the text at first glance offers an impenetrable and often alienating experience, and more likely than not the page will be divided almost equally between the primary text and notes devoted to annotation and explication. Besides using diverse languages (including several kinds of English or, in Pound's phrase, "Amurican langwidge," as well as Greek, Latin, Italian, French, Provençal, German, Chinese, and Portuguese), Pound also uses the languages of science, economics, and politics (*Selected Letters* 252). Furthermore, his geographical and linguistic quests (his method, as he notes in canto 59, is that of the *periplum*: "not as land looks on a map / but as sea bord seen by men sailing") take him not only to the Mediterranean basin but also to Africa, China, and beyond (*Cantos* 324). Accordingly, his allusions to events, persons, and texts range through prehistory, ancient China, classical Greece and Rome, Hellenistic times, Byzantium, Renaissance Italy, the United States of the Founding Fathers, modern England, and war-torn Italy. Even the most learned of readers or teachers may never hope to keep pace with Pound's range and erudition, surface erudition though it sometimes might be.

Pound himself had no doubt about the difficulty of his texts and was not concerned about readers who might expect the writer to do their work for them. In a letter of 12 October 1907, he acknowledges that "[m]ost of the stuff I write does not pretend to make itself intelligible to anyone who has not done a certain quite large amount of reading" ("Letters to Viola Baxter Jordan" 108). We have chosen this telling sentence from the first issue of *Paideuma*, the Pound journal founded by Carroll F. Terrell, as a keynote to Pound's understanding of his own work and of a reader's responsibilities. *Paideuma* often did the work Pound insisted his readers must undertake before attempting to read him.[1]

Difficulty, nonetheless, is a theme that can be used in the classroom as intellectual stimulation, to infuse courses on modernism with both the complexity and the satisfaction deriving from paradigmatic readings of Pound's texts. In this fashion, Pound's work becomes a site for analyzing difficult texts by a range of poets while learning about the history, form, aesthetics, and cultural contexts of modernism. The essays collected in this volume are designed to meet the pressing need among teachers (and students) to present Pound and his difficulties as opportunities for learning about modernist literature by exploring aesthetic, historical, cultural, social, economic, and ethical issues relevant to Pound's world and to our own. They view Pound's manifest difficulty not as a problem but rather as a challenge and even a reason for studying his work.

Reading Pound means encountering what theorists have labeled "oppositional discourse"; but it is precisely engaging in such discourse through Pound that teaches us critical thinking. Balance and context in teaching the conflicts should not only characterize any discussion of Pound but should become a new kind of organizing principle. Conflict becomes a form of common ground in approaching Pound. If, as Graff argues, "good teachers . . . *want* their students to talk back," Pound wants his readers to do the same (*Beyond the Culture Wars* 9). Apathy is not an option when reading Pound; readers need to speak out.

Teaching the Controversial Poet

In his own critical work and poetry, including *The Cantos*, Pound rages against reductive pedagogy that fetishizes biographical critiques; yet his work is essentially and substantially personal, ingrained with biographical experience. Ira B. Nadel's essay "Teaching Celebrity Pound" traces the exchange between Pound's autobiographical practice, especially its focus on his American roots and creative expression, and the works.

Designed to explore the highly gendered rhetoric of modernist aesthetics (often constructed as a powerful and clarifying masculinity that dominates over an ineffectual and mystificatory femininity), Jennifer Moxley's essay "'Free from Emotional Slither': Gender, Sexuality, and Pound's Ejaculations" offers syllabi and approaches appropriate for a number of pedagogical settings. Situating Pound's ideas about femininity, masculinity, and sexuality in their historical context and against the backdrop of the fight for women's reproductive rights, plus the eugenics movement's anxiety around inheritance and race, Moxley invites readers and students to question and elucidate Pound's positions and those of other modernist writers.

Susan McCabe addresses constructions of women in Pound's poetry from a contemporary feminist angle in "Pound among the Women," offering strategies for resisting facile generalizations about Pound's misogyny and for establishing productive classroom discussion. McCabe's essay also analyzes Pound's relationships with women such as H.D., Harriet Monroe, and Dorothy Shakespear Pound, in the context of his poetic development and theirs.

Trevor Sawler, in "Anti-Semitism, Racism, and Conspiracy Theories in Pound's Rome Radio Speeches," confronts the pedagogical authority of Pound's ideology, which reached its most extreme and excessive articulation in the Rome Radio speeches delivered on behalf of the Fascist regime in Italy during

World War II. The speeches' frenetic, stylized mode of authorial insistence, employing modernist, paratactic rhetoric masquerading as argument, is also the mode of large expanses of the later cantos. Sawler weighs the arguments for and against addressing these issues with students and offers an overall estimation of Pound's more controversial ideas and their impact on the author's worldview, work, and life.

Apart from the twelve and a half years of imposed repatriation at St. Elizabeths in Washington, D.C., Pound's cosmopolitism coincided with his nomadic existence in Europe. As John Gery explains in "'Out of Key with His Time': Pound as Poet in Exile," this protracted estrangement had a profound effect on Pound's aesthetic, cultural, and political thinking. Beginning with some of Pound's early poetry and *Hugh Selwyn Mauberley*, Gery helps students begin to think about the nature of Pound's exile and his journeys farther and farther away from home.

In "Pound and Difficulty," Leonard Diepeveen and J. Matthew Huculak use early poetry and prose by Pound to discuss the poet's own statements on difficulty, his reception history, and his modernist complexities in general. The basis of the discussion is Pound's assumed difficulty ("I shall have to learn a little greek to keep up with this," he writes in canto 105, "but so will you, drratt you") compared with his early and sustained emphasis on directness in writing (*Cantos* 770).

Pound's Aesthetics

Stephen J. Adams employs two methodologies, one historical and the other prosodic, in "Pound's Prosody for the Classroom" to demonstrate Pound's concept of rhythm as being rooted in practices of translation and literary history. Pound's global influences are emphasized and his use of quantitative meter elaborated; in addition, approaches to free verse metrical analysis are presented with examples from *The Cantos.*

Sara Dunton recounts an undergraduate seminar's hands-on investigation of prosodic allusion to Greek classical texts over Pound's entire career in "Patience for the 'Ancients': Studying Classical Allusions in Pound's Prosodic Practice." She explains how, beginning by taking to heart Pound's call for slowing down and demonstrating patient perseverance, students without training in classical Greek can investigate the Hellenic roots of Pound's prosody and the classical debts that helped shape and direct twentieth-century prosodic innovation.

In Rebecca Beasley's contribution, "Pound and the Early-Twentieth-Century Visual Revolution," the link between Pound and innovations in the visual arts becomes the focus, joined to original pedagogical practices reflecting individual course structures. Importantly, the visual arts provide models for Pound's multiple styles and content. To understand the aesthetic heritage and use of that material by Pound is the goal. The poet's connections with, and commitment to, the artistic milieu of early-twentieth-century London and Paris become critical in, for example, comparisons between "In a Station of the Metro" and the paintings of Kandinsky. Key terms like *imagism* and *vorticism* receive extended discussion, with references to Pound's essays on art from *The Egoist* and *The New Age*, early collections of poetry, *Hugh Selwyn Mauberley*, and selected early cantos.

Jennifer Ryan-Bryant uses selections from *Cathay*, *The Cantos*, *The Chinese Written Character as a Medium for Poetry*, Pound's Japanese Noh drama, and his translations of Confucian texts to illuminate the influence of Chinese and Japanese literature and culture on Pound's poetry. Her essay, "Vorticism, the Palimpsest, the Ideogram, and Pound's Understanding of Chinese Historiography in *The Cantos*," discusses the transmission of poetry from Li Po to Pound's time, explicates and clarifies Pound's Orientalism, describes an in-class translation exercise, and argues for the importance of acts of translation in Pound and in the poetic theory of the twentieth century.

Zhaoming Qian's pedagogical method in "Pound's China: Teaching 'The River-Merchant's Wife: A Letter' and Canto 49" uses Pound's intentional misrepresentations, and his preservation of errors in Fenollosa's text, to study the poet's theories of translation and of vorticism. Qian's discussion will clarify for instructors and their students some common misconceptions about Confucianism and Daoism while identifying in modernist poets linkages to, and a revolt against, the hegemonic Orientalism of their predecessors and peers. His approach allows students to participate in the reconceptualization of Orientalism using concepts of comparative literature, translation, and transnational cultural production and transmission.

In "Pound's Economics and Politics," Alec Marsh provides a historical and archival contextualization of the question of Pound's Fascist, anti-Semitic, and racial allegiances. Using a few of the money pamphlets, *Guide to Kulchur*, sections of *The Cantos*, and also, most importantly, Pound's economic poetics, Marsh guides students (and teachers) through the development of Pound's controversial economic ideas.

Classroom Contexts

In his graduate seminar dedicated to reading *The Cantos* sequentially while tracing Pound's shifting aesthetic and thematic concerns, Brian Reed considers how a nonlinear model of reading may complement, enhance, and interrogate traditional methods of annotation. His metacognitive reflection "*The Cantos* in a Quarter" lays out and evaluates learning outcomes, resources, and teaching strategies and ultimately challenges accustomed models of graduate instruction.

Anderson Araujo's essay "Using Electronic Resources and Information Technologies to Teach Pound's *Guide to Kulchur* and Canto 45" demonstrates how electronic media utilizes Web links to create experiences similar to the epiphanies, the bursts of insight, Pound and other modernists believed could be ignited in their readers' minds. Enlisting a range of information and communication technologies, Araujo employs and interrogates learning management systems and online literary resources in order to facilitate students' engagement with Pound's difficult, allusive, paratactic, polyvocal rhetoric and content.

Peter Nicholls, in "Usury, Poetry, and Art: Canto 45," presents canto 45 as an exception to the allusive and oblique nature of the majority of the poem. Noting that Pound's invective against banking interests sounds remarkably contemporary and resonant for students, Nicholls shows how to contextualize the issue in Pound's time. He then guides students through Pound's shift in cantos 47 and 49 to a possible world without usury and to canto 51's reprise in modern language—yet with important differences—of the themes of canto 45.

In "Pound as Noh Student: The Lessons of *Hagoromo*," Carrie J. Preston uses Pound's controversial translation of the Noh play *Hagoromo* (羽衣; *The Feather Mantle*) to help students examine "the role of translation, cultural transmission, and exoticism in modernism." Preston shows how *Hagoromo* can be used to teach Pound's aesthetics and to clarify such Poundian notions as those of the Chinese ideogram and modernist allusion; and her interdisciplinary approach examines the play as a collaborative cultural transmission and textual production; challenges the sense of the modernist poet as a sole, inimitable "genius author"; and invites discussion of the politics and intricacies of translating between languages.

In "Pound and Periodicals: Editing Modernism," Craig Monk guides students through the history of modernism as it is told through Pound's relationship to periodicals and his interactions with publishers, editors, and fellow artists. Providing a nuanced view of the literary world in Pound's day, this approach also illuminates Pound's role as a conduit through which the work of so many of his associates and ancient texts appeared.

Alan Golding, in "'Poundian Ambition on the Semester System': Pound, the Avant-Garde, and the Academy," undertakes to pay specific attention to the ways Pound's views about pedagogy have impacted three areas of post–World War II poetry and education: first, the poet-edited classroom anthology; second, the poetry and criticism of postmodern poets who have taken on in their work—overtly and explicitly—Pound the teacher; and, third, institutional programs in which Poundian pedagogy has been embraced and enacted. A case study of Poundian pedagogy in action at Black Mountain College, founded in 1933 in North Carolina based on Pound's 1914 call for a college of arts made up of teacher-practitioners, demonstrates the spirit of what Moxley has called "Poundian ambition" as it has, and continues to be, experienced by the academy.

From the wide-ranging teaching resources, critical methods, biographical sources, social theories, and cultural studies applied in this volume, it is clear that Pound's poetry and prose continue to engage and challenge, offering students and instructors the means to explore not only his world but their own, a source of confirmation and contraction, much like Pound's.

NOTE

[1] Terrell's line-by-line annotation of *The Cantos*, published in two volumes as his *Companion to* The Cantos *of Ezra Pound*, extended his initial investigations and those appearing in the journal.

TEACHING THE POETRY AND THE CONTROVERSIAL POET

Teaching Celebrity Pound

Ira B. Nadel

In his critical work and poetry, Ezra Pound consistently objects to, and often rages against, reductive pedagogy that fetishizes biographical criticism. This contradicts his own practice, however, where biography plays an important part in his aesthetic. Indeed, Pound thought of himself, and promoted himself, as a celebrity. He demonstrated an early awareness of what he believed to be his fame, publishing "How I Began" at the age of twenty-eight and then "A Retrospect" at age thirty-three. Through didactic titles like "How to Read" or *Guide to Kulchur*, and capitalizing on his increasing role as the promoter of modernism, Pound defined and celebrated his own importance as a celebrity poet more conspicuously than did any of his elders (Thomas Hardy, W. B. Yeats) or peers (T. S. Eliot, William Carlos Williams). And biography, as a form of self-promotion, became his means of endorsing and sustaining this role.

This essay traces the exchange between Pound's use of biographical experience, especially his American roots and European experiences, and his opposition to it. Though Pound, like Eliot, would like us to view his entire oeuvre as impersonal, relying on masks, personae, or other voices, his work is essentially and substantially personal. In the classroom, this dimension of Pound needs to be addressed and at times exposed.

Conceptually, Pound resists the biographical, but in practical terms he employs it. He remains centered in the biographical circle through his writing forming his own prominence, whether it be his narratives of American history, his accounts of life in Fascist Italy, or memories of his early life in London. Personal reactions to events in the Second World War, as in the so-called Italian cantos (72 and 73), further his biographical practice in the final volumes of

The Cantos: *Section Rock-Drill*, *Thrones*, and *Drafts and Fragments*. Throughout these last volumes, there are frequent personal remarks, often about the author's own failures. One of his most moving passages is the following from canto 120:

> I have tried to write Paradise
>
> Do not move
> Let the wind speak
> that is paradise.
>
> Let the Gods forgive what I
> have made
> Let those I love try to forgive
> what I have made.
> ("Notes for CXVII et seq." [*Cantos* 822])

Here and elsewhere, Pound embraces the biographical, becoming the hero, if not the celebrity, of his own poem.

Pound's antipathy to biography most likely originated in his undergraduate days at the University of Pennsylvania and Hamilton College. In letters to his parents, he expressed comic pleasure in his studies, writing from Hamilton College in the fall of 1904 that "with double French, Anglo-Saxon, Spanish, analytics & three hours of Prex's hot air I expect to come home a corpse" (*Ezra Pound to His Parents* 23).[1] But readings such as Browning's *Sordello* and Taine's lectures on art and literature failed to satisfy his appetite for direct study of poetic language (27). His criticism of American writing was entirely focused on language—"'They,' the American brood, have ears like elephants and no sense of the English language"—and he argued that the biographical emphasis of British and European literary history produced a moribund engagement with texts that did not survive or live on their own (*Selected Letters* 15).

In his earliest poetry, however, Pound could not escape himself. At sixteen, he fell in love with Hilda Doolittle, the fifteen-year-old daughter of a professor of astronomy at the University of Pennsylvania, where he was a freshman. His first collection of poems, *Hilda's Book*, relied on myth to convey his feelings for the young woman who would later be known as H.D. In a blend of pagan legend and Christian mysticism, Pound sublimated his personal desires through the use of myth or mythological figures, calling H.D. "The Dryad" since, as he wrote in "Rendez-vous," "[s]he hath some tree-born spirit of the wood / About her" (*New Selected Poems* 17).

Highly stylized, these poems, composed between 1905 and 1907, reflect the impact of Dante's *La vita nuova* (poems to the author's love, Beatrice) and the works of Dante Gabriel Rossetti. Soon seeking a new aesthetic, however, Pound kept only "The Tree" for inclusion in *Collected Early Poems*. The poem confronts the transformation of the human into the mythopoetic while the poet maintains his own identity, speaking through an observing mind. A classroom discussion of the personal metamorphosis Pound incorporated into the stories of Apollo and Daphne, Baucis and Philemon ("I stood still and was a tree amid the wood") may establish certain signatures of his early poetry: his remaking of the classical into the personal, and a dialogue between the subjective and the objective.

When he left for Venice and then London in 1908–09, Pound sought to free himself from the sway, if not the influence, of Rossetti and the Pre-Raphaelites. Browning's dramatic monologues and Yeats's confrontations with history became his new guides in the search for an objective style. In London, he found models such as Yeats, Eliot, and James Joyce who rejected the subjective and personal for the power of the impersonal; and after a visit in 1911 to the writer and editor Ford Madox Ford, who laughed uproariously at his new poems, Pound renounced all poetical affectations. The elaborate rhetoric and imagery of "Xenia" (1909), as in the opening lines, "And / Unto thine eyes my heart / Sendeth old dreams," stand in stark contrast to the more immediate and natural style of "The Picture" (1912): "The eyes of this dead lady speak to me."

During his early days in London, Pound delivered a series of lectures that became the basis of his first work of literary criticism, *The Spirit of Romance.* Familiar with his poetry, the London Polytechnic asked Pound to give a full course on Romance literature. He agreed but only after Ernest Rhys persuaded J. M. Dent to publish the lectures as a book. The essays in that volume indict the philological approach to literary study and advocate instead for a "history of masterwork[s]." Reacting against the study of literature as "hero-worship" (5), Pound claims to want to study poetry *as poetry* and not as biography, although autobiography pervades the lectures, even to the extent of defending his competence to deliver them, which he attributes in part to his compliance with the University of Pennsylvania's regulation that required completion of one's assigned lecture reading (7). Later in the series, in "Psychology and Troubadours," Pound emphasizes biographical elements in Dante, the poet he invoked throughout his life, from youthful poems such as "Histrion" (1908) to his decades-long project, *The Cantos.* A useful class assignment would be to analyze the importance and function of biography for his argument in this early essay.

"Histrion"—whose title means "actor"—engages with the poet's inheritance of the voices of his predecessors, among whom Pound particularly acknowledged Dante and the French medieval poet François Villon: "Thus am I Dante for a space and am / One François Villon, ballad-lord and thief." By studying and translating works from the Provençal troubadour tradition in poems such as "Sestina: Altaforte," Pound discovered the freedom of the dramatic monologue through the creation of personae, seizing on a valuable tool for sublimating biography. In 1909 he published a poetry collection with the provocative title *Personae of Ezra Pound*, suggesting a series of false fronts or identities for the self.[2] He also recognized the alternate subjectivity provided by personae in the early writings of Eliot and Joyce, although he would disagree with Eliot's declaration in "Tradition and the Individual Talent" that "it is not in his personal emotions . . . that the poet is in any way remarkable or interesting" ("Tradition" 51). For Pound, it is quite the reverse; for him, personality becomes identity.

Pound continually reconstructed his own identity through self-invention, and in this engagement with the biographical he was always his own best subject. His elaborate American manner, stressing the old West, played well in London, where he was immediately perceived as an outsider, a role he enjoyed. Unlike Henry James or Eliot, he did not try to fit in. He aimed to stand out. His dress, his speech, his mannerisms displayed a brash, uncouth, and hopefully rugged Americanism. He spoke with a drawl and wore cowboy boots or a sombrero and colorful cape. And he built the myth of his origins with autobiographical works such as "How I Began" and his self-inscribed entries in *Who's Who*. The first of these, from 1915, begins, "Pound, Ezra, M.A.; vorticist." The author then summarizes his education, notes that he is the literary executor of the American sinologist Ernest Fenollosa, and ends with "Recreations: fencing, tennis, searching *The Times* for evidence of almost incredible stupidity."

For the 1919 edition, Pound revised his recreations to include dissecting "the public taste and that of Sir Owen Seaman," who was a parodist and editor of *Punch* from 1906 to 1932. By 1920, he had altered his identity again, replacing "vorticist" with "poet and constructive critic" but keeping the reference to Seaman. Five years later, he identified himself as "poet and hack writer" and eliminated the reference to Seaman. His occupation in 1929 shifted to "poet and composer." These adjustments to his self-image and biographical awareness are also reflected in various autobiographical notes sent to numerous editors and publishers. A class exercise in charting these changes would be of immense value in understanding shifts in Pound's poetic style and personal image.

Pound's reference to Fenollosa, for example, should be understood to signify an aesthetic revolution. Asked by Fenollosa's widow in London to take over her husband's papers, Pound quickly absorbed the scholar's aesthetic. In the process of overcoming his early imitative verse and subjectivity, Pound found his poetic voice in translating Chinese poetry and in the hard-edged writing of the newly formed modernists (organized around the imagist movement initiated by Pound), which included H.D. and Richard Aldington. The sculptor Gaudier-Brzeska had taught Pound to "cut direct," to remove the frivolous, the distracting, the useless words (Pound, *Gaudier-Brzeska* 19). Pound saw the idea that language and form should embody the essence of the thought manifested in the spare style of Japanese Noh theatre and more thoroughly in Fenollosa's writings. *Cathay*, Pound's translation of fourteen poems from the Chinese with the aid of Fenollosa's notes, immersed him in the world of objectivity and allowed him to mask personal impulses through dramatic monologue at the additional remove of a foreign language and style.

Pound edited and published Fenollosa's important essay *The Chinese Written Character as a Medium of Poetry*, a critical statement of his own poetics.

Fenollosa stresses the value of the Chinese character as a sign: Chinese poetry, he writes in Pound's version, "speaks at once with the vividness of painting, and with the mobility of sounds. It is in some sense more objective than either, more dramatic." In reading such poetry, we do not juggle "mental counters" but seem "to be watching things work out their own fate." The ideograph in Chinese poetry is "a verbal idea of action," a goal for Pound in his own use of language (Pound, *Chinese Written Character* [*Early Writings*] 309).

Pound took as the subject of his 1920 poem *Hugh Selwyn Mauberley* an artist who could not adopt a spare, objective style. In Mauberley, he created a character whose inability to sacrifice the biographical for the new formalism of his time caused his downfall and exile, placing him "out of step with the decade" (132). Mauberley never learns how to transform a "consciousness disjunct," a phrase at the core of the modernist project, into art (141). The allure of the romantic will not leave him. Pound, however, as he states in *Mauberley*, manages to reject "the suave bounding-line" for a precise, exact style, even if his protagonist cannot (142).

Hugh Selwyn Mauberley marks a shift for Pound away from the device of personae. In it, the author shows the dangers of the biographical and subjective in the trapped poet Mauberley, but also demonstrates his own release from the clotted writing of the Victorians and Georgians. In place of "maudlin confession" (140), he discovers a new sense of self that does not interfere with his writing but enhances it. This self is critical, distant, and objective yet integrates the personal and biographical with the aesthetic. Poetic integrity is achievable but only through a persona that avoids the confessional.

Pound availed himself of further personal/interpersonal interventions through the use of *simultanéisme*, a technique of superimposing simultaneous voices that originated with the avant-garde poet Henri-Martin Barzun. In sections of *The Pisan Cantos* (see cantos 74 and 77), simultaneous conversations compete for the reader's attention. For Pound, this becomes a contest between the personal-biographical and the objective-reportorial, as in canto 74:

> and the guards op/ of the . . .
> was lower than that of the prisoners
> "all them g.d.m.f. generals c.s. all of 'em fascists"
> "fer a bag o'Dukes"
> "the things I saye an' dooo" (*Cantos* 456)

Later, in canto 80, he brings biography directly into the text:

> so that leaving America I brought with me $80
> and England a letter of Thomas Hardy's
> and Italy one eucalyptus pip
> from the salita that goes up from Rapallo (520)

The Cantos are a dialogue of Pound with history and with himself. Memory is the link—as Williams understood:

> a kind
> of accomplishment
> a sort of renewal
> even
> an initiation, since the spaces it opens are new
> places
> inhabited by hordes
> heretofore unrealized
> (*Paterson* 77)

As Pound writes at the end of canto 116,

> Many errors,
> a little rightness,
> to excuse his hell
> and my paradiso.
> . . . .
> To confess wrong without losing rightness:
> Clarity I have had sometimes,
> I cannot make it flow thru.
> A little light, like a rushlight
> to lead back to splendour.
> (*Cantos* 817)

He ends with a confessional and biographical statement: "The dreams clash / and are shattered— / and that I tried to make a paradiso / terrestre" ("Notes for CXVII et seq." [822]). The personal gives urgency, intensity, and authenticity to his admission.

Indeed, just as Dante's political life formed the backdrop for the *Divine Comedy*, so too did Pound's for *The Cantos*. His own life, he came to realize, had currency and purchase in his work; the personal and the biographical reciprocally enhanced his writing even as he sought the objectivity and hardness he identified as characteristic of the modern.

Pound's voice is never absent from his criticism, which gives the latter a certain, and occasionally offensive, authenticity. He was fired after only three months of working for the *Athenaeum* because of an intemperate review and often encountered challenges, if not insults, in response to his unrestrained commentaries. But as a critic and reviewer, he was always bracing if not revitalizing. Two sentences from *The Spirit of Romance* demonstrate this: "Here the preciseness of the description denotes, I think, a clarity of imaginative vision" (105 ["Lingua

Toscana"]). The "I think" is telling. From "The Quality of Lope de Vega": "From my scant knowledge of the English religious plays I should say that they are more vigorous than those written in Spanish" (182). This is a personal opinion informally qualified. Instructors should select at least three essays from *The Spirit of Romance* and identify, as well as discuss, the importance of the personal as a means for Pound to advance his arguments.

Later, in "Translators of Greek," Pound declares, "I do not imagine I am the sole creature who has been well taught his Latin and very ill-taught his Greek" (249). "I believe" or "I think" is the repeated refrain of Pound's "Credo" from "A Retrospect," a work that argues for a style "austere, direct, free from emotional slither" (12) in a voice that is nevertheless overtly personal: "I would much rather lie on what is left of Catullus' parlour floor and speculate the azure beneath it and the hills off to Salo . . . than discuss any processes and theories of art whatsoever. I would rather play tennis" (9). As an early critic noted in a two-sided remark, "in his prose Pound is all personality and no form" (Kirk 702). To test this claim, students should read "Proença" in *The Spirit of Romance* (39–63) and determine and identify Pound's reliance on personality to make his case for the importance of Arnaut Daniel, Provençal poetry, and the troubadour tradition.

Readers of Pound's multitudinous autobiographies will observe the predominance of the life over the literature with few exceptions.[3] Interviews with Allen Ginsberg, Donald Hall, and James Laughlin, in which Pound recanted his anti-Semitism and worried over his critical reception and the financial well-being of Olga Rudge, reflect his biographical concerns at the end of his life rather than his aesthetic ones (Reck; Hall; Nadel, "E.P."). A comparative reading of these interviews would provide students with an in-depth opportunity to assess Pound's complex career and his drive to sustain his celebrity status in cooperation with his publishers, New Directions and Faber and Faber, who kept his works in print throughout his lifetime and beyond. Louis Menand's essay "The Pound Error" also provides a provocative discussion point for a class engaged with an energetic debate on Pound's reputation.

The trick to teaching and reading Pound is, as he himself emphasized, to stay with the text, with the language, and to concentrate on the objective, hard-edged, crystalline expressions. But being alert to biography is also necessary. Pound does not write against the self but with the self, although sometimes in disguise. The "I" is the combination of his own and other presences, such as Dante and Villon. Such a strategy, he explains at the end of canto 84, the last of the *Pisan Cantos*, essentially creates "distinctions in clarity" (*Cantos* 559). What really matters, he believes, is "only the total sincerity, the precise definition" (canto 77 [488]). "Ego scriptor" ("I, the writer") may be Pound's most important statement, a simultaneously biographical and critical declaration matched in importance only by his marginal note on the manuscript of "Histrion": "I do not teach I awake" (canto 74 [478]; *Collected Early Poems* 299).

NOTES

[1] Prex was M. W. Stryker, the president of Hamilton College.

[2] Pound expanded the text and altered the title in 1926 to read *Personae: The Shorter Poems of Ezra Pound.* Included were *Cathay*, *Hugh Selwyn Mauberley*, "Three Cantos," and eight uncollected poems.

[3] One recent exception is A. David Moody, whose expert three-volume life focuses on Pound's poetry and his career as a writer.

"Free from Emotional Slither": Gender, Sexuality, and Pound's Ejaculations

Jennifer Moxley

"Even oneself has felt it," Ezra Pound asserts, "driving any new idea into the great passive vulva of London, a sensation analogous to the male feeling in copulation" (*Pavannes* 204). This casting of his London years (1908–20) in a sexist metaphor, along with his pseudoscientific claim that it is "more than likely" that the image-making brain is a "great clot of genital fluid" and that the "spermatozoide is precisely the power of exteriorizing a form," would seem to be adequate evidence that Pound was a male chauvinist pig (203–04). A *Google* search of "Pound + gender" gives as a top hit the text where these statements first appeared, the postscript to his 1921 translation of Rémy de Gourmont's *Natural Philosophy of Love* (1903), now hosted on the Modern American Poetry Web site. The site titles the postscript "Pound on Gender," as if these singular musings sum up the issue. Yet the issue is not so simple. "I am certainly neither writing an antifeminist tract," Pound clarifies, "nor claiming disproportionate privilege for the spermatozoide" (*Pavannes* 204). Nor did he claim special privileges for men in literary ventures, in which he championed women writers (such as H.D. and Marianne Moore) and had meaningful collaborations with women editors (namely Dora Marsden, Amy Lowell, and Margaret Anderson).[1] Pound was also quick to amend his thinking on "genital fluid." Only a year later he was "happy to dismiss" the above statements and "was speculating about a possible chemical basis of intelligence" in the pineal gland (Moody, *Epic Years* 10–11). In other instances of the published record Pound explicitly censures "those writers . . . who find the source of illumination . . . centred solely in the philo-progenitive instinct" (*Spirit* 94). Nevertheless, despite his lively support of literary women, and his change of mind concerning one offensive tract, Pound was a man of his time and as such was prone to gender-biased language that can be difficult to reconcile with today's values.

The instructor who includes Pound in a course can exclude instances in his oeuvre that are embarrassing, outdated, or offensive (particularly anything to do with gender, politics, or gender politics), or that might disturb students; but such a course would be both historically inaccurate and a missed opportunity. Teaching Pound's core ideas about genius, poetry, and the creative mind through the lens of gender, on the other hand, is a powerful way to energize today's students by meeting them where they live: in a time when questions of gender and sexuality are once again thought to be central to who we are—as makers, and as social and political beings.

Pound was a child of the Victorian era. Beginning a course on modernism with a brief unit on late-Victorian aesthetics contextualizes Pound's male chauvinism, attraction to the rhetoric of aggression, and focus on a Roman-derived idea of virtue (from the same Latin root, *vir,* as *virility*) or manliness as central to the artist (see, for example, "A Retrospect," "I Gather the Limbs of Osiris," "Manifesto 1," "Manifesto 2").

Reading Friedrich Nietzsche's *The Case of Wagner* and Max Nordau's *Degeneration* helps students appreciate what was at stake for masculinity, and thus for Pound, at the dawn of the twentieth century. Though there is "no direct evidence that Pound admired either Nietzsche or Wagner," he most certainly "imbibed Wagnerism and Nietzscheanism at second and third hand" (Surette, *The Birth of Modernism* 175, 178). Pound did read Nordau in 1912 and even claimed that he found Nordau's conclusions "fairly sound," even if he didn't agree with his reasoning (176).

In *The Case of Wagner,* Nietzsche argues that Wagner—whom he had formerly championed—is dangerous because he is an "*artist of decadence*" whose music "corrupts our health." Nietzsche thinks that Wagernism is a disease: "Is Wagner a human being at all? Isn't he rather a sickness?" (164). Wagner's music is an expression of "physiological degeneration" and a form of "hystericism" that appeals to "pale, breathless" youths (169, 172). "Hystericism" is code for feminization. Wagner's music sickens young men by feminizing them. It denies male youths "light feet, wit, fire, grace," in short, "*la gaya scienza*" or "joyous science" (from the Provençal *gai saber*) of the troubadours' "art (or technic) of poetic song" (Babich 98). Pound will echo Nietzsche's use of the troubadours as a sunlit "cure" for a Victorian aesthetic malaise with his deep study of the Provençal poets, *The Spirit of Romance* (see also Pound, *Personae,* and Moody, *Young Genius* 21–22).

In *The Spirit of Romance* Pound argues that the chivalric love code invented during the twelfth century tapped into the "fluid force" of the "germinal universe" (92), otherwise described as "the flowing," an energy where "we find sex, or some correspondence to it" (93). While neither misogynistic nor macho, Pound's ideas in *The Spirit of Romance* use procreative language and assumptions about the poetic mind as akin to the "vital universe." They also tacitly accept, and arguably even promote, gender stereotypes about the robust male artist and "his lady" (92–93), illustrated best in his homage to the troubadour Bertran de Born, "Sestina: Altaforte," where Pound equates opposition to violence with femininity, bloodlessness, and rot: "The man who fears war and squats opposing / My words for stour, hath no blood of crimson / But is fit only to rot in womanish peace" (*Personae* [rev. ed.] 27).

"The arts are not passive, nor static, nor, in a sense, are they reflective," wrote Pound (*Spirit* 222). According to Nietzsche, passivity, stasis, and reflection are all symptoms of the sickness produced by Wagner's music. And while he never says it explicitly, he implies that this sickness is a *gender* sickness: the feminization of men to the point of impotence. Nietzsche complains that Wagner's heroes "condescend to the level of women" and that his heroines, though redemptive, are sterile. They never manage to produce children (161, 159).[2]

Good art, according to Nietzsche and Pound, is art that is generative, which "makes [us] fertile" (Nietzsche 158); it is not degenerative but revivifying. Or, as

Pound would later put it, it can "prevent ennui" and "revive the mind" (*Spirit* 6). Though Nietzsche prescribed Bizet's *Carmen* as an inoculation against the Wagner virus (159–60), Pound's later call for a poetry that would be "austere, direct" and "free from emotional slither," that would "move against poppy-cock," "be harder and saner" and as "as much like granite as it can be" ("A Retrospect" 12) proved just as powerful. Pound's critique of Christianity as a feminizing religion, and his advocacy of poetic objectivity and experiment modeled on science ("[c]onsider the way of the scientists" [6]), are also prefigured in *The Case of Wagner* with Nietzsche's lambasting of Wagner's hypocritical "Christian sighs" and the composer's view that "it is a crime against what is highest and holiest to be scientific" (Nietzsche 169, 161).

Four years after *The Case of Wagner*, Max Nordau's screed against decadence, *Degeneration*, also raised the specter of a sick art infecting robust masculinity. Nordau's chapter on Symbolism lays into Stéphane Mallarmé with a rhetoric reminiscent of Pound's "unmitigated gall" ("I Gather the Limbs" 21). Following a lengthy quotation of Mallarmé concerning the aesthetic superiority of suggestion over direct naming, Nordau gloats, "If the reader does not at once understand this combination of vague words, he need not stop to solve them. Later on I will translate the stammerings of this weak mind into the speech of sound men" (115). Calling the Symbolist poets "imbeciles" (a buzzword among eugenicists at the time), Nordau claims that decadent artists are ruled by emotions rather than ideas and "cannot make use of definite words of clear import, for their own consciousness holds no clearly-defined univocal ideas which could be embodied in such words" (118).

Nordau accuses Symbolist poets of having a sickness that results in weak, emotional, and vague (i.e., feminine) poems. "The healthy man can tell what he thinks . . . the mystic imbecile thinks merely according to the laws of association" (118). "[D]efinite words of clear import" and knowing one's mind are central to Pound's poetics, from his call for a "direct treatment of the thing" in "A Retrospect" (3) to his assertion that "[a]s long as the poet says not what he, at the very crux of a clarified conception, means, but is content to say something ornate and approximate, just so long will serious people, intently alive, consider poetry as balderdash—a sort of embroidery for dilettantes and women" ("I Gather the Limbs" 41). Nordau's ideas regarding poetry are buffoonish while Pound's are deeply informed, yet the former's claim that European society was undergoing a wide-scale degeneration, and that "art for art's sake" and the dandified men who practiced it had something to do with this downfall, overlapped with Nietzsche's critique of Wagner's music. The 1895 arrest, trial, and imprisonment of Oscar Wilde on charges of "gross indecency" (code for homosexual acts) gave further evidence to fears that European art was undergoing a crisis of masculinity. It was into such a climate that Pound arrived in London—a cock-of-the-walk, red-blooded American male free of aesthetic sickness—ready to drive "new idea[s]" into the city's "great passive vulva."

The key points in *The Case of Wagner* (the equation of aesthetics with gender sickness and the infertility of Wagner's heroines) can be introduced, and a passage from the chapter on Symbolism in *Degeneration* shared (100–44), during the first class meeting of a graduate seminar or advanced undergraduate course. In addition to the Nordau material above, the following passage provides ample fodder for discussion of the assumptions encoded in such words as *infertility*, *production*, and *capacity* about so-called healthy masculinity versus congenitally sick masculinity:

> [Mallarmé] is the most curious phenomenon in the intellectual life of contemporary France. Although long past fifty years of age, he has written hardly anything . . . yet he is esteemed as a very great poet, and the utter *infertility* of his pen, the entire absence of any single work which he can *produce* as evidence of his poetical *capacity*, is prized as his greatest merit . . . This statement must appear so fabulous to any reader not deranged in mind . . . (128; italics added)

To prepare students for this lecture, assign Willa Cather's 1905 short story "Paul's Case," a portrait of an American youth who has been stricken by this European sickness. Paul is a dandy who wears "an opal pin in his neatly knotted black four-in-hand," is revolted by the specter of the reproductive middle-class American family, and feels that "the natural nearly always wore the guise of ugliness" (111, 120). Like Wilde, who believed that "all bad art comes from returning to Life and Nature," Paul's idea of the beautiful requires "a certain element of artificiality" (Wilde 319; Cather 120). Paul's way leads not to life, vigor, health, and reproduction, but to death—and the story ends with his suicide.

These readings bring to the foreground themes that are essential to any discussion of gender and sexuality in Pound and his contemporaries: anxiety about masculinity being threatened by feminization; and anxiety about generation, both in the sense of a group born at the same time and in the sense of procreation. Michel Foucault's theory that during the Victorian period certain perversions became identities—that "the sodomite had been a temporary aberration" but "the homosexual was now a species"—helps explain how threatening any sexuality that was seen as unnatural had become (43). Those who feared this new "species" might have imagined it as the queer Scylla to the female Charybdis that was the fight for women's rights during the first two decades of the twentieth century. The women's suffrage movement exemplifies this struggle, but the fight for birth control and reproductive rights was also well underway. Christina Hauck, in "Abortion and the Individual Talent," provides an overview of how the declining birthrate in England created a crisis of sexual reproduction. "Reproductive failure," she argues, underlies the tendency of male modernists to cast their aesthetics in metaphors of sexual potency and reproductive success (226). Thus, when Pound recalls "driving" his new ideas "into the great passive vulva of London," or calls himself the male midwife ("Sage Homme") who "performed the caesarean Operation" on the imperiled fetus that was T. S. Eliot's *The Waste Land*, what he is in fact recalling is his role as a much-needed fertility doctor to a culture that found itself increasingly unable to bring an artwork or idea to term (*Selected Letters* 170). Is it any wonder, then, that in his 1913 essay "The Serious Artist" Pound compares the dishonest artist who "falsifies his report as to the nature of man" to a doctor who "falsifies the reports of a maternity hospital" (43)? The stakes were high, and the rhetoric fraught; but few contest that Pound did, in fact, succeed at revitalizing the health of poetry and giving birth to entirely fresh and still relevant ways of thinking about the poem.

The "explicitly masculine and even phallic rhetoric of literary fitness" as "fundamental to Pound's and Eliot's aesthetic project," and the connection of this rhetoric to eugenic discourse, is brilliantly analyzed in Daylanne English's book *Unnatural Selection: Eugenics in American Modernism and the Harlem Renaissance* (68). While Eliot comes under especial scrutiny, Pound's role as interlocutor in Eliot's poetics of sexual containment and racial anxiety is informative, as is the excellent chapter on Gertrude Stein's early writing (93–116). Placing Pound alongside his female contemporaries helps students understand how gendered (and racialized) language, as well as a sexualized understanding of human creativity, was not solely the province of men. For example, we see the casualness with which such assumptions could be employed when Stein asserts in her 1909 trilogy *Three Lives* that her character Anna had "a german woman's feeling for the masterhood in men" or that her character Melanctha's friend Rose "was never joyous with the earth-born, boundless joy of negroes. . . . [h]er white training had only made for habits, not for nature. Rose had the simple, promiscuous unmorality of black people" (29, 60).

Janet Lyon's chapter "Militant Allies, Strange Bedfellows: Suffragettes and Vorticists before the War" in her book *Manifestoes: Provocations of the Modern*, is an excellent analysis of the militant rhetoric of male modernists like Pound, Filippo Marinetti, and Wyndham Lewis as contrasted with the actual militancy of the suffragettes (92–123). While Marinetti advocated "scorn for women" and the "hygiene of war," and Pound and Lewis advised in 1914 that they would give the suffragettes their vote if these women would "SOYEZ BONNES FILLES" (be good girls) and agree to "LEAVE ART ALONE" (Lewis), these resolutely "bad girls" were practicing civil disobedience, breaking shop windows, disrupting parliamentary meetings, and slashing art.

The modernist poet Mina Loy's 1914 "Feminist Manifesto"—a direct riposte to Marinetti—is a good example of a woman using incendiary, *Blast*-like rhetoric regarding sex, gender, and identity. Similar to Pound and Lewis, Marinetti claimed he "supported the suffragists" yet "maintained that whatever came of their crusade, the average woman would continue to exist within the 'closed circle' of femininity, 'as a mother, as a wife, and as a lover'" (Burke 178–79). Loy's manifesto counters this gender-role imprisonment by calling for the demolition of the division of women into the roles of "mistress" or "mother" (153). The discomfort students may feel encountering Loy's eugenically tinged call for "[e]very woman of superior intelligence" to "realize her race-responsibility," as well as Loy's astonishing demand for the "unconditional surgical destruction of virginity" at puberty, can lead to meaningful classroom debates (155). Loy's sex essentialism—along with her rejection of the rhetoric of equality—may challenge contemporary feminist and gender studies orthodoxy, but they also align with and help put into perspective similar views embraced by Pound.

A close reading of Pound's postscript to *The Natural Philosophy of Love* alongside H.D.'s 1919 *Notes on Thought and Vision* can work similarly to Loy's manifesto and provoke an edifying classroom debate about the relationship of sexuality to creativity. Though snickers may arise, today's students are uniquely equipped to appreciate the importance of sex hormones. As all who have gone through puberty know, hormones affect our emotions as well as our ability to think. Growing awareness of the experience of transgender people, as well as the idea of transitioning from one gender to another, a process that may include hormone therapy, adds further evidence to a connection between sex hormones and identity.

Pair these ideas with the ancient belief that "poetical rapture" (as Ben Jonson calls it), like sexual love, cannot be accounted for by reason alone—articulated by Plato in the *Phaedrus* as "if any man come to the gates of poetry without the madness of the Muses . . . he and his works of sanity with him [will] be brought to nought" and by Emily Dickinson as "Much Madness is Divinest sense"—and suddenly Pound's claims that "[t]hought is a chemical process" and that "the brain is thus conceived not as a separate and desiccated organ, but as the very fluid of life itself" seem less farfetched (Jonson 414; Plato 492; Dickinson 278; Pound, *Pavannes* 206, 214).

Pound compares the "spermatozoide's" power to exteriorize a form (i.e., to inject a life-form into what he calls the "ovular bath") to the brain's power to do the same as a "maker or presenter of images" (*Pavannes* 204–05). His fellow imagist H.D. connects sexual function to image-making in a similar way in her *Notes*, though instead of validating her ideas with pseudoscientific jargon, H.D. frames them in the language of personal experience: "If I could visualise or describe that over-mind in my own case, I should say this: it seems to me that a cap is over my head, a cap of consciousness over my head, my forehead, affecting a little my eyes" (18). H.D. outlines three states of life, "body," "mind," and "overmind," and argues that "men and women of temperament" (i.e., artists) must cultivate "certain definite physical relationships" in order to "develop" their talent sources. As she experiences it, the jellyfish-like cap that sits over her head shoots long feelers down and out from her body. The jellyfish mind can also be visualized as "centered in the love-region of the body or placed like a foetus in the body" (19). "The brain and the womb are both centres of consciousness, equally important," she writes, and these two centers are connected to image-making, each producing a different kind of "vision" (21).

More mystical than Pound's postscript, H.D.'s *Notes* stress the importance of sympathy and love to her theory, revised after her sessions with "a scientist, a psychologist" (specifically, Freud, for whom she would later write the remembrance *Tribute to Freud*). Employing language similar to Pound's from *The Spirit of Romance*, H.D. concludes, "These jelly-fish . . . are the 'seeds cast into the ground.' But as it takes a man and woman to create another life, so it takes these two forms of seed, one in the head and one in the body to make a new spiritual birth" (50). Though H.D.'s *Notes* could be read as reducing "gender" to "sex," it is helpful to remember that their author chose a life partner who, though labeled female at birth and named Winifred, had no doubt that she was, in fact, male, and thus changed her name to the gender-nonbinary Bryher. She also "cautioned H.D., as Gertrude Stein had her friend Alice Toklas, never to refer to her as a 'she.' That would be a pronoun of opprobrium, and would cast an illicit shadow on their relationship" (Guest 122).

The H.D. biographer and poet Barbara Guest's dismissal of the *Notes* as little more than "D.H. Lawrence at his philosophic worst" overlooks this unique text's attempt to honestly examine the link between the mind, sexual love, and vision in poetry, a trio of interconnected influences that H.D. remained committed to throughout her life, notably in her hymn to Eros, *Vale Ave*, but also very powerfully in her masterpiece *Trilogy* (Guest 120). Writing about the second sequence of the *Trilogy*, *Tribute to Angels*, the poet Robert Duncan stresses H.D.'s commitment to the power of sexual love through the figure of Earthly Aphrodite. H.D., he notes, makes an "impassioned evocation" to "'re-light the flame'" where "venery and the venerous (the body of *heat*) are called forth from the body of fire and re-related to venerate, venerator in the name of Venus-Aphrodite." Duncan sharply contrasts the steadfastness of H.D.'s commitment to this principle with Pound's later sublimation of his allegiance to the élan vital by turning the goddess of sexual love as articulated in *The Spirit of Romance* into the desexualized Heavenly Aphrodite "of the higher intellect" captured in "the protection of crystal." Pound desexes his Aphrodite, breaking the link between body and mind so passionately articulated in his early writings: "The spirit of romance is supplanted by the spirit of the schools. Philosophers, not poets, form the great tradition; and among philosophers, those who seek the victory of the mind over the passions are now Pound's master" (302–03).

Of course, Pound's poetry is the most powerful resource we have when seeking to complicate any simple reading of the "man speaking to men" ambience that so permeates his writings on poetry. As a counterbalance to the bloodlust of Bertran de Born that he deftly channels in "Sestina: Altaforte," enter into evidence section 4 of *Hugh Selwyn Mauberley*. Few poems are as moving in their critique of the dehumanizing effects of modern warfare on young men. The delicacy of the central image of "In a Station of the Metro" betrays little of the author's macho credos, and his masterful version of Rihaku's "The River-Merchant's Wife: A Letter" compassionately inhabits a female narrative voice.

Setting these much-anthologized pieces alongside "The Condolence"—a critique of machismo and protest against male stereotyping—is an excellent way to help students see that discomfort with gender stereotypes existed even when cultural ideas about "maleness" and "femaleness" were more codified. "The Condolence" is an apostrophe to songs of youth, called "fellow sufferers":

> O my fellow sufferers, songs of my youth,
> A lot of asses praise you because you are "virile,"
> We, you, I! We are "Red Blood"!
> Imagine it, my fellow sufferers—
> Our maleness lifts us out of the ruck,
> Who'd have foreseen it?
>
> O my fellow sufferers, we went out under the trees,
> We were in especial bored with male stupidity.
> We went forth gathering delicate thoughts,
> Our "*fantastikon*" delighted to serve us.
> We were not exasperated with women,
> for the female is ductile.
>
> And now you hear what is said to us:
> We are compared to that sort of person
> Who wanders about announcing his sex
> As if he had just discovered it.
> Let us leave this matter, my songs,
> And return to that which concerns us.

The "asses" who praise Pound's early songs on the basis of gender conformity (they are "virile," have "Red Blood!" and so on) irk the poet in exactly the way women poets have been irritated from time immemorial when valued solely on the basis of culturally approved supposed female strengths, such as empathy or maternal warmth.

At the same time, we might question why Pound, while rejecting male stereotypes, promotes a generalizing idea about women. What does he mean when he writes, "the female is ductile"? He is bored by "male stupidity," which reads here as rigidity, and prefers the supposed plasticity of women; yet Pound seems unmindful of how a statement reducing all woman to one quality is just the sort of thing that might be uttered by "that sort of person / Who wanders about announcing his sex / As if he just discovered it." On the other hand, being "ductile" is arguably one of the ways art can reach across boundaries and inhabit the "personae" of the other. Does this mean that Pound is *identifying* with this supposedly female quality, along with those "delicate thoughts" he seems to value two lines above?

"The Condolence" is a fascinating instance of Pound's engagement with the gender puzzle and illustrates modernist writers' engagement with sex and gender as directly linked to their aesthetics and creative potential. Pound's frustration emerges from the fact that he wanted to work against "male stupidity" by taking what he believed to be the feminine route: "gathering delicate thoughts" to build his "*fantastikon*" (a Greek term, also used by Yeats in *A Vision*, which refers to the real world created through image and imagination).

Here are other questions that can be used to stimulate classroom discussion: A condolence is an expression of sympathy, usually on the occasion of a death. What or who has died, or needs sympathy, in this poem? Who—men or women—does Pound imagine as the audience or reader for this address? Do the poem's final lines, "Let us leave this matter . . . and return to that which concerns us," betray the privilege of a false universal that would allow Pound to address or ignore the issue of gender at his convenience? Does the poem anywhere indicate for what qualities, if not for virility, Pound would have preferred that his "fellow sufferers" be praised?

Perhaps "delicate thoughts" were exactly what was bulldozed by the stark reality of World War I. In the first sections of *Mauberley*, Pound elegizes his own youthful naïveté, his or his "mask's" attempt to wring "lilies from the acorn." In sections 4 and 5, however, he turns from his attempt "to resuscitate the dead art / of poetry" to the art of death as perfected by modern warfare (*Personae* [rev. ed.] 185):

> Died some, pro patria
>   non "dulce" non "et decor" . . .
> walked eye-deep in hell
> believing in old men's lies, then unbelieving
> came home, home to a lie,
> home to many deceits,
> home to old lies and new infamy;
> usury age-old and age-thick
> and liars in public places.
>
> Daring as never before, wastage as never before
> Young blood and high blood,
> fair cheeks, and fine bodies;
>
> fortitude as never before
>
> frankness as never before,
> disillusions as never told in the old days,
> hysterias, trench confessions,
> laughter out of dead bellies. (188)

Here we see Pound's almost feminized description of the young male soldiers as having "fair cheeks" and "fine bodies." They are driven to "hysterias"—a female nervous condition—not by Wagnerian decadence, but by the "frankness" of "trench confessions," a kind of truth pressured by war horrors. This loss of "a myriad, / And of the best" was occasioned by masculine mendacity, the fault of "old men's lies." And for what? "For an old bitch gone in the teeth, / For a botched civilization" (188).

Some students may reject the sentiment Pound is expressing here because of his decision to use harsh, gendered language. But it is worth debating why he chooses to personify Western civilization in this manner. In Pound's critique, it is the commercialization of life, the fact that the "pianola" has replaced "Sappho's barbitos," that has caused the rot. The language of "an old bitch gone in the teeth" points backward, toward a Chaucerian register. From the point of view of melopoeia, the sequence of "bitch," "teeth," and "botched," followed by the Latinate "civilization," is very affecting. But behind the word "botched" there also lies a whiff of obstetric malpractice. In other sections of *Mauberley*, Pound's critique regarding the morbidity of the "old bitch's" aesthetics employs metaphors of reproductive failure: "The English Rubaiyat was still-born," or "Among the pickled fetuses and bottled bones" (*Personae* [rev. ed.] 189–90). An excellent way to help students work through this difficult and reference-filled poem is to have them make a gender map of Pound's diction, distinguishing between instances when he is writing about real men and women (or gods and goddesses) and when he is employing gendered language metaphorically. Of course, what constitutes "gendered" language is, like gender itself, fluid, a discovery that provides another pedagogical opportunity.

I love teaching, at all levels, Pound's most famous imagist poem, "In a Station of the Metro." The central image is delicate and beautiful: "The apparition of these faces in the crowd / Petals on a wet, black bough" (*Personae* [rev. ed.] 111). Students are quick to recognize that the image has a racial component, insofar as the contrast of the petals to a "black bough," conjures pink or white faces. Well-read students also have no trouble seeing Pound's use of the word "apparition" as a cue to "shades," drawing an analogy of the Paris Métro to the Greek underworld. But is this little masterpiece "gendered"? One way to think about this question would be to teach "In a Station of the Metro" alongside H.D.'s "Heat," which begins, "O wind, rend open the heat, / Cut apart the heat / Rend it to tatters." In contrast to the presentation of the image in Pound's poem, H.D.'s image is an imperative, calling for violence. She goes on:

> Fruit cannot drop
> through this thick air—
> fruit cannot fall into heat
> that presses up and blunts
> the points of pears
> and rounds of grapes.
>
> Cut the heat—
> plough through it,
> turning it on either side
> of your path.

"Heat" poses a challenge to Pound's definition of the image as "that which presents an intellectual and emotional complex in an instant of time" ("A Retrospect" 4). Pound's poem punctuates time in an attempt to stop linearity. By contrast, H.D.'s poem seems singularly uninterested in "an instant of time." Rather, the cyclical nature of temporal experience is embodied in the image of the over-ripe fruit longing for release. Julia Kristeva's essay "Women's Time," which examines cultural and political ideas about time and gender, could prove a useful frame for an advanced discussion of imagism and temporality: "As for time," Kristeva writes, "female subjectivity would seem to provide a specific measure that essentially retains *repetition* and *eternity* from among the multiple modalities" (191). How do H.D.'s and Pound's poems, both defined as "imagist," help us think about assumptions we might draw between temporality, image-making, and gender in poetry?

NOTES

[1] Pound, who advocated for a poetry "free from emotional slither," described H.D.'s work in a letter to Harriet Monroe as "the sort of American stuff that I can show here in Paris without its being ridiculed. Objective—no slither; direct—no excessive use of adjectives; no metaphors that won't permit examination. It's straight talk, straight as the Greek!" ("A Retrospect" 12; *Selected Letters* 11).

[2] This is not strictly true. In *Die Walküre*, Sieglinde becomes pregnant by her twin brother, Siegmund, and gives birth to Siegfried, though she dies in childbirth.

Pound among the Women

Susan McCabe

Ezra Pound's relationships with women were, if nothing else, complex. While Pound thought of himself as a self-made troubadour, his dependencies were many, including several fiancées, a wife and her celebrated mother, his own mother, collaborators, admirers, a wife, a mistress, their child, and his early London patron, Margaret Cravens. Alongside personal affairs, Pound needed the productive modernist female editors of his day to shape modernism. In essence, Pound construed the creative process as bound up with women, not as agents or actors, but rather as muses, ideals, or drudges. He can be taught most insightfully through his relationship to H.D., who was seeking a poetics almost in polar opposition to Pound's, one where muse and artist overlapped. Both their courtship and its finish reflect on the contradictory attitudes, with extremes of adoration and disdain, Pound held toward women even as he relied upon them for inspiration and support. This essay outlines ways instructors and students can approach the women in Pound's work and life.

In 1901, H.D., born Hilda Doolittle in 1896, met Pound through her brother Gilbert and her friend Margaret Snively, a day before his sixteenth birthday, at a fancy dress Halloween ball. From there, she embarked on a literary courtship with the flamboyant Penn student. A year older than H.D., born 30 October 1885 in Boise, Idaho, Pound rarely acknowledged his maternal New England ties, even his distant relation Henry Wadsworth Longfellow, the first American to translate Dante's *Inferno*. His family moved to Philadelphia, where his father, Homer, working at the Mint, fueled Pound's obsession with poetry and money. Meeting H.D. for furtive kisses in the woods, Pound called her his "Dryad," a tree spirit. H.D. broke her engagement with Pound in 1908, after he found new muses in a less Philistine country. Nevertheless, H.D. told her friend Viola Jordan that it was Pound who had first given her the life-changing sight of Dante's *Vita nuova* and its frontispiece, Dante Gabriel Rossetti's "Dante's Dream."

The template Pound discovered in Dante's *Vita nuova* for his psychic relationship to women spurred *Hilda's Book*, a work that illuminates the contrary approaches to mythology and poetics taken by Pound and H.D. (as well as many other women writers). For Pound, Dante's book offered two mutually exclusive roles, the poet and his elevated muse; H.D. rejected this dualism for a more invocatory poetics. Any of H.D.'s poems in her 1916 *Sea Garden* illustrate this "where sea-grass tangles with / shore-grass" in a geography of tearing wind, broken shells, and a rose, "marred and with stint of petals" ("Hermes of the Ways," "Sea Rose"). H.D. read Rossetti and especially Algernon Charles Swinburne for all their queerness, rather than as models of poet-heroes such as Odysseus, who in Pound's canto 1 relishes sailing and writing with "Circe's this craft" but, descending to the underworld, comes upon his mother, Anticlea, "whom [he] beat[s] off" (*Selected Poems* 96, 97). Pound embodied Odysseus, evading and powered by Circe's magic, absent at sea when Anticlea dies.

Pound drew deeply from *La vita nuova*, finding in its devotion to beauty and truth, embodied in Beatrice, the dreamed ideal that would also compel Yeats and H.D., though in different directions. A. David Moody considers that while at the University of Pennsylvania and then at Hamilton College, Pound's main subject was "desire for women redirected—painfully, joyfully, skeptically toward the sublime" (*Young Genius* 18). Pound's psyche, run by Beatrice, feeds upon the decadent tea-shop women, or the whores "dropping in for a word" in his "Lake Isle," revisionary of his hero, W. B. Yeats. Eve Sedgwick's important scholarship has made it evident that love for a woman often fuels homoerotic bonding between two men; this dynamic played out in the way Pound originally used the Shakespear mother and daughter to get to Yeats: Olivia Shakespear, mother to Dorothy, provided the calling card to Yeats, whom Pound then considered the greatest living poet.

Moody writes that Dorothy Shakespear's notebooks between March 1909 and April 1910 "show her struggling to understand and imitate him, writing her own *Vita Nuova*," while "Pound could not sustain H.D. as muse ideal; she was too active and probing" (*Young Genius* 85). Dorothy played a better Beatrice than H.D., and Pound updated *Hilda's Book* for Dorothy in a sequence called "The Dawn," much of which was lost (85–87). In *Personae*, poems such as "La Donzella Beata," "Era Venuta" (retitled "Camaraderie"), and "The Tree," a poem deeply bound up with Pound's walks with Hilda in the Pennsylvania woods, were retooled for Dorothy—and her mother ("Hilda's Book" 68).

Pound's *Selected Poems* or, if more time can be spent, the *New Selected Poems and Translations*, edited by Richard Sieburth, should be taught alongside *Paint It Today*, *End to Torment*, and H.D.'s *Selected Poems* to lay out the literary work that grew out of, to some extent, the short-lived romance between two poets who were mutually shaped by Dante, Swinburne, and Rossetti. A fruitful dialogue emerges between "The Tree," for example, with its instantaneous metamorphosis—"I stood still and was a tree amid the wood / Knowing the truth of things unseen before"—and the author's sense of H.D. as Dryad. Pound's later monologue translation "The River-Merchant's Wife: A Letter" creates a Penelope-like figure, on the alert for her husband's return. These poems work in a dialogue with H.D.'s "Hermes of the Ways," "Sea Rose," "Oread," and especially "Garden," where the speaker violently replies to betrayal, "if I could break a tree, I could break you." It juxtaposes with Pound's "Garden," which depicts an upper-class woman walking in Kensington Park, "dying piece-meal / of a sort of emotional anemia."[1] One might say Pound's early "personae" poems led to H.D.'s early poems using personae such as Helen, scapegoat for the Trojan War, who "could only be loved, / white ash amidst funereal cypresses" ("Helen"). This poem recoiled from the masculine poetics that made Helen a muse, a phantom to be fought over.

H.D. recorded in her 1920 unfinished *Paint It Today* the aftereffects of romancing with Pound, "feeling that someone had tampered with an oracle, had banged on a temple door, had dragged out small curious, sacred ornaments, had not understood their inner meaning," focusing instead on "their outer value, their perfect tint and caring." An "irreverent male youth," he had not "stolen" these "but left them, perhaps worse, exposed by the roadside, reft from the shelter and their holy setting" (7). By the time she wrote these words, she was in a relationship with the modernist producer Bryher, born Annie Winifred Ellerman, and Pound saw her as too sexually indeterminate a poet to play the lesser parts he assigned women close to him—wives, muses, patrons, editors, all bound to his early formulation to his mother on 1 January 1910: "If the artist must marry let him find someone more interested in art, or his art, or the artist part of him, than in him. After which let them take tea together three times a week" (*Ezra Pound to His Parents* 209). This was the married life Dorothy walked into: he was the art, the artist; he was himself; she was cast as the eternal Penelope. For H.D.'s part, she recognized Pound's talent but thought he lacked humility. Pound's influence worked through antagonism, fueling H.D.'s search for a female-centered eroticism that reconciled love and art.

After setting up Pound's early biographical engagement with H.D. as his "Dryad" who broke away, I use *Paint It Today* and *End to Torment* (composed thirty-eight years later, in 1958) to show the biographical arc and historical backdrop of H.D.'s relation to Pound. Although Pound's romance with H.D. had ended by the time he became embroiled with Olivia and Dorothy Shakespear, and with Olga Rudge, who would become his mistress, Pound seized H.D.'s work as an exemplar of his imagist vision. H.D. recounts 26 September 1912, when, now married to Richard Aldington, she convened with Pound at the British Museum tearoom. There a significant bit of literary history came into being as H.D. exposed a sheaf of poems. Pound resolved that day to send to Harriet Monroe, editor of *Poetry*, "Hermes of the Ways," signed by him with the flourish "H.D. *Imagiste*": letters crisp, curt, leaving the author in potential anonymity, though it was a stroke of brilliance ("Doolittle" didn't sing). H.D. recounted the incident 1958 as if it had happened the day before:

> We all read in the British Museum reading room. Dark walls and statues that looked dingy. Frances had gone home. I could wait till mother wrote, "We could meet in Genoa." I had my own allowance now. Drifting? "But Dryad," (in the Museum tea room), "this is poetry." He slashed with a pencil. "Cut this out, shorten this line. . . ." And he scrawled "H.D. Imagiste" at the bottom of the page. (*End* 18)

Pound may have appreciated and appropriated H.D. for his developing and short-lived imagist movement, but he saw his forming definitions epitomized in his past love's poems. His muse was, in fact, a poet, and he wanted the credit for making her one. H.D. embraced the initials: they gave Pound's theories praxis. The capture of an "image" as an "intellectual and emotional complex in an instant of time" played out even in her hieroglyphic name as well as in her chiseled poems (Pound, "A Retrospective" 4).

Though Pound was influential in providing H.D. with initial acclaim, H.D.'s work, relying on many similar sources as that of Pound, ultimately created a feminist counterpart to Pound's patriarchal tendencies. Thus, in teaching Pound, it is necessary to teach H.D. and other producers of modernism—Bryher, Monroe, Amy Lowell, Moore, and Loy, to name a group—as a foil, borrowing and building upon or alternating from Pound's mythic modernism. His 1916 essay "Psychology and Troubadours" was influential upon H.D.'s thought, particularly its visceral sense of myth:

> I believe that Greek myth arose when someone having passed through delightful psychic experience tried to communicate it to others and found it necessary *to screen himself from persecution*. Speaking aesthetically, the myths are explications of mood: you may stop there, or you may probe deeper. Certain it is that these myths are only intelligible in a vivid and glittering sense to those people to whom they occur. I know, I mean, one man who understands Persephone and Demeter, and one who understands the Laurel, and another who has, I should say, met Artemis. These things are for them *real*. (*Spirit* 92)

Pound mentions no women poets conversing with gods, he finds reality in these essentially female myths, eliding the fact that women poets also identified with these mythic personalities; what Pound contributes, however, is a matter-of-fact poetic truth: poets find mythologies inspiring and are moved to re-embody them.

After a close reading of H.D. and Pound's dialogic relationship, teaching Pound among the women would err if it did not include Pound's role as a powerful impresario, often named editor-at-large, igniting magazines. He sought out strong women editors, most useful to him at a distance, such as Monroe, in Chicago. His letters about the "new" poetry shaped many of her decisions, and he became the magazine's foreign correspondent in London. In a 1919 essay in *Poetry*, Monroe's detailed reflection upon the various sonic inventions, tones, even instruments, available to modern poets (Vachel Lindsay she links to "the organ, or even a jazz band, at his pleasure," Lowell to Bach's fugues), called for more liberty: "And shall Ezra Pound, composing nocturnes and fantasias as delicate as Chopin's, be reminded that the public prefers Strauss waltzes?" ("What Next?" 239). She heeded Pound's insistence that "'[t]hey,' the American brood, have ears like elephants" (*Selected Letters* 15), publishing his prescriptive "A Few Don'ts by an Imagiste." With this edict, Pound took on a paternal mantle, both generative and foreclosing to women.

Pound's interaction with Monroe is suggestive of one of his more positive professional relationships with women. Pound promoted the work of H.D., Loy, and Moore. His wonderful short piece "Marianne Moore and Mina Loy" recognized these poets' inventiveness as *logopoeia*, "a dance of the intelligence among words," distinct from the other two modes of poetry: *melopoeia* (his own brand of poems driven by "music") and imagism, its visual form. Significantly, he selected two of the most characteristically unsentimental women poets as subjects: in Moore, he can "detect traces of emotion," and in Loy, "no emotion whatever." These observations, intended as praise, reveal his discomfort with both poetry and women that elevated emotion over intellect. He welcomed Lowell as an imagist when they met in 1913 in London, after Monroe had given her a letter of introduction, and he accepted "In a Garden" for *The New Freewoman*; but as her work became increasingly female-centered, he dismissed her for turning *his* imagism into "Amygism." Indeed, Lowell brought together a band of poets—H.D., Moore, Robert Frost, John Fletcher, D.H. Lawrence, and Aldington—in successive imagist anthologies.[2]

Aldington and H.D. liked Lowell and tried to get her to change her anthology title *Some Imagist Poets* to "The Six" when Pound threatened legal attacks; he owned imagism, he argued. Meanwhile, Gertrude Stein called Pound "a village explainer," mocking his expansive braggadocio; she, too, was making a new poetics, even more divorced from his precursors than was H.D.'s. Friends with Lowell, Stein, and Alice B. Toklas, H.D. could straddle the two polarities of Pound and Stein. In teaching these allegiances and divergences, it is best to present imagism as Pound saw it—and then also through others in the imagist circle.

Pound was guided by his drive to engender a new poetics, to break out of inherited sentimentalities; he also bluntly expressed the generalized misogyny that dominated his time period. His early essay "I Gather the Limbs of Osiris" (published in December 1911 and February 1912 in *The New Age*[3]) formulated his key modernist principle: "the method of luminous detail" (21), a method that registered with readers of all genders. In Pound's effort to infuse more visceral embodiment into poetics, he relied on masculine principles of creativity, amplified in his introduction to his translation (begun in 1913) of Remy de Gourmont's *The Natural Philosophy of Love* (he devoted a special issue of *The Little Review* to Gourmont in 1919). For the pagan-minded Gourmont, the brain acted as a repository of seminal fluid that charges and recharges creativity, and Pound writes in his introduction that "the power of the spermatozoid is precisely the power of exteriorizing a form," alluding to Plato's placement of a male "shaping principle" as necessary for art, with women relegated to a passive function. Pound's introduction links "phallic religions" and everyday London life for the male dandy: the creative process amounts to "the phallus or spermatozoid charging, head-on, the female chaos. . . . Even oneself has felt it, driving any new idea into the great passive vulva of London, a sensation analogous to the male feeling in copulation" ("Natural Philosophy" 144). In teaching Pound alongside women, I set forth this introduction and other theories of the creative process, including H.D.'s own in *Notes on Thought and Vision*, where she sees creativity as stemming from womb-vision, tracing herself back to Sappho and writing directly counter to Pound's phallic vision.

In teaching Pound's imagism, as well as these dual ideas of the creative process, I direct students to his most famous poem, "In a Station of the Metro," which in some ways enacts both the still shot of imagism and the active eye of the male spectator plunging into the "passive" station. The dynamics of imagism can then be more broadly studied in relation to Peter Nicholls's persuasive argument that modernism rested on a divide between the subjective (presumably male) gaze directed at the female as object in an effort to gain "a contrasting disembodiment" (*Modernism* 3), using the exemplary "To a Red-Haired Beggar Girl" by Charles Baudelaire. It could be argued that imagism was Pound's until Lowell inserted a less binary use of the gaze. Certainly, in teaching Pound and his representations of women, it is imperative to place his poetic decrees alongside those of female practitioners as well as the poetic theories that buttressed influential notions.

In Pound's view, editorial work suited women's talents and usefully diverted their attention away from the politics of suffrage and women's rights. Bonnie Kime Scott writes that "the journalistic world was often more welcoming to women than the literary world—a condition exemplified by Pound's wresting of *The New Freewoman* from its feminist-socialist-environmentalist basis to the modernist literary cause" (190). *The Egoist* (a telling revision of *The New Freewoman*) closed down the original journal's feminist aims, with H.D. serving as "acting editor" only when Aldington, her then husband and fellow imagist, was sent to the Front.[4] In teaching Pound generally, but specifically in regard to women, it makes good sense to lay out the publishing scene in Europe and in America, and to discuss how Pound inspired modern women editors while keeping them in check.

Pound was devoted to his art above all else, and his elevations and deflations of women in his world and in myth help us understand his modernism. Like T. S. Eliot's, many of his early poems idealized or vulgarized women. "Praise of Ysolt" in *Personae* shows three women, each driving the poet to song such that "one gathers that 'the woman of the sun' is his new *donzella beata* and ideal muse" (Moody, *Young Genius* 89). The problem lies in the distance between artist and muse; watching Pound trying to make her into a muse, H.D. considered that the process might work better if the muse were active, in dialogic relation. Indeed, Moody concludes, "One might say that his genius is to be the idealization of beauty, not the actual presence of a woman" (89). "An Idyl for Glaucus," for instance, presents a lover lamenting that her beloved has been turned into a sea-god; about this poem he writes mathematically to his father, Homer, subtly placing male poetic power akin to a grander beauty than the lover can know, that "the equation ought to hold good in any case where the man's further and subtler development of mind puts a barrier between him & a woman to whom he has become incomprehensible" (qtd. in Moody, *Young Genius* 91).

Pound's early "Portrait d'une Femme," like the "Portrait of a Lady" poems by William Carlos Williams and Eliot, attacks a stereotyped socialite of the time—like the one in his "Garden," decorative, inessential, here with "[i]deas, old gossip, oddments of all things"—with the slight, "You have been second always." Secondary though they might have seemed to Pound, women claimed his imagination throughout his career, from his own identification with Daphne in "A Girl" to all the city women in "The Tea Shop" ("The girl in the tea shop / Is not so beautiful as she was") or his catalogue in "Shop Girl" (his triumph over earlier male "objectivists"):

> For a moment she rested against me
> Like a swallow half blown to the wall,
> And they talk of Swinburne's women,
> And the shepherdess meeting with Guido.
> And the harlots of Baudelaire.

The major feminine types in Pound's cosmology are most notably arrayed in his major poem *Hugh Selwyn Mauberley*. If *Mauberley* was Pound's attempt "to condense the James novel," he would not have had far to look for a narrative, living as he did in a "*marriage-blanc*," as Alec Marsh puts it, with his wife's mother along with his mistress (*Ezra Pound* 31). The opening of the poem is accordingly self-critical: "Wrong from the start—" (*New Selected Poems* 111). The poet goes on to recount his London life with the Rhymer's Club, eventually disdained; the Pre-Raphaelite followers; and even his relation to Ford Madox Ford—all portrayed through the lens of the decadent femme fatale. He positions "the stylist" who has withdrawn from public view, taking "shelter . . . [w]ith a placid and uneducated mistress," near the tea salons and Lady Valentine (one who might procure some connections for him, or patronage): she's a "possible friend and comforter" (117). In the sequence's otherwise moving war poems, Pound describes European civilization in the wake of World War I as "an old bitch gone in the teeth," as if to say that what was destroyed was already decadent and feminine. It is also not a long shot to see this image as a reference to Queen Victoria, who died in 1901. The point is that Pound feminizes decay, already starting to scapegoat women and what he considered effeminized Jews as culpable (like H.D.'s "Helen") for the awful catastrophe of war.

Mauberley is a crossing point in Pound's career, showing him leaving behind the romanticism of Yeats for the sharper role he cultivated for himself as he sought a bolder way to engage the edginess of modernity. In the first sequence of *Mauberley*, the poet is torn between preferring "the elegance of Circe's hair" and his "true Penelope"—in the poem, not Dorothy but "Flaubert," allowing for a homoerotic literary bond (*New Selected Poems* 111). He bids farewell to the closed drawing rooms of portraits where Rossetti's muse with that "faun's head of hers / Became a pastime for / Painters and adulterers" (114). He rejects "the perfect glaze" of the Pre-Raphaelites and their "[t]awn fore-shores / Washed in the cobalt of oblivions" (122). Thus this poem rejects a feminized London, one where poets were still striving for a beauty no longer possible with the old lore and sentiments of Swinburne, who must go the way of the Rhymer's Club in Pound's search for a harder, more classical poetics.

By the end of World War II, Pound had been confined in St. Elizabeths Hospital after pleading insanity to the charge of treason brought on the basis of his Rome Radio broadcasts excoriating Jews, elevating Mussolini, and spouting racist, xenophobic assertions. H.D. had suffered a nervous breakdown from her experiences living through the Blitz: she thought she could communicate with the R.A.F. pilots killed in the Battle of Britain through table tapping and stop a third world war. She was treated at Kusnacht in Zurich from May to November 1946 and recovered though nutrition, writing, and reuniting with Bryher, who had lived through the war with her and had helped Jewish refugees. In 1958, as Pound's release was imminent, Norman Holmes Pearson, the Yale professor who collected H.D.'s work, urged H.D. to write a memoir of their early relationship to help sustain Pound's reputation and to keep the name "H.D." from erasure. Recovering from a painful hip operation, H.D. was terribly fearful of being "caught, caged, confined," and linked her predicament both to an earlier "confinement," her experience of childbirth, and to Pound's imprisonment in his cage in Pisa and at St. Elizabeths. She could not understand how he had gone so far afield.

Bryher was adamant that Pound not visit H.D.; she had seen friends murdered by Fascists. H.D. agreed, however, at Pearson's behest and for the sake of setting her own history down, to write *End to Torment*, a daily record from March to July in the year of Pound's release, a nonlinear meditation rousing her memory trail: "Dr. Erich Heydt injected me with Ezra, jabbing a needle into my arm, 'You know Ezra Pound, don't you?" (20). H.D. employed Freud's method in her memoir of Pound, working through associative memories in a potentially cathartic process of narrating her parallel but distinct life. She imagines that she could have been Dorothy and is happy to have escaped marriage to Pound. She reflects upon their opposed allegiances during the war—hers on the side of the Allies and his on the side of the Axis—and on the horror of his broadcasts. She suggests that Pound would have "destroyed" her and "the center they call 'Air and Crystal' of [her] poetry" (35). She also doesn't let him off the hook on lighter matters: "I suffered excruciatingly from his clumsy dancing" (49). Her basic sense of Pound had not changed from the time of writing *Paint It Today*, where she portrayed him as savaging a shrine. No doubt she had pity for Pound's insanity, especially in reading *Pisan Cantos*, composed while caged, at his most humble, confessing, as might have H.D., "When the mind swings by a grass-blade / an ant's forefoot shall save you" ("From Canto LXXXIII" [*Selected Poems* 228]).

In this period of crisis, some were disinclined to accept Pound's "greatest poet ever" calling card. Such a person was Bryher, who helped shore up modernism's margins through her vast funds (her father, the shipping magnate Sir John Ellerman, was the richest man in England when he died in 1933), though she was carefully erased, and self-erased, from most public history, likely because of her transgenderism. After Pound's death, an academic begged Bryher to contribute to a "tribute for great men," in particular, for an honorary occasion devoted to Pound; but H.D.'s intimate attachment to Bryher constituted an alternative path away from "great men." Long before, in February 1925, Pound had contacted Bryher—recalling the aid she had given H.D. with her "fatherless" child in 1919—about the "disposition of X" and his "secretismo," that his mistress was with child: "Will you now take on your parental functions and look about for some suitable lying-in hospital or maternity home or whatever, in French Switzerland?" (Letter to Bryher). Pound was averse to any overflow of emotional energy from his work; in part, his work depended upon not conforming to marriage conventions, leading to his crass assumption that Bryher would want to handle, as he put it, "the goods." He would later fault H.D. for not seeking monetary aid for him from Bryher just after Ellerman's death.

Bryher wrote to Moore a letter that strikes me as a fitting ending to exploring how Pound might be recast among the women. After Pound visited H.D. in 1920, he found Bryher alone in the pair's flat and pronounced her quite dull; she shared the same view of him. Moore recounted to her brother about Bryher's meeting Ezra, "Bryher said, 'I let him in; I thought it was the bread or the potatoes and I was very sorry I had. He talked to me an hour about a Saxon king and a Danish chief and how one wanted to carry off the other's wife and things went on till but one was left. He said afterward I didn't stand up very well without H.D.'" (*Selected Letters of Marianne Moore* 43). Pound's anecdote about the exchange of wives signals the paternal control artists like H.D., Moore, and others had to overcome. Yet in a larger picture of Pound among women, he *is* inciting; he shows how various links can be made, even to the obscure Bryher, who helped shape H.D.'s ethical poetics.

It would be a mistake to teach Pound without reference to his political controversy, which hinged upon women supporting his vision. Only by laying his biases out can we appreciate any of his poems. Defenses continue to be made. Mary de Rachewiltz, Pound's daughter, wrote in *Discretions*, "By the beginning of 1943 the hope that England would, like France, surrender and America make peace with the Axis had almost vanished" (159). De Rachewiltz never considered that her father could be wrong:

> I had hoped that someday, if I followed him closely, I might understand everything he said and wrote. . . . I felt sure he was enunciating eternal truths. The beauty of it was that he believed it too. It never occurred to me at the time that the Axis might not win. But "victory" had become something so abstract that it seemed not to matter which side won. (135)

Victory, it might be remembered, would have mattered greatly to political dissidents or prisoners, to the French, to the English, to the Americans.

Pound struggled against "humanity" in its want: "with a painted paradise at the end of it / without a painted paradise at the end of it" (canto 74 [456]). He catches the error in trying to totalize the fragments of civilization; perhaps he counted the moral cost. He confesses at the end of *The Cantos*: "I cannot make it cohere" (canto 116 [816]). The hope lies here. In teaching Pound among the women, their "incoherences," and innovations, speak to his best writing.

Indeed, the twenty-first century is not an age exclusively of "great men." In order to understand women's roles in Pound's poetry and life, we must first consider the above biographical facts along with his misogyny and active anti-Semitism, making his appeal as a high modernist less attractive. However, for any class devoting time to exploring early practitioners of modernist poetry, Pound is a necessary figure, sounding the call to "make it new" and writing deftly restrained yet heady poems that marked the need to throw over hyper-romanticism. There is a reluctance, especially by feminists, to teach Pound due to his disparagement of women and his anti-Semitic attacks. But teaching Pound among the women is really tantamount to revealing him as foil, even initiator, for female rebellion. This is not a pretty story, but I think it is one teachers and students should know.

NOTES

[1] This essay cites the 1971 New Directions edition of *Personae*.

[2] Published annually between 1914 and 1917, all four of the imagist anthologies (1914–1917) are now available through the Modernist Journals Project (MJP) at modjourn.org.

[3] All thirty volumes of *The New Age* are available through the MJP.

[4] Both journals are available through the MJP.

Anti-Semitism, Racism, and Conspiracy Theories in Pound's Rome Radio Speeches

Trevor Sawler

Anyone who teaches Ezra Pound's poetry will at some point be faced with the problem of how best to deal with the poet's fascism and its attendant anti-Semitism. A pivotal figure in modernism, Pound nevertheless remains a controversial and problematic writer, in large part because of the overt anti-Semitism that colors so much of his work. It can be challenging to broach this topic in the classroom. In this essay, I suggest that in seeking to help students come to terms with this issue, it is important to acknowledge the widely divergent points of view among the critics, to place Pound's anti-Semitism in context, and to let Pound speak for himself. This last point will be explored using technology as a pedagogical tool by presenting electronic selections from Pound's poetry, his prose, and his infamous Rome Radio broadcasts.

There is no denying that Pound had anti-Semitic views, and that he was not at all hesitant to express them. In "Radio Broadcasts," Benjamin Friedlander usefully explains that Pound's anti-Semitism should not be viewed simply as a critique of World Wars I and II but is rooted in his theories about war and its underlying causes; Friedlander adds that Pound's approach and thinking are organized along two basic lines, economic and racial, with the former dominating his imagination. This double argument, expressed in language whose stiffness and crudeness are as distinctive as they are painful and reprehensible, also dominates Pound's radio speeches.

Ever the teacher, Pound offers an argument in his Rome Radio speeches, but also in the rest of his work and correspondence, according to which "[t]here is no understanding of history without some understanding of finance" (*"Ezra Pound Speaking"* 262). An "understanding" of usury as the immoral and criminal manipulation of currency leads to economic enslavement brought about by war: "Wars in old time were made to get slaves. The modern implement of imposing slavery is DEBT. Usury is an instrument for increasing debt, and for keeping the debtor in debt perpetually or at least for the longest possible period" (261). "The Jews have worked out a system [of debt manipulation through the banking system], very neat system, for the ruin of the rest of mankind, one nation after another" (257). This plain truth of the "Jewish problem" is not evident to the ordinary citizen because "The Economist [the media] does NOT elucidate, because it belongs to the Jews, that is to Rothschild, and its editors serve their owners" (256).

Believing that Jews, as usurers, deliberately cause war and profit from it, Pound regards them and those in their debt with anger and contempt, cultivating a rhetoric of racial hatred extending to a call for annihilation. So, as Friedlander summarizes, in his radio speeches Pound offers a series of variations on the theme and on the word *kike*: "Kikery, kikocracy, kikette, kikeria, kikosophy" (120). In a speech delivered on 27 April 1943, Pound can go as far as to call for the execution of President Roosevelt along with that of many Jews: "I think it might be a good thing to hang Roosevelt and a few hundred yidds IF you can do it by due legal process, NOT otherwise. Law must be preserved. I know that this may sound tame, but so it is. It is sometimes hard to think so. . . . Sometimes one feels that it would be better to get the job done somehow, ANY how, than to delay execution" (*"Ezra Pound Speaking"* 289).

Ignoring the Rome Radio speeches as some critics do does not solve or soften the problem of Pound's anti-Semitism since the same ideas and rhetoric infect the poetry. Important examples of Pound's irascible and erroneous thinking include *The Cantos*, which, in the words of Massimo Bacigalupo in *The Forméd Trace*, "in many ways . . . belong in those shops that sell swastikas and recordings of Mussolini's speeches, for they are, among other things, the sacred poem of the Nazi-Fascist millennium which mercifully never eventuated" (x). One example of this kind of argument can be made in connection to the opening page of canto 52, which was printed for decades after its initial publication in 1940 with the word "Stinkschuld" used twice in one line and redacted, and then with the final five lines also redacted. Here is the earlier version:

> sin drawing vengeance, poor yitts paying for
> paying for a few big jews' vendetta on goyim
> . . . .
> Remarked Ben: Better keep out the jews
>   or yr/ grand children will curse you
> jews, real jews, chazim, and neschek
> also super-neschek or the international racket
>
> (257)

We know that the publishers (New Directions and Faber and Faber) wished to avoid libel suits and requested that Pound agree to delete "Stinkschuld" as well as the final five lines of this page, made up largely of virulent anti-Semitic slurs. Pound, however, refused to do so and suggested that they be blacked out instead. Moreover, the remark made according to Pound by "Ben," that is, by Benjamin Franklin, is based on a document that, as Carroll F. Terrell notes, "has been exposed as a forgery; Franklin never said anything of the kind" (*Companion* 2:201).

These views have resulted in much controversy among the critics, and that controversy is perhaps best identified through two widely divergent and mutually exclusive points of view: on the one hand, that Pound should be read and taught in spite of his championing of fascism and his animus towards Jews, simply because his work is so good; and, on the other hand, that his attitudes are so objectionable that he ought not to be taught at all. The first group consists largely of defenders and apologists, with Hugh Kenner acting as the chief spokesperson, while Robert Cassillo best characterizes the second one.

The approach of the apologists is in many ways similar to that of the New Critics of the mid–twentieth century: pay little or no attention to the artist; instead, focus exclusively on the art itself. All that matters is the poetry, which functions as a self-contained, self-referential aesthetic object. Introducing students to T. S. Eliot's essay "Tradition and the Individual Talent" at this point explains, but does not justify, the position taken by Pound critics who apply Eliot's comments—for instance, his claim that "Honest Criticism and sensitive appreciation are directed not upon the poet but upon the poetry"—in order to absolve Pound from his ethical responsibility or the foolishness of succumbing to the illusory temptations of totalitarianism, racial pigeonholing, and conspiracy-mongering (7). Pound does not want his readers to miss the point; he speaks with authority and is determined to praise (and mourn) Mussolini; to decry the corruption of the central banks, often organized or directed by Jews; and to criticize modern democratic society as an "old bitch gone in the teeth" (*Hugh Selwyn Mauberley* 191). Such is the argument made by Kenner in *The Poetic Achievement of Ezra Pound* and in *The Pound Era* and by many of those who followed him and this direction. It's an argument that makes it possible for the poet Donald Hall, as late as 1999, to equivocate, "'I know the horrendous things that Pound did, and I also know that he was a great American poet" (qtd. in Ellison). That is the conundrum, the dilemma, faced by all readers of Pound.

The approach of the denunciators, in turn, is equally spirited. In *The Genealogy of Demons: Anti-Semitism, Fascism, and the Myths of Ezra Pound*, Casillo argues that anti-Semitism was central to Pound's outlook and not merely a "suburban prejudice," as Pound described it to Allen Ginsberg in 1967, or an incidental by-product of his economic theories about usury (Wilhelm, *Ezra Pound, the Tragic Years* 344). Casillo suggests that anti-Semitism was an essential element of Pound's thought and permeated the entirety of his work. Casillo, and others like him (for instance, Leon Surette in a number of publications, including *Pound in Purgatory: From Economics Radicalism to Anti-Semitism* and the more recent *Dreams of a Totalitarian Utopia: Literary Modernism and Politics*), argue that nearly the entirety of Pound's work is tainted by his fascist, anti-Semitic attitudes—the implication being that it has no place in the classroom.

Students find this critical divide disturbing and challenging. Like the opening to his Rome Radio broadcasts ("Europe calling, Ezra Pound speaking"), the man himself, his work, and the critical divide are a kind of siren song, equally inviting and repellent (*"Ezra Pound Speaking"* 20). To allow students to think about this divide and its complexities, I direct them to the aptly called "Book in Controversy" section in *Make It New*, the electronic journal of the Ezra Pound Society, where they can follow a number of critical responses to Matthew

Feldman's recent archival study, *Ezra Pound's Fascist Propaganda, 1935–45*. We read these reviews and discuss them as representing a variety of opinions and reactions to Pound's fascism and anti-Semitism.

Feldman, a historian whose book is the first sustained foray into the archival application of the Rome Radio broadcasts, clearly states that

> [f]or too long, Pound's fascist activism has simply been dismissed as either mad or bad, the product of political naiveté or misplaced economic idealism. Some or all of these factors may apply but, in short, this misses the wood for the trees. All too often lacking in supporting evidence, this tradition will be directly countered by the archivally driven view advanced here: Pound was a committed and significant English-language strategist and producer of fascist [including anti-Semitic] propaganda before, and during, Europe's most destructive war. (ix)

In his review, an outraged Surette claims Feldman demonstrates "no idea of the genesis of the views and beliefs that Pound embraced between his college years in New England, his poetic apprenticeship in Old England, his early cultural and literary criticism and his radicalization by Major Douglas' Social Credit ideas during and immediately after World War I" (8). The other two reviewers, Alec Marsh and Greg Barnhisel, are more circumspect in their criticism and also allow for the utility of Feldman's methodology and argument. For instance, Marsh notes that

> Feldman's evidence is unequivocal. And most of it comes from the Beinecke rather than squirreled away in obscure archives. . . . Feldman has discovered that Pound's radio propaganda 1940–1945 includes not hundreds, but thousands of items, from the relatively well-known speeches collected by Doob and Mary de Rachewiltz in the 1960s to a plethora of speeches to be read by others or performed by "personae" that Pound invented, to give his radio-work variety. There are also squibs, fake pro-Axis letters and, perhaps most damning of all, letters that show Pound actively crafting his propaganda efforts to the needs of the regime. . . . For those of us who have wondered how Pound supported himself during the war years when royalties and remittances were stopped from coming into Italy, the answer is that Pound was working steadily for EIAR, the Axis radio. . . . Feldman reports that "at a conservative estimate" Pound earned about 250,000 lire between 1940 and 1945 as a fascist radio propagandist, worth about $185,000 today. (11–12)

Meanwhile, Barnhisel opens his review with this:

> Matthew Feldman would like us to face up to the facts: Ezra Pound was a fascist and an anti-Semite. In [his book], Feldman, a scholar of "fascist ideol-

> ogy and the contemporary far right" . . . shovels some new manure on top of the stinking heap of Pound's political beliefs and activities before and during World War II. By doing so, he seeks to force readers—and, more importantly, scholars—to confront just how feculent that pile really is. (13)

Finally, I ask students to read a brief rejoinder to Surette's review by A. David Moody, Pound's celebrated biographer, who wonders, "What is it that makes some of us so uncritically ready to believe the worst about Pound and to have it eclipse what is of permanent value in his work?" ("On Matthew" 51).

Our discussion of these recent, telling reviews also takes into consideration the history Surette thinks must be known by anyone wishing to discuss (let alone in a book) Pound's fascism and anti-Semitism and their heavy personal cost to the poet in the aftermath of World War II. I therefore offer students a brief history of Pound's enduring commitment to economic reform (in Tony Tremblay's words, he wished to promote an economic system "that promised to democratize credit and to create economic justice through a fairer distribution of goods" [83]) that led to his early espousal of C. H. Douglas's social credit and later to his support of Benito Mussolini's brand of fascism. These involvements informed the radio broadcasts that, I explain, resulted in his indictment for treason by a grand jury in the United States on 25 July 1943, followed by his imprisonment at the end of the war at the United States Army Disciplinary Training Center in Pisa for six months. Next was a trip to Washington, D.C.; a trial, and the finding in court of mental unfitness (which certainly saved his life); and his subsequent commitment to St. Elizabeths Hospital for the Criminally Insane, where he remained until the spring of 1958.

In order to familiarize students with this story, I ask them to read a report written for the attorney general of the United States, dated 14 October 1942, on Pound's activities in Italy (Proposed Indictments 5). It was received by the criminal division of the United States Department of Justice on 22 October 1942. Appearing today under "Frequently Requested Records: Ezra Pound," this is a one-page document in part one of a six-section Pound collection that runs for at least two hundred pages and includes, along with many other relevant documents, transcriptions of Pound's speeches on which the indictment for treason was based.

After the students read this letter, I ask them if the facts in it are correct. In the ensuing discussion we discover that in some ways the writer of this report does an excellent job in assembling scattered pieces of information regarding Pound's life (especially in Italy) and his work, but he also gets some details wrong and is ignorant of some basic facts, like the year of Pound's departure from the United States (1908). It's easy to feel superior and notice only the errors of fact and interpretation. More fruitfully, I use this and similar reports from this collection to test students' knowledge of Pound's life and situation but also to discuss how such reports must have been composed based on a system of communication that depended on the mail service.

Pound had been invited in November 1939 by the Italian Ministry of Popular Culture to submit scripts. He made his initial broadcast in person in January 1941. On 16 July 1941, the FBI reported that the State Department was aware of his whereabouts and circumstances and that "A record is being maintained of his case upon the possibility that subsequently it may be found that other action against him may be taken" (*Ezra Pound's Justice Department Criminal Division File* 2). The FBI record is the work of several hands and a response to a 13 October 1942 memorandum to the bureau's director from Wendell Berge, the assistant attorney general:

> Re: Dr. Ezra Pound
> The above subject, an American citizen, has been reported to the Criminal Division to have been broadcasting enemy propaganda from a Rome, Italy radio station.
>
> It is requested that you obtain, if possible, transcripts of his broadcasts and transmit the same to this Division, together with any information you may have regarding this subject. (4)

Making these materials available to students, and directing them to a few key letters, reports, and transcripts of Pound's speeches, prepares them for an informed discussion of Pound's fascism and anti-Semitism. Therefore, rather than investigating the convoluted and ethically complex history of World War II and presenting it as Pound would have his readers understand it, I choose to bring a variety of texts (and audio recordings) to the classroom and present each as a kind of ideogram, without critical comment or explanation. Included among the texts are selections from Pound's infamous Rome Radio broadcasts, where his anti-Semitic views are abundantly clear. Supplied with little more than Pound's own words (but in the context of the critical divide), students are asked to respond both to the poetry and to the problems presented by Pound's attitude toward Jews.[1]

I also suggest that it is important in any effort to come to terms with Pound's anti-Semitic views to place them in context and to see how they changed over the course of his career. For example, as already mentioned, in 1967 Pound told Allen Ginsberg that "the worst mistake I made was the stupid suburban prejudice of anti-Semitism. All along, that spoiled everything" (qtd. in Wilhelm, *Ezra Pound, the Tragic Years* 344). The use of "suburban" is remarkably apropos; Pound came of age in an America when Jews were banned from country clubs, many colleges, and even retirement homes. His early work has no more anti-Semitic content than that of T. S. Eliot or William Carlos Williams. There are a few scattered references that might be deemed inappropriate from the perspective of a modern reader, but it is clear to this writer that Pound's work prior to the 1930s can be labeled casual or social anti-Semitism.

After placing Pound's attitudes in context, the question I next pose to students is one that has been thoroughly examined by many critics: what triggered Pound's obsession with, and hatred toward, Jews? Rather than falling back on the critics, though, I let Pound speak for himself. I assign selections from *Jefferson and/or Mussolini*, some of the Pound-Agresti letters (*I Cease Not to Yowl*), *Hugh Selwyn Mauberley*, "A Visiting Card," and "What Is Money For?" Lastly, I ask them to read canto 52, in both its redacted and complete forms, as well as canto 81. With the exception of the material from *The Cantos*, which is under copyright, this material is distributed electronically on a course Web site (see appendix).

Students are asked to read the material and then post a response to cantos 52 and 81 on the Web site. The questions they are asked to respond to are simple: How would you characterize Pound's anti-Semitism in canto 52, and is canto 81 an apology of sorts? What appears to be at the root of his hatred towards Jews? Has Pound changed his mind to any degree when he writes the *Pisan Cantos*? At this point in the course, students have not been asked to read any of the criticism surrounding the poem, only the materials listed above. All the students' responses are made available to the entire class, and students are encouraged to read each other's work.

A subsequent lecture presents students with both the text and audio versions of Pound's "Books and Music," his radio broadcast from 26 October 1941 (*"Ezra Pound Speaking"* 7–10). The broadcast is made available in class and on the course Web site. A hypertext format presents the textual version of the broadcast with various sections linked to Pound's other writings and to relevant criticism. The students' initial reaction to the radio broadcasts is a combination of bewilderment and disgust. The content of the broadcast is wide-ranging, eclectic, and fragmented. Mussolini is without doubt praised, and is often represented as more democratic than Roosevelt because Pound understood his policies to be far more in keeping with the intentions of America's founding fathers than were those of the sitting American president.

Pound's anti-Semitism in the text of these speeches is self-evident. The names he gives to Roosevelt, for example, make this vividly clear: he is at times called "Jewsfelt," "Roosenstein," and "Rosefield." In addition, racial slurs abound, and it is easy to understand why so many students new to Pound focus upon this aspect of his work. At no point do I offer a defense of Pound's words, nor do I condemn him. Instead, I ask the students to consider the content of "Books and Music" in the light of the other materials they have previously read. I also ask them to review the annotated version of the broadcast that is available on the course Web site, and to incorporate the additional information found in the annotations in their analysis. There is also consideration of the impact of listening to as opposed to reading the broadcast.

As expected, the results are provocative. For example, the students find that reading the opening section of the broadcast is unsettling:

> Mr. Churchill, EVEN Mr. Churchill hasn't had the brass to tell the American people WHY he wants 'em to die to save what.

> He is fighting for the gold standard and MONOPOLY. Namely the power to starve the whole of mankind, and make it pay through the nose before it can eat the fruit of its own labor.
>
> His gang, whether kike, gentile, or hybrid is not fit to govern. And the English OUGHT to be the only people ass enough, and brute enough to fight for him.
>
> Now as to my personal habits, the few of you who know that I exist know that I have given most of my time to muggin' up kulchur, that I have writ a few books, and spent my spare time trying to learn musical composition, or else playin' tennis and floatin' round the gulf of Tigullio, in which act I make, so far as I know, a nuisance of myself to no one whatsoever.
>
> (*"Ezra Pound Speaking"* 10)

In general, students' first reaction to this passage is that the broadcast is little more than the rambling diatribe of a disturbed individual. Clearly, Pound has concerns with Churchill and money, but the racial slurs are the most disturbing. Yet there is far more going on here. For example, in the latter part of this excerpt, Pound includes, seemingly without reason, references to playing tennis, to writing books and music, and to swimming in the "gulf of Tigullio" on the Ligurian Sea: Pound had continued to live in Rapallo, on the Ligurian sea, since 1925.

Links embedded in the electronic version of the text can shed light for students. For example, the reference to playing tennis is revealed as ironic by an annotation directing readers to Surette's *Pound in Purgatory*, where they will learn that Pound's tennis partners included Harold Loeb and Louis Zukofsky, both of whom were Jewish. Zukofsky later said, "I never felt the least trace of anti-Semitism in his presence. Nothing he ever said to me made me feel the embarrassment I always have for the 'Goy' in whom a residue of antagonism to a 'Jew' remains" (qtd. in Surette 241). Similarly, the reference to Gulf of Tigullio links to Massimo Bacigalupo's article "Ezra Pound's Tigullio" and to its occurrence in *The Cantos*, as in Pound's memory, in canto 77, of Yeats's reaction to the place: "'Sligo in heaven' murmured uncle William / when the mist finally settled down on Tigullio" (493).

Rapallo, Pound's home at the time he gives this broadcast, is at the center of the Tigullio region in northwest Italy, east of Genoa, and biographical information might be included online for the students' review as well. In the same way, Pound's vitriolic outburst against Churchill at the opening of the broadcast links to the relevant sections of "What Is Money For?" and "Gold and Work," both of which offer considerable insight into Pound's economic thought at the time.

After reviewing the online materials, students are asked to produce another response paper to the two cantos, addressing the same questions they were asked the first time. Obviously, my goal at this point is for the students—many of whom saw canto 81 as an apology of sorts—to realize that when Pound says, "Pull down thy vanity," he is not speaking of himself (521). Instead, he is addressing the American soldiers in the Disciplinary Training Center at Pisa. Far from being apologetic, he is railing against his captors. Pound laments what has been lost, but he does not regret his actions.

Finally, students are asked to respond to another frequently quoted defense of Pound: Marjorie Perloff's post to a Pound discussion group, wherein she offers not so much a defense of the poet's anti-Semitism as an acknowledgment of it, followed by the observation that racism and anti-Semitism were widespread in much of the Western world at the time, and that there were many other writers who were far worse than Pound. Perloff's message is posted to the course Web site in its entirety, but the section most likely to receive a response from the student is the following:

> I still believe—and I speak here as a refugee from Hitler whose family fled the morning of the Anschluss (March 12, 1938) of Austria—that Pound's 'fascism'—most of it completely nonsensical, juvenile, and failing to understand how government works—was not nearly as dangerous as Heidegger's willed, conscious, perfectly 'reasoned' Fascism.
>
> ("Re: Pound and Fascism")

Perloff's defense is straightforward: Pound may have been anti-Semitic, but so were so many others at the time, and there were many who were worse. Students are asked to respond to Perloff's defense and, after having reviewed at least some of Pound's poetry, prose, and radio speeches, to come to their own determination. Given that the material presented has been carefully selected to include Pound's definition of usury, elements of his economic thought, and discussion of what he understood to be the appeal of Mussolini, it is hoped that they will begin to realize that Pound's anti-Semitism, usually directed at bankers, such as the Monds and the Rothschilds, may not have been simple racial prejudice. Although this is hardly a defense of the poet, it at least makes it clear that neither the apologists nor the denunciators have a credible argument.

This difficult dimension of Pound, based on the material outlined above, becomes one of the most engaging encounters for students who, initially disturbed by confronting Pound's prejudicial and unreasoned views, learn at least to listen to, if not to understand, his position. Agreement is not sought, only comprehension of, first, Pound's articulated and often didactic positions and, second, the contradictory readings and reactions of the critics. The classroom becomes an arena of debate as well as dialogue, based on original documents that state Pound's problematic views. Determining how to judge them and their impact on his writing is the very essence of students' examination and evaluation of Pound the poet, essayist, editor, and modernist.

APPENDIX
Digital Sources

Jefferson and/or Mussolini
archive.org/details/JeffersonAndOrMussoliniPound1935

"Ezra Pound Speaking": Radio Speeches of World War II
archive.org/details/EzraPoundSpeaking-RadioSpeechesOfWorldWarIi

Hugh Selwyn Mauberley
www.modernistweb.com/page/poem/19/Ode+pour+l%27election+de+son+sepulchre

"What Is Money For?"
www.modernistweb.com/page/prose/19/What+is+Money+For%3F

Fragments from Rome Radio Speeches
archive.org/details/EzraPoundAFewWwiiBroadcastRecordings/EzraPound-power.mp3
archive.org/details/EzraPound1942
archive.org/details/movies?and[]=Ezra%20Pound

From the Rome Radio Speeches, Jan. or Feb. 1942
writing.upenn.edu/pennsound/x/Pound.php

"Re: Pound and Fascism"
writing.upenn.edu/epc/authors/perloff/perloffpound.html

Recorded by the Foreign Broadcast Intelligence Service of the Federal Communications Commission, 12 February 1942
web.archive.org/web/20041013164136/http://www.umit.maine.edu/~ben.friedlander/Pound.htm
web.archive.org/web/20190111094444/www.english.illinois.edu/maps/poets/m_r/pound/radio.htm

NOTE

[1] At web.archive.org/web/20041013164136/http://www.umit.maine.edu/~ben.friedlander/Pound.htm, Friedlander makes available to students materials including canto 46, "The Pattern," "With Phantoms," "E. E. Cummings," and "Violence," and adds what he calls "Pound's Invective: A Sampler."

"Out of Key with His Time": Pound as Poet in Exile

John Gery

Approaching Pound: "Frankness as Never Before"

Besides the phrase, "out of key with his time" (185), which Ezra Pound uses to describe "E.P." in the first line of *Hugh Selwyn Mauberley*, another phrase that haunts that long poem is Pound's rant against the sacrifice of Great Britain's soldiers in World War I in parts 4 and 5 of the "E.P." sequence. Though discussed less often than the more allusive sections that surround them, these two sections anticipate the vitriolic cantos 14–15, where Pound depicts the war as Dante's hell. In part 4, he laments not only those slaughtered at the front but also those who survived the war, only to come

> home to a lie,
> home to many deceits,
> home to old lies and new infamy;
> usury age-old and age-thick
> and liars in public places.
>
> Daring as never before, wastage as never before.
> Young blood and high blood,
> fair cheeks, and fine bodies;
>
> fortitude as never before
>
> frankness as never before,
> disillusions as never told in the old days,
> hysterias, trench confessions,
> laughter out of dead bellies. (188)

Pound's juxtaposition of the deceit of "liars in public places" (here aligned with "usury" for the first time in his poetry) and the "frankness" of the martyred soldiers provides a provocative entry into his poetry. Before asking students to confront Pound's later associations with Italian Fascism or his anti-Semitism, it may be helpful to ask them how the same poet who gives his early poems such arcane titles as "In Exitum Cuiusdam" and "Nils Lykke" (*Collected Early Poems* 182, 121)—and the same poet who composes such mannered lines as "He had passed, inconscient, full gaze, / The wide-banded irides / And botticellian sprays implied / In their diastasis; // Which anaethesis, noted a year late, / And weighed, revealed his great affect, / (Orchid), mandate / Of Eros, a retrospect" (*Hugh Selwyn Mauberley* [*Personae* (rev. ed.)] 198)—could also praise his younger contemporaries' "frankness as never before." Where, exactly, in Pound's own poems, which Edward Thomas dismissed for their "turbulent opacity" (Tryphonopoulos and Adams 115), is such candor to be found?

One reply to this question that epitomizes a prevalent paradox in Pound's writing is "Everywhere!" In fact, despite what may seem an impenetrable poetics to students encountering him for the first time (outside of "In a Station of the Metro"), Pound is nothing if not true to his word. In his 1913 essay "The Serious Artist," he writes:

> Bad art is inaccurate art. It is art that makes false reports. If a scientist falsifies a report either deliberately or through negligence we consider him as either a criminal or a bad scientist according to the enormity of his offence. . . .
>
> If an artist falsifies his report as to the nature of man, as to his own nature, as to the nature of his ideal of the perfect, as to the nature of his ideal of this that or the other . . . , then that artist lies. If he lies out of deliberate will to lie, if he lies out of carelessness, out of laziness, out of cowardice, out of any sort of negligence whatsoever, he nevertheless lies and he should be punished or despised in proportion to the seriousness of his offence. (43–44)

While the layers of allusions, assumed poses, phrases from multiple languages, and coined terms found throughout Pound's poetry may frustrate a new reader, who may label him a pedant or an elitist, that same reader might agree with Pound that the first obligation in writing poetry is to the poet's own mind. For Pound, such fidelity begins with a poem's technique as much as with its subject: "I believe in technique," he declares in "A Retrospect," "as the test of a man's sincerity; in law when it is ascertainable; in the trampling down of every convention that impedes or obscures the determination of the law, or the *precise rendering of the impulse*" (9; my italics).

As a case in point, *The Cantos* follows less the pattern of a conventional epic poem that traces the odyssey of a single figure or signifies a people's origins and character than the intricate peregrinations of one poet's mind as he explores those concerns. As Marjorie Perloff explains, the "eclectic nature" of *The Cantos* is at least as important as its subject matter, "not because it provides us with a vision of Reality but because its processes imitate the processes of the external world as we have come to know it"; specifically, she argues, the epic's "capacity to assimilate all kinds of material and to incorporate many voices . . . makes more sense when we read Pound's text against, say, the *Satyricon* or *Le neveu de Rameau* than when Pound's 'poem including history' is compared to *The Prelude* or *Song of Myself*" (*Dance* 22).[1] One way in the classroom to demonstrate Perloff's point about *The Cantos*, for instance, is to compare the opening lines of other epic-length texts to the opening of canto 1, "And then went down to the ship, / Set keel to breakers, forth on the godly ship, and" (1). While Pound's lines render into English the opening of book 11 of *The Odyssey*, they also allude to the first lines of Virgil's *Aeneid*, Dante's *Inferno*, Robert Browning's *Sordello*, and Elizabeth Barrett Browning's *Aurora Leigh*, as well as a host of other epics. Yet canto 1 equally introduces the poet's own experience when it later turns to a reading of Andreas Divus's sixteenth-century Latin translation of Homer, as well as to the Anglo-Saxon poem "The Seafarer." In this way, Pound also aligns his poem to William Wordsworth's *The Prelude* and Walt Whitman's *Song of Myself* as an author-centered work.

When considered as a poem of the intellect, *The Cantos* parades a pageant of the poet's associations, lexicons, and predilections, if not his obsessions, that cumulatively can seem mysterious, indecipherable, or just other. Yet for all its idiosyncrasies, *The Cantos* triumphs as a profoundly social poem—a public work of art—whose vision comes alive most vividly through conversation and debate, through outside reading and broad speculation, more than through secluded analysis. For all its erudition, obscurities, subjectivities, weird grammar, and crags, the poem is designed to be read and discussed aloud. Those who read the poem with any sympathy, in effect, become linked not only to the plethora of figures who populate the epic, but also to those on whom its multifaceted speaker finally depends—namely, his global audience.

Pound as a Poet in Exile

One practical way to understand the candor in Pound's poetry, then, is to examine how the conditions of exile, even a self-styled exile, inform and clarify his work, especially for new readers, but even for one, like Pound's "ideal teacher," who may approach it "*almost* as if he had never seen it before" (*ABC of Reading* 86). Not only is acknowledging Pound's exile preliminary to gaining a perspective on his poetics, but it also situates his work in the context of other exiled modernists—Robert Frost, Gertrude Stein, T. S. Eliot, H.D., Ernest Hemingway, Claude McKay, F. Scott Fitzgerald, Stephen Crane, Mina Loy, Laura Riding, Langston Hughes, Thornton Wilder, and James Baldwin—as well as in contrast to the likes of Wallace Stevens, William Carlos Williams, Marianne Moore, and William Faulkner, for instance. What are the particular features of this poet's early identity, or multiple identities, in exile? Given Pound's departure from the United States in 1908 and his foreign residence through the next four decades, how does a consciousness of exile shape his method?

Except for his nearly thirteen-year incarceration at St. Elizabeths in Washington (1945–1958), Pound lived most of his life, from 1908 until his death in 1972, outside the United States. On an eight-month-long return visit in 1910, during which time he considered moving back, Pound "surveyed the American scene" and observed a "passion for achievement and getting things done" that chimed with his own. But, as Noel Stock writes, "in another sense, the people everywhere around him with whom the future lay were not his people and he decided to leave" (*Life* 95). Despite a well-orchestrated celebration in the Philadelphia newspapers of Pound's successes in London, other American writers he met that year found him "surly, supercilious and grumpy" (Stock 95; Carpenter 151), and at least one reviewer considered his poems "erratic utterances" lacking "the voice of a poet" (qtd. in Moody, *Young Genius* 129). After visiting New York, notes Ira Nadel, Pound "felt commerce controlled its culture, while the architecture seemed inauthentic" (*Cambridge Introduction* 8). Trying at first to replicate his literary experience in London by meeting such poets as Joyce Kilmer, Bliss Carmen, and Witter Bynner (Carpenter 150), Pound became convinced "that poetry in America would find no audience and that a poet would be isolated" (Nadel, *Ezra Pound* [Palgrave MacMillan] 51), a view which anticipated by forty years his comment to Eustace Mullins about his incarceration at St. Elizabeths: "The insane asylum is the only place I could have lived, in this country" (qtd. in Mullins 297). In other words, from 1910 onward Pound chose external, rather than internal, exile.

In fact, after departing for Europe on 22 February 1911, he would not return for twenty-eight years (Stock 95), during which time an almost entirely new generation would arise in the United States, leaving Pound far behind contemporary mores and fashion. Yet Pound felt equally out of place in London, "a city without much of an avant-garde tradition," where "tolerating the bohemian was about as far as it would go" (Nadel, "Introduction" 21). As John Tytell observes, Pound irritated other writers in London as much as he had in New York, "antagonizing the English, with aplomb and lots of self-assurance," one of the reasons Yeats, for one, liked him (86). By 1914, even though Pound had asked her daughter to marry him, Olivia Shakespear was urging him to leave London because "Englishmen don't understand your American ways" (Tytell 100). In London, "Pound had embraced the causes of the extreme fringes of radical art. Besides this ideological choice, Pound's manners were purely American. His casualness and frankness in speech made the English cringe" (158).

Despite what critics have argued about Pound's antics in London, and despite the fact that his departure from the United States was voluntary, his prolonged estrangement would have an unshakable impact on his aesthetic, cultural, and political vision—alternately, and sometimes simultaneously, resulting in brilliant insights and enormous blind spots. Reflecting on Pound's long exile, Dorsey Kleitz identifies its most salient features: "Forced exiles and voluntary exiles share some of the same characteristics which have changed very little since Classical times: a desire to address in some way the cause of the exile, a loss of authority, and an estrangement from one's mother-tongue. These characteristics applied both to Ovid on the Black Sea and to Pound on the gulf of Tigullio" (1–2). Concerning "estrangement from one's mother-tongue," for instance, Kleitz recalls that Mary Oppen, when visiting Pound in Rapallo with her husband, George, in the early 1930s, was struck by how removed from contemporary American English Pound's own speech had become, to the extent that he asked her what the terms "girlfriend" and "boyfriend" meant. "New words were entering the language," writes Oppen, "and he didn't hear them from the tongues of those who were giving them their meanings" (qtd. in Kleitz 4).

Kleitz further argues that Pound's exile "infused his entire poetic practice," leading him to create "a dynamic rhetoric, one that grew organically from his life to reflect his nomadic impulse" (6). Indeed, not only does Pound's isolation from American speech explain his highly stylized rhetoric, but the other tendencies of the exiled writer Kleitz lists—seeking "the cause of the exile" and dealing with "a loss of authority"—predominate as themes. Despite the varied voices, diverse languages, erudition, mixed tones, dandyism, and sometimes obscure subject matter of his early poems, these recurrent themes seep through. Ironically, however, Pound's being "out of key with his time" also fostered his allure, even as it risked alienating his readers. Still, it is from his exile, in short, that Pound derives his singular poetic technique.

Teaching Pound as Exile outside the English-Speaking World

Having taught Pound's work outside the United States to both American and non-American students, I have developed a seminar on his poetry that inevitably takes up exile as a central tenet of his vision. Since 1990, I have periodically taught seminars at the unique site of Brunnenburg, a restored castle in northern Italy that since 1947 has been the home of Pound's daughter, Mary de Rachewiltz, together with her son Siegfried de Rachewiltz and his family; this beautiful locale on the slopes of the Italian Alps near Austria is also where Pound was to "retire" after his release from St. Elizabeths in 1958, though he lived there only briefly. Over the years, I have also taught Pound and modernism elsewhere in Italy and in Serbia, Spain, and China. In these settings, without having to emphasize Pound's exile, but just by delving into his early poetry, I have discovered that reading his work as that of an exile instills in students, regardless of their nationality, a receptivity to his sometimes visionary, sometimes remote, thinking as both American and global, thereby encouraging them not to be distracted or intimidated by his erudition.

This fairly straightforward approach to Pound involves close readings of his early poetry but also draws on his translations, criticism, political essays, and letters to gloss it. It further requires, of course, considering the contrasting cultures of the United States and the rest of the world during the first decades of the twentieth century. But reading closely such poems as "Na Audiart," "Sestina: Altaforte," "Guido Invites You Thus," and "Apparuit" introduces students to Pound's innovative interpretations, as himself an outsider, of Provence, the troubadours, and François Villon, as well as of classical and Italian Renaissance poetry. "Apparuit," for instance, exemplifies Pound's technique when he adopts sapphics to render Dante's first sight of Beatrice in chapter 2 of *La vita nuova*.

In practice, Sappho's syllabics share nothing inherently with Dante's strictly composed sonnets and canzones. Yet without hesitation, Pound splices these diverse forms as though from one source:

> *Gol*den *rose* the *house*, in the *por*tal *I* saw
> *thee*, a *mar*vel, *car*ven in *sub*tle *stuff*, a
> *por*tent. *Life* died *down* in the *lamp* and *flick*ered,
>   *caught* at the *won*der.

Only a poet with no particular stake in either Greek or Italian culture would so readily forge such a hybrid poem. Similar anachronistic juxtaposition of techniques invaluably informs readings of Pound's poems derived from Latin, Chinese, medieval, Renaissance, imagist, and vorticist contexts, in a panoply of modernist experimentation, as Hugh Kenner was first to note.[2]

Nevertheless, despite Pound's indiscriminate meshing of various personae, forms, and eras, readers continuously encounter exiled voices in his early poems. To complement them, his "American" poems, such as "A Pact," "Cantico del Sole," "To Whistler, American," and "The Rest," express Pound's estrangement directly, so that by the time of *Homage to Sextus Propertius* and *Mauberley*, the crisis of the poet's displacement has already become a prominent motif, including in the early cantos. For students, Pound's recasting of these voices creates a foundation for reading his method—whether as imagist, vorticist, or ideogrammic—as that of a poet situated both inside and outside his American legacy, establishing a fundamentally transnational premise that necessitates reading him as both doggedly American and inventively global. Furthermore, interpreting Pound through his exile liberates someone teaching his poetry from having to dwell excessively on the stringent left-right polarities that can rob his work of its richness, despite the fascist and anti-Semitic forays that appear later.

To suggest how Pound's exile provides a context for the vivid yet often taxing variety of his personae, consider the opening lines of poems from the first fifty-three pages of *Personae*, the section "Poems of 1908–1911," or what basically might constitute a first week's assignment.[3] These poems Pound himself selected to preserve in 1926, so their order does not accurately reflect the chronology of their composition. Still, removed from context as first-person lines that might resonate with a reader not familiar with Pound's arcane sources, they demonstrate a tone remarkably consistent with what Kleitz identifies as the exile's preoccupation with the "cause for exile" and "loss of authority." Furthermore, they anticipate the self-transformation, as well as the search for the solace of home, any displaced person may experience. Here are several examples:

> Bah! I have sung women in three cities,
> But it is all the same. (6 ["Cino"])

I, even I, am he who knoweth the roads
Through the sky, and the wind thereof is my body. (17 ["De AEgypto"])

I am homesick after mine own kind,
Oh I know that there are folk about me, friendly faces,
But I am homesick after mine own kind. (19–20 ["In Durance"])

"Lappo I leave behind and Dante too,
Lo, I would sail the seas with thee alone!"
(24 ["Guido Invites You Thus"])

"Being no longer human, why should I
Pretend humanity or don the frail attire?"
(30 ["Paracelsus in Excelsis"])

O strange face there in the glass!
. . . . .
I? I? I?
And ye? (33 ["On His Own Face in a Glass"])

Once a reader accommodates the learned infrastructure of Pound's poetics, his speakers' shared anxiety in these monologues emerges. The excessive attention given to wandering, longing, lack of control over fate, fear of erasure, and the frailty of meaning anticipates these same concerns recurring throughout the next three sections of *Personae*: "Poems from *Ripostes* (1912)," "Poems from *Blast* (1914)," and "Poems from *Lustra* (1913–1915)," as, for instance,

When I behold how black, immortal ink
Drips from my deathless pen—ah, well-away!
Why should we stop at all for what I think? (55 ["Silet"])

May I for my own self song's truth reckon
Journey's jargon, how I in harsh days
Hardship endured oft. (60 ["The Seafarer"])

I would bathe myself in strangeness. . . . (66 ["The Plunge"])

You say that I take a good deal upon myself;
That I strut in the robes of assumption. (76 ["Monumentum Aere, Etc."])

The lateral vibrations caress me,
They leap and caress me. . . . (77 ["Before Sleep"])

Three spirits came to me
And drew me apart. . . . (92 ["April"])

Take thought:
I have weathered the storm,
I have beaten out my exile. (94 ["The Rest"])

Although in later volumes Pound's Browningesque personae figure less prominently, his portrayal of exile, in fact, becomes more pronounced. And as readers come to recognize Pound's signature use of personae, they can start to scrutinize the poet in his poems, though not in any conventionally confessional sense.[4] Rather, Pound emerges in his early poems as the "serious artist" finding his way, building his own world from whatever applicable materials he finds at hand.

One anecdote from my teaching abroad that illustrates this point involves a comment from an American graduate student at Brunnenburg studying Pound for the first time. Wondering why a poet would choose again and again to adopt the stylized voices of (to her) obscure figures and hide behind a veil of foreign phrases, inaccurately translated lines, and archaic diction, she asked repeatedly, "Where is the *real* Ezra Pound in all these poems?" To make matters worse, or so it seemed, we next came to *Cathay*, in which "Exile's Letter" and "Lament of the Frontier Guard," among other poems, further portray exile, in yet another remote guise. We then embarked on a lengthy explication of "The River-Merchant's Wife: A Letter," Pound's brazen version of Ernest Fenollosa's translation of the Li Bai original that freely leaps across time, language, and culture—as we discussed, for instance, what those infamous "blue plums" in "the village of Chokan" might signify, or exactly how far Chokan is, or was, from "Cho-fu-sa" (*Personae* 134).[5] After considering how Pound in this poem fashions a young woman's writing in a voice dramatically different from the monologues of Bertran de Born, Peire Vidal, Arnaut de Marvoil, Guido Cavalcanti, Sappho, Daphne, Simon Zelotes, the Seafarer, Catullus, and others we had read, the class gradually began to see how, in spite of her modesty, self-deprecation, and discretion, the river-merchant's wife expresses, by poem's end, utter desperation at her husband's prolonged absence and the loss of a way of life she has come to desire. At that moment, I reminded the class of the poem's greatest irony, that once the wife seals her letter, she cannot actually post it, since she has no idea where to send it, nor whether her husband is even alive.[6]

After a pause and a collective sigh from the class, the ever-skeptical graduate student slowly lifted her eyes from the poem and exclaimed, "Ah! So *here*, at last, is the *real* Ezra Pound!" Where could she possibly find the *real* Ezra Pound in this poem? Yet the other students broke into laughter, recognizing immediately what she meant. And I knew, too, that she had "gotten" it. Despite our questions about the accuracy of Pound's translation of the Chinese; the poem's stereotyping of cultural and gender differences; and the barriers of aesthetics, historical scholarship, and literary traditions, all negotiable over time, Pound's candor resonates in "The River-Merchant's Wife" through his sincerity of style. In his zeal for his art, his determination, as he writes in "I Gather the Limbs of Osiris," to "have a simplicity and directness of utterance, which is different from the simplicity and directness of daily speech" (41), he asserts in this poem a "frankness as never before" (*Hugh Selwyn Mauberley* 188). His ambition for a verse "which exalts the reader, making him feel that he is in contact with something arranged more finely than the commonplace," derives conspicuously from his own exile as a poet ("I Gather the Limbs" 41). If nothing else, exile creates at least two conditions: *displacement* from a home from which the exile becomes increasingly estranged, and *suspension* in the present environment, wherever that is, whether by virtue of its language, customs, politics, or mores. Displacement can precipitate posturing, or inventing personae, whether to sustain one's identity with the lost home or to transform oneself altogether; suspension, meanwhile, can precipitate the opposite—silence, speechlessness. But for the poet, neither inventing personae nor remaining silent can suffice: the former can result in lies, false representations, a crime for which Pound believes the poet "should be punished or despised in proportion to the seriousness of his offense" ("A Serious Artist" 44), while the latter can result in the erasure of identity altogether, a state of being equally untenable. Paradoxically, by combining these conditions, by creating, especially in *Mauberley*, a poetry of displacement whose very technique suspends identity, Pound achieves a candor by depicting himself, in the third person, no less, as "out of key with his time." What better self-portrait for an irascible American poet in London—much as he cannot possibly be, yet most assuredly is, the river-merchant's wife—than to entomb E.P. while in the same moment he becomes, though without becoming, Mauberley?

To approach Pound as an exiled poet, whether with students who are themselves "in exile" or not, is to demonstrate tangibly, poem by poem, how displacement and suspension can shape an artist's sensibility, not only in determining the choice of subject matter but also in shaping the artist's assumptions about place, time, and identity. Whether reading Pound sympathetically or skeptically, those who recognize the impact of his exile on his poetics are more likely to engage receptively with the inventive variety of voices throughout both *Personae* and *The Cantos*. Such readers are better equipped to interpret Pound's work not as dichotomous, erratic, or politically extremist, but as emerging from a lifelong struggle to realize a vision not bound by a single nation, tradition, or language. To search for and work through "the *real* Ezra Pound" in his early poetry can help prepare the diligent student to grapple with the substantive contradictions that animate his work throughout and continue to challenge even his most sustained readers.

NOTES

[1] *Satyricon*, a novel by Gaius Petronius written during Emperor Nero's reign, provides a raucous account of Roman practices and indulgences, composed in varied forms and structures. *Le neveu de Rameau*, a satiric novel by Denis Diderot, depicts a series of conversations between Moi ("Me") and Lui ("Him"), lampooning the French elite of the time.

[2] Describing the development of vorticism before World War I, Kenner writes, "At 28 Pound was immersed in the orchestration of a new sensibility, decisive and blocked and faceted, a vortex of vortices, in touch with Li Po and Provence and Chou bronzes and Uccello and Flaubert and *Feng Shui*, the Chinese geomancer's art of detecting the rhymes

and unrhymes of the local cosmos. Unimpeded by fussy 'tradition,' *virtù* free as light in space could intersect (with precision, with immediacy) any tradition it chose" (*Pound Era* 245–46).

[3] This essay cites the revised edition of *Personae* published by New Directions in 1990.

[4] Of course, with the surfeit of Pound biographies, despite the impact of postmodern theory, both students and critics readily speculate over the "real" sources of Pound's monologues, a practice that has almost become canonized in the footnotes in teaching anthologies that include *Mauberley*, for instance.

[5] For an explanation of the poem's geography, see Guiming Wang's *A Study of Ezra Pound's Translation: An Interpretation of* Cathay (249–50).

[6] Concerning the poem's title, Wang notes that "A Letter" is Pound's emendation, whereas the poem's original Chinese title identifies it as a lyric. Pound substitutes "A Letter," where "other translators . . . render it 'The Tune of Chang-gan'—a literal version of the Chinese original (the character '行 xing' was a song-tune in ancient China, meaning 'The Tune of . . . or The Song of . . .')," according to Wang, "but the content of the poem is really like a letter from a wife to her husband. Pound may not have intended the poem to be congruent with the formal elements (the original title does not indicate the narrative mode of the poem), as he considered that a new title may fit the monologue mode which frees the protagonist to express her loneliness and how she misses her husband" (239).

Pound and Difficulty

Leonard Diepeveen and J. Matthew Huculak

When they first read works like *The Cantos*, many students find them difficult and react the same way as did many of modernism's first readers: with resistance, anger, anxiety, and, occasionally, ridicule. We look at how one might make students' reactions a useful part of understanding Ezra Pound's work as well as high modernism in general. Turning to the initial reception of these works, we have students consider not only these initial emotive responses but also the defenses of difficulty that other first readers of modernism employed to counter them. Our pedagogical strategy does several things at once: it provides students with the beginnings of Pound's reception history, and it puts that history to work as an engagement with their own responses. Pound's reception history should be understood in terms of his desire to connect with his readership. When Pound moved to London in 1908, he had contributed just five articles to magazines; by 1918, he had written over 117 (Scholes and Wulfman 5). In his essay "A Retrospect," Pound calls for language that is "austere, direct, free from emotional slither." Students should be aware that Pound *wants* to be understood and that his apparent difficulty is a reaction against the "painted adjectives" surrounding modern readers in their mass media universe (12).

Our strategy also encourages students to think about difficulty not just as an attribute of texts but also as a way of reading. We want students to learn that an understanding of Pound and high modernism is not just a knowledge of facts and textual details; instead, it is a knowledge of protocols and an ability to put them to use.

We begin by bringing students to 1909 and a reviewer of *Book News Monthly* who turned to the first book of an unknown poet and commented, "The academician bristles all over his work. French phrases and scraps of Latin and Greek punctuate his poetry and prose, and the carelessness that attends the swift birth of an idea marks his every line. He affects obscurity and loves the abstruse." Disappointed by the poetry, the reviewer nevertheless held out for the possibility of improvement once the poet had "learned that simplicity and greatness are synonymous" (Review). The work was *A Lume Spento*; the poet was Ezra Pound; and the presaged simplicity, according to most of his subsequent readers, never arrived. May Sinclair, writing of Pound's work in 1920, reported that "All the approaches to this twentieth century poet are difficult" (662); in 1938 Herbert Palmer referred to the "enormous incomprehensibility" of *The Cantos* (353). In his 1999 *Cambridge Companion to Ezra Pound*, Ira B. Nadel begins by noting that "Understanding Pound has never been easy" (1).

We then show students how Pound's difficulty was part of a larger cultural situation in the earlier twentieth century that profoundly shaped how his work was read. Harold Child, reviewing Ezra Pound's *Ripostes* for the *Times Literary*

Supplement (*TLS*), relates the poetry's difficulty to the response generated by the 1910 postimpressionist exhibition in London: "At the Post-Impressionist exhibition some spectators may be seen dancing with fury, others quaking with laughter, others indiscriminately worshipping and a few using their brains coolly. Mr. Ezra Pound's book will have the same effect, no doubt, upon its readers" (94). During the years 1910–1950, years that saw the formation of the Anglo-American modernist canon and the establishment of its texts and writers in the university curriculum, readers overwhelmingly sensed that difficulty was central to what was beginning to be called modernism. And it was modernism writ large, for people commonly perceived that modern music and visual art as well were radically more difficult than their predecessors, and writers used the same arguments for these arts as those they employed to discuss literary difficulty. The 1910 London postimpressionism exhibit, the scandal that erupted at the Paris premiere of Stravinsky's *Le Sacre du Printemps*, the furor over the New York 1913 Armory show—all these galvanized the public because of their difficulty. The simultaneous appearance of modernism and the discussion about difficulty was not coincidental: difficulty allowed modernism to rise, and it was central to how modernism—including Pound's modernism—shaped the canon. Pound's work and its difficulty cannot, then, be explained just as a series of unique aesthetic properties; rather, it needs to be understood socially and in the context of the rest of modernism.

Attack on Difficulty

For many critics, Pound's difficulty was the product of a technique, a stunt, a formal game—and because it was easy to produce, it had no aesthetic value. Conservative anthologist Marguerite Wilkinson, who described Pound as someone who wrote "alarmingly clever" poetry and was "too clever to be a poet" (183), registered her disapproval of such writing by claiming that "poetry is not, after all, an intricate puzzle game for sophisticated intellects" (9). The problem with Pound, Wilkinson argued, was that he thought it *was*, with unfortunate results: "Very likely Mr. Pound does not expect or even wish his poems to give pleasure to many readers" (183). For readers like Wilkinson, the difficult text, lacking in emotion or self-expression, produced a non-humanistic pleasure, technical, cold, and deliberate—the pleasures of a game. F. R. Leavis granted that *Hugh Selwyn Mauberley* was a "great poem," but he grumbled that "the Cantos appear to be little more than a game—a game serious with the seriousness of pedantry" (155).

Defense of Difficulty

Difficulty's omnipresence could more efficiently be explained by its necessity in modern life. Difficulty was realistic, mimetic, both of the human mind and of modern civilization. Artists were necessarily difficult because of the peculiarities of modern culture. As T. S. Eliot was famously to note, "it appears likely that poets in our civilization, as it exists at present, must be *difficult*" ("Metaphysical Poets" 65). Pound, then, was typical of his peers when, in a review of Cocteau's *Poesies*, he noted, "The life of a village is narrative; you have not been there three weeks before you know that in the revolution et cetera, and when M le Comte et cetera, and so forth. In a city the visual impressions succeed each other, overlap, overcross, they are 'cinematographic,' but they are not a simple linear sequence. They are often a flood of nouns without verbal relations" (110).

We then call on students to address what might be the implicit view of contemporary life offered by Pound's statement—the difficulty engendered by "a flood of nouns without verbal relations"—and how that leads to an apparent separation from the past and the difficulties of modern life. The developments in communication, transportation, and entertainment technology during Pound's modern age are starting points for students' reflections on similar phenomena in their own lives and on how these are mirrored in a text like canto 4, where difficulty suddenly takes off.

Closely related to this argument was the assertion that modern difficulty mirrored the processes of the human mind. Herbert Read, acknowledging the "insuperable difficulties" of *The Cantos* while yet being "convinced of the greatness of the poem as a whole," argued that poetic obscurity could be positive, that it could arise from "a fundamental obscurity in the actual thought process involved—an obscurity due to the honesty and objectivity of the poet" ("Ezra Pound" 273, "Obscurity in Poetry" 99–100). As its association with the human mind might suggest, one way of approaching the difficulty of Pound and his fellow modernists was to argue that all new art is difficult. As Pound testily maintained in 1928, "A new language is always said to be 'obscure', the dastard Gifford said Keats was obscure" ("Berlin" 114). Difficulty is part of the regenerative power of poetry as the mind interacts with it. Thus, when Dudley Fitts argued that "*The Cantos* will baffle people who are willing to be baffled; but this is so of any considerable poem" (253), he was merely participating in a general argument made by many of high modernism's apologists that "much poetry in every age has been 'difficult'" (qtd. in Rodman 31).

These arguments help prepare students to critically intervene in this general poetic discourse of difficulty: Is it true that earlier works, like *The Faerie Queene*, are just as difficult as *The Cantos*? What is different about Pound's difficulty compared to earlier works with which students are familiar? What do *The Cantos* and *Hugh Selwyn Mauberley* reveal about the qualities of Pound's "mind" in how he makes connections between the present and past? How would students compare Pound's mind as a poet with that of another writer? Moreover, who is the "I" speaking in *The Cantos* or *Hugh Selwyn Mauberley*? Students can explore the shift in lyric poetry from earlier works like "Ballad of the Goodly Fere" or "Portrait d'une Femme" in *Personae* to the disjointed speakers of the *Cantos*, and they can do so in the context of other difficult modernist writers, such as

Eliot, Marianne Moore, and Gertrude Stein—whose texts rewrite and complicate lyric expectations in different ways, at times shifting the poetic voice from singular to multiple, or decentering the subject, or turning to popular culture. One could ask, for example, how the narrator in his opening canto relates to the voices of *The Waste Land.* Students typically note that Pound's narrator seems to be from an earlier time (in form, diction, and subject matter), and the changes in voice in Pound are generally much more harsh or jarring than in Eliot's work. That said, we recommend that these questions be seen as opportunities for opening up the texts to multiple interpretations from students, whose own communication environments—mobile phone applications, Web-based communication, etc.—are changing rapidly from day to day. Students understand the tonal shifts required for various audiences from one digital application to another and are thus poised to decode Pound's tonal shifts in oftentimes surprising ways.

Difficulty as Professionalism

One way in which modernist creation differed from that of earlier times was its association with the artist as a new kind of professional—and not as amateur. Leavis argued in *New Bearings in English Poetry* that "not only poetry, but literature and art in general, are becoming more specialized: the process is implicit in the process of modern civilization" (213). Professional specialization and its resultant difficulty therefore had a cultural necessity—it was not merely one option among many. Particularly for a writer like Pound, there was to be no wavering. From the professional side of what often looked like a cultural divide, Pound praised the poet Lionel Johnson "in part for his hardness, in part for his hatred of amateurness" ("Lionel Johnson" 363).

Hidden within this belief were, of course, a series of implied attitudes to art, to modern culture, and to readers. But modernism's defenders praised the virtues of professionalism because it supposedly had no hidden agendas, it sprang from pure motives, and it was above politics and class. There was remarkable unanimity that *technique* was the specialized object of enquiry for writers, composers, and artists. As Eliot argued, in response to a *TLS* attack on professionalism, "Surely professionalism in art is hard work on style with singleness of purpose" ("Professional" 61). Technique usefully marked out the profession's territory; it separated aesthetic professionals from those who were eager to assert the spiritual claims of art but who were less adept at articulating the devices that might put those claims into play. Consider Pound's claim: "The touchstone of an art is its precision. This precision is of various and complicated sorts and only the specialist can determine whether certain works of art possess certain sorts of precision" ("The Serious Artist" 48).

Precision, development, a group identity—particularly when coupled with difficulty—such concepts made inevitable that "seriousness" would be a hallmark of modernist art. In his 1913 essay "The Serious Artist," mentioned above, Pound asserted that "[t]he arts, literature, poesy, are a science, just as chemistry is a science. Their subject is man, mankind and the individual" (42). This similarity between the artist and the poet, Pound claimed, meant that "the serious artist is usually, or is often as far from the *aegrum vulgus* as is the serious scientist" (47). After urging would-be poets to follow "the way of the scientists," Pound pointed out what was crucial in the scientific method: "The scientist does not expect to be acclaimed as a great scientist until he has *discovered* something. He begins by learning what has been discovered already" ("A Few Don'ts" 203–04). Modernism's developmental newness had direction that was so ingrained that it was a professional obligation to assist it. And once that direction was accepted, difficulty could seem inevitable.

Having provided students with this background, we invite them to address the following questions: What in the reviews and the literary texts signals that this writing or reading comes from (or is opposed to) a professional mindset? Why might one read or write professional literature, and what makes a given example of professional writing good professional writing? If Pound's professionalist stance is a change, a difficult newness, what is the direction of that change? What problems does the difficult newness solve? This is a good time to present students with a Georgian poet, such as Lascelles Abercrombie, whose "The Sale of Saint Thomas" opened *Georgian Poetry* (3), and compare it to *The Cantos*. Teachers can then ask how *The Cantos* are a rebuke to a poem like this. Is Pound's implied argument (that art should be professional and developmental) fair?

Replacing Pleasure with Labor

What kind of reading did serious art require? High moderns didn't deny reading's strenuousness; instead, they often acknowledged, rightly, that difficult texts required hard work, that the effort of reading high modernism encountered resistance. Difficulty's defenders, searching for a physical analogy for a mental process, argued that their texts called for vigilance and energy. Pound, implicated more than most in high modernism's vigor, noted that "Intense emotion causes pattern to arise in the mind—if the mind is strong enough" ("Affirmations" 374). Instead of passively drifting along, readers and writers of difficult work needed to remain constantly alert. As Maxwell Bodenheim asserts, the real task of reading Pound is to reach the "kernel" which "lies beneath the hard shells." And this requires "a mind that is not averse to labouring" (206). First-time readers of Pound in the classroom may feel frustrated by this laboring since his poetry does not look like the easily digestible reading matter of the mass market. Teachers may have to instill in the reader a sense that the labor required to find the kernels of meaning is part of the modernist reading experience. Reading Pound is not a passive, lazy experience but rather an active, energetic practice that may require initiation in the classroom—the hard work *is* the pleasure.

Strategies of Reading

When they discussed how to read his difficult work, Pound's contemporaries most often addressed two strategies: the first, a difficulty based on the knowledge Pound's poetry apparently called on its readers to draw on, and the second, a difficulty of Pound's technique, a technique that hid meaning, particularly through parataxis—its juxtapositions and ellipses. In the first case, readers had to ask, without knowing his sources, *was* the act of reading Pound useless? Pound's defenders gave differing answers. The most basic strategy conceded that although one might not have full knowledge of the poem's sources, reading Pound could still be a profound experience. John Peale Bishop, writing about *The Cantos* for *Vanity Fair*, circumvented his own lack of knowledge in the following way: "I shall have to learn at least three more languages and read seven years before I shall pretend to recognize all the references, but patchwork of erudition, of phrases in five tongues and paraphrased as it is, it still contains much that is pure poetry" (208). Bishop typifies Pound's supporters, who believed that there had to be a way into his difficult texts that did not require specialized knowledge. In his 1917 *Ezra Pound: His Metric and His Poetry*, Eliot, nodding to the uncertain or negative reception accorded much of Pound's work, inflected it in the following manner: "Few readers were prepared to accept or follow the amount of erudition which entered into *Personae* and its close successor, *Exultations*, or to devote the care to reading them which they demand" (165). But Eliot's conclusion was not that Pound's work therefore had little value. Rather, he argued the following:

> It is here that many have been led astray. Pound is not one of those poets who make no demands of the reader; and the casual reader of verse, disconcerted by the difference between Pound's poetry and that on which his taste has been trained, attributes his own difficulties to excessive scholarship on the part of the author. "This," he will say of some of the poems in Provençal form or on Provençal subjects, "is archaeology; it requires knowledge on the part of its reader, and true poetry does not require such knowledge." But to display knowledge is not the same thing as to expect it on the part of the reader; and of this sort of pedantry Pound is quite free. (165–66)

Yet the effects that contemporary readers valued in Pound included those visceral reactions and responses to difficulty which eventually made dominant the ideas that poetry—indeed, all of art—is best understood as a site of struggle. In order to engage adequately with Pound's poetry, students need to see difficulty as a methodology of asking questions rather than that of providing answers. This history of reactions to Pound's difficulty shows that his difficulty is not going to disappear. The difficulty is not resolvable, and students and teachers need to search for ways to make it productive, to understand its peculiar hold. This kind of response is integral to a search to find ways of making Pound's difficulty expressive, and to begin to understand its peculiar hold.

This is a good time to ask students to describe a particular canto and explain what it might mean without having any knowledge of the sources for the poem. Carroll F. Terrell's *A Guide to* The Cantos *of Ezra Pound* can then be used to help students explore Pound's sources more fully. Classroom discussion can center on the problem of reading practices dependent on annotations. Students can consider if research is a formal reading practice. Does difficulty always demand research? How might the crises Pound's difficulty creates be useful for students? Is it simply irritating, or does it serve another purpose? Is good literature always difficult? Students can consider the hierarchies of value applied to these difficult texts.

Difficulty and the Digital

One of the ways into these questions of reading practices is to turn to Pound's own writing on reading. Pound saw himself as a pedagogue, and he used the periodical genre to instruct his readership in the ways of reading modernism. Pound was not ignorant of the difficulty his poetry and prose presented, and he made a concerted effort to teach his readers how his poetry should be read. In both the *ABC of Reading* and his periodical contributions, he exhorts readers to take the stance of the "scientist" whose methodical observations are necessary to decode the modernist "age of science and of abundance" (*ABC of Reading* 17). Part of this abundance was the glut of print produced by periodicals in the modern age, peddled by what Pound called the "noose-stands" on the street corners and railways stations (Scholes and Wulfman 2). Pound has a paradoxical relationship with periodicals: he expropriates the everydayness of the periodical to instruct uninitiated audiences on how to read, while simultaneously challenging readers to appreciate the difficulties of modernist thought.

Students have a bevy of resources available online in these acts of reading and rereading. With online collections like the *Modernist Journals Project* (*MJP*) freely accessible, students are able to read Pound's early poetry alongside his pedagogical notes on how difficult modernist poetry should be approached (modjourn.org). We first ask students to read Pound's "A Few Don'ts by an Imagiste," published in Harriet Monroe's *Poetry* (March 1913) and now available at the *MJP*, in which Pound exhorts his ideal reader to recognize the "complex" nature of modern poetry and warns them not to "think any intelligent person is going to be deceived when you try to shirk all the difficulties of the unspeakably difficult art of good prose" by simply following standard formulae in writing (200–02). Pound's twelve-poem "Contemporania" series appears in the next issue of *Poetry* (April 1913), which contains his famous imagist/vorticist "In a Station of the Metro," as well as "A Pact," to Walt Whitman. We ask students to read these poems next to "A Few Don'ts," to unpack Pound's sparse "poesy," and to judge whether or not he succeeds in creating the "complex" and "difficult" images he outlines in his essays.

It is also helpful to have students apply Pound's tips on writing to their own essays and classwork. The writing process in higher education is always difficult; our classrooms have their own codes of conduct and writing styles, which students must labor to perfect. This is a good time to discuss the writing process as well as the difficulties of writing for the classroom environment. Sometimes students think that writing an English essay is easy, or they may be tempted to write a paper the night before it is due. Teachers can use Pound's difficulty to foreground everyday writing as a difficult process and as a discipline. For example, we ask students to change one aspect of Pound's poetry (perspective, verb tenses, nouns, etc.) to make it different as a way of showing them how Pound's poetic choices while crafting his poems actually effect readers' responses.

We also assign students to work in pairs and ask them to edit each other's essays as if they were Pound. Students pull out pertinent sentences from "A Few Don'ts," including "Use no superfluous word, no adjective, which does not reveal something . . . Go in fear of abstractions" (201), and apply these instructions to their own writing. This helps students understand that the writing process includes revision and highlights the fact that difficult writing is deliberate—there is reason to obscurity and difficulty. For those teaching Eliot's *The Waste Land*, this is a productive time to discuss Pound's role as editor on making that poem the version we read today. Showing page images from *The Waste Land: A Facsimile and Transcript of the Original Drafts Including the Annotations of Ezra Pound* is a great way to show students how Pound applied his technique to the work of others. It is good to show students that even great writers need to go through extensive editing and rewriting processes.

Another example of Pound's magazine writing on difficulty is the essay "Vorticism," which appeared in the *Fortnightly Review* in 1914. Though this essay is useful in explaining vorticism to students, it is also a good place to have them question Pound's success as a pedagogue in explaining his difficulty. In this work, Pound speaks directly to the "ordinarily intelligent undergraduate" while also attempting to explain the "four different intensities of mathematical expression" that "make up the language of philosophy" (461–71). Ask students to consider where Pound succeeds and fails as apologist and teacher. Once students have been properly introduced to vorticism, reading *Blast* on the *MJP* site will allow them to see Pound's work placed in a larger context of modernity and manifesto writing. The manifesto instructs its readers how to read the magazine, and the large fonts coupled with distinctive page layouts still seem unusual (and exciting) to the contemporary reader.

The digital archive also affords students the ability to create their own annotated editions of Pound's work and gives them new ways of experiencing Pound's difficulty. Gail McDonald's essay "Hypertext and the Teaching of Modernist Difficulty" outlines ways for students to create their own editions of *The Cantos* by hyperlinking to other resources online. Not only does this practice ask students to engage directly with the text, but it also encourages them to produce annotated editions that can be used by their peers in the classroom. One way of nurturing collaborative activity is to ask students to choose a short poem (or a section of a longer poem) and create an annotated edition together in class. A free *WordPress* or *Google Docs* account will allow students to work together online simultaneously and link to pictures, resources, and other pages on the Web to create an interactive learning environment. As students practice making editorial decisions about what should be annotated and what should not, the teacher gains information about which references students understand and what may need more explaining in lecture.

By using resources like the *MJP* as well as collaborative editing environments, teachers can help students read Pound in his original context instead of in potentially alienating anthologies, which may amplify the difficulties students experience when first encountering Pound. Students learn that Pound was very careful to explain himself (sometimes unsuccessfully) and wanted to teach people how to read difficulty—not for difficulty's sake, but to be "equipped for modern thinking" (*ABC of Reading* 17). For Pound, modernity, not his poetry, is difficult: his poetry inoculates readers against the difficult mental and verbal environments created by the conditions of modernity.

POUND'S AESTHETICS

Pound's Prosody for the Classroom

Stephen J. Adams

From the beginning, Pound's poetry has been praised for its distinctive rhythms. His advice to young writers is quoted endlessly—"compose in the sequence of the musical phrase, not in the sequence of a metronome"; "master all known forms and systems of metric" ("A Retrospect" 3, 9); ditch pentameter, that's "the first heave" (canto 81 [*Cantos* 538]). These memes are cited as self-evident, or used to impress or mystify. But Pound's practice demonstrates that he meant something specific by these verbal gestures, and coming to terms with his meaning is important for both the scholar and the aspiring poet today. My reflections on this question go back many years, to my frustration with the inability of Pound's admirers to get at the concrete reality behind his talk about rhythm. My efforts to demystify them describe only one avenue among a very few others that have been tried, but I present them here as teaching points—imagining an ideal class already equipped with a basic grasp of English prosody. I understand, too, that the teaching of prosody is double-edged: presenting the abstract principles is easy; encouraging the student to "hear," to discover these ideas at work in real poems, is far more difficult.

Pound began his career with two large convictions. First, he fetishized technique. Don't imagine "that you can please the expert before you have spent at least as much effort on the art of verse as the average piano teacher spends on the art of music," he declared, throwing the gauntlet down at the aristocratic notion of poetry as something any educated person might produce as a pastime ("A Retrospect" 5). To the middle-class American Pound, poetry was a profession that demanded expertise, as much as did musical composition or carpentry. He even put a moralistic spin on it: good technique, he said, is "the test of a man's sincerity" (9). Or, as his Kung pronounces in canto 13, without character one cannot "execute the music fit for the odes" (*Cantos* 60). This fetish is, according to Stephen Cushman, a trait common to American poets, who everywhere tend to "overvalue the formal aspects of their art, investing those aspects with tremendous significance"; like all the canonical American poets, Pound is "not only, or even primarily" a poet of statement but one "of style and form" (4, 12).

In Pound's case, technical expertise extended beyond English prosody to that of human languages globally. Pound, as I impress on students, is the first Western poet with a truly global world view. In terms of prosody, each language has its own exclusive field of melopoeia, its potential for emotional expression through word music. These many different fields of sound devolve into a few prosodic systems. Stress-timed languages develop accentual systems that regularize the number of accents per line, leaving slack syllables free, as in Anglo-Saxon. Syllable-timed languages regularize the number of syllables per line, as in French. Modern English has developed a complex accentual-syllabic hybrid, basically accentual but also regulating the syllabic count in specific ways. Classical languages, Greek and Latin, regulate vowel "quantity," a feature barely perceptible in English but a phantom ideal for classically trained English poets since the Elizabethan era.[1] Chinese, being ideogrammatic, monosyllabic, and intonational, brought a different set of principles into Pound's ken, though they mainly affected his sense of syntactic rhythm.[2] The general principle is that the poet writing in English can always learn from the melopoeia of any language; the "artist should master all known forms and systems of metric" ("A Retrospect" 9). Pound drew on all of these systems in his own practice, although I do not know of any instance where he employed strict syllabics.[3] "I have never read half a page of Homer," he said, "without discovering melodic invention" (*ABC of Reading* 43). "Dissect the lyrics of Goethe coldly into their component sound values" ("A Retrospect" 5). In his early Osiris essays, he speaks of a certain element in Anglo-Saxon that has "transmuted the various qualities of poetry which have drifted up from the south," which have "enriched and made them English" ("I Gather the Limbs" 24).[4]

My second point is that poetic rhythm for Pound conveys not just feeling but very particular meaning. This is the point of his declaration in his introduction to *The Sonnets and Ballate of Guido Cavalcanti*, "I believe in an absolute rhythm as I believe in an absolute symbol or metaphor" (*Translations* 23). This was the crux of his dispute with Amy Lowell, who delighted at the discovery of free verse and advocated fighting for it "as for a principle of liberty" (qtd. in Jones 135). But Pound replied, in an important letter, that "Rhythm MUST have meaning. It can't be merely a careless dash off, with no grip and no real hold to the words and sense" (*Selected Letters* 49). For Pound every rhythm, every slight nuance, conveys a specific cognitive meaning. In his early years, he took this notion to literalist extremes: "I believe that every emotion and every phase of emotion has some toneless phrase, some rhythm-phrase to express it." This belief, he concluded, "leads to *vers libre* and to experiments in quantitative verse"

(*Gaudier-Brzeska* 84). Therefore, the poet uses free verse not to liberate poetry from the rules of prosody but to access and discover new rhythms in the language beyond conventional prosodic limits, so that emotions previously inexpressible might be found. Emotion in poetry is tied to its sound and rhythm; onomatopoeia, Pound declares, "is not a mere trick of imitating natural noises, but is a mastery in fitting the inarticulate sound of a passage to . . . that mood or passion which the passage describes or expresses" (*Spirit* 160).[5] This valuation of sound and rhythm has been a convention of poetry from earliest times, of course, but it has always been explained in much looser terms. "Every passion has its proper pulse," said Coleridge (181). But Pound's beliefs are hyperliteralist, bound with an almost mystical theory of correspondences, like Yeats's belief in an "absolute symbol," or the common talk in early-twentieth-century criticism of an oxymoronic precise emotion. Belief in such literal correspondences may not bear scientific scrutiny, but it has a literary heritage that may be traced to concepts of correspondences in sources like Baudelaire and Swedenborg.

The free verse epic, or "long poem," is the major poetic genre of the twentieth century, and Pound's *Cantos* created the template against which subsequent examples must be compared. *The Cantos*, for all their formal liberties, established certain formal expectations that later poets have imitated, extended, or sometimes violated. For a poetic genre is tied to its metrical form, and as Renato Poggioli argued in his important essay "Poetics and Metrics," it is a rule of literary history that "the apparition of a new literary genre is always accompanied by the invention or the exclusive adoption by that genre of a definite verse form." The association of genre and meter is, at first, part of the "unwritten poetics" of that genre, and always, "legislation comes after, rather than before, the fact" (347).

When Pound set to work on his *Cantos*, he was unsure himself about the verse form. One of the less frequent observations about his discarded ur-cantos is that they are written not in free verse but in a loosened form of blank verse. The following lines in ur-canto 3 mark the transition into the Nekuia passage that now stands as canto 1. The first two lines are free, as are the two short lines, but the rest (including the last) are pure iambic pentameter:

> Uncatalogued Andreas Divus,
> Gave him in Latin, 1538 in my edition, the rest uncertain,
> Caught up his cadence, word and syllable:
> "Down to the ships we went, set mast and sail,
> Black keel and beasts for bloody sacrifice,
> Weeping we went."
> I've strained my ear for *-ensa*, *-ombra*, and *-ensa*
> And cracked my wit on delicate canzoni—
> Here's but rough meaning:
> "And then went down to the ship, set keel to breakers . . ."
> ("Three Cantos" 250–51)

Pound's translation of Homer through Divus's Latin has long been recognized as a multilayered demonstration of cultural transmission, translation, and preservation, and the significance of its allusion to Anglo-Saxon alliterative tradition is also well known. Less frequently recognized is Pound's interplay of lines with alliterative stress rhythms in canto 1 ("Bore us out onward with bellying canvas") and lines of ordinary pentameter ("A sheep to Tiresias only, black and a bell sheep") along with phrases marked by the adonic pattern (-˘˘-˘) found at the end of every line of dactylic hexameter ("heavy with weeping," "jamming the tiller," "black and a bell-sheep") (*Cantos* 3–4). I suspect that Pound's remark about iambic pentameter—"that was the first heave"—actually refers to this moment when he cut loose the meter of his future "poem of no known category" from its metrical moorings (*Pound/Joyce* 102). Meter could now enter freely or disappear, and its presence would become a self-conscious allusion to a particular complex of cultural feeling.

Poggioli's dictum as applied to the free verse epic assumes that free verse is in fact a metrical form, not merely the absence of form. Free verse has its own conventions.[6] When I first set my mind to consider, many years ago, how to present this phenomenon to students—quite apart from Pound's idiosyncratic practice—my first instinct was to survey all the different kinds of free verse and attempt to classify them. I was unable to do so, and when I looked at earlier efforts, I found them unsatisfactory as well. There are too many variations and, by definition, there are no rules. Handbooks were no help at all—authors of such books are usually hostile to free verse or baffled by it. Finally, in my own handbook (*Poetic Designs: An Introduction to Meters, Verse Forms, and Figures of Speech*), I discovered that if one could not enumerate all the kinds of free verse, one could enumerate the methods of free verse analysis that various scholars have attempted. I isolated three approaches that have produced meaningful results. (There is no reason others may not be found.) Specific passages of free verse respond more or less well to one or another approach. First is attention to the line break and enjambment. Second is attention to syntactic form, syntactic parallelism, and the rhetorical schemes. Third is the use of known metrical forms as a reference point or a point of allusion that may appear or disappear at will.

Free verse in *The Cantos* lies on a scale of more or less free; that is, Pound uses many different kinds of free verse there, and the types range from fully metered verse at one extreme (Cavalcanti's "Dona mi prega" in canto 36; "Tudor indeed is gone" in canto 80) to ordinary prose at the other (*Cantos* 177–79, 536). By mixing verse forms, juxtaposing them ideogrammatically, according to vorticist principles, Pound points up their significance *as verse forms*. John Hollander, in *Vision and Resonance*, has advanced a concept of the "metrical contract"—the purely conventional aspect of a given work whose function "involves the elements of convention which link a metrical style or type to the whole poetic genre and, hence, a poet's choice of metre to a larger intention" (188–89).[7] Hollander's concept assumes that the poet's choice of meter is made once at the beginning of composition, the way Milton chose blank verse rather than the more conventional rhymed couplets for *Paradise Lost*. Pound's innovation was to make this "contract" conditional on subject and tone. The shifts, the juxtapositions of meters in *The Cantos* become a meta-commentary on their own versification.

Free verse in *The Cantos* varies on a scale between a more or less crude, rough-hewn prosaic tone and lyric evocations of the paradisal. This scale is controlled by a sense of decorum, to use an old-fashioned word: when the subject is crude, so are the tone, diction, and versification; when the subject is transcendent, the poetry shifts accordingly. It is in these passages, the obviously poetical passages usually favored by anthologists, where Pound's most idiosyncratic rhythms appear, and these call for the most complex explanation.

My clues to this explanation are drawn partly from earlier work by classicists like James A. Powell and D. S. Carne-Ross, combined with a concept of analysis advanced by Annie Finch in her book *The Ghost of Meter*. Finch draws her title from T. S. Eliot's remark that "the ghost of some simple metre should lurk behind the arras in even the 'freest' verse; to advance menacingly as we doze, and withdraw as we rouse" (Eliot, "Reflections" 34–35). Her subtle analyses reveal the lurking presence of iambic pentameter in both Walt Whitman ("I celebrate myself and sing myself"; "Look up in perfect silence at the stars") and Eliot ("Like a patient etherized upon a table"), and finds elements of iambics embedded in Whitman's longer lines: she calls this "meta-free verse" (102–03). Charles Hartman describes it as not vers libre but "*vers liberé*" (111–17). In this type, poets write freely and yet maintain both rhythmical equilibrium and a felt contact with metrical traditions. But Pound complained that Eliot continued to write "as if all meters were measured by accent" ("T. S. Eliot" 421). When Pound wrote that "every phase of emotion has some toneless phrase, some rhythm phrase to express it" (*Gaudier-Brzeska* 84), he noted that this fact led not only to "*vers libre*" (a logical step) but "to experiments in quantitative verse" (a personal leap). That is, Pound's personal search for new rhythms to express emotions previously uncaptured by English meters led him to classical quantities.

Pound attempted pure quantitative meter in English only once, in "Apparuit," written in the sapphic stanza. When Pound wrote this poem in 1912, he expected most readers to have some training in Latin and maybe Greek, and to have been acquainted with quantitative meters. Since we can no longer expect that of our students, or indeed of teachers, I present the sapphic paradigm that Pound used. The sapphic quatrain uses three lines containing five quantitative feet, with liberty only in the second position, which may be trochee or spondee:

- ˇ / - ˇ / - ˇˇ / - ˇ / - -

- ˇ / - - / - ˇˇ / - ˇ / - -

And a final line of two metrical feet, dactyl and spondee:

- ˇˇ / - -

This last line, a double foot called an adonic, is also found at the end of every epic dactylic hexameter line of Homer and Virgil, so it is a very recognizable pattern. I have elsewhere offered full scansion and discussion of Pound's "Apparuit" ("Metrical Contract"), but here are the first and third stanzas for illustration:

- ˇ /- ˇ/ - ˇ ˇ/ - ˇ /- -
Golden rose the house, in the portal I saw
- ˇ/ - ˇ / - ˇ ˇ / - ˇ / - -
thee, a marvel, carven in subtle stuff, a
- ˇ / - - / - ˇ ˇ /- ˇ / - -
portent. Life died down in the lamp and flickered,
- ˇ ˇ / - -
caught at the wonder.

- ˇ / - ˇ / - ˇ ˇ /- ˇ/ - -
Green the ways, the breath of the fields is thine there,
- ˇ / - ˇ /- ˇ ˇ / - ˇ /- -
open lies the land, yet the steely going
- ˇ/- - / - ˇ ˇ / - ˇ /- -
darkly hast thou dared and the dreaded aether
- ˇ ˇ /- -
parted before thee.

Notice certain features: First, as with the majority of attempts to write quantities in English, long and short syllables are (in most instances) simply replaced by accented and unaccented syllables. Second, the fragments that commonly reappear in Pound's practice are the adonic itself, - ˘˘ / - - , and the second half of the longer line, - ˘˘ / - ˘ / - - . A third fragment called the choriamb, - ˘˘ - , a truncated version of both of the others, is also common to classical prosody and Pound's rhythms, but far less frequent in most English poetry.

Pound's paradigmatic "quantities" in this poem, however, raise theoretical issues. Although he generally lets English accent serve for quantity, he occasionally allows English accent and classical quantity to strain against each other, as in the lovely effect of the phrase "glamorous sun," where the final syllable of "glamorous" is long but unaccented, or the phrase "frail alabaster," where the first syllable of "alabaster" is accented but short. "Remember," he wrote to Iris Barry, "the SWAT must strain against the duration now and again" (*Selected Letters* 262).[8] Thus, Pound's determination of English "quantity" is intuitive and inconsistent. It is an illusion, dependent on foreknowledge of the textbook paradigm. The relevance of this to Pound's general practice in *The Cantos*, then, is debatable, since in free verse there is no paradigm. As James A. Powell puts it, the classical meters in Pound's free verse are a "useful fiction which can help us to understand the way Pound manipulates and combines rhythmic patterns" (27). The interplay of adonics, choriambs, and other rhythmical fragments serves both as an allusive point of reference and as a ghostly reminder (to classicists' ears) of rhythms not commonly found in English poetry.

Here is Powell's scansion of a passage from canto 23. Notice, he uses the accent mark, not the classical macron, for "long" syllables:

> Where a man might carry his oar up,
> And the boat there in the inlet
> As we had lain there in the autumn
> Under the arras, or wall painted below like arras,
>
> And above with a garden of rose-trees,
> Sound coming up from the cross-street;
> As we had stood there,
> Watching road from the window,
> Fa Han and I by the window,
> And her head bound with gold chords.
> Cloud over mountain; hill-gap, in mist, like a sea-coast. (108)

Certain principles need clarification: First, since there is no guiding paradigm, scansion of free verse is always intuitive and subject to divergence from one reading to the next. There is no use arguing about a "correct" scansion. Second, there is no need that every syllable conform to a pattern for patterns to emerge. Prosodists habitually think of a meter as a kind of abstract grid that controls every syllable of a piece of verse; but in this kind of free verse, patterns emerge freely among a number of less patterned syllables. Pound was aware of this when he wrote,

> I doubt if we can take over, for English, the rules of quantity laid down for Greek and Latin, mostly by Latin grammarians. I think one should write vers libre only when one "must," that is to say, only when the "thing" builds up a rhythm more beautiful than that of set meters, or more real, more a part of the emotion of the "thing" . . . than the measure of regular accen-

tual verse. . . . I think progress lies rather in an attempt to approximate classical quantitative meters (NOT to copy them). . . .
("A Retrospect" 12–13)[9]

Just as the Anglo-Saxon meter of canto 1 suggests but does not duplicate the rules of its source, so Pound's classical meters are free and yet allusive. The pattern that does emerge very frequently here is the adonic, mainly placed at the end of end-stopped lines marking phrasal closure: "under the arras," "garden of rose-trees," "there in the inlet," "there in the autumn," "cloud over mountain." Longer fragments of the sapphic line also appear: "man might carry his oar up," "painted below like arras," "watching road from the window." As well, frequent spondees in these paradisal passages not only slow down the pace but make room for Pound's inventive noun compounds—"cross street," "gold chords," "rose-trees"—for, as he advised Mary Barnard, "[t]he best *mechanism* for breaking up the stiffness and literary idiom *is* a different meter, the god-damned iambic magnetizes certain verbal sequences" (*Selected Letters* 260). Meter and diction always interact.

Here is another sample, the beginning of canto 17:

So that the vines burst from my fingers
And the bees weighted with pollen
Move heavily in the vine-shoots:
    chirr—chirr—chir-rikk—a purring sound,
And the birds sleepily in the branches.
ZAGREUS! IO ZAGREUS!
With the first pale-clear of the heaven
And the cities set in their hills,
And the goddess of the fair knees
Moving there, with the oak-woods behind her,
The green slope, with white hounds
            leaping about her . . .   (*Cantos* 76)

Again the adonic pattern recurs, and serves for closure at the end. Again, spondees predominate. As usual in this kind of verse, Pound limits the number of slack syllables between accents to two, though he violates that practice once in line 9. Most curiously, lines 3 and 5 (as I hear them) replicate a feature that I mark with a macron over the letter *y*, suggesting that Pound hears this unaccented vowel as a long quantity forming two more adonic patterns: "heavily in the vine-shoots," "sleepily in the branches." If I am correct (and my point is necessarily subjective), then this is an instance where Pound strains the limits of English prosody by allowing quantity to supersede accent. But, as Pound himself cautioned, "I do not think one can use to any advantage rhythms much more tenuous and imperceptible than some I have used" ("A Retrospect" 12–13).

In *The Cantos*, however, this kind of free verse is reserved for those visionary, paradisal passages. Elsewhere, Pound's versification loosens into a more conventional stress-timed accentual free verse common to many poets—English is, after all, a stress-timed language, as Pound well understood. His fascination with quantity was motivated in large part by a desire to counteract the natural accentual rhythm of the language, and he delighted in releasing quasi-syllable-timed Greek patterns as a countermotion. But in passages resembling narrative or exposition, a loose accentual meter serves:

```
      /   /          /
The ship landed in Scios,
        /   /         /
       men wanting spring-water,
            /           /         /          /
And by the rock-pool a young boy loggy with vine-must,
            /      /          /           /
       "To Naxos! Yes, we'll take you to Naxos,
 /     /           /
Cum' along lad." "Not that way!"
 /      /          /
"Aye, that way is Naxos."
          /                  /       /
      And I said: "It's a straight ship."
       /   /             /
And an ex-convict out of Italy
         /        /         /
       knocked me into the fore-stays,
         /          /               /
(He was wanted for manslaughter in Tuscany)
                 /     /       /
       And the whole twenty against me,
 /         /       /    /
Mad for a little slave money.    (Cantos 7)
```

This passage illustrates a kind of phrasal free verse, where the lines conform to the phrase-units of the language, which speakers instinctively punctuate with slight pauses. Another signal is the different handling of slack syllables—rarely more than two in succession in more controlled passages, left free in looser passages. This phrasal free verse is in fact the commonest kind, rationalized by its earliest practitioners with the generic word *cadence*. John Hollander also notes the "powerful effect" in Pound's passage of the "graphic schema of the broken line," a device he believes is borrowed from "the scholarly space added between half-lines of early Germanic poetry" (236–37).

In its simplest form, this cadenced free verse tends to avoid enjambment. Elsewhere in *The Cantos*, however, this loose versification enjambs more freely, here in canto 25 for comic effect:

> THE BOOK OF THE COUNCIL MAJOR
> 1255 be it enacted:
> That they mustn't shoot crap in the hall
> of the council, nor in the small court under
> pain of 20 danari, be it enacted:
> 1266 no squire of Venice to throw dice
> *any*where in the palace or
> in the loggia of the Rialto under pain of ten soldi
> or half that for kids, and if they won't pay
> they are to be chucked in the water. (*Cantos* 115)

Here, the verse lines play against both the phrasal cadence and the syntactic parallelism, the visual force of the line breaks creating moments of hesitation and heightened emphasis. (Pound, however, rarely uses the extremes of enjambment practiced by William Carlos Williams.) Later in the same canto, Pound modulates into his now familiar lyric rhythms:

> / ˘ ˘ / ˘ / ˘ / ˘ ˘ / ˘
> Which is to say: they built out over the arches,
> ˘ ˘ / ˘ / / ˘ ˘ / ˘ /
> and the palace hangs there in the dawn, the mist,
> ˘ ˘ / ˘
> in that dimness,
> ˘ ˘ / ˘ / ˘ / ˘ ˘ / ˘
> or as one rows in from past the murazzi
> ˘ / / ˘ ˘ / ˘
> the barge slow after moon-rise
> ˘ ˘ / ˘ ˘ / ˘ ˘ /
> and the voice sounding under the sail. (117)

Canto 25 is a clear example of the principle of metrical juxtaposition and metrical decorum used throughout *The Cantos*.

In canto 45, Pound uses another principle to structure his versification: simple syntactic parallelism and anaphora, like that found everywhere in Whitman:

> With usura hath no man a house of good stone
> each block cut smooth and well fitting
> that design might cover their face,
> with usura
> hath no man a painted paradise on his church wall
> *harpes et luz*
> or where virgin receiveth message
> and halo projects from incision,
> with usura
> seeth no man Gonzaga his heirs and his concubines
> no picture is made to endure nor to live with
> but it is made to sell and sell quickly
> with usura, sin against nature,
> is thy bread ever more of stale rags
> is thy bread dry as paper,
> with no mountain wheat, no strong flour
> with usura the line grows thick
> with usura is no clear demarcation
> and no man can find site for his dwelling. (*Cantos* 229)

Here the repetitions give the entire passage a sense of gravity, while the catalogue makes the litany of usura's bane appear endless, all-encompassing. The primary control of the verse is syntactic, though lineation and cadence also play an important role. The accents fall into no recurrent pattern, either of English iambs or classical metra.

In sum, Pound's free verse responds to the same kinds of analytical approaches as any free verse—control of line endings, control of syntactic patterning, allusion to known metrical practices, approximating but not conforming to their rules. His major innovation is verse that approximates not English meters but classical quantitative metra, though accommodated to English stress. In *The Cantos*, too, his meters are governed by an instinctive decorum between form and content. Meters are juxtaposed as well as ideas and images. The slack syllables between stressed syllables may be looser as the verse approaches prose, or stricter as it approaches conventional meter. Pound's choice of meter for any particular passage enters the reader's understanding of both his meaning and his intention.

NOTES

[1] Quantity exists in English, but it almost never enters into meaning as it does in Greek and Latin, so it goes largely unnoticed.

[2] At the time of *Cathay* (1915) Pound seems unaware that his Chinese originals used meter and rhyme, but his later translations of *The Confucian Odes* reflect these elements.

[3] A possible exception is "A Song of the Virgin Mother" in *Exultations*, translated from Lope de Vega (*Collected Early Poems* 122).

[4] In "A Case for Pound's 'Seafarer,'" I point out that Pound's translation, alone among several examined, captures not only the sounds of the language but also the falling rhythmic patterns of the original (132).

[5] There is a large body of philosophic discourse in musical aesthetics about the relation of sound and meaning, but surprisingly little in poetics, discouraged by dogma that insists on arbitrary relationship of signifier to signified. A comprehensive theory of onomatopoeia is much needed. Pound's explanation of onomatopoeia seems analogous to Susanne Langer's definition of music as an "unconsummated symbol" that "articulates subtle complexes of feeling that language cannot even name, let alone set forth" (189).

[6] I found books by the following scholars most useful: Jonathan Culler, Stephen Cushman, Annie Finch, Veronica Forrest-Thomson, and Charles O. Hartman.

[7] See also Hollander's "Blake and the Metrical Contract" for an earlier version of this argument.

[8] Pound's correspondences with Iris Barry and Mary Barnard supply much understanding to his experiments with classical meters. "Apparuit" also conforms to advice Pound gave Iris Barry: he does not always use spondee for the second foot "like that Blighter Horrace" (*Selected Letters* 252).

[9] Pound meticulously dates this passage to August 1917, the month when his third ur-canto appeared in *Poetry*.

Patience for the "Ancients": Studying Classical Allusions in Pound's Prosodic Practice

Sara Dunton

In his prefatory comments to the *ABC of Reading*, pointedly titled "How to Study Poetry," Pound refers to the teachers who may read his self-described textbook: "I am not idly sowing thorns in their path," he declares; "I should like to make even their lot and life more exhilarating and to save even them from unnecessary boredom in class-room" (11). Surely, no teacher—or student—would choose boredom over exhilaration, or could resist Pound's exuberance. However, when analyzing his metrics, students soon realize the merit in Pound's more tempered counsel, namely that they must slow down and "HAVE PATIENCE" (49). Brave and keen students of modernist literature are not deterred by this approach or by the prospect of studying notoriously difficult texts. Nevertheless, counting myself as one of those brave ones enrolled in an honors seminar on modernist poetry, I felt some trepidation at discovering that half the course material concentrated on Pound's poetry and prose.[1] The assigned works by Pound (especially *The Cantos*) and the course syllabus (promising analysis of the prosodic practices of the poet's Hellenic precursors) were equally daunting.

Stirring deeper anxiety was the list of issues inherent to studying the modernists, including their debts to Homer and others; the use of allusion, quotation, citation, and textual appropriation; and the place of these poems in twentieth-century prosodic innovation. Both Pound's "exhilarating" textbook, the *ABC of Reading*, and his *Literary Essays* (edited by T. S. Eliot) were assigned readings; and explorations of Pound's contributions to journals—*The Egoist*, *The New Age*, and *Poetry*—were strongly encouraged.

I came to this course equipped with a solid background in English literature, a basic understanding of prosody, and very little knowledge of the classical authors—"the ancients," in Pound's words ("A Retrospect" 11). Tackling Pound's material was intimidating enough without Homer in the mix; my nervousness was compounded when I encountered another Poundian gem, the opening statement on the reading list he prescribes in *ABC of Reading*: "Let the student brace himself and prepare for the worst" (41). Fortunately, the professor's approach to presenting what he termed the inscrutable "papyrus effect" of Pound's layered allusions and prosodic appropriations of classical texts was inventive and well designed. In this essay, I do not recount my personal experience; instead, with other anxious students in mind, I reconstruct the path of discovery that the teacher plotted. His main objective was to initiate a patient close study of Pound's prosodic methods: first, to identify Pound's appropriations of classical poetry; then, to recognize the interfaces between prosody and allusion in Pound's poetry; and, finally, to contemplate the interplay of all these as primary markers of his practice.

The assigned readings were presented in a sequence designed to trace Pound's purposeful adaptations of classical forms: beginning with the early poem "Apparuit," an original composition in sapphic stanzas; moving on to section 4 from part 1 of *Hugh Selwyn Mauberley*, in which Pound echoes a passage from Bion's classical lament; and then to canto 1, where he layers allusions to Homer's *Odyssey* and his *Hymns to Aphrodite.* The textbook for the course was Stephen J. Adams's indispensable *Poetic Designs: An Introduction to Meters, Verse Forms, and Figures of Speech*, which begins with Adams's reassurance that his "ultimate goal is to heighten the experience of prosody." The best way for students of poetry to achieve that goal, he insists, is to embrace the technicalities of meter and form, to "acquire an intellectual understanding of them," to learn the rules that will enable them to better see, feel, and hear that experience (1).

At the outset of the first seminar, the professor urged the students to be stirred rather than deterred by the "comprehensiveness and capaciousness" of *The Cantos*, paraphrasing George Kearns's reminder that a proven obstacle to reading the epic is the "demand to know too much too soon" (*Pound* 8). Directed to resist the temptation to dive into companions and online resources, students were required to read poems aloud—to hear them—before studying them. This emphasis on aural experience was not intended to exempt students from researching the prosodic practices and texts of classical writers but to enforce the pedagogical slant established by Adams. Thus positioned, students considered Pound's preferred definition of poetry as the "composition of words set to music," a key dictum appropriated from Dante, and reconfirmed that poetry, like scored music, has a hidden technical structure that the untrained audience may not detect, even when attuned to the sounds and rhythms of verse (*ABC of Reading* 31). Once alerted to that structure, and introduced to the "visual coding" (i.e., scansion) of poetry texts, students began to realize how (and why) prosody depends upon the senses (Adams, *Poetic Designs* 1n2).

Considerations of Pound's dictum and hidden structure then incited discussion of allusion, which, broadly speaking, is a "more artful and resonant literary device than our critical vocabulary has allowed us to appreciate" (Machacek 535). Introducing Pound's use of the device, the professor cited J. A. Cuddon's claim that a writer, "[w]hen using allusions . . . tends to assume a literary tradition, a body of common knowledge with an audience sharing that tradition and an ability on the part of the audience to 'pick up' the reference" (27). As part of an audience far removed from Pound's tradition of Greek and Latin languages and literature, the seminar students were not yet ready to "pick up" references, but were, at least, ready to pursue Pound's trail. Ellen Stauder offers a useful signpost: Pound alludes directly to an articulation from Dante that "arrived at what, for Pound, was a crucial turning point in European literary history" when poets "stopped making poems in the ancient tradition, started by the Greek lyric poets and extending up through the medieval period. That ancient practice understood poems to be a joining of music and words . . ." (23). Digesting this insight alongside Pound's critical *ABCs* prompted the realization that the adopted

Dantean credo, like many of Pound's dicta, is seemingly modern in spirit and tone but is meant to alert readers to precedent forms and paradigm shifts in literary history. Braced for detection of such allusions and primed to scan Pound's verse, the class was poised for further preliminaries, namely, Pound's innovative classification of modern poetics into three "poeias"—phanopoeia, melopoeia, and logopoeia.

Putting the Poeias into Perspective

One of the most appealing aspects of reading Pound's oeuvre is the energetic language of his critical prose. Writing with alternating looseness and precision, Pound effectively practices what he preaches. In "A Retrospect" his tone is almost biblical: "Let the neophyte know assonance and alliteration, rhyme immediate and delayed, simply and polyphonic, as a musician would expect to know harmony and counterpoint and all the minutiae of his craft" (6); in a letter to a young translator seeking advice, he shouts, "THE JOB of the writer of verse is to get the LIVE language AND the prosody simultaneously. Prosody: articulation of the total sound of a poem (not bits of certain shapes gummed together)" (qtd. in Gordon 171); and, with characteristic flair, in "How to Read," he pronounces, "It is as important for the purpose of thought to keep language efficient as it is in surgery to keep tetanus bacilli out of one's bandages" (22).

Class debates centered on Pound's declarations about living language, musical harmony, and clinical efficiency before turning to the three essential "kinds of poetry" Pound outlines in "How to Read" (25). The Greek roots of Pound's terms *phanopoeia*, *melopoeia*, and *logopoeia* reinforce the importance of the classical tradition he sought to revive: *phanos* and *melos* signal the sensory characteristics that can be connected, respectively, to the familiar imagist credos and Pound's appropriated Dantean dictum. Phanopoeia, the professor remarked, occurs when the best writers tell readers, through unornamented language, how they see things, making their vision "translatable into English." The sound of poetry, melopoeia, he suggested, is accessible but not as easily translatable. Although poems and words "charged . . . with some musical property" (25) may inspire an aural response, they are also arranged in an inaudible metrical pattern that, in Pound's view, is particularly dependent upon Greek prosody. Peter Liebregts's comments on "why Pound [so] valued ancient Greek poetry" are particularly helpful here: "[Pound] regarded it as a prime example of *melopoeia*, a perfect aesthetic marriage between sound and sense, which was enhanced by the wide range of metrical patterns, a second reason for Pound's interest since he believed the study of Greek prosody could expand the possibilities of English verse" ("Classics" 175).

The third prefix, *logos*, is in itself allusive since it implies that knowledge is meant to be detected. Pound's notorious "dance of the intellect among words" (*Literary Essays* 25) is arguably the more complex "kind" of poetry and provoked a robust class discussion. In a secondary reading, *Ezra Pound's Early Poetry and Poetics*, Thomas Grieve contends that logopoeia, "as Pound maintained with only a few qualified and hesitant exceptions, is the discovery of the modern writer" and that "this is so because it is a dimension of poetic language that required the modern poet to become self-conscious concerning his status as beneficiary and victim of a traditional literary language before it could come into being" (104). The professor, however, prompted students to consider that ancient poetry itself contains logopoeia, derived from its authors' inherited knowledge—oral tradition and mythological narratives—which they in turn remade into their own syntactical and rhetorical patterns.

Before delving into prosodic analyses of Pound's poems, the class was reminded that Pound's turn to the classics arose neither from his admiration for the rigor of classical studies nor from his desire to return to traditional ways of teaching. "Among Pound's criticisms of the educational system," Liebregts explains, "we find him objecting to the way Latin and Greek were taught as objects in themselves, rather than as keys to worlds whose discoveries and philosophies about the human condition were still valid for an understanding of the modern world." Indeed, Pound's "ultimate aim in reading and learning," Liebregts emphasizes, "was not to live the scholar's life of texts, but to search for life in texts" ("Classics" 174).

"Apparuit": Pound's "Delicate Attempt" and Deliberate Appropriation

Pound's "Apparuit" is a fitting though anomalous introduction to his indebtedness to classical poetics, constituting his sole composition in the quantitative meter form of sapphic stanzas. The Latin title, meaning "she appeared," comes from Dante's vision of Beatrice in his *Vita nuova*, a work revered by Pound; more significantly, it is also Pound's tribute to "Poikilophron," an ode to Aphrodite written by the ancient Greek lyric poet Sappho, one of the few writers Pound names on his "list of the minimum that a man would have to read if he hoped to know what a given new book was worth" (*ABC of Reading* 41). Adams refers to the "wholly artificial" poem as Pound's "delicate attempt" at adapting the quantitative metrical system to the English language (*Poetic Designs* 66). Despite the inherent difficulty of this system, Adams suggests, "It is helpful . . . to be aware from the beginning of the full range of metrical possibilities" (69). To underscore Adams's recommendation, the professor highlighted this pair of Pound's crucial convictions from "A Retrospect":

> I think the artist should master all known forms and systems of metric, and I have with some persistence set about doing this, searching particularly into those periods wherein the systems came to birth or attained their maturity. (9)

> I mean I do not think one can use to any advantage rhythms much more tenuous and imperceptible than some I have used. I think progress lies rather in an attempt to approximate classical quantitative metres (NOT to copy them) than in a carelessness regarding such things. (12–13)

These statements—even in isolation—underline the importance of Pound's experimenting with structure to remake modern vers libre; they also illuminate his strategy of using an ancient prosodic form, such as the sapphic stanza design of "Apparuit," as an allusion. Here Pound is preparing his audience for the modern practice of poetics that he envisions enacted by writers who master prosody, critics who detect prosodic play, and students who are trained in Latin and Greek.

Nevertheless, one century later, the fact remains that students who are not advanced, whose ears are not naturally tuned to the rhythm of quantitative meter, still need to understand why the prosody and lyricism of Sappho hold relevance. At this juncture, the professor referred to Christine Froula, whose description of "Apparuit" and its meter is accompanied by images of the metrical patterns under consideration:

> The Sapphic stanza, associated with passion and elegiac solemnity, consists of three eleven-syllable lines (hendecasyllabics) followed by one five-syllable line [i.e., the adonic foot]. In English, accented and unaccented syllables substitute for Greek long and short syllables. . . . The difficulty of the form lies in its relative inflexibility, for the poet must follow this pattern as closely as possible, and in doing so, forgo the powerful effects of rhythmic variation. (*Guide* 40)

The "Sapphic stanza" lyric quatrain, then, works like this: lines 1–3, ¯˘ | ¯¯ | ¯˘˘ | ¯˘ | ¯¯ or ¯˘ | ¯˘ | ¯˘˘ | ¯˘ | ¯˘ (eleven syllables); and line 4, "adonic foot": ¯˘˘¯˘ or ¯˘˘¯¯ (five syllables).

Students were asked to comment on Froula's observation about rhythm after they had read "Apparuit" aloud. Despite their initial perceptions of plodding lines and awkward enjambments, their appreciation for the rhythm and melody of Pound's language grew. Quantitative meter notwithstanding, Pound successfully evokes the ethereal character of the speaker's voice and vision in the first stanza:

> Golden rose the house, in the portal I saw
> thee, a marvel, carven in subtle stuff, a
> portent. Life died down in the lamp and flickered,
>   caught at the wonder.

Turning to the scansion of the first two stanzas of "Apparuit" shown in *Poetic Designs* (68–69), the class read aloud again, this time emphasizing the stressed syllables and listening for quantity in the English vowel sounds. Next, they imposed the pattern of the sapphic stanza upon the first verse of "Apparuit" to reveal an almost perfect fit:

> – ˘ | – ˘ | – ˘ ˘ | – ˘ | – –
> Golden rose the house, in the portal I saw
> – ˘ | – ˘ | – ˘ ˘ | – ˘ | – ˘
> thee, a marvel, carven in subtle stuff, a
> – ˘ | – – | – ˘ ˘ | – ˘ | – ˘
> portent. Life died down in the lamp and flickered,
> – ˘ ˘ | – ˘
> caught at the wonder.

The teacher punctuated this exercise with a reminder: in praising Sappho's "Poikilophron," Pound says that he "knows of no better ode" (*ABC of Reading* 47). Students were then asked to contemplate the purpose of "Apparuit." Is it meant to be a translation as well as a prosodic copy of Sappho's ode? Prompted to compare Pound's poem with an English translation of Sappho, "Prayer to Aphrodite," by Vayos Liapis, students discerned that while Liapis's tone and diction—"golden" and "swift"—echo Pound's evocation, there is no overriding evidence of similar contextual meaning. Most notably, the Liapis translation has no consistent sapphic stanza patterns. This raised another question: has Pound effectively "translated" metrical pattern by imposing it on his verse, just as the teacher had imposed the scansion marks from Sappho's verse on "Apparuit"? How does Pound convey the same sensations as Sappho and Liapis by following a prosodic pattern of quantitative measure that might occlude the sensuousness of language and rhythm?

The professor then revisited Liebregts's observation that Pound "regarded [ancient Greek poetry] as a prime example of *melopoeia*, a perfect aesthetic marriage between sound and sense" ("Classics" 175). With this in mind, how might students assess "Apparuit"? Certainly *how* poems mean instead of what they mean, or, more precisely, the meaning of poems other than their paraphrasable ones, is Pound's subject here; moreover, melopoeia, meaning, "words are charged, over and above their plain meaning, with some musical property, which directs the bearing or trend of that meaning," is his method. While Pound claims that melopoeia "is practically impossible to transfer or translate . . . from one language to another, save perhaps by divine accident, and for half a line at a time," nevertheless, he accomplishes the near-impossible ("How to Read" 25). What he attempts to "translate" in "Apparuit" is not simply a specific poem by Sappho but also the prosody of the sapphic stanza. The professor's summation was memorable: the poet, his ear full of Sappho's melopoeia, composes the poem in a "delicate attempt" to repeat not the thematic content but the melodic and rhythmic quintessence of her work. By striving for English quantities, not just letting accent stand for quantity, Pound works not by rule but by aural intuition.

Mauberley 1:4: The Ancient Lament Enlivened

With "Apparuit" Pound demonstrates that scansion can reveal classical form and stir readers to hear the poems with a modern ear: prosodic allusion and melopoeia interact to signal Sappho's methods and enliven Pound's free verse. A similar interaction with different key components occurs in the next assigned reading—part 4 of section 1 of *Hugh Selwyn Mauberley*—in which Pound pays homage to *Lament for Adonis*, an ode from the second century BCE written by another ancient cited in his "must read" list:

> The Bion is separated by centuries from the Homer and Sappho. In studying the earlier parts of this list, the attention would, I think, have gone to the WRITING, to the narrative, to the clarity of expression, but would not have naturally focused itself on the melodic devices, on the fitting of the words, their SOUND and ultimately their meaning, to the tune.
>
> (*ABC of Reading* 41–42)

Following "Apparuit," students expected enlightenment from spoken readings and scansions of the *Mauberley* excerpt. Instead, they were asked to take Pound's lead and focus on the devices that leap from the first ten lines:

> These fought in any case,
> and some believing,
>   pro domo, in any case . . .
>
> Some quick to arm,
> some for adventure,
> some from fear of weakness,
> some from fear of censure,
> some for love of slaughter, in imagination,
> learning later . . .
> some in fear, learning love of slaughter. . . .
> (*New Selected Poems* 112–13)

The teacher distributed an extensive list of rhetorical figures to accompany the twenty-seven-line section under study. Reassuring students that they would not be responsible for memorizing the sixty-four definitions therein, he asked them to identify Pound's use of figures. The first of these is obvious: the pattern of repeating "some" as first word—epanaphora—is dramatic, with the opposition of "fear" and "love" emphasizing the effect. The repetition of "in any case" and "as never before" exemplifies epistrophe. Throughout the segment, Pound plaits his words: "as never before" and "some" appear mid-line; "home" acts like its eye-rhyme "some" and appears at the beginnings and midpoints of lines; "blood," "lies," and "slaughter" are repeated; "as never before" is interwoven with the emphatic alliteration of "fair cheeks, and fine bodies; / fortitude as never before / frankness as never before." All these devices of repetition accentuate the uneven rhythm and momentum of the lines, which seem to stall and then charge ahead.

Why, the professor asked, did Pound arrange these lines in alternating lengths, with rising and falling counts of syllables? How does this metrical maneuver enhance the meaning of the lament? These questions segued to the excerpt from Bion's *Lament for Adonis* in which the poet describes the ritual preparation of Adonis' body for burial. Students were asked to visually examine Bion's Greek text (as it appears in J. M. Edmonds's edition, accompanied by his translation), heeding its punctuation and pauses:

> χὢ μὲν ὀστώς,
>
> ὃς δ'ἔβαλλεν, ὃ δε πτερόν, ὃς δὲ φαέτραν·
>
> χὢ μὲν ἔλυσε πέδιλον Ἀδώνιδος, οἳ δὲ λέβητι
>
> χρυσείῳ φορέουσιν ὕδωρ, ὃ δὲ μηρία λούει,
>
> ὃς δ'ὄπιθεν πτερύγεσσιν ἀναψύχει τὸν Ἄδωνιν. (lines 81–85)

> This flung upon him arrows, that a bow, this a feather, that a quiver. One hath done off Adonis' shoe, others fetch water in a golden basin, another washes the thighs of him, and again another stands behind and fans him with his wings. (387)

Next, students were asked to rearrange Bion's lines, relying upon the appearance and structure of Edmonds's translated version, to create a poem that reflects the lineation of Pound's *Mauberley*:

> χὢ μὲν ὀστώς,
>
> ὃς δ'ἔβαλλεν,
>
> ὃ δε πτερόν,
>
> ὃς δὲ φαέτραν·
>
> χὢ μὲν ἔλυσε πέδιλον Ἀδώνιδος,
>
> οἳ δὲ λέβητι χρυσείῳ φορέουσιν ὕδωρ,
>
> ὃ δὲ μηρία λούει,
>
> ὃς δ'ὄπιθεν πτερύγεσσιν ἀναψύχει τὸν Ἄδωνιν.

Although unable to read Bion's Greek, students could see and appreciate the syntactical (and typographical) repetition of the ancient text's rhetorical thrust.

Pound adapts the controlled layout of Bion's consistent structure of uninverted, uninterrupted syntactical arrangements to reflect the orderly, ceremonial form of the lament. Pound's adaptation of prosody here is a graphic one, but it is also a purposeful allusion to Bion's classical form, not to the essence of his narrative. Instead of translating Bion's linguistic code (the lexical meaning), Pound ingeniously reproduces the rhythms of the passage's syntactical and rhetorical patterns and thus its logopoeia. In "How to Read," the class was reminded, Pound declares that logopoeia "does not translate; though the attitude of mind it expresses may pass through a paraphrase" (25). Through appropriation of prosody, Pound paraphrases Bion's "attitude of mind" toward the lament, but, tellingly, he does not echo the restrained tenor of the ode. *Mauberley* is a modern lament that releases Pound's embittered rail against the blood, lies, and slaughter of World War I.

The final class discussion on *Mauberley* and Bion centered on the significance of Pound's gestures. Students agreed that while prosodic allusion can distance the writer from the text, it can also point overtly to the writer's intention. As Stauder argues, Pound was motivated "to foreground the present moment of the past through a poetics of fragmentation and juxtaposition that emphasizes not the personality of the poet but the poet's medium" (25). Despite the pervasiveness of Pound's personality, exemplified by the didactic voice of his *ABC*s, Stauder's comment enforces the notion that the poet's overriding intention was to promote his "poeias" and revive the medium; it also reasserts the importance of Pound's tactic of using his lens into the classical age while eyeing the remaking of his craft. The celebrated passage from Pound's "Credo" confirms his intentions and reveals another allusion to Bion's rhetoric of repetition:

> My pawing over the ancients and semi-ancients has been one struggle to find out what has been done, once for all, better than it can ever be done again, and to find out what remains for us to do, and plenty does remain, for if we still feel the same emotions as those which launched the thousand ships, it is quite certain that we come on these feelings differently, through different manners, through different nuances, by different intellectual gradations. ("A Retrospect" 11)

Pound concludes with an open-ended question—"What is there now, in 1917, to be added?"—which the professor rephrased and redirected to his students: "What is there now, in 2012, to be learned from Pound's indebtedness to the 'ancients'?" Would they be willing and able to "paw over" what Pound had "done" in *The Cantos* through "gradations" of knowledge they were still painfully aware of lacking?

Canto 1: Prosodic Portal to Pound's "Endless Poem"

Lack of familiarity with ancient languages, prosody, and epic poems often undercut students' confidence and raised doubts—how much of the technical character of Pound's metrics did they really need to know? Ironically, it was Adams, the expert on prosody, who echoed their concern with the plea, "What can we poor Greekless readers do?" in his essay "The Metrical Contract of *The Cantos*" (61). To aid readers, Adams alerts them to the "Poundian metrical fingerprint" (*Pavannes* 177) that appears throughout Pound's "endless poem" (Cookson xvii): namely, "the noble epic meter of Homer's *Iliad* and *Odyssey*" (Adams, "Metrical Contract" 63), the dactylic hexameter,

–⏑⏑ | –⏑⏑ | –⏑⏑ | –⏑⏑ | –⏑⏑ | – –

1 2 3 4 5 6

and the more familiar adonic pattern encountered in "Apparuit." This visualization of Pound's prosodic strategy eased students' entry into canto 1, his celebrated appropriation of a passage from book 11 of Homer's *Odyssey.* As "Greekless readers," students needed to recognize the descent of Odysseus as "a crucial episode in the Western epic" (Froula, *Guide* 128); but they also needed to grasp the significance of Pound's reconstruction of the passage, his pleating of "a translator's modern English version of . . . Homer's Greek, [and] the Latin of the translator Andreas Divus, whose text mediates between Pound and the Greeks" (129). And so, reading patiently, students detected Pound translating Divus's text, retaining the prosodic ghost of the Greek text in his head, which he then replicates in English, twice removed from Homer.

Tasked with identifying a classical metrical pattern in the opening ten lines of canto 1, students named the familiar iambic pentameter, as it appears in line 5; however, the stress pattern here does not produce the standard rhythm expected from the meter:

– ⏑ | ⏑ – | ⏑ ⏑ | – ⏑ | – ⏑

Heavy | with weep|ing, and | winds from | sternward

Analyzing this as a tactical adaptation, the teacher described Pound as advancing toward and retreating from the iambic pentameter he is resisting; the lines can be scanned as pentameter, but the alternating strong stress meter of another near-ancient hallmark—the alliterative Anglo-Saxon verse—interrupts the regular stress patterns expected by modern ears. Pound's famous declaration from canto 81—"To break the pentameter, that was the first heave"—comes long after canto 1; nevertheless, it reconfirms his primary prosodic maneuver (*Cantos* 538).

Accepting that these lines from canto 1 exemplify the "heave," students then discovered another layer of prosodic allusion—the adonic foot that ends the sapphic stanza (and constitutes part of the pattern of dactylic hexameter) and emerges from lines 5, 6, 8, and 10 as shown in these fragments:

– ⏑ ⏑ – ⏑
Heavy with weeping
– ⏑ ⏑ – ⏑
Bore us out onward
– ⏑ ⏑ – ⏑
Bellying canvas
– ⏑ ⏑ – ⏑
Jamming the tiller
– ⏑ ⏑ – ⏑
Sun to his slumber (*Cantos* 3)

These half-lines, alluding to Sappho and to Homer's epic meter, act as "prosodic hint[s] that the poetry is more than a translation of a translation" (Sawler 173). By drawing attention to the act of making poetry in the echoes of classical traditions, Pound also alludes to his role as modern innovator or, as Peter Nicholls describes it, to his "process of increasing emphasis on the way poems stage the dynamic process of making as their central concern" ("The Poetics of Modernism" 54). The professor noted that while Pound's process has received significant critical attention as regards his translations of classical texts, it has received far less attention in relation to his transmissions of prosody. In canto 1, Pound writes an obvious homage to Homer's text, but it is built from fragments of prosodic and syntactical patterns that allude to classical works, Old English poetics, and the modern verse he envisions. He creates a collage of juxtaposed structures that interact with each other, making a visual exercise of the writing and reading of his own text.

The closing class discussions on canto 1 included review of William Cookson's "Anthology of Statements by Ezra Pound on the *Cantos*." The first of these, from a 1917 letter to James Joyce, is a critical portal: "I have begun an endless poem, of no known category, Phanopoeia (light or image-making) or something or other, all about everything" (Cookson, *Guide* xvii). With these notions of open-endedness and image-making in mind, prepared to see the patterns of prosody emerging from Pound's text, students were directed to canto 17, which (in the professor's words) continues to "translate the rhetoric of the Odyssey," and to canto 23, which finds Pound translating a lesser-known "ancient," Stesichorus. Here Pound continues to exhibit his seemingly paradoxical intent to create something "of no known category" while practicing his "process of reclaiming the past" (Longenbach, *Modernist Poetics* 127). Given that class conversations had often addressed students' estrangement from this past (both Pound's time and the ancients'), recent critical commentary was particularly helpful. Michael Dirda, for example, claims that "[a]mbitious fiction and poetry—'language charged with meaning to the utmost possible degree'—matter in this increasingly noisy and trivialized world" (8). These words provoked a lively exchange on the production and reception of ambitious writing—both ancient and modern—in the world Dirda implies is weakened by the "internet generation"

(8). This is an exchange, both students and professor concluded, that Pound himself would have welcomed, and likely would have claimed as a direct consequence of his own determination to "save us from unnecessary boredom in class-room."

NOTE

[1] The course described is The American Long Poem in the Twentieth Century, a seminar taught by Demetres P. Tryphonopoulos at the University of New Brunswick, Fredericton, in the 2012 winter term. Classes were held weekly, in three-hour sessions. My recollections of the course are drawn directly from class notes. This essay does not address the analyses of other modernists' works (H.D., T. S. Eliot, and William Carlos Williams) that constituted the second half of the course. Their interconnectivity with Pound's work was a central thread, but not the sole focus of discussion.

Pound and the Early-Twentieth-Century Visual Revolution

Rebecca Beasley

Teaching Ezra Pound's poetry in relation to contemporary innovations in the visual arts has several pedagogical advantages. Visual analogues to Pound's poetry help categorize and make more accessible diverse aspects of his poetic technique; students are introduced to modernist culture beyond the literary text; and comparison of Pound's art and literary criticism encourages students to reflect on and historicize their own literary values.

I have taught Pound's poetry both as a section (typically one or two lectures or classes) in longer undergraduate modules on modernist literature and as a part of specialist undergraduate and graduate courses on modernism and visual culture. Three roughly chronological clusters of material reappear in slightly different forms in all these courses. The first examines the emergence of modernist poetry and imagism in relation to aestheticism and changing conceptions of beauty. The second explores Pound's engagement with modernist art movements, particularly vorticism. (I often combine aspects of these two clusters into one class.) The third is based on *The Cantos*' engagement with the visual arts and its status as a visual text, where the aim is to distinguish *The Cantos*' different aesthetic modes and to provide students with techniques for interpretation.

As Mary Ellis Gibson discusses in *Epic Reinvented: Ezra Pound and the Victorians*, Pound's early poetry is written in two largely separate styles, influenced by what he saw as two distinct traditions in English poetry. "The first strain, the Keatsian, flows for Pound through Keats, Tennyson, Swinburne, and the Pre-Raphaelites to the Georgian aesthetes, including the early Yeats," Gibson writes. "The second is represented by Browning, by Landor and Beddoes, possibly by Wordsworth, and by the 'harder' language of Yeats's middle period" (66). Though the visual arts provide models for Pound's poetry in both styles, the poems written in the Keatsian style most straightforwardly demonstrate Pound's changing use of the visual arts and show imagism's debts to a fin de siècle cult of beauty. As well as the literary models Gibson lists, Pound looked to nineteenth-century painters such as Edward Burne-Jones, J. M. W. Turner, John Waterhouse, and James McNeill Whistler for analogues for his own poetic project (Zinnes 287; Pound, *Spirit* 162). Whistler is the most important of these early models: comments in letters and early essays from Pound's student days at the University of Pennsylvania attest to his interest in both Whistler's painting and his collection of art criticism, *The Gentle Art of Making Enemies*. After having moved to London, Pound visited an exhibition of Whistler's works at the Tate Gallery that resulted in a poem, "To Whistler, American," and the declaration that "what Whistler has proved once and for all, is that being born an American does not eternally damn a man or prevent him from the ultimate and highest achievement in the art" (Zinnes 2, 217).

While a course that includes nineteenth-century poetry might use these connections as a way forward into Pound's early work, I tend to work back to this aestheticist heritage from an extended analysis of Pound's imagist poetry. Students of all levels find imagism—and Pound's combative definitions of it—accessible and engaging, and beginning with a comparison between Pound's archetypal imagist poem, "In a Station of the Metro" and the earlier "Piccadilly" enables students to draw out many of the characteristics of imagist poetry.

Discussion begins by noting the change from archaic to conversational diction, from rhyme to unrhymed verse, from (relative) length to extreme brevity—and students usually notice the similarity of "In a Station of the Metro" to Japanese haiku. Few modern editions of Pound's poetry have preserved the typographical layout the author insisted on for the first publication of "In a Station of the Metro"; but showing students that version, easily accessed through the *Modernist Journals Project* Web site, will generate discussion of the poem as a visual artefact, which is particularly useful if the class later studies *The Cantos*.[1]

Once students have developed their own ideas about imagism's innovations, we turn to look at Pound's definitions. The most easily accessible is "A Few Don'ts by an Imagiste," published in the previous number of *Poetry* and reproduced in Pound's later compilation of early essays, "A Retrospect." Here, we focus in particular on the definition of the image as "that which presents an intellectual and emotional complex in an instant of time," in order to discuss how "In a Station of the Metro" works: are the faces and petals "images" in this sense? Or is it the whole poem that constitutes the "image," triggering the "intellectual and emotional complex"? Is Pound's image a visual image at all?

It is at this point that students find it helpful to think about the visual arts context of the poem. Pound directs us to specific artists and works in his essay "Vorticism," written as he was rebranding imagism as the poetic wing of Wyndham Lewis's art movement of that name. In this essay for the *Fortnightly Review*, he tells the story of how he came to write "In a Station of the Metro," and I either set the essay as background reading or look at a long passage in class ("The image is the poet's pigment . . . as the symbolists bid us" [465–66]).[2]

Pound refers here to the expressionist painter Wassily Kandinsky's treatise *Über das Geistige in der Kunst* (*Concerning the Spiritual in Art*), which had just been translated into English as *The Art of Spiritual Harmony*. The book contained black-and-white reproductions of several of Kandinsky's paintings, including *Improvisation No. 29 (The Swan)* and *Small Pleasures*; Pound had seen the original *Improvisation No. 29* alongside two more paintings by Kandinsky the year before at the Allied Artists' Association exhibition. The essay also refers positively to cubism, to Picasso in particular, and to artists associated with the vorticist movement: Pound compares his poem "The Return" to sculptures by Jacob Epstein (*Sun God*) and Henri Gaudier-Brzeska (*Boy with a Coney*, which Pound owned, and which is reproduced in his *Gauder-Brzeska: A Memoir* [figs. 7, 8]), and he praises Edward Wadsworth's lost work *Khaki* and Lewis's portfolio of drawings *Timon of Athens* ("Vorticism" 464, 466, 464, 470).

Asking students why Pound might want his poetry seen in the context of these artworks can open up a number of issues central to modernism. Comparison of "In a Station of the Metro" and Kandinsky's paintings invites us to think about the extent to which poetry can be abstract: Pound's description of the image in "A Few Don'ts" suggests that the placing of word pictures against each other may generate an effect that lies outside verbal articulation. Is there a sense in which the "intellectual and emotional complex" triggered by the image might "look like" the abstraction of Kandinsky's *Improvisation No. 29*? Pound writes that "'The Return' . . . is an objective reality and has a complicated sort of significance, like Mr. Epstein's 'Sun God' or Mr. Brzeska's 'Boy with Coney'"—a rather gnomic pronouncement that becomes clearer when set alongside Pound's negative statements about impressionism and Italian futurism: "'[F]uturism,' when it gets into art, is, for the most part, a descendent of impressionism. It is a sort of accelerated impressionism" ("Vorticism" 464, 461). As with his approving remark about the "ice-block" quality of Picasso's cubism, Pound is distancing his poetry from the strain of modernism that takes the representation of subjectivity as its starting point and is consequently preoccupied with shifts in perception, with time (466). Pound's variety of modernism, by contrast, seems to look to the visual arts as a model for its experiments with form, with space. Helpful distinctions can be made here from the work of Joyce and Woolf; I use Monet's series of *Stacks of Wheat* paintings to illustrate impressionism's interest in changing perception over time, and the *States of Mind* series by the Italian futurist Umberto Boccioni to show futurism's representation of changing consciousness. Boccioni's *Unique Forms of Continuity in Space* makes an even more precise comparison with Epstein's *Sun God*: where Epstein emphasizes the solidity of sculpture, Boccioni works to overcome it. Discussion of other imagist poems by Pound—"Liu Ch'e," "The Garden," and "The Encounter," for example—highlights the way visual apprehension is predicated on the distance of the speaker from the subject (*Poems and Translations* 43, 36, 42).

At this point, the class may rightly express skepticism about Pound's analogies. If the image is presenting "an intellectual and emotional complex in an instant of time," it cannot be quite so easily separated from a subjective modernism, and the fact that so many imagist poems are written in the first person suggests there is, after all, an interest in individual perception. Is Pound deliberately overstating the similarity between his poetry and the visual arts? This provides an opportunity to discuss modernist self-fashioning, and I draw on Lawrence Rainey's article "The Creation of the Avant-Garde: F. T. Marinetti and Ezra Pound" to show how imagist poetry draws on visual art movements to advertise its modernity and increase its audience.

Having begun the class by thinking about the innovations of imagist poetry, we now return to "In a Station of the Metro" and "Piccadilly" to draw out continuities that can be traced back to the tropes of nineteenth-century symbolist poetry and painting. Indeed, Pound had published a version of his story about the composition of "In a Station of the Metro" a year before "Vorticism," in which he implied that "Piccadilly" might be seen as an early version of "In a Station of the Metro": "I waited three years to find the words for 'Piccadilly,' it is eight lines long and they tell me now it is 'sentiment'. For well over a year, I have been trying to make a poem of a very beautiful thing that befell me in the Paris Underground. I got out of a train at, I think, La Concorde. . . ." ("How I Began" [*T.P.'s Weekly*]). If students have read "Vorticism" in its entirety, they may remember that the essay begins not with the modernists Kandinsky or Picasso but with the nineteenth-century aesthetes Whistler and Walter Pater. It is to Whistler, in fact, that Pound attributes the break with representation and the move to formalism in painting ("Vorticism" 461). We look at Whistler's *Nocturne in Grey and Gold—Piccadilly*, which depicts a crowd on Piccadilly, with details lit up by the street lamps, and consider the extent to which this impressionist painting represents the experience of "In a Station of the Metro" as well as of "Piccadilly."

What happens to this aestheticist strain in Pound's oeuvre? A concluding section of a class on imagism, or a bridge to beginning work on *The Cantos*, might focus on Pound's 1920 poem sequence, *Hugh Selwyn Mauberley*. Pound later remarked that *Mauberley* was the product of his and T. S. Eliot's decision that imagism and its free verse form had become diluted, that a "general floppiness had gone too far and that some counter-current must be set going. . . . Remedy prescribed [Théophile Gautier's] 'Émaux et Camées' (or the Bay State Hymn Book). Rhyme and regular strophes" ("Harold Monro" 590). Pound still draws on a nineteenth-century model (the Parnassian poet Gautier), but the polished perfection of the form will now be a vehicle with which to critique aestheticism and imagism.

Mauberley is a difficult poem for undergraduates. I give my students a handout with a brief section-by-section explanation that draws on guides to the poem by Peter Brooker, John Espey, and Christine Froula (*To Write Paradise*). Since usually there is not time to work through the whole poem in class, my focus is on providing students with the interpretative tools with which to read it themselves. We begin with section 2, "The age demanded an image," to work out the section's argument that the twentieth century has replaced the cultural forms of the past with inferior versions; we then look at section 6, "Yeux Glauques," which discusses the Pre-Raphaelite painters and poets more ambivalently. The particular artists and writers named—Dante Gabriel Rossetti, Burne-Jones, and Algernon Charles Swinburne—influenced Pound's early poetry, and his admiration for them is registered in the poem. Burne-Jones's painting *King Cophetua and the Beggar Maid* is praised: the eyes of the beggar maid "still, at the Tate, . . . teach / Cophetua to rhapsodize." Yet these eyes, while beautiful, lack power: they are "[t]hin like brook-water, / with a vacant gaze" (*New Selected Poems* 114). This is a beauty that belongs to the past, that has failed to remain relevant to the changing world; and it is this criticism that Pound levels at the poets of the 1890s in the next section ("Siena Mi Fe', Disfecemi Maremma"), at the "stylist" of section 10 (usually taken to be a portrait of Ford Madox Ford), and at "E.P.," the poet's alter ego, who is the subject of the first section, "E.P. Ode pour l'élection de son sépulchre." This first section suggests that E.P.'s poetic project, "to maintain 'the sublime'/ in the old sense" was "wrong from the start"; his commitment to the past results in him "pass[ing] from men's memory" at the age of thirty (Pound was thirty-five in 1920). E.P.'s failure is not simply attributed to a decline in culture, as we might expect after having read section 2: the poem argues that E.P.'s poetic project itself was misguided—he was "unaffected by 'the march of events.'" Rather than commending this commitment to tradition, the poem concludes by telling us that E.P.'s "case presents / No adjunct to the Muses' diadem" (111). The lesson of the first part of the sequence is not that the twentieth century is to be deplored for its lack of interest in beauty but, rather, that beauty has not maintained its relevance in the new century: a new art is required.

However, *Hugh Selwyn Mauberley* provides no example of what that art might look like. The second part of the poem, "Mauberley 1920," portrays the fictional poet Hugh Selwyn Mauberley, whose poetry is presented as the quintessence of beautiful irrelevance, drawing closely on models by visual artists that Pound admired (Jules-Ferdinand Jacquemart, Piero della Francesca, Pisanello, Sandro Botticelli, and Benardino Luini are all mentioned by name). A year after publishing the poem, Pound made perhaps the clearest statement of his dilemma at this point in his career:

> The symbolist position, artistic aloofness from world affairs, is no good now. . . . In a world politically governed by imbeciles and knaves, there remain two classes of people responsible: the financial powers and the men who can think with some clarity.
>
> (Don't imagine that I think economics interesting—not as a Botticelli or Picasso is interesting. But at present they, as the reality under political camouflage, are interesting as a gun muzzle aimed at one's own head is interesting; when one can hardly see the face of the gun holder and is wholly uncertain as to his temperament and intentions).
>
> (Review of *Credit Power and Democracy* 1)

"The symbolist position" here seems to include not only the French symbolist movement specifically, nor even the broader nineteenth-century aestheticist impulse of which it was a part, but also Pound's own early career. In *Mauberley* Pound bids farewell to "the symbolist position" and resolves to write poetry that is affected by "the march of events": *The Cantos*. As this quotation makes clear, even if artists and art works appear in *The Cantos*, they are not the only or the most relevant models for the poet.

Though Pound remained interested in visual culture throughout his career, his involvement with the short-lived vorticist movement (1914–17) was his most significant engagement with modern art. He signed the vorticists' manifesto, promoted them in his criticism, published poetry in the two volumes of their journal, *Blast*, helped organize their exhibitions, and bought their work. Vorticism, and Pound's interaction with it, is well documented, and teaching Pound through vorticism is a means of introducing literature students to the major art movements of the twentieth century—Italian futurism, German expressionism, and cubism—on which the British movement drew.[3] It can also constitute a case study through which to think about interdisciplinarity and inter-art influence.

I introduce students to vorticism primarily through *Blast*, both volumes of which are available on the *Modernist Journals Project* Web site. Usually, this will follow a class discussion of imagism during which we've read the *Fortnightly* "Vorticism" essay, looked at one or two representative examples of futurism, expressionism, and cubism, and talked about the role vorticism played in imagism's self-marketing. We look at the cover and introductory pages of the first issue of *Blast*, where the typography is particularly striking; students often note that the magazine's appearance is more like a tabloid newspaper than it is like the restrained pages of *Poetry*, and this observation can lead to a productive discussion of modernism's audience.

In introducing the class to vorticist art, I start with the reproductions in the journal—I want students to see the art in context—but I also show color images of works by the vorticists from the Tate Web site. I have usually developed the European art context through a course anthology, either *Modernism: An Anthology of Sources and Documents*, which has relevant extracts by Marinetti, Kandinsky, Guillaume Apollinaire (on cubism), Lewis, and Clive Bell, or—for the graduate course on visual culture—*Art in Theory, 1900–2000*, from which I assign the extracts by Kandinsky, Marinetti, Boccioni, Lewis, Gaudier-Brzeska, Apollinaire, and Albert Gleizes and Jean Metzinger. Since my courses focus particularly on the introduction of modern art to Britain, we look at paintings shown in Roger Fry's postimpressionist exhibitions of 1910 and 1912 (here I find J. B. Bullen's *Post-Impressionists in England* and Anna Gruetzner Robins's *Modern Art in Britain, 1910–14* indispensable). A course oriented towards modernism in the United States might focus instead on the 1913 Armory show. The Smithsonian has an excellent repository of primary materials and bibliographies to download from their Web site ("The Story of the Armory Show").

Despite Pound's close involvement with vorticism, it is by no means straightforward to demonstrate a relation between his poetry and vorticist art works. His own manifesto, "Vortex, Pound," gives H.D.'s imagist poem "Oread" as an example of vorticist poetry: its imagery appropriately (and unusually for imagism) recalls vortices. Pound wrote only one poem directly modeled on vorticist painting, published in the second issue of *Blast*, "Dogmatic Statement on the Game and Play of Chess (Theme for a Series of Pictures)," through which we discuss the techniques a poet uses to imitate a work of visual art. At this point, it is helpful to look at a quotation from another of Pound's essays on vorticism, "Affirmations II: Vorticism":

> And vorticism, especially that part of vorticism having to do with form—to wit, vorticist painting and sculpture—has brought me a new series of apperceptions. . . . I have my new and swift perceptions of forms, of possible form-motifs; I have a double or treble or tenfold set of stimulæ in going from my home to Piccadilly. What was a dull row of houses is become a magazine of forms. There are new ways of seeing them. There are ways of seeing the shape of the sky as it juts down between the houses. The tangle of telegraph wires is conceivable not merely as a repetition of lines; one sees the shapes defined by the different branches of wire. The lumber yards, the sidings of railways cease to be dreary.
>
> The musical conception of form, that is to say the understanding that you can use form as a musician uses sound, that you can select motives of form from the forms before you, that you can recombine and re-colour them and "organise" them into new form—this conception, this state of mental activity, brings with it a great joy and refreshment. (278)

While this statement repeats Pound's point in "Vorticism" that he is interested in "arrangements" of form and color, there are two additional points to note. One is the emphasis on individual perception. The individual's "mental activity" is both the origin of vorticist art (in the second paragraph) and its effect (in the first). The other is the structural lesson Pound attributes to vorticism in the second paragraph. Both these points have significance for *The Cantos*, which Pound begins planning in 1915, during his interaction with the vorticists.

The major difficulty in reading *The Cantos* is not its referentiality—making available the notes to a canto from Brooker's, Froula's, or Carroll F. Terrell's guides largely solves that problem—but its structure. How can students move beyond the decoding of local details to construct the poem's larger arguments? Here, knowledge of Pound's involvement in visual culture provides initial assistance. Pound's description of vorticist art in terms of arrangements, patterns, and motifs alerts us to his method of repeating ideas, images, and qualities across the poem, and it provides us, as it provided Pound, with a vocabulary for describing that method. Early interpretations of *The Cantos* read the poem through imagism and vorticism in just this way, arguing for its structural unity (see Frank; Kenner, *Poetry*). More recent criticism has emphasized its disunity but still finds the visual arts a useful explanatory model: Marjorie Perloff makes the much-quoted remark that "Pound's basic strategy in the *Cantos* is to create a flat surface, as in a cubist or early Dada collage, upon which verbal elements, fragmented images, and truncated bits of narrative, drawn from the most disparate contexts, are brought into collusion" (*The Poetics of Indeterminacy* 181). Such statements are liberating and enabling for students of *The Cantos*: they provide a way to discuss the poem's form without requiring mastery of its arguments and details.

They also encourage students to consider the poem as a visual artefact. This approach is not without its pitfalls: arguments about authorial intention are complicated by the fact that the published editions are inaccurate versions of Pound's typescripts, as Ronald Bush and David Ten Eyck have discussed. But *The Cantos* nevertheless clearly draws attention to its visual dimension in its use of space and its inclusion of ideograms, pictograms, signs, and a section of musical score (see, for example, cantos 22, 75, 88, 94, 100, 112).[4] Does modern art provide accurate analogues for this visual artifact, though? The first three editions of *The Cantos* were illustrated with illuminated capitals by the artists Henry Strater, Gladys Hynes, and Dorothy Shakespear, Pound's wife. Only Shakespear's capitals appear modern; Strater's and Hynes's present the poem in the guise of a medieval manuscript or, more accurately, the late-nineteenth-century revival of the medieval style by printers such as William Morris's Kelmscott Press. A quotation from Jerome McGann's *Black Riders* directs the class to think about how the appearance of the page places the text in a bibliographic tradition, transferring the poem's argument about language use in history into a visual form:

> *The Cantos* summons up the power and authority of the most elementary forms of language, its systems of signifiers, and it apprehends these signifiers as historical artifacts. The graphic presentation of Pound's books is thus made an index of their aims. Through book design Pound makes an issue of language's physique, deliberateness, and historicality. (80)

Certainly, Pound's aesthetic decisions in these early editions suggest that he was more interested in relating the poem to past traditions than in alerting readers to its modernity.

Ultimately, analogies between the form of *The Cantos* and its modern art context are of limited use: they overemphasize the visual arts as a structural model for the poem. Despite Pound's interest in cubism and Dadaism, there is no record of him praising collage techniques, and even vorticist art was only one source for Pound's experiments with combining repeated forms into larger frameworks (equally important are Japanese Noh drama, the Chinese ideogram, and fugue). More helpful in developing students' observations on the poem's form into a discussion of its argument is the analogy of sculpture. This is a venerable approach to *The Cantos*: Donald Davie's *Ezra Pound: Poet as Sculptor* masterfully demonstrates Pound's ideological investment in conceiving the writing of verse as carving ("the 'sculpture' of rhyme," as he called it in *Mauberley*, alluding to Théophile Gautier [*New Selected Poems* 111]). I give students Hugh Kenner's list of *The Cantos*' "two contrasting streams of imagery" from the end of the very first book on Pound, *The Poetry of Ezra Pound*:

Cut	Lumpy
Clear	Opaque
Defined	Soggy
Sculptured	Confused

Stone	Mud
Water	Murk
Volition	Drift
Light	Gloom (314)

With this list on hand, we compare the imagery of canto 16 (the first of the two hell cantos) and canto 17 (one of the paradise cantos). In the latter we notice the prevalence of stone: the cave of seaworn rock, the sand "as of malachite," the forest of marble trees (*Cantos* 77). I also show photographs of the elongated marble and wood pedestals in the studio of Pound's friend during the 1920s, the sculptor Constantin Brancusi, and the famous photograph of Gaudier-Brzeska carving the *Hieratic Head of Ezra Pound* ("Intérieur"; Benington).[5] We discuss how the verse formally embodies the disorder (canto 16) and order (canto 17) it describes in its subject matter, and how the aesthetic of the "arrangements" we saw in imagism and vorticism here constructs paradise: "prow set against prow, / stone, ply over ply" (canto 17 [*Cantos* 78]).

Discussion of *The Cantos'* hell and paradise, however, must be complemented by discussion of its purgatory, where the aesthetic oppositions are far less clear. The Malatesta cantos, cantos 8–11, are the group of poems we focus on. Although the cantos deal with the fifteenth-century ruler of Rimini, Sigismondo Malatesta, Pound's experience of modern art is central to their conception. They were written between late spring 1922 and July 1923, when Pound's theory of art was changing and crystallizing, and they introduce a new technique of writing—copying out chunks of text from primary sources—that was a major breakthrough in the poem's composition. Indeed, Perloff's characterization of *The Cantos* as collage refers specifically to the Malatesta cantos.

After they have become familiar with the aesthetic oppositions of the hell and paradise cantos, students are able to get some way toward establishing aspects of the argument in these cantos. The fact that Sigismondo is involved in the construction of a building and that he is providing work for artists aligns him with the poem's positive values. The precision of his and his employees' comments about the building we know to value too. But there is much about the building itself that is at odds with the sculptural aesthetic we expect from Pound's favorite works of art. How can Sigismondo's Tempio, portrayed at the end of canto 9 as "[t]he filigree hiding the gothic, / with a touch of rhetoric in the whole," relate to Pound's involvement in modern art (*Cantos* 41)? To answer this question, I show the class the title page to *Guide to Kulchur*, where Pound writes that "If the Tempio is a jumble and junk shop, it nevertheless registers a concept. There is no other single man's effort equally registered" (i). The Tempio's attraction for Pound can best be understood if we see it as a work of conceptual art.

This is not as anachronistic as it sounds. While living in Paris in the 1920s, Pound became close to the pioneers of conceptual art, the Dadaists (see Beasley 154–204). Though their literary and visual artworks seem at odds with Pound's cultivation of beauty, he admired their constant invention as evidence of intelligence and personality. Furthermore, as we saw in *Mauberley*, by 1920 Pound had become aware of the limitations of art as beauty, rebuking the artist "aloof from world affairs," and was now interested in "the men who can think with some clarity" (Review of *Credit Power and Democracy* 1). These Pound found among the Dadaists: the best-known work—and perhaps most useful example in this context—is Marcel Duchamp's *Fountain*, accompanied by Duchamp's comment on it, "The Richard Mutt Case." There Duchamp writes that, "[w]hether Mr. Mutt with his own hands made the fountain or not has no importance: He CHOSE it. He took an ordinary article of life, placed it so that its useful significance disappeared under the new title and point of view—created a new thought for that object" (5).[6] Discussion of Dada (especially of Duchamp's readymades and Francis Picabia's drawings of machines) can be extended to include Pound's short essay "Machine Art," where the aesthetic values of vorticism are aligned with the new focus on the artist as inventor or engineer. The beauty of machines, Pound remarks, is "chiefly to be found in those parts of machines where the energy is most concentrated . . . it is here that the inventors' thought, or more probably the thought of a whole series of inventors has been most concentrated" (57). The essay also mentions Pound's brief experiment with cinema (he worked with the painter Fernand Léger, the composer George Antheil, and the filmmaker Dudley Murphy on the 1924 film *Ballet Mécanique*), again locating the film's value in the experiments of the filmmakers rather than in the medium itself.

In this context, Sigismondo becomes legible not as a Whistlerian or vorticist maker of arrangements or a Kandinskian creator of patterns but as a Dadaist conceptual artist, an inventor, an engineer. Like Duchamp, he takes a readymade, in this case the thirteenth-century church of San Francesco, and creates "a new thought for that object" by having it encased in a classicist façade by Leon Battista Alberti and remodeled inside by Matteo de' Pasti and Agostino di Duccio. It is of course what Pound is doing in *The Cantos* too: quoting ready-made passages, putting them into new relationships, and by that method conveying "new thoughts," his arguments.

The sculptural metaphors and allusions in *The Cantos* thus help students discover the work's two major aesthetic modes. Formal beauty, which we saw Pound first associating with the Pre-Raphaelites and later with abstract art and Brancusi's sculpture, remains an ideal, but as such it is primarily encountered in the paradise cantos. In the cantos that work their way through history, it is Pound's other aesthetic mode that is predominant, the "single man's effort" that recalls Lewis's vorticist individualism and Dadaist found objects. Pound's use of the visual arts was historically specific: the appearance of different artists, works, and interpretations in his criticism and his poetry served his changing intellectual requirements. So too does our use of visual art analogies in criticism serve our changing intellectual requirements. In every class, my aim is to teach students to see every analogy with the visual arts—Pound's, the critics', their own—not as an illustration but as an argument: "The history of culture is a protracted struggle for dominance between pictorial and linguistic signs, each claiming for itself certain proprietary rights on a 'nature' to which only it has access," writes W. J. T. Mitchell. "The point, then, is not to heal the split between words and images, but to see what interests and powers it serves" (43).

NOTES

[1] For Pound's instructions about "In a Station of the Metro" to the editor of *Poetry*, Harriet Monroe, see Parisi and Young 57–58. The *Modernist Journals Project* Web site shows the original layout at library.brown.edu/pdfs/1205845053374034.pdf.

[2] This essay is also reproduced in *Early Writings* (278–91).

[3] See especially Cork, Edwards, Antliff and Klein, Dasenbrock, and Sherry.

[4] In *The Cantos of Ezra Pound*, canto 22 falls on pp. 101–06, canto 75 on pp. 470–71, canto 88 on pp. 597–609, canto 94 on pp. 653–62, canto 100 on pp. 733–42, and canto 112 on pp. 804–5.

[5] For further information, see Rainey's *Ezra Pound and the Monument of Culture* and the chapters on Pound in North, *The Final Sculpture*, which are particularly relevant to the issues discussed in this essay.

[6] *The Blind Man*, the journal in which "The Richard Mutt Case" appeared, is digitized as part of the International Dada Archive at the University of Iowa.

Vorticism, the Palimpsest, the Ideogram, and Pound's Understanding of Chinese Historiography in *The Cantos*

Jennifer Ryan-Bryant

Readers of Ezra Pound's poetry and essays can readily identify the principles of composition that he laid out in such works as "Vorticism" and *Guide to Kulchur.* One of Pound's best-known maxims is "Make it new," a simple imperative that he derived from the Chinese emperor Ch'êng T'ang, founder of the Shang dynasty, who had these words inscribed on his personal washbasin (Terrell 205). As Pound notes in canto 53,

> For years no water came, no rain fell
>   for the Emperor Tching Tang
> grain scarce, prices rising
> so that in 1760 Tching Tang opened the copper mine (ante
>   Christum)
> made discs with square holes in their middles
>   and gave these to the people
> wherewith they might buy grain
>   where there was grain
> . . . .
> Tching prayed on the mountain and
>   wrote MAKE IT NEW
> on his bath tub
>   Day by day make it new
>
> 新
>
> (*Cantos* 264–65)

This convergence of aesthetic principle and historical metaphor provides one key example of the strong influence that Pound's interpretations of Chinese and Japanese literature and history exercised over his emerging theories of poetics. In particular, he identified the central tenets of both vorticism and imagism, precursors to his high modernist poetics, in concert with his study of traditional Chinese poetry, Chinese dynastic history, Confucian philosophy, and Japanese Noh drama. A substantial critical assessment of Pound's relation to Asian cultural history exists: it analyzes his Orientalist perspectives on the literature and his difficulties in translating either Chinese or Japanese writings directly from the original language (see, for example, Nicholls, "Experiment"; Qian, *Orientalism*; Kern, Hayot, and Yao, "Toward a Prehistory"). However, his poetry from World War I through the latter years of *The Cantos* benefited significantly both from the precepts that arose from the work of Ribaku and Mei Sheng, among others, and from his increasingly complex understanding of the ebbs and flows of Chinese dynastic power as metaphors for contemporary political conflict.

When I teach selections from *The Cantos* and individual poems from *Cathay* in an undergraduate poetry course for English majors, American Poetry after 1900, or in a graduate topics course, American Long Poems, I focus class discussion on the ways in which Pound's creative translations of Asian literature and his advocacy of Confucianism helped consolidate his theory of modernist poetics. One of our first topics of conversation is the problems intrinsic to translation. Eric Hayot explains that Pound translated *Cathay* in part from Ernest Fenollosa's notes, with the result that Fenollosa's misreadings are added to his own (518). However, he was often so successful in capturing the poems' tone and meaning in a modernist idiom that T. S. Eliot called him, famously, "the inventor of Chinese poetry for our time" (Introduction [*Literary Essays*] xvii). Although he only began his formal study of Chinese two decades after the publication of *Cathay*, Pound used his work with Fenollosa's notebooks as a means by which to articulate his ideas about poetry's social and aesthetic functions. Yao suggests, in fact, that Pound introduced "unprecedented possibilities for the practice of translation as a mode of literary production" through his work in *Cathay* and, later, *The Cantos* ("Toward a Prehistory" 137). Pound's careful treatment of the eighteen poems of *Cathay* built upon the imagist tenets he had already formulated in 1912 and 1913, while his expanding interest in Chinese historiography and Confucianism prepared the ground for the modernist innovations whose limits he would test in *The Cantos*.

Among the standards for poetic composition that Pound identified through his study of Chinese and Japanese literature are his consistent interest in clear-cut, sharply focused images; his poetic speakers' tendency toward emotional association rather than direct statement; *The Cantos'* experiments with unconventional spellings, spacing, typesetting, and other visual elements; the epic's palimpsestic assemblage of literary, historical, and cultural allusions; juxtapositions of seemingly unrelated topics and voices that inform one another; and the occasional use of ekphrasis. Pound's concerns about his literary legacy, his critiques of capitalist excesses, his belief in the cyclical nature of history, and his advocacy of an expressive precision that could lead to real social change grew in part out of his admiration for the political models that the Chinese emperors represented. My students and I explore the delineation of these ideas in the poems by first identifying the historical and mythological sources of a particular canto and then performing close readings that incorporate both these literary inspirations and the poem's formal qualities. Looking at not only semantic but also structural contexts allows us to consider Pound's political views and aesthetic biases as only two dimensions of the work as a whole. As we do these analyses, I remind the students of Yao's concern that *Cathay* both "promotes an ahistorical, racialist notion of Chinese identity" and also "conflates differences between Chinese and Japanese as distinct languages, thereby enacting an early textual version of Asian American racialization" ("Toward a Prehistory" 135). This assignment helps us gather ideas about the sources of Pound's fascination with Asian literary culture and keep in mind the danger, common in the period, of romanticizing Eastern identities.

In class, we shape our initial interpretations of Pound's poetics by consulting Fenollosa's famous essay *The Chinese Written Character as a Medium for Poetry*, which defines qualities that set Chinese ideogrammic poetry apart from its Western counterparts. Fenollosa points to, for instance, the poetry's combination of synchronic and diachronic notions of time (Saussy et al. 45); its syntactical constructions as transfers of power that "bring language close to *things*" by articulating cause and effect (48); its reliance upon the multiple linguistic functions of Chinese characters, which disregard distinctions between object and action (51); its ability to lay bare "what is said, not what is merely meant" (53); its complex use of metaphor as a means of expressing abstract concepts as well as concrete actions (54); the etymologies contained in the ideograms' pictorial representations (55); and the accumulation of "maximum meaning into the single phrase" through the use of object nouns and transitive verbs (58). Fenollosa elucidated these properties of the Chinese ideogram after having studied classical poetry and the *Book of Changes* with Ariga Nagao, Mori Kainan, and Michiaki Nemoto (Saussy 14). Fenollosa's second wife, Mary McNeil Fenollosa, sent her late husband's notebooks to Pound; he revised, edited, and annotated Fenollosa's work even while developing his own compositional strategies. Pound's concentrated interest in the expressive potential of the ideogram shaped both the collage-like style of the early cantos and the sequence's increasingly fragmentary, antinarrative organization in the later poems.

After analyzing with my students the primary components of the Chinese ideogram according to Fenollosa, I give them a creative assignment: each is asked to create, using at least three of the principles that Fenollosa identified in *The Chinese Written Character*, a new version of one of the poems he translated. I encourage my students to employ concrete verbs, to focus on the connection between the object perceived and the action performed, to examine actions and processes as they occur in nature, to reveal the poem's meaning by creating metaphors that express relations between concrete things, and to keep in mind the etymologies of their poems' primary subjects. Students often choose one of the shorter poems in order to focus the project more carefully. Their new translations include synonyms to replace words from the original translation; few to no conjunctions, articles, or other connective words; and moments of reflection achieved through caesurae, additional line breaks, and juxtaposition of nouns and verbs in combinations unfamiliar to conventional Western poetry. After the students share and discuss their own compositions, we study the ways in which these elements of the Chinese ideogram find their earliest expression, in Pound's work, in the translations of *Cathay*. Though these poems' signification in English often varies substantially from their original meanings, as many critics have observed, Pound succeeded in re-creating the texts' focus on object, action, and effect. His "Poem by the Bridge at Ten-Shin," for instance, proceeds as a series of specific images—such as "[p]each boughs and apricot boughs," "head gear glittering," "dragon-like horses," and "yellow dogs"—that both generate the poem's action and reflect his imagist commitments (36). For Pound and Fenollosa, the cultural richness of Chinese literature mandated that it enter Western traditions as both translation and original work.

Other poems in *Cathay* argue on behalf of the compositional elements that resonate within both Eastern and Western traditions, and they illustrate the issues inherent in translation practices. To elucidate such concerns, I read with my students translations of Li Po's "Two Letters from Chang-Kan" by W. J. B. Fletcher, Amy Lowell, Shigeyoshi Obata, Witter Bynner, and Wai-Lim Yip, highlighting these writers' varying attention to voice, meter, tone, image, historical context, and other poetic elements ("Other Translations"). We consider Pound's own work as translator through his transformation of Li Po's verse in "The River-Merchant's Wife: A Letter," which focuses on the emotional intensity of the speaker's experience. The translation's focus on objective statement without overt narrative direction is another trait held in common with contemporary imagist examples.

After my students and I have discussed Pound's work on translations, we turn to the roots of his compositional style in the theory of vorticism, which he defined as a component of imagist poetry ("Vorticism"). Pound reviewed the early traits of imagism he had presented in "A Few Don'ts by an Imagiste," including "[d]irect treatment of the 'thing,' whether subjective or objective," "to use absolutely no word that does not contribute to the presentation," and "to compose in sequence of the musical phrase." More relevant to our study of the *Cathay* translations is his definition of an image as a vortex, "a radiant node or cluster . . . from which, and through which, and into which, ideas are constantly rushing" ("Vorticism"). This description evokes the economy of expression that Fenollosa recognized in the Chinese ideogram, replacing the typical Western reliance on linear narrative with images whose interconnections produce energy. Pound's interest in the etymological roots visible in the ideogram also pointed him toward the palimpsest, a surface or document on which one piece of writing has been superimposed on another so that the earlier text is partially effaced, as a suitable metaphor for a record of history that is at once permeable and dynamic. Since traces of both texts remain visible, ideas contained in one comment on the other. This concept informed Pound's work until the end of his life; as he notes in canto 116, "But the record / the palimpsest— / a little light / in great darkness—" (*Cantos* 815). The palimpsest and the vortex remain his work's two signature figures for representational denseness.

My students and I explore the modernist index of ideogrammic elements by reviewing Pound's imagist principles, which he clarified in collaboration with H.D. and Richard Aldington. The compositional techniques that he pursued throughout his career included a reliance on "juxtapositional" rather than "connected meanings," which gave the poet a sharpened, more precise method by which to perceive the world (Barbarese 300–01). Though Pound famously eschewed the formulaic "Amygism" that he came to associate with Amy Lowell's substantial books of short poems, he continued to write poems centered on images, actions, multiple historical narrators, and metaphor rather than employing the traditional lyric voice. He often organizes his poetry's sequences of concrete actions, sensations, and objects in collage-like form.

For Pound, the ideogrammic approach is consistent with the performance practices of Japanese Noh drama, which portrays multiple actions through a single, unmoving scene, reducing plot to the level of image. Peter Nicholls notes that Pound appreciated this form's "high degree of stylization" and its rejection of earlier drama's "conversational realism" in favor of dance and mime performances; these traits contributed to his overall conceptualization of the *Cantos* ("Experiment" 2). Noh often includes a moment of climax that does not lead to a conclusion, producing instead a gesture toward the cyclical nature of human birth and death (4). In parts of *The Cantos*, these features prompt Pound to emphasize the need for precise expression, one means by which both to capture a particular moment in time and to gesture toward the larger outlines of human existence.

One key pedagogical tool that I use in teaching Pound's work is Carroll F. Terrell's *A Companion to the* Cantos *of Ezra Pound*, which I require my graduate students to purchase and my undergraduates to check out from the library. I also assign compendia by William Cookson, George Kearns (*Pound*), and John Hamilton Edwards and William W. Vasse, among others. Though Terrell's analyses sometimes reflect a conservatism characteristic of an earlier time period, I find his translations and his identifications of Pound's sources invaluable; my students appreciate the ease with which they can access many different types of information in a single source. In canto 60, for instance, in the course of describing Emperor K'ang Hsi's commitment to advancing cultural knowledge, Pound suggests that one of the emperor's greatest achievements existed in determining the true nature of his language. In typically Poundian style, he presents this goal to his readers in both colloquial English and the original French: "He ordered 'em to prepare a total anatomy, et / qu'ils veillèrent à la pureté du langage / et qu'on n'employât que des termes propres / (namely CH'ing ming)" ("and / that they looked to the purity of the language / and that one should use only suitable terms / . . . to regulate the names" [*Cantos* 332–33; Terrell 256]). These lines are followed by the ideograms for "right" and "name," which recur throughout the sequence as reminders of Pound's investment in precise expression and morally sound government.

In order to expand our focus on the artistic genealogies that Pound helped create, I point out to my students that successful Noh drama depicts synchronic time, also a key element of literary modernism. Chronology in *The Cantos* is marked by a similar divergence from linear narration, a technique that aligns Pound's work with other modernist epics like T. S. Eliot's *The Waste Land*, William Carlos Williams's *Paterson*, and H.D.'s *Helen in Egypt*. The acts of interpreting and translating Noh plays helped Pound reimagine the form and temporal function of poetry, providing a "structural conception of time which would allow him to progress from the momentary intuitions of imagism to the complex and extended structures of *The Cantos*" (Nicholls, "Experiment" 2). One compositional device that helped to enable this new conception of time in the work is ekphrasis, which evokes an extended history of Western poetry even as it encourages the reader to linger on discrete, allusively rich passages. In canto 49, for instance, the seven lakes canto, Pound's eight brief stanzas emerge from his readings of eight Chinese and eight Japanese poems contained in the Japanese text 瀟湘八景 (*Shosho hakkei; The Eight Scenes of Xiao-Xiang*). The poems were inspired by "eight famous paintings of scenes along a river in China which pours into Lake Dotei"; Pound's parents owned a book containing these poems (Terrell 190). Using minimalist language and short, paratactic sentences, approaches that recall his earlier imagist efforts, Pound evokes the immediate visual impact of the paintings' landscapes. In passages like these, I underline for my students Pound's precise use of punctuation. Where in the more narratively sprawling cantos the poetic syntax and style appear erratic, here frequent semicolons and periods regulate the poem's pacing and differentiate one stanza's visual source from that of the next. The lines "Rain; empty river; a voyage, / Fire from frozen cloud, heavy rain in the twilight / Under the cabin roof was one lantern" create a series of carefully measured perceptions in the first stanza that contrast with the fleeting impression captured later on (*Cantos* 244). These examples illustrate the compressed chronologies that inform Pound's poetics.

Every class on *The Cantos* must remark on the sheer scope of the poems' literary, historical, and cultural allusions, the rapid successions of which produce the sequence's famously collage-like structure. Though these allusions permeate every poem, their diverse subjects and reliance upon other languages increase in the latter parts of the sequence. Nicholls points to the roots of this phenomenon in Noh drama as well: Pound's persistent use of "superposition," closely juxtaposed ideas and themes, helps to create "a formal hiatus or pause, a gap between two parts of the poem, a space in which a reader might construe relationship" (9). This reflective space originates in the tendency within Noh to represent time as retroactive and reminiscent, the act of understanding one's emotions rendered possible only through memories of past experience (8). Thus I illustrate for my students the ways in which Pound includes Chinese ideograms in order to invoke directly the functions of memory. Ideograms appear in more than thirty of the cantos, including all of the Confucian sequence except 58. In particular, the ideograms for "right" and "name" recur at the conclusions of 51 and 60 and within the text of 64. These words return the reader to the focus on precise expression that serves as a guiding principle for the epic while underscoring the fundamental imprecision of translation in relation to the many passages of Greek, French, and Italian.

Once my students and I have reviewed the formal components of *The Cantos*, identifying in them some key elements of Pound's theory of modernist poetics, we turn to the sequence's historical and philosophical dimensions. Because so much of *The Cantos*' thematic design and narrative structure relies upon Confucian beliefs and Chinese history, my students usually voice concerns about Pound's potentially Orientalist attitudes. In *Orientalism and Modernism*, his study of Asian influences in the careers of Pound and William Carlos Williams, Zhaoming Qian argues that the use Pound made of his "found" or translated Chinese texts was primarily informational and structural, not diagnostic or prescriptive. In other words, he created "a style of superposition" in *The Cantos* that overlays "not just imagery upon emotion, but Wang Wei upon de Gourmont/Laforgue; Kung upon Malatesta/Adams—in short, past upon present and Eastern culture upon Western culture" (109). While on the one hand this devotion to Asian poetry merits recognition within the history of modern verse, on the other such reimaginations of Chinese and Japanese literature undercut the existence of the originals altogether (Kern 156). In later years, Pound turned to an "anti-literal stance" in which he reproduced precise Chinese characters within the text of his poetry, rather than in translation—an attempt to achieve greater fidelity to the cultural values and artistic practices in the original texts (Kern 170). As I explain to my students, it is possible to be an inaccurate translator while respecting the work's history and structure. This profound curiosity about Chinese and Japanese literature remains central to *The Cantos*.

The structural concepts that Pound derived from his study of Chinese poetry and Noh drama laid the groundwork for the political critiques he articulates in the mode of Chinese historiography. While he makes reference to specific periods in modern European history as commentary on current events throughout *The Cantos*, his references to Chinese dynastic history in particular organize the sequence's arguments about what traits just rulers should possess. For instance, in keeping with the notion that rulers act with a people's best interests at heart when they follow the precepts and examples of Confucian thought, Pound explicates the ethics of the Confucian system in cantos 52–61. Hong Sun suggests that Pound was attracted by Confucianism's "persistent search for the origin of social order," which gave him a guide to follow in his own journey toward truth and in his attempts, alongside those of other scholars, to maintain "peace and harmony . . . in the world" (99). One key example of the moral lessons that today's heads of state—and, by extension, today's writers—glean from the past can be seen in canto 53, which provides a catalogue of Chinese "mythical kings" and emperors who embodied ethical practices and also introduced forms of knowledge that became central to Chinese cultural life (Terrell 203). Among the leaders Pound cites are "Yeou" (Yu Tsao-chi), who "taught men to break branches" in the service of building houses; "Hoang Ti" (Huang Ti), who began the practice of historiography; and "Yu" (Ta Yü), who founded the Hsia dynasty (*Cantos* 262; Terrell 203–04). These men's choices as rulers favored their people's accumulation of knowledge and access to resources, both natural and manufactured. Historians describe their reigns as periods of increased political stability and intellectual freedom. As a result of their efforts, "Exchange brought abundance, the prisons were empty" and "'Peace and abundance bring virtue'" (*Cantos* 268).

As model rulers, Yu Tsao-chi and his successors exemplify a promise of harmonious existence. My students and I explore the apparent structural and thematic dissonance between this idea and the overall scope of *The Cantos* in order to locate Pound's specific interpretations of Confucian ideals in relation to supposedly exemplary leaders in the West. Sun notes that cantos 52 and 62 in particular articulate the shared beliefs of, and the divergences between, the founding moments of American and Chinese nationhood. Both countries originate, for example, in "models of enlightened civic order" and in families whose members participated in moments of national revolution. At the same time, however, "one culture stretches back into a mythological past," in contrast to the other's recent beginnings (Sun 109–10). Their vastly different historical time lines shape contrasting notions of what cultural products should constitute success, even as they both make a "constructive effort" to achieve positive change and self-improvement (Sun 110). This comparison puts *The Cantos*' American origins on full display, since Pound valorizes Confucius and John Adams as exemplars of democratic government.

Throughout the sequence, Pound reserves his sharpest critiques for the European "usurers" whose poor choices condemned their subjects to penury or, at the very least, to corrupt models of human existence. I suggest to my students that these critiques stand in direct contrast to Pound's depictions of Chinese rulers as models for contemporary readers even when they fall prey to similar faults. For Pound, these figures' cultural foundations in Confucianism position them as superior alternatives to Western degeneracy. Though my students accept this justification for Pound's compositional choices, they are generally interested in discussing the romanticization of Asian culture that this preference suggests—what they see as Pound's Orientalist, even if celebratory, attitudes—and in comparing these critiques of modern European government to postbellum American conditions. Several of them have noted that Pound seems, perhaps arbitrarily, to favor one legal system over another. In canto 65, for instance, the mercenary decisions of Li Chi, a ninth-century governor in Kiang-nan who "accumulated and hoarded the treasure of six departments," meet opposition from Hsien Tsung, an emperor known for his fair and careful regulation of the country's finances (Terrell 227). However, Tsung struggled with his own adversaries, the court eunuchs; at the end of his life, "he died of the elixir, / fooled by the eunuchs, and more Tou-san (tartars) / were raiding" (*Cantos* 291). Legislative vulnerability develops when the nation's ideal principles, which Pound saw as emerging from both Confucian philosophy and the period of the American revolution, yield to "the disciplinary society of a capitalist market economy" (Bell, "Middle Cantos XLII–LXXI" 104). Although Pound observed the capitalist tendencies of the United States firsthand, he associated these shortcomings with the centuries-long decadence of European rule rather than with the originary promise of American government.

In keeping with his formulations of alternately corrupt and superlative models of rule, Pound advances a theory of history that links order and governance to the cycles of human existence. This theme recurs throughout *The Cantos* and offers students another means by which to think about the notion of synchronous time. Focusing on representations of synchronous time also illustrates the many narrative parallels that exist even among cantos that are chronologically and spatially separate. Canto 64 starts with the invocation "So that," the same words that conclude canto 1 (where they point the reader toward the continued narrative in canto 2) (275, 5). At the start of canto 64, this phrase draws attention to the accomplishments of "Tien-tan" (T'ien Tan), a soldier who rose to commander in Emperor Chi's army and became known for his innovative strategies in battle (Terrell 213). His presence here resonates with that of Odysseus, subject and narrator of canto 1, who designed the Trojan horse ruse that helped the Greeks win the war and who, on the journey home, speaks to the dead. Both T'ien Tan and Odysseus are successful because they understand the rules within which their respective societies flourish, and they use creative tactics to win wars without violating those rules. The parallel that Pound draws between these two moments in *The Cantos* suggests a telescoping of the time that separates them; this notion of time evolves in part from the Noh cycle, in which time "turns back on itself, always seeming to begin again" (Nicholls, "Experiment" 5). Events that recur across time add another dimension to the work's palimpsestic construction.

This cyclical conception of history begins from Pound's vision of dynastic China as a paradigm for modern rule. Canto 64 offers an elegant example of the ways in which Pound sometimes considers several concerns central to his poetics in the same piece. Here, for example, in addition to the axiomatic comparisons that he uses to illustrate the ideal principles of Chinese government, we see him return to the notion that the best art is that which "makes it new." In reference to "Fou-Y" (Fü I), a minister under Emperor Kao Tsu who argued for the abolition of Buddhism within the empire (Terrell 224), Pound advocates moderation and measured action: "Fou-Y saying they use muzzy language / the more to mislead folk. / Kung is to China as is water to fishes. / War, letters, to each a time" (*Cantos* 285). The point here is not to denigrate one school of thought in favor of another; rather, the poem suggests, "Kung" (Confucius) supports and enriches Chinese culture without the need to oppose Buddhism actively. History—in the forms of "war" and the "letters" that record it—accommodates all things in their proper places. In fact, another theme that recurs throughout the entire sequence is the notion that words themselves, through the acts of writing and transmission, can change the world. As Pound suggests in canto 67, cultural achievements arise at the intersections of act and speech; even rulers, like "Hien Tsong" (Hsien Tsung)—easily swayed by his eunuchs yet responsible for repairs to the Great Wall (Terrell 245)—who overcome political weakness can bring about genuine accomplishment. Though Tsung may have declared his goal to be merely "the transmutation of metals" (echoed on the page in the ideogram P'ien, "metamorphosis"), he was also "seeking a word to make change" (*Cantos* 313). This phrase is one of the epic's most concise statements of Pound's poetics. It reflects the modernist principles that the poet derived from his study of Chinese translations and ideograms as well as his dedication to the Confucian belief that humans' earthly experience prepares them for ascension to a higher plane of existence.

In my classes, I conclude our studies of Pound's Asian influences by discussing the need to read *Cathay* and *The Cantos* in relation to the historical context of the two world wars and the deep-seated anxieties that the period's losses generated for modernist writers. In canto 13, a calm interlude before the violence and the scatological imagery of the hell cantos, Confucius articulates the principles of rule and order that many of the other poems seek to follow. Alluding to the self-cultivation, self-discipline, and self-reliance that his disciples practice, Confucius notes, "If a man have not order within him / He can not spread order about him;" he recognizes that errors are human, yet observes that "[a]nyone can run to excesses, / It is easy to shoot past the mark, / It is hard to stand firm in the middle" (*Cantos* 59). These admonitions urge readers themselves to seek the knowledge represented in the text even as they refuse conformity. "Make it new," the aesthetic law that Pound borrowed from Ch'êng T'ang, also resonates in the poet's approach to composition and in his assessment of the interwar climate. This phrase recurs in canto 54 in the ideogram for "new" and in the passage "Sin / jih / jih / sin," which translates to "make new, day by day, make new" (278; Terrell 216). By returning again and again to this concept, which renders canto 13 "the pivot of the whole epic," and by making it a watchword in his other writings, Pound explains the fundamental nature of his life's work: "a poem in which, ideally, one text might overlay another without effacing it" (Sun 114; Nicholls 12). The compositional principles that he derives from Chinese literature thus allow him to insert himself into the very history he frames for his readers. Canto 13 concludes with a long-established symbol of Confucian teachings as Confucius's voice and Pound's become one: "The blossoms of the apricot / blow from the east to the west, / And I have tried to keep them from falling" (*Cantos* 60). As a conclusion to our studies, my students and I review the modernist anxiety about legacy and reputation that this passage articulates. We assess Pound's compositional and literary-historical achievements at the end of the sequence and draw conclusions, which have differed widely by class, about the relative success of his efforts to compile a new vision of Western history from the fragments of the old. Finally, we note that even as he compiles a tremendous span of human knowledge in this masterwork, Pound tempers his achievement with a realization of the mortality that literature—like its authors—will face.

Pound's China: Teaching "The River-Merchant's Wife: A Letter" and Canto 49

Zhaoming Qian

In a globalizing age it seems less and less justified to study American literature in isolation from the rest of the world. Our students growing up in the twenty-first century have instant access to the entire world—Europe, Asia, Africa, Oceania, and the Americas—through streaming video, Internet search, social media, and music and sports journalism. It is no longer possible for anyone to ignore the global vision of American literature. Within American literature are worlds beyond the nation's borders and across the Atlantic, the Pacific, and the Gulf of Mexico. American literature is essentially transatlantic, transpacific, and transhemispheric.

Going for the new and the other has always been a part of the national character of the United States. This is especially true of American literary masters, from Melville to Morrison and from Poe to Pound. Pound's poetry and prose make "other" the worlds of China, ancient Greece, medieval Provence, and modern France. Pound described China in his essay "The Renaissance" as "a new Greece," an interesting and dynamic model that will bring about a renaissance in twentieth-century Europe and America (*Literary Essays* 215). Indeed, China is crucial to Pound's development from imagism to vorticism, and from early modernism to high modernism. Pound's China-related poems should be included in literary studies at both the undergraduate and graduate levels.

The first two sections below will show how I introduce undergraduate and graduate students respectively to Pound's China and early modernism by teaching his *Cathay* poem "The River-Merchant's Wife: A Letter." In a third section I shall demonstrate how I lead discussions at the graduate level of Pound's canto 49, of his use of the ideogrammic method, and of his delving into the world of East Asia at once through textual, visual, and interpersonal means.

Teaching "The River-Merchant's Wife: A Letter" at the Undergraduate Level

In an undergraduate introduction to poetry or American literature class, "The River-Merchant Wife: A Letter" from Pound's *Cathay* may be used along with his other poems of the 1910s to teach imagism. Pound's early masterpiece *Cathay* owes a heavy debt to Ernest Fenollosa, a Harvard-trained scholar who spent fifteen years in Japan teaching Western philosophy and studying East Asian art and literature. He died of a heart attack in 1908, leaving to his widow, Mary

Fenollosa, ample notes for a Chinese poetry anthology, a Japanese Noh drama anthology, and an essay on the Chinese character. It was Pound's "In a Station of the Metro" in the April 1913 issue of *Poetry* that convinced Mary Fenollosa to choose him as her late husband's literary executor. Out of Fenollosa's Chinese poetry notes Pound made *Cathay*.

"In a Station of the Metro," the haiku-like poem that helped Pound win Mary Fenollosa's trust, may serve as an excellent example of imagist poetry; but this one-image poem does not tell us all about Pound's imagist principles: "Direct treatment of the 'thing,' whether subjective or objective"; "To use absolutely no word that does not contribute to the presentation"; and "As regarding rhythm: to compose in sequence of the musical phrase, not in sequence of the metronome" ("A Retrospect" 3). To learn more about the workings of these principles, students should move from the metro poem to "The River-Merchant's Wife." It is in the latter that the image—a flower, a lowered head, the river of swirling eddies, or a pair of butterflies—really comes to the reader's mind as "the speech itself," and a cluster of pictures corresponding to dynamically related, shifting sensations—innocence, shyness, love, and desperation—becomes "a VORTEX, from which, and through which, and into which, ideas are constantly rushing" (*Gaudier-Brzeska* 92). The poem's swiftly changing moods are easily accessible through its swiftly changing images. "The River-Merchant's Wife" can be used more effectively than most other Pound poems to teach vorticism, a term Pound and his fellow vorticists used to refer to advanced or intensified imagism. A close reading of "The River-Merchant's Wife" will help students understand what Pound means by "a VORTEX."

Pound's poetry should be taught beside his critical prose. Two Pound texts of particular importance to the reading of his China-related poems are "Vorticism" and "Chinese Poetry." In "Vorticism" Pound spells out his imagist and vorticist doctrines; and in "Chinese Poetry" he makes clear why he translates Chinese poetry: it is "because Chinese poetry has certain qualities of vivid presentation; and because certain Chinese poets have been content to set forth their matter without moralizing and without comment that one labors to make a translation" (*Ezra Pound's Poetry* 3: 84). For Pound, Chinese poetry's lively images, what he calls *phanopoeia*, can be translated without much difficulty, whereas Chinese poetry's melodic property, what he calls *melopoeia*, is hardly translatable ("How to Read" 25). Accordingly, in selecting poems from Fenollosa's Chinese poetry notes, Pound kept only those that mirrored and challenged his imagist principles, and in re-creating them he focused almost entirely on their "vivid presentation." As a result, despite numerous misrepresentations, Pound succeeds in recapturing the poems' overall sense and sentiment, disregarding their "rhymes" and "tones" while following their verbal constructions and methods of presentation.

Teaching "The River-Merchant's Wife" at the Graduate Level

At the graduate level, we need to address several contextual dimensions beyond imagism and vorticism. In a graduate class, I usually require students to read half a dozen *Cathay* poems before exploring two or three of them in the classroom. "The River-Merchant's Wife" and "Lament of the Frontier Guard" are suitable texts for this purpose and available in the *Norton Anthology of Modern and Contemporary Poetry* (Ramazani et al. 352, 353). With tools such as my introduction to Ezra Pound's *Cathay: The Centennial Edition* and Ira B. Nadel's *Cathay: Ezra Pound's Orient*, students should be able to present the poems' background, situating them in the contexts of imagism, vorticism, and antiwar sentiments.

Prior to having them published in a slim volume by Elkin Mathews, Pound had sent versions of "Lament of the Frontier Guard" and other antiwar *Cathay* poems to fellow vorticist Henri Gaudier-Brzeska, then fighting in the trenches of World War I. The French sculptor, soon to be killed, wrote Pound after reading them, "The poems depict our situation wonderfully" (*Gaudier-Brzeska* 58). With the World War I context in mind, students will acquire a better understanding of the antiwar emotion expressed in such lines as "Bones white with a thousand frosts, / High heaps, covered with trees and grass" (Qian, *Cathay* 38), an emotion shared by the eighth-century Chinese poet Li Bai ("Rihaku" in Japanese) and Pound.

In providing the background against which *Cathay* was made, instructors should be wary of two tendencies: either to take *Cathay* as a translation or to consider it as original poetry. They might open a class discussion by asking the question, "Is *Cathay* original poetry?" Students in favor of *Cathay* as a translation will cite Pound's consistently retained subtitle *Translations by Ezra Pound for the Most Part from the Chinese of Rihaku, from the Notes of the Late Ernest Fenollosa, and the Decipherings of the Professors of Mori and Ariga* (*Cathay* 25). Those in favor of *Cathay* as Pound's original poetry will call attention to the inclusion of Pound's re-creation of the Anglo-Saxon "Seafarer" both in the original *Cathay* and in *Selected Poems of Ezra Pound*. Students who have compared Pound's text to Fenollosa's corresponding notes, however, will approve of neither view. As their comparison will reveal, some of Pound's lines are highly inventive whereas others are quite close to the word-for-word translation provided by Fenollosa. T. S. Eliot aptly asserts in his introduction to *Selected Poems of Ezra Pound* that to consider Pound's "original work and his translation separately would be a mistake" (*New Selected Poems* 368). In "Vorticism," an essay contemporaneous with *Cathay*, readers will find proof that Pound wanted the 1915 volume to be read both as a translation and as original poetry. While calling "The Seafarer" and the other *Cathay* poems translations, he meant them to be his personae: "I began this search for the real in a book called *Personae*, casting off, as it were, complete masks of the self in each poem. I continued in long series of translations, which were but more elaborate masks" (*Gaudier-Brzeska* 85).

Cathay: The Centennial Edition will serve as an ideal tool to facilitate this discussion. Made available in that edition are not only the transcripts of all the relevant Fenollosa notes kept at the Beinecke Library of Yale University but also the corresponding Chinese originals, with each character aligned with Fenollosa's English equivalents.

Having traced "The River-Merchant's Wife" to Fenollosa's notes, students will be able to make a comparison, ascertaining where Pound is inventive, where he introduces a mistake from Fenollosa, and where he penetrates through the surface of the Fenollosa notes to the original meaning. Pound has been ridiculed for presenting a line meaning, "You came by on a bamboo stick horse" as "You came by on bamboo stilts, playing horse" (*Cathay* 33), and another line rendering "It is impossible to traverse in the fifth month" as "And you have been gone five months" (34). While the latter misrepresentation was Pound's, the former was derived from Fenollosa's faulty gloss (75). The comparison will also help testify to Pound's gift for occasionally catching original meanings from the context. Fenollosa is not wrong to describe the River-Merchant's Wife as "at first covering my brows" (75); but it is Pound's "my hair was still cut straight across my forehead" (33) that really captures the original image of a hair style associated with innocence.

Students can build on their knowledge of the *Cathay* text and its corresponding notes to explore Pound's complex strategies intended to make it new and avant-garde. Two useful essays for this exploration are Barry Ahearn's "*Cathay*: What Sort of Translation?" and Marjorie Perloff's "The Search for 'Prime Words': Pound, Duchamp, and the Nominalist Ethos." Ahearn introduces Lawrence Venuti's distinction between two modes of translation—domestication and foreignization—highlighting Pound's use of both (37); and Perloff brings in modernist artist Marcel Duchamp's concept of "maximum precision" or "infra-thin difference" to offer insight into Pound's preference for foreign proper names (56–57). Armed with the concepts spelled out in these two essays, students will be able to identify Pound's juxtaposition of foreignization and domestication in "The River-Merchant's Wife." Pound's typical technique is to overlay a foreign proper name on his idea in English. Thus, in "The River-Merchant's Wife," the couple grew up together in "the village of Chokan" (*Cathay* 33), and when the husband "went into far Ku-to-Yen, by the river of swirling eddies," the wife wanted to meet him "[a]s far as Cho-fu-Sa" (34). For Perloff, Pound's Japanese-sounding Chinese proper names are attempts to render the *Cathay* poems at once genuinely and remotely Chinese. Her essay will enable students to account for why Pound insists on using "Cho-fu-Sa" for the port Fenollosa glosses as "long wind sand" (81). "Cho-fu-Sa," with its "infra-thin difference," as Perloff shows, "takes on an aura despite the emptiness of the signifier in question" (47).

Cathay anticipates Pound's more frequent use of the "make it new" technique in *The Cantos*. An example given in my introduction to *Cathay: The Centennial Edition* is in the opening section of canto 85, where the Confucian character 靈 ("a great sensibility") appears as a heading above such names and phrases as "the time of I Yin 伊尹," "Galileo index'd 1616," "Wellington's peace after Vaterloo," Queen Bess, who "translated Ovid," and Cleopatra, who "wrote of the currency" (*Cantos* 563). The character 靈 takes on nuanced meanings when juxtaposed with Chinese and Western proper names and anecdotes.

Teaching Canto 49

Canto 85 has 320 lines with 104 Chinese characters, alluding to scores of Chinese and Western personages, six (I Yin, Galileo, Wellington, Elizabeth I, Ovid, and Cleopatra) in its first eleven lines alone (*Cantos* 563). In my experience of Pound's China-related cantos, canto 49 best suits exploration in a graduate class. Also known as the "seven lakes" canto, canto 49 can be used to extend students' knowledge of Pound to his "ideogrammic method" or verbal collage of concrete images as a way to express abstract ideas. In addition, canto 49 is an exceptional poem that illustrates three types of East-West exchange: through text, through image, and through personal interaction. According to J. Hillis Miller, "Cultural studies tend to assume that a work of art, popular culture, literature or philosophy . . . has its best value or purchase on the world if it remains understood in relation to some specific and local people, a people defined by language, place, history and tradition" (*Illustration* 14–15). Canto 49 is a rare example that exhibits Pound's active interaction with an East Asian interlocutor "defined by language, place, history, and tradition."

Two meetings of a biweekly graduate class may be devoted to canto 49.[1] During the first meeting two students might be invited to give presentations, one on canto 49's background information and the other on that canto as Pound's split response to the poems and pictures of 瀟湘八景 (*Shosho hakkei*; *The Eight Scenes of Xiao-Xiang*), a screen-book in his possession. Two key tools are an oral translation by Zeng Baosun of the screen-book's eight Chinese poems, copied out by Pound in an unmailed letter to his father, and the reproductions of the book's eight ink paintings, three of which are reproduced (in black and white) in the next few pages. The transcript appears in my *Ezra Pound's Chinese Friends: Stories in Letters*, and the images are reproduced from photographs by Richard Taylor, courtesy of Mary de Rachewiltz. For full-color reproductions of all eight ink paintings accompanied by the poems in Chinese and in Japanese, see Maria Costanza Ferrero de Luca. Among other useful supplementary materials are Wai-lim Yip's *Pound and the Eight Views of Xiao Xiang*, "Pound's Seven Lakes Canto" in my *The Modernist Response to Chinese Art*, and Sanehide Kodama's essay on "The Eight Scenes of Sho-Sho."

In presenting canto 49's background information, students are expected to cover three contextual aspects derivable from the supplementary materials. First, drafted between 1928 and the early 1930s and published in 1937, canto 49 is an exercise of the "ideogrammic method," a collage of eight Chinese waterscape poems, two ancient Chinese songs, some historical narratives, and the poet's interposed voice. This sequence of seemingly unrelated sections of poetry brings some tranquility after the anger and frustration of canto 45, the usura canto, and look ahead to cantos 52–61, the Chinese history cantos. Second, the eight waterscape poems, introduced by the line, "For the seven lakes, and by no man these verses" (*Cantos* 244), are based on the pictures and poems of the screen-book Pound received from his parents in 1928. A relic from Japan, the fourteen-fold screen-book consists of eight ink paintings, eight poems in Chinese, and eight poems in Japanese, mutually representing eight classic views of the Xiao and Xiang (Sho-Sho in Japanese) rivers in south central China. According to Sanehide Kodama, a 1683 book by Genryu entitled 八景詩并歌 (*Hakkei shi awase uta; Poems in Chinese and Japanese on the Eight Famous Scenes*) "contains exactly the same version of the Chinese and Japanese poems on *Shosho hakkei* that Pound's manuscript book contains" (134). Pound's screen-book could be an eighteenth- or nineteenth-century copy of the 1683 relic by Genryu, though. It would be best if the presenter could check out a library copy of Ferrero de Luca's facsimile edition of the screen-book and pass it around the class. Third, the screen-book is a simulation of a nine-hundred-year-old tradition of both visually and verbally representing the eight views of the Xiao and Xiang rivers. Pound's awareness of this tradition is evidenced by a letter he wrote his father, dated 30 May 1928: "They are poems on a set of scenes in Miss Thseng's part of the country, Sort of habit of people to make pictures & poems on that set of scenes" (qtd. in Qian, *Ezra Pound's Chinese Friends* 15). Thirty of canto 49's forty-seven lines are, therefore, extracted from Pound's experience of verbally and visually conceiving the eight scenes in his source book.

Without the assistance of a Chinese or Japanese native speaker—the "Miss Thseng" referred to in the letter quoted above—Pound would not have been able to decipher the poems in the screen-book. It happened that a lady in Rapallo had done missionary work at a girls' academy in the Xiao-Xiang region, and in early 1928 she told Pound of an expected visit from her former employer, the president of the academy. "D[orothy] is up a mountain with a returned missionary," Pound told his mother on 1 March 1928. "Yes Chinese book arrived, berry interestin', returned missionary promises us a descendent of Confucius on a month or so, who will prob. be able to decipher it" (qtd. in Qian, *Ezra Pound's Chinese Friends* 15). Zeng, the academy president, whom Pound met in April, turned out to be a descendent of Confucius's disciple Zeng Xi, or Thseng-sie in canto 13, who "desired to know: 'Which had answered correctly?'" (*Cantos* 58). To Pound's amazement, Zeng had resided in London during his imagist years, studying for a degree in biology from 1913 to 1917 at London University's Westfield College. The two discussed Chinese poetry and Confucianism (Zeng Baosun,

Zeng Baosun Huiyilu 98). At Pound's request Zeng offered an oral translation of the eight Chinese poems in his screen-book. Her rough translation, copied out by Pound in the unmailed letter to his father of 30 July 1928, should serve as proof of her role in the making of canto 49 (Qian, *Ezra Pound's Chinese Friends*, 15–17; see also *Ezra Pound to His Parents*, 662–64).

Against this background, the second presenter can compare the first thirty lines of canto 49 at once with Zeng's translation and with the paintings of the screen-book. The images in the opening lines, for example—"[r]ain," "empty river," and "[s]mall boat"—are all taken from Zeng's translation (*Cantos* 244). Nothing in Zeng's version, however, suggests line 5, "The reeds are heavy; bent." It could only be derived from the screen-book's first ink painting, "Night Rain," whose three bold strokes across slanting strokes signify small boats amid bent reeds (fig. 1). Similarly, canto 49's images for "Autumn Moon" in lines 7–12—"moon," "hills," and "evening cloud"—are copied from Zeng's version of the second poem in Chinese. What remains unseen in Zeng's text is the image of line 11, "sharp long spikes." It seems drawn from the screen-book's second ink painting, whose image of a tall tree, like "sharp long spikes," pierces through strokes that embody clouds (fig. 2). Nothing in canto 49 is more removed from Zeng's version than lines 13–14, where Pound disregards what is elaborated in six lines of imagery and explanation and freely responds to his fancy evoked by the detail from the screen-book's third ink painting (fig. 3). The pictorial speech of "Evening Bell" brings about the dynamics in the fourth scene, "Sailboats Returning." Here is a line neither from Zeng's version nor from the painted spectacle but rather from the poet's imagination: "Sail passed here in April; may return in October" (line 15).

In a discussion that follows the presentations, the instructor might cite J. Hillis Miller's reference to Walter Benjamin's view that original works of art "will have aura, or 'speak'" (*Illustration* 35). Indeed, canto 49 mimics the screen-book's pictorial language so intensely that its lines will become audible or "speak" whenever a source image breaks muteness. When this occurs first in reference to "Night Rain," the text, "the bamboos speak as if weeping" (line 6), conveys the sorrow suggested in the first two painted scenes. Next, when line 12, "Behind hill the monk's bell," turns "audible," again it conveys the tone of its source picture: its resonance awakens us to a sense of serenity and contentment that is subsequently supported by the silent views of "[s]un blaze," "wine flag," "a people of leisure," and "[w]ild geese." When line 30, "the young boys prod stones for shrimp," "speaks," it echoes the sequence's final note of joy. Thus, by way of translating the changing tones of the pictorial composition, the first thirty lines of canto 49 signify a theme of transformation from solitude to liberation through uniting with nature.

During the second meeting, the class may explore canto 49 as an intercultural, interpersonal encounter before they uncover hidden links between its seemingly unrelated sections. Did Miss Zeng from the Xiao-Xiang region offer Pound nothing more than a rough translation of the eight poems in Chinese? Is it right to

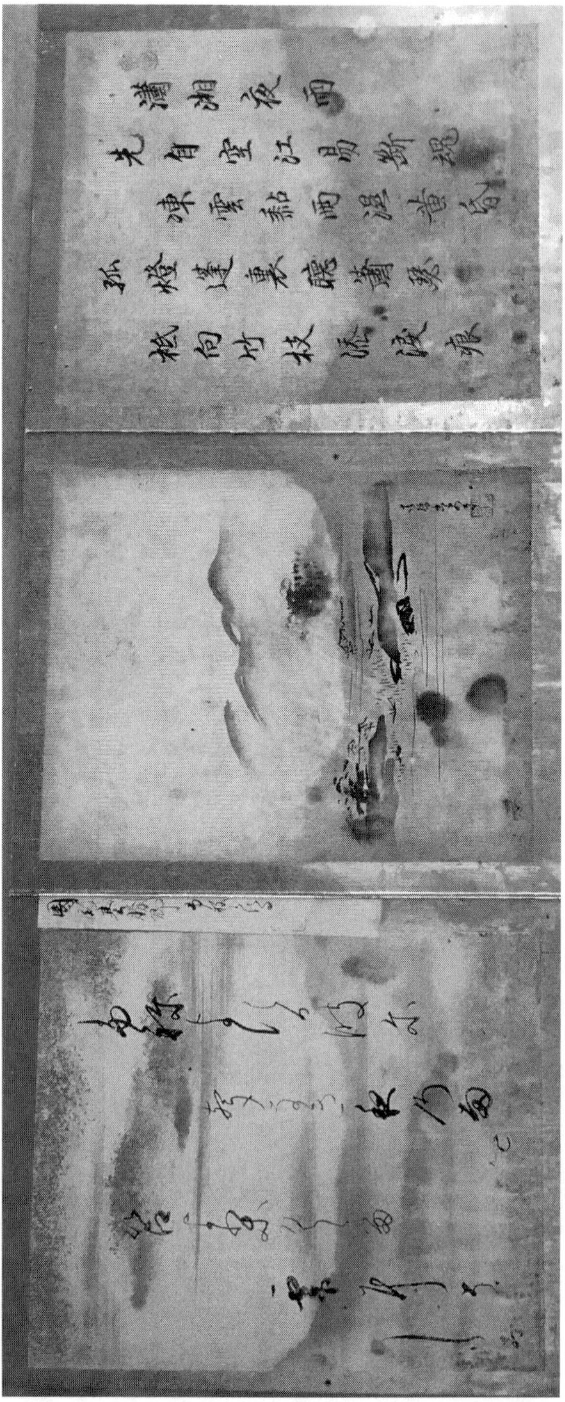

Figure 1. "Night Rain," a scene accompanied by a poem in Chinese (right) and a poem in Japanese (left) from Ezra Pound's screen-book. Photo by Richard Taylor (courtesy of Mary de Rachewiltz).

Figure 2. "Autumn Moon," a scene from Ezra Pound's screen-book. Photo by Richard Taylor (courtesy of Mary de Rachewiltz).

see canto 49 merely as Pound's split response to the image and the text of this source book? These questions will encourage students to consider larger issues of cross-cultural exchange. Reading Pound's 1928 letters to his father such as the one referring to the screen-book as "a set of scenes in Miss Thseng's part of the country" (qtd. in Qian, *Ezra Pound's Chinese Friends* 15) will enable them to see that canto 49 also represents Pound's response to the intuitive commentary of Zeng, an interpreter from the target culture informed of its language, place, history, and tradition. Indeed, a native Chinese speaker less conversant with classic poetry about the Xiao-Xiang region would not have referred to the

Figure 3. "Evening Bell," a scene from Ezra Pound's screen-book. Photo by Richard Taylor (courtesy of Mary de Rachewiltz).

eight scenes of Xiao-Xiang as the "seven lakes." "Seven lakes" (七澤, or *qi ze*, in Chinese) is an example of an auratic reference used only by a small number of local experts within a culture or subculture. The phrase *qi ze* entered literature in the second century BCE, in the rhyme-prose writer Sima Xiangru's masterpiece "On Sir Vacuous." There, *qi ze* or "seven lakes" refers to lakes both in the Xiao-Xiang region and north of it. The expression occurs juxtaposed with Xiao-Xiang alone in Li Bai's famous poem "Song of Dangtu Deputy Magistrate Zhao Yan's Landscape Painting." In subsequent writing, "seven lakes" is paired specifically with Xiao-Xiang, thus securing its association with that region. In a version of the eight views of Xiao-Xiang by the fifteenth-century Ming emperor Zhu Zhanji, "seven lakes" occurs three times to allude to Xiao-Xiang: first in "Night Rain," then in "Snowfall on the River," and finally in "Sailboats Returning." As a learned Xiao-Xiang scholar knowing most if not all of those poems, Zeng probably referred to the eight views not by their common name, "Xiao-Xiang," but by the literary epithet "seven lakes." She is likely to have spoken of the eight scenes as "seven lakes," leading Pound to do the same in canto 49.

How are the eight scenic poems connected to the two ancient Chinese folk songs, "KEI MEN RAN KEI / . . . / TAN FUKU TAN KAI" and "Sun up; work / . . . / Dig field; eat of the grain" (*Cantos* 245)? The rustlings the speaker hears from the bamboos in "Night Rain," the first scenic poem, allude to the sobs of E-huang and Nü-ying, daughters of legendary King Yao (in canto 53, "Yao like the sun and rain") and consorts of King Yao's successor, Shun ("Chun to the spirit Chang Ti"), mourning the sudden death of Shun on a tour of inspection to the Xiao and Xiang rivers (*Cantos* 262, 263). As the legend goes, the two consorts' copious tears stained the bamboos by the Xiang River with purple spots; so lines 37–44 echo the opening section's nostalgia for lost ancient leaders. "KEI MEN RAN KEI . . ." and "Sun up; work . . ." record "The Auspicious Clouds Song" of Shun's time and "The Soil-Hitting Games' Song" of Yao's time. Without his April 1928 parley with Zeng, Pound would not have dug up these ancient songs from Fenollosa's notes. Nor would he have produced a line so approximate to the original in effect: "the bamboos speak as if weeping."

Between the last scenic poem and the first ancient song in canto 49 is some historical narrative: "In seventeen hundred came Tsing to these hill lakes. / A light moves on the south sky line" (lines 31–32; *Cantos* 245). The reference is to Kangxi ("Kang Hi"), the second emperor of the Qing or "Tsing," who toured the hill lakes of the Yangtze delta rather than those of the Xiao and Xiang rivers. But does Pound's mix-up matter? Lines 31–32 are a tribute to the Confucian governance that made the good old times possible. Just as the songs of Yao and Shun anticipate the opening of the Chinese history cantos, "Tsing" prefigures the last four cantos of that sequence (cantos 58–61).

The poet's voice is then heard: "State by creating riches shd. thereby get into debt? / This is infamy; this is Geryon" (*Cantos* 245). This brings us back to the usura canto, reminding us that the world without Geryon and without wild beasts is but a vision out of the blue from the "infamy" of Western powers that depended on borrowing money from individuals to create wealth. Canto 49 concludes with two lines, again in the poet's own voice: "The fourth; the dimension of stillness, / And the power over wild beasts" (245). For Wai-lim Yip the "stillness" alludes to the "Free Flow of Nature." "Only when the subject retreats from its dominating position—i.e. not to put 'I' in the primary position for aesthetic contemplation," explains Yip, "can we allow the Free Flow of Nature to reassume itself" (158).

If time permits, the instructor might ask the class yet another important question: what distinguishes Zeng as an influence from the influences of the screen-book's text and image? What should be recognized is the local expert's capability of interacting with Pound face-to-face while explicating the poems in Chinese. The screen-book's text and image cannot interact with Pound the way she does, through sound, gesture, and facial expressions—from the speech-act theorists' perspective, indispensable components of speech acts that suggest subtle meanings beyond words. Furthermore, a live interlocutor can be interrupted for clarification or elaboration.

To read Pound's China-related poems and cantos is to contemplate East-West exchange in the twentieth century. It is to be aware of transnationalism and interculturalism within modern American literature. In the twenty-first century it makes little sense to teach American literature purely as a national literature and not at once as a national literature and as a subset of world literature. In a globalizing age it is no longer acceptable to shun Pound's China or his China-related poems and cantos in a literature class at the graduate or undergraduate level.

NOTE

[1] While the page numbers in the following discussion come from *The Cantos*, New Directions' *Selected Poems of Ezra Pound* is a less expensive option for classroom study of canto 49 (189–90).

Pound's Economics and Politics

Alec Marsh

Ezra Pound is regarded as a crank about economic matters, especially about money. In fact, Pound thought long and hard about economics, almost as much as he thought about poetry, and our task in the classroom is to understand why economics attracted him and how it affected his poetry and prose. Ezra's father, Homer, was an assayer at the Philadelphia Mint during a period when "the money question" was *the* issue in American politics. Seemingly abstruse questions concerning the virtues and defects of metallic and paper currency, gold and silver money, monetary signs and symbols were dinner table conversation. Years before his celebrated conversion to C. H. Douglas's social credit, young Ezra was a Republican Progressive, impressed by the reformer Theodore Roosevelt and dreaming of economic reform and limits on personal wealth. Impelled by the prolonged economic crisis of the 1930s, his readings of Confucius and Mencius, the distributive mechanism of Sylvio Gesell's *Schwundgelt* ("shrinking money"), and the so-called new economists attracted to A. R. Orage's magazine *The New Age*, Pound evolved his own syncretic economic philosophy, volitionist economics, with which he tried to interest Mussolini, whom he saw as the Theodore Roosevelt of the Italian Peninsula. The question of just what the phrase means becomes the catalyst for classroom discussion and debate.

Pound was most interested in the contradictory nature of money, which is the language of economic exchange. His researches into money continued during his incarceration at St. Elizabeths to find startling if obscure expression in the difficult late cantos, most strikingly in his "reading through" of Alexander Del Mar's *History of Monetary Systems* in canto 97. Pound's belated discovery of Del Mar's work, a direct intervention into the monetary controversies of the late nineteenth century, brought his economic thinking full circle. For clarity, students are encouraged to review Del Mar's text on their own.

But economics had surfaced in Pound's epic long before. Canto 12 is dedicated to "money business" (*Cantos* 53). In canto 18, Kublai Khan's invention of paper money is set against war profiteering, establishing a crucial nexus in Pound's thought confirmed years later by the social credit adage "War is economic peace. Peace is economic War" (Munson 226). Social credit is taken up explicitly in canto 38 with the inclusion of Douglas's foundational "$A + B$ theorem" (discussed below). Douglas himself appears in canto 22 as "C.H." in a debate with John Maynard Keynes ("Mr. Bukos") and again in canto 46. Canto 33 quotes extensively from Karl Marx's *Capital*, while Vladimir Lenin surfaces in cantos 74 and 80. Students should select any one of these cantos and study its historical references and how Pound interpreted, or misinterpreted, his sources.

Pound's fugitive economic writings remain for the most part out of print. Fortunately, his *Selected Prose 1909–1965*, edited by William Cookson, contains a representative sampling, including crucial essays like "Mang Tze," an appreciation of Mencius, which contains Pound's exposition of the "nine fields system" (103), otherwise known as the well-field system, and his theory of taxation (discussed below). *Selected Prose* also samples pamphlets like "What Is Money For?," "Gold and Work 1944," and "The Economic Nature of the United States," as well as the *ABC of Economics* and *Social Credit: An Impact.* Roxana Preda's useful collection *Ezra Pound's Economic Correspondence 1933–1940* gathers many letters whose economic dicta are also found throughout *The Cantos*.

Pound's obsession with a sane economics is part of his lifelong antiwar stance, a fact that may startle some too eager to label Pound "fascist" and so avoid looking into his economic philosophy. To Pound, the "anglo-judaic war against Europe"—what we call World War II—was precipitated by fascist threats to the liberal economic system dominated by the Bank of England, the bank's subsidiary British Empire, and an international financial elite, whom Pound preferred to imagine as "Jews," whether individual bankers were Jewish or not.[1] The taint of anti-Semitism, though well-deserved, has unfortunately occluded Pound's important insights into the undeniable predatory and criminal propensities of finance capitalism still evident today.

"The State-Finance nexus," as David Harvey calls it, has many names (46). Dwight D. Eisenhower called it "the military-industrial complex." Harvey, whose credentials as the leading expositor of Marx and *Capital* might mark him as antithetical to Pound, observes how "the privileged banking establishment has managed to monopolize everyone's credit, enabling the few to exploit the many through their partiality in allocating credit, by charging usury (disguised as 'interest') and increasingly exorbitant fees, and by rewarding politicians for their service in promoting their interests" (Harvey 48–49). Pound calls this establishment the "usocracy," labeling its ethos "usura." His famous chant against "usura" helps make canto 45 the most memorable of *The Cantos* and one of the great poems of the twentieth century. Yet Pound's critique from the right has strong affinities with leftist anticapitalism, one reason why Lenin's *Imperialism: The Highest Stage of Capitalism* remains an important touchstone for Pound. At this point Lenin's economic views become the focus of classroom discussion. Pound's critique of capitalism evolved over time, shaped on the one hand by historical events and on the other by his historical and economic research.

Pound worked in the Jeffersonian tradition of American politics and economics. Thomas Jefferson remains a radical figure, known for his deep distrust of big government and his scorn for banks and the English financial system, which he justifiably felt had been foisted on the new American republic by his political rival, Alexander Hamilton. Jefferson had a horror of debt, which reached from the past into the present like a skeletal hand. Pound never tired of quoting from Jefferson's 1813 letter to John Eppes about the dangers of debt, with its famous phrase, "The earth belongs to the living"; that is to say, everyone deserves to be born free of debt (canto 77 [*Cantos* 488], *Jefferson* 115–17, *Guide* 181). Jefferson believed that farming was probably the only truly productive activity, all else being merely traffic; so did Pound (*Jefferson* 45, 63). Jefferson saw a world of producers—farmers and craftsmen doing immediately useful labor—pitted against an exploitative commercial class who merely shifted and exchanged other people's product for their own profit. Commerce was a tyranny controlled by bank credit and disciplined by debt. Following Jefferson, Pound saw history as a class struggle between a mass of producer-debtors and a clique of predatory creditors.

Jefferson was friendly with many French physiocrats, whose writings defined all wealth as coming from the earth. Physiocracy, the first systematic economic scheme (see Gay 349), derives directly from the writings of Confucius, which were translated into Latin and then French in the seventeenth and eighteenth centuries. Pound's lifelong obsession with Confucius, whom he translated periodically from the 1910s onward, may have been influenced by his own Jeffersonian predilections. Both Confucius and Jefferson were agrarian thinkers with vast practical experience in government, and a classroom debate between Confucians and Jeffersonians would ensure a lively engagement, uncovering many commonalities amid conflicting economic theories.

Pound's early economics is in the moralistic Ruskinian mode. Like John Ruskin, and all economists, Pound is interested in "wealth." But fundamentally, wealth, from *wele*, or weal, cannot be defined as money or even riches ("Wealth"). Wealth can only be what is good for life. From this perspective, what are generally considered riches tend merely to be useless goods bought with money. Money itself does not constitute riches but only the power to purchase "goods"—Ruskin insists we remember the meaning of the word. Seen broadly, wealth must include the vast commonwealth of cultural and technical achievements, among them the work of poets and artists. The cultural commonwealth is the sum of its achievements as a culture. Cultural failures, among them poverty, ignorance, and war, all life-denying, obviously count against a culture's wealth. Ruskin went so far as to call them "illth" (6–9).

Progressive reform is very much the mood of Pound's early economics as well. No wonder, then, that he was open to the economic currents flowing through the *The New Age* when he arrived in London in 1908. A. R. Orage, the journal's visionary editor, also was formed in the Ruskin–William Morris crucible of the late nineteenth century. Before publishing Douglas, Orage had written an important work on guild socialism, a trend within socialism that showed the influence of the *corporazione* idea later adopted by Italian Fascism.[2] Pound's close friend in the 1930s, the Hungarian intellectual Odon Por, who also wrote for *The New Age*, later promoted guild socialism in Italy. Por imagined in several books a linkage between guild socialism and Mussolini's nascent Fascism, which originally had no economic program except violent anticommunism. In the 1930s, Pound and Por helped each other: Por arranged for Pound to appear on Rome Radio and Pound was the English translator of Por's *Italy's Policy of Social Economics 1939/1940*. The thrust of Pound's early economics and curiosity about Italian Fascism shows that he was interested in improving society through a more equitable distribution of the total wealth of the community, including tangible and intangible cultural assets. In Italy, Pound saw the summer concert series of modern and classical music he arranged in Rapallo in the 1930s as a distribution of cultural wealth. Students at this point will investigate the combination of music and economics, beginning with research into what music was actually performed in the series and how large were the audiences.

Primed by Orage, by the time he met Douglas at *The New Age* at the height of World War I in 1917, Pound had become interested in the economic causes of war. He saw the conflict presented in the press as a clash between Teutonic *Kultur* and French *civilisation* instead of as a product of obscure economic interests. Douglas, a Scottish engineer, had been running an aircraft factory since the war began. He noticed that the state could mobilize for war in ways it would never mobilize for projects under peacetime conditions. He is remembered as an economic reformer with an idea, social credit, that deserves to be taken seriously.

Pound's reviews of Douglas's *Economic Democracy* both quote this powerful insight: "Real credit is a measure of the reserve energy belonging to a community." "Real credit" is a community's "social credit," in other words its productive potential, including artistic and cultural production, the "cultural heritage." Douglas observes that the "power to draw on the productive capacity to do work is clearly subject to the control of its owners through the agency of credit" (qtd. in Pound, "Probari Ratio" 179). Thus, "it must be perfectly obvious to anyone who seriously considers the matter that the State should lend, not borrow" from private banks like the Bank of England, or quasi-private entities like the Federal Reserve; "in this respect as in others the Capitalist usurps the function of the State" (qtd. in Pound, "Economic Democracy" 181). In canto 97, Pound will refer to this statement in Del Mar: "The right to coin money has always been . . . the surest mark of sovereignty" (66). When the banks control the currency—or in modern times, credit—they call the shots, while the government must borrow its own money and pay interest on it. Seen in this light, the supposed sovereignty of the United States rests with the banks, represented by the unelected Federal Reserve Board, rather than with elected officials or even the Constitution of the United States. At this point, students should reread the Constitution to determine the limits and freedoms of banking in the United States. They will discover an intriguing, quasi-literary text with extraordinary ramifications for Pound.

Douglas also deserves credit as one of the discoverers of the emergent consumer culture. "The only object of production is consumption," he wrote—not profit, as Marx had claimed in *Capital* (*Social Credit* 124). By the twentieth century, the problem of production had been solved, but the problem of consumption had scarcely been formulated. It was assumed that everything produced would be consumed; yet history has shown that war remains the only perfect consumer; no one has yet figured out how to make capitalism sustainable in times of peace. Whether the problem is called overproduction or underconsumption, the basic tension remains: productive capacity overwhelms society's ability to consume (*Social Credit* 124). The problem is not a lack of the will to buy but a lack of the means to buy with, that is, money. Douglas defined money as "effective-demand," or the power to buy, because without it no demand for goods could be fulfilled, however pressing (*Social Credit* 149). This contradicts one of the most famous maxims of nineteenth-century economics, Say's law of markets, which states in effect that "the total supply of goods and services in a free market economy will equal exactly the total demand during any given time period," an early-nineteenth-century fallacy that nonetheless withstood the pressures of economic reality for a century (Say 132–40). Douglas's critique of Say's law is expressed in his famous $A+B$ theorem, which is the heart of his analysis of what ails capitalism. It was so important to social credit and to Pound himself that he wrote it almost verbatim into canto 38:

> A factory
> has also another aspect, which we call the financial aspect
> It gives people the power to buy (wages, dividends
> which are power to buy) but it is also the cause of prices
> or values, financial, I mean financial values
> It pays workers, and pays *for* material.
> What it pays in wages and dividends
> stays fluid, as power to buy, and this power is less,
> per forza, damn blast your intellex, is less
> than the total payments made by the factory
> (as wages, dividends AND payments for raw material
> bank charges, etcetera)
> and all, that is the whole, that is the total
> of these is added into the total of prices
> caused by that factory, any damn factory
> and there is and must be therefore a clog
> and the power to purchase can never
> (under the present system) catch up with
> prices at large. (*Cantos* 190)

The poet's asperity is typical: Pound never could understand why people became confused by economic data he found self-evident. Douglas had noticed that the purchasing power distributed by his factory in the form of wages, salaries, and dividends A was smaller than the price of the factory's product, since the latter also included other expenditures B—the costs of materials and tools, interest on bank loans, depreciation of the plant, logistical costs, waste, and scrap. Obviously, "A must be smaller than $A+B$" (see Marsh, *Money and Modernity* 89–94). A was in practice a fraction of B, which reflected most of the cost of doing business. Outlining these propositions on a whiteboard will enhance students' understanding of these details.

By Douglas's reckoning, the conclusion was inescapable: purchasing power could never keep up with prices. So far the world had made up the difference through loans against future production and by dumping abroad; that is, by subsidizing production so that products could be sold abroad below fair market value, which Pound (and Lenin) saw as a key cause of war. Only technological innovation and cheaper raw materials, which lowered costs of production, stemmed the rush towards permanent indebtedness and an ultimate credit crash. But technical innovation decreased the cost of labor too. Workers were displaced by machines, thereby further decreasing *A*, the distribution of purchasing power, even as it lowered *B*, production costs. Now add in the "infamy"[3] of taxes needed by governments to pay off loans, which further stripped consumers of purchasing power. As a result, progress caused poverty. If Douglas is right, capitalism as we know it is unsustainable unless ways can be found to augment consumer purchasing power. Indeed, the decision by the Bank of England after the Great War to return to the financial status quo ante bellum by reimposing the gold standard was disastrous economically, ultimately creating conditions precipitating the famous stock market crash of 1929. Foreseeing the disaster, Pound's correspondent Arthur Kitson charged a "bankers' conspiracy" in a pamphlet of that title he sent to Pound. Kitson would later send Pound *The Protocols of the Elders of Zion*, a popular and highly toxic piece of anti-Semitism that reimagined the bankers' conspiracy as a Jewish conspiracy. Pound doesn't appear to have read the book till World War II, but he, like Douglas, Kitson, Hitler, Henry Ford, and millions of others, believed the fable of an all-seeing, all-knowing Jewish conspiracy using universal debt as a weapon to hijack history, with Russia its first victim and the Communists as its first tools.

Postwar England in 1919 was well lubricated with money, but prices seemed high and the "high cost of living" became a journalistic byword. The return to the gold standard reflected bankers' policy to deflate the economy by withdrawing credit. This would lower prices and increase the value of creditors' debts since each unit of money was worth more. When prices are low, a pound note buys more goods. But the contraction of the economy also meant higher unemployment just when demobilized veterans were looking for work. The social credit adage "Peace is economic war; war is economic peace" captures well this dilemma to which orthodox economics had—and still has—no answer. Pound himself would state the problem in canto 22 ("And C. H. [Douglas] said to the renowned Mr. Bukos [i.e., Keynes]: / 'What is the cause of the H. C. L. [High Cost of Living]?' and Mr. Bukos, / The economist consulted of nations, said: / 'Lack of Labour.' / And there were two million men out of work") as a kind of philosophical dialogue between Douglas and Keynes (*Cantos* 101–02). Keynes was not yet the famous author of *The General Theory of Employment, Interest and Money* (in which he pays a handsome tribute to Douglas and Gesell) but was still an orthodox economist, which is to say he believed in Say's law of markets. What would make Keynes a Keynesian is precisely the rejection of Say's law.

Ironically, Pound's *Social Credit: An Impact* records the impact, not so much of Douglas's social credit ideas, which had already made an indelible mark on Pound, but of Silvio Gesell, author of *The Natural Economic Order*.[4] Though Pound had been aware of Gesell's work since 1932, when he had seen it in action in the Austrian town of Wörgl, it was only upon reading Hugo Fack's 1935 American edition of Gesell's book that he realized that Gesell provided a mechanism for achieving some of Douglas's goals. Pound's pamphlet is designed to bring Douglas and Gesell together and in so doing to criticize Marx, English leftists, and American New Dealers. Pound epitomizes Douglas's economic critique of finance capitalism by stating, "WORK is not a commodity. Money is not a commodity. The state HAS credit, and does not need to rent it from banks" (14). With this statement, Pound draws a distinction between work and labor: work is what one person does, labor is a mass phenomenon governed by market forces. He adds, with emphasis, a quote by Gesell: "'*Marx found nothing to criticize in money,*'—S. Gesell" (15).[5]

He continues, "Many vast and heavy books have ended in muddle from failure to see that property and capital are radically different. Property does not imply the enslavement of others. There is a difference between durable and perishable goods, in fact there are all degrees of durability, from that of the fresh-plucked fruit to that of the art works of Chaldea" (15). The heavy books certainly include the three volumes of Marx's *Capital*, where indeed Marx has little to say about money. Following the classical economists Adam Smith and David Ricardo, Marx subscribes to the labor theory of value, which is measured by money. According to Pound, once the true nature of money is understood, by way of thin pamphlets like his own, economics can be rendered in pithy maxims rather than pages of recondite algebra or difficult economic theory.

Pound rejected the labor theory of value but believed in the value of work. Gesell's innovative *Schwundgeld*, sometimes called "stamp scrip," based on "work done" (*Arbeitswert*), offered a way to monetize work without first creating debts. A kind of "work money," stamp scrip can be issued when and wherever work needs to be done; it never needs to be borrowed and thus puts banks out of the picture. It has emerged periodically in many places where a shortage of circulating currency has brought economic exchange and necessary public works projects to a halt for lack of cash. At this point we digress to discuss the history of banks in three countries: Italy, England, and the United States, all countries directly bearing on Pound.

A peculiarity of *Schwundgeld*, literally "shrinking money," is its virtue of losing value over time. It is purely a medium of exchange, not a store of value, as money usually is. Gesell envisioned money whose value would decay at a fixed rate like most of the commodities for which it was exchanged; hoarded, it should rot like so many uneaten potatoes. Such money demands to be kept in circulation since there is no point in hoarding it, or letting banks speculate with it by alternately hoarding, then investing in other sectors, often overseas. If not spent, *Schwundgeld* loses value at a fixed rate of a certain percentage per month: it oxidizes, so to speak. Gesell recommended stamps to indicate the lowered value of his money, an awkward, fiddly feature. But as David Harvey points out, with the electronic money in use today, such a regulated degradation of value could easily be managed without fuss (35).

Pound regarded *Schwundgeld* as a temporary expedient, a "half-way house" on the way to a full Douglasite reform of the money system (*Social Credit* 14, 20). But he saw it could be used to manage another result of a social credit economy. If the state can lend, in theory it should also pay dividends to its citizens. In the form of stamp scrip, such dividends would circulate rapidly, offering a sudden stimulus to any economy.

The "infamy" of taxation is a constant in Pound's economic agitation. "Mang Tze," his essay on Mencius, pushes for a tithing but not a taxation system. If there must be taxes, Mencius said, let them be taken as a small portion of what is produced, a tithe. Fixed taxes, levied without regard to production, meant ruin for producers unable for one reason or another to sell their products. Obviously Mencius, writing in the third century BCE in China, was thinking of the plight of peasant farmers, oppressed by fixed tax rates regardless of their crop yields; but the principle can be extended even if, as the physiocrats and Jefferson noticed, "mercantilism is incompatible with Mencius" and his system (91).

Pound's syncretic economic philosophy melding Douglas and Gesell, leavened with his Confucian and Jeffersonian bias towards agrarian societies, matured in the 1930s as volitionist economics. The following were its key premises:

> All wealth is ultimately rooted in the generosity of nature.
>
> The "cultural heritage" includes all the arts—the poet is as much a producer as a farmer or a machinist.
>
> All history is the class struggle between a mass of debtors and a few creditors.
>
> The resolution of that struggle is the understanding that:
> money is not a commodity; it is a means of exchange; and
> labor is not a commodity, it is life itself.
>
> Class-collaboration, directed by responsible individuals willing the national good by welcoming civic responsibility, is the road to prosperity.

This last expresses the "volitionist" part of Pound's program. Truly responsible individuals want the national good, not private profit.

Pound's title *Jefferson and/or Mussolini* neatly encapsulates his political economy in the 1930s. Pound believed that volitionist reforms steered by a genius at the top (Mussolini or Franklin Roosevelt) could reform capitalism and save Europe and America from financial and therefore political disaster—that is, a bankers' war against civilization. "Usocracy makes wars in succession," he wrote in "Gold and Work." "It makes them according to a pre-established plan for the purposes of creating debts" (338)—because under the perverse canons of value promoted by "demoliberal ideology" (the myth of the free market and free trade, based on convertible gold), debt is equivalent to wealth (*Guide to Kulchur* 26). He foresaw that a second global war would be necessary to save the liberal economic system and wanted to forestall it. To do this it would be necessary to install "a sane economic system somewhere," anywhere, as a check on the lie that liberal capitalism and democracy were compatible systems. Pound hoped that Fascism under the pragmatic direction of Mussolini might adopt his economic scheme and thereby take economic steps toward an ideal republic—at bottom, an agrarian autarchy saturated with the wisdom of Confucius, where the classes collaborated on the social good and the economic program promoted productive labor and saw to it that goods were distributed justly.

In *ABC of Economics*, he proposed:

> Both in England and America the new party should be a MATERIAL PARTY with three parts to its platform:
>
> When enough exists, means should be found to distribute it to the people who need it.
>
> It is the business of the nation to see that its own citizens get their share, before worrying about the rest of the world.
>
> (If not what is the sense of being "united" or organized as a state? What is the meaning of "citizen"?)
>
> When the potential production (the possible production) of anything is sufficient to meet everyone's needs, it is the business of the government to see that both production and distribution are achieved. (264)

The distributive mechanism would be Gesell's stamp scrip. In this way, the state lends against its own credit and pays no interest to anyone. Taxes would be minimal and the state could, in principle, pay dividends to its citizens.

Pound's utopian dream was never realized; he thought Fascism flopped for lack of Confucian probity. By war's end, Europe was devastated, its eastern half swallowed by the Soviet empire. Years later, incarcerated at St. Elizabeths Hospital, having translated virtually all of Confucius, Pound was still at work agitating for a sane economic system. The key, he felt, was proper money. To issue money was to assert control over the value of things, and this was the true nature of sovereignty. "Civilisation," he had written in his essay on Mencius, "consists in the establishment of an hierarchy of values" ("Mang Tze" 90). Money is one way of measuring this hierarchy. Much of Pound's writing in the late cantos is concerned with establishing a proper scale of values, with ratio and "proportion" (canto 90 [*Cantos* 625]). For example, while reading Alexander Del Mar in the 1950s Pound came upon the "nummulary theory" of value. "Value is not a thing," Del Mar reasons, "not an attribute of things; it is a relation, a numerical relation, which appears in exchange. Such a relation cannot be accurately measured without the use of numbers, limited by law and embodied in a set of concrete symbols, suitable for transference from hand to hand. It is this set of symbols which, by metonym, is called money" (7–8). In short, "Money is a Measure and must of necessity [be] an Institute of Law" (8). This theory of monetary value means that the ratio of value between coins within the same monetary system is legislated. If money is a measure, it can never be a commodity, any more than miles or kilograms can become commodities. "Nummulary theory" brings the discourse of law and the discourse of money intimately together as a principle of cohesion in the final group of cantos. Pound's turn to Del Mar in canto 97 and the law in his very late cantos (cantos 107–109) reflects this development of his economic thought.

The Cantos is a global epic, not only telling "the tale of the tribe" (*Guide* 194) but also constituting "the poem including history" (*ABC of Reading* 46). Economic arrangements, institutions of exchange and its language—money—are integral to any responsible history. In explicitly making economics a theme in his epic poem, Pound was only making plain what was implicit in other epics. All epic poets are economists of a sort, some more, some less openly. Like most twentieth-century reformers of consequence, Pound is something of an economic determinist, believing that the restructuring of our economic arrangements is the surest way to reform society for the good. His proposals, like his poetry, deserve our close attention. When we give it, we discover that teaching Pound's economics means asking radical questions about the basic assumptions underlying economics as usually taught.

NOTES

[1] Pound to Congressman Jerry Voorhis, 13 September 1939: "Only England and the yidds are driving for any such extension. It is in great measure an anglo-judaic war against Europe."

[2] Fascist *corporazione* were more like guilds than our corporations. Italian Fascism is a mode of state capitalism, binding formerly private businesses closely to the state. It was a way of reorganizing all sectors of production in a particular industry, to reduce or control conflicts between management and workers.

[3] See Pound, *Hugh Selwyn Mauberley* (*New Selected Poems* 113).

[4] The discussion of Gesell is based on Marsh, "Social Credit: An Impact."

[5] This was not true, but nobody knew it until the belated release of Marx's nine-hundred-page *Grundrisse der Kritischen der Politischen Őkonomie* (*Fundamentals of Political Economic Criticism*), not published in full until 1951. The massive (more than five hundred pages) "Rough Draft" or "outline" was published in 1857–58. English translations of Marx's German text would not be available until the 1970s.

The Cantos in a Quarter

Brian M. Reed

While in graduate school, I took several courses on modernist poetry, but I encountered Pound's *Cantos* only piecemeal, a few cantos here, a few there. When preparing for my PhD orals, I resolved to read the entire epic. My committee, after all, consisted of not one but three experts on the work: Marjorie Perloff, Albert Gelpi, and George Dekker. To my surprise, they recommended that I put less than a third of the poem on my examination lists, the sections originally published as *Draft of XXX Cantos* and *The Pisan Cantos*. Were *The Cantos* so formidable that not even an advanced doctoral student could do them justice?

I disregarded my committee's advice and, over the course of a year, made my way through Pound's long poem, from the first canto's "And went down to the ship" (*Cantos* 3) to the last's "A little light, like a rushlight / to lead back to splendour" (817). The experience was transformative. I had to consult numerous commentaries and secondary texts; I had to learn to read a terrifically challenging poem; and I had to wrestle with fundamental questions about the nature and purpose of literature and the relationship between aesthetics, ethics, and history.

I also thought about pedagogy. Could a productive, immersive engagement with a text as long as *The Cantos* take place in a classroom setting within the constraints of the academic calendar? James Laughlin, for one, doubted it. In 1965 he wrote Pound to advocate an abridged version of the poem: "We are constantly getting requests . . . for such a selection from the professors who teach the modern courses in literature in colleges here. They want to teach the 'Cantos' but find the big book too bulky and expensive for their students" (qtd. in Barnhisel, *James Laughlin* 168).[1]

If the answer to my first question about a course on *The Cantos*—could it be done?—appeared to be yes, one still had to ask, Should it be done? Pound is guilty of every sin that 1990s New American studies equipped me to ferret out in literary texts: misogyny, homophobia, racism, anti-Semitism, even overt fascism. Dare I ask students to tackle eight-hundred-plus pages of verse whose themes could be objectionable, even toxic? There are defensible reasons to introduce new readers to *The Cantos*, not least its influence on writers such as Susan Howe, Christopher Okigbo, and J. H. Prynne, all of whom employ Pound's compositional techniques toward different political and moral ends. But why assign the whole poem, when volumes such as Richard Sieburth's 2003 edition of *The Pisan Cantos* provide an opportunity to concentrate in depth on just one section of the epic? Students could gain an appreciation for the work's merits and demerits without having to chart its every meander, shoal, and rapid.

My own cover-to-cover reading of *The Cantos* suggested, though, that there are aspects of the poem's design that can only come into view after extended reading. Moreover, I have found a thorough knowledge of *The Cantos* to be remarkably useful whenever writing or teaching about twentieth-century poetry and poetics. It has served me as a point of reference, a primer, a sine qua non, and a ne plus ultra. In fall 2007, I decided, as an experiment, to teach a graduate seminar in which we read the entire work.

What follows is a retrospective metacognitive reflection, an after-the-fact personal narrative intended to help myself and other educators "learn about and improve" pedagogical practices by "turning experience into knowledge about teaching" that can then be transferred to other occasions and situations (McAlpine and Weston 364). I have ordered my reflections based on Nancy Joseph's observation that "metacognition includes planning, analyzing resources, being open to feedback, and assessing the effectiveness of one's actions" (111). While the immediate goal is to advance conversations about the teaching of *The Cantos*, the hope is also to contribute to a relatively new, preliminary discussion, the theorization of "how graduate students are (or should be) taught" (Khost et al. 20).[2]

Planning

After I committed to teach a graduate seminar on *The Cantos*, I drew up a list of learning outcomes. I resolved that, by quarter's end, the students—masters-level and doctoral students from the departments of English and comparative literature—would

> gain a sense of *The Cantos*' overall design, recurrent motifs and themes, and changes in style and subject as Pound released new sections over the decades;
>
> demonstrate a mastery of Pound's rhetoric and compositional strategies through close readings of individual passages;

articulate what *modernism* meant to Pound as he wrote *The Cantos* and explain whether that definition is portable to other contexts;

develop a critique of *The Cantos*, that is, a dynamic appreciation of the historical, political, economic, and literary preconditions that enable and shape its composition, including European anti-Semitism, the social credit movement, and Italian Fascism;

synthesize what they have learned by writing a paper on a topic of their choice that requires research into primary and secondary sources.

Finally, although it did not exactly constitute a learning outcome, I was also conscious of needing to provide opportunities to discuss the affective experience of reading *The Cantos*. Students would likely resent Pound's elitism, obscurity, crankiness, and fascist hero-worship. The syllabus would have to publicize the kind of material that we would be reading, and prospective students had to hear that the occasional impulse to chuck *The Cantos* into a fire pit was not only healthy but in fact something they should take seriously and analyze whenever it struck.

Having established goals, I had to figure out how we might get there. There were two immediate obstacles. First, my home institution follows the quarter system. Fall, winter, and spring quarter each last roughly twelve weeks. These students would have to read the Mount Everest of modernist long poems and write a polished paper in three months or less. How could it all be crammed in? The second obstacle was my lack of prior comparable instructional opportunities. I had primarily taught Pound at the undergraduate level, where I had generally limited myself to cantos 1, 2, and 4. Could I scale up from, or take away any hints from, that relatively dissimilar mise-en-scène?

I reviewed the ways cantos 1, 2, and 4 had served as a means of introducing novice readers of poetry to the epic. Canto 1, for example, encourages a teacher to talk about Homer's *Odyssey* and the Western epic tradition and to cover techniques such as beginning *in media res*, in the middle of things, and concepts such as *nekyia*, the summoning of the spirits of the dead to learn hidden knowledge. On display too is Pound's peculiar insistence on the nitty-gritty details of textual transmission—for example the fact that he interrupts his narrative to inform readers that he has been freely translating Andreas Divus's Latin translation of the *Odyssey*. And there is no need to coax students to think about gender politics. The speaker's rejection of mothers (the ghost of Anticlea) and his embrace of Aphrodite, the eternal feminine in her guise of lover and seducer, are fundamental to the canto's plotline—and they establish a pattern for how women will be treated throughout the remainder of the long poem.

Canto 2 allows an instructor to redirect attention to poetic form, that is, to explain techniques such as parataxis (the serial accumulation of materials) and subject rhyme (the juxtaposition of two or more persons, places, or things that Pound perceives as sharing essential attributes). Canto 4 then introduces *The*

Cantos in its sublime and visionary mode: "The silver mirrors catch the bright stones and flare, / Dawn, to our waking, drifts in the green cool light; / Dew-haze blurs, in the grass, pale ankles moving" (*Cantos* 13). They also take in its Ovidian moral that an encounter with the divine is violently transformative, even deadly, as in the case of the hunter Actaeon, who glimpses the goddess Artemis bathing and in punishment is turned into a deer and torn apart by his hounds: "The dogs leap on Actaeon /. . . / Spotted stag of the wood" (14). Finally, overture-like, canto 4 announces the poem's geographical sprawl, presenting vignettes set in classical Greece, Confucian China, troubadour-era Provence, and Renaissance Italy. In theory, after reading cantos 1, 2, and 4, undergraduates are sufficiently keyed in to Pound's characteristic themes and formal devices to continue exploring *The Cantos* on their own.

Could this pedagogical strategy—letting *The Cantos*, as it unfolds, teach students how to read it—be adapted for a graduate course? My syllabus started slowly, assigning no more than five cantos per class. The number of pages per day thereafter increased, on the assumption that the students would gradually grow more familiar with *The Cantos*' style and substance. Once we reached *The Pisan Cantos*, though, the syllabus again slowed the pace. From there onward, the number and frequency of textual borrowings greatly escalate, and correspondingly greater time and effort are required to comprehend the poetry's progress. The syllabus also tried to respect the divisions between the poem's constituent sections. Here is the day-by-day breakdown of twice-weekly meetings over ten weeks:

Summon the Dead	Canto 1
Overtures	Cantos 2–7
The Malatesta Cantos	Cantos 8–11
A Dirty Joke, Confucius, Hell, and Venice	Cantos 12–17
The Italian Renaissance and Russian Revolution	Cantos 18–30
From Jefferson to Mussolini	Cantos 31–41
"Not by Usura"	Cantos 42–51
The China Cantos	Cantos 52–61
The Adams Cantos	Cantos 62–71
Pisan Cantos 1	Cantos 72–77
Pisan Cantos 2	Cantos 78–80
Pisan Cantos 3	Cantos 81–84
Rock-Drill 1	Cantos 85–89
Rock-Drill 2	Cantos 90–95
Thrones 1	Cantos 96–98
Thrones 2	Cantos 99–103
Thrones 3	Cantos 104–09
Drafts and Fragments 1	Cantos 110–15
Drafts and Fragments 2	Cantos 116 etc.

I planned to facilitate discussion during the first two weeks so I could illustrate ways of charting, explaining, and close-reading individual cantos and runs of cantos. Thereafter, I hoped to limit myself to providing clarification, supplemental information, and direction toward available resources, as well as, occasionally, a *mise au point*, an overview, from my perspective, of what students had been saying during discussion and how a given conversation connected to earlier ones and to larger course themes. One or two students per class meeting would take the lead. I invited them to bring in handouts, audiovisuals, or secondary materials that might help them summarize the day's readings and indicate directions for classroom inquiry.

Analyzing Resources

Like other high modernist texts—T. S. Eliot's *The Waste Land*, James Joyce's *Ulysses*, Marcel Proust's *Remembrance of Things Past*—*The Cantos* has long attracted exegesis. It is possible to publish monographs on isolated sections of the epic, such as Dan Ten Eyck's *Ezra Pound's Adams Cantos*, as well as studies that illuminate only one aspect of the long poem, such as Alec Marsh's *John Kasper and Ezra Pound*. In recent years too digital humanities initiatives such as the Modernist Journals Project have made many once-scarce primary texts readily available. How does one make effective use of these specialized resources in a course that focuses on having students experience, for the first time, a profound work of literature in all its aesthetic complexity? Nietzsche warns in *On the Use and Abuse of History for Life* that too much commentary robs a text of the vitality that makes it worthwhile in the first place (19–20). Could this course provide an enabling sufficiency, while avoiding a disempowering superfluity, of supporting information?

I thought back over the history of *Cantos* criticism. Although Pound's first cantos began appearing in *Poetry* in 1917, serious academic criticism on the poem did not gain momentum until after the 1948 Bollingen Prize. In the 1950s and 1960s scholars such as Walter Baumann, Guy Davenport, Clark Emery, Eva Hesse, and Hugh Kenner were responsible for invaluable pioneering work, tracing recurrent themes and images in Pound's work in progress and exploring its developing artistry and accumulating allusions. The first reference work—John Hamilton Edwards and William W. Vasse's *Annotated Index to the* Cantos *of Ezra Pound*—appeared in 1957; then, in 1964, the publication of cantos 1–109 brought together for the first time all the separately published installments of the epic. In 1970, after *Drafts and Fragments* was added to produce a near-final version of the long poem, would-be analysts had access both to a convenient, complete primary text and to a sufficiently large body of secondary criticism to orient their reading. In 1971 Kenner's *The Pound Era* rewrote the story of literary modernism with *The Cantos* as its implied culmination, and Carroll F. Terrell began the work of institutionalizing Pound studies by founding the National

Poetry Foundation at the University of Maine, Orono. A year later, Terrell launched the journal *Paideuma* to give old-guard and aspirant Poundians a venue in which to share ideas and build community.

In 1975, at a conference in Orono, scholars decided the time had come, not simply to update the *Annotated Index*, but to replace it with a work that, canto by canto, provides a bibliography of Pound's sources and of existing commentaries and then annotates the poem on a near-line-by-line basis. After prodigious work by Terrell and others, *A Companion to the* Cantos *of Ezra Pound* appeared in 1980. The preface explains that the *Companion*'s primary purpose is pedagogical:

> In the end, whether Pound will be assigned a place in the hierarchy as a major poet will depend on a fuller if not final critical evaluation of *The Cantos*. Before that can be accomplished the text must be made more broadly accessible. . . . [T]he text of *The Cantos* must be made more easily comprehensible to a sizable audience of students and professors as well as critics. Although some progress has been made, it becomes clearer, as time goes on, that the problems are not so much in the abstruse levels of thinking as in the extraordinary and wide-ranging fields of reference. The 'luminous details' or 'gists and piths' or 'ideas in action' which Pound gives us in his epic are drawn from sources quite outside the humanist tradition in which literary scholars have been trained; hence the need for *A Companion to the Cantos*. (ix)

Terrell also presents *A Companion* as no more than a temporary stop along the way to producing the "definitive variorum edition of *The Cantos*" (x). A generation later, though, no such edition exists. One could say that the first, heroic phase of textual criticism on *The Cantos* came to a close with the *Companion*. While its annotations are neither complete nor unfailingly accurate, and its citations are outmoded, it has never been updated or superseded. Projects such as Sieburth's *Pisan Cantos* represent important advances, but since 1980 large-scale editorial endeavors have tended to concentrate not on *The Cantos* but on other aspects of the Pound canon, for example assembling the eleven volumes of *Ezra Pound's Poetry and Prose: Contributions to Periodicals* (1991).

After reviewing the history of criticism on *The Cantos*, I decided that *A Companion* represents an ideal classroom resource, comprehensive yet venerable enough to generate skepticism about its authority. Moreover, every true Poundian owns a copy. Reading *The Cantos* with the *Companion* would provide students with the same foundation of knowledge shared by a generation of experts, which should in turn make it possible for them to follow more recent, more highly specialized scholarship.

Openness to Feedback

For the *Cantos* seminar I offered, we did end-of-the-quarter numerical and written evaluations, which in aggregate were strong—students were grateful for this chance to immerse themselves in a canonical modernist text—but any recommendations for improvement present in those evaluations came too late to help reshape the course while it was still in process. Thankfully, some of my students displayed independent initiative. About a month in, a group of female students met with me to express concerns about the classroom climate. They felt that a gendered dynamic had emerged that left them feeling uneasy, even silenced. I too had sensed something was off, but I was unsure precisely what. On a near-daily basis we had been analyzing passages from *The Cantos* in which misogyny, homophobia, and racism come to the fore, sometimes as thematic content and at other times as assumptions that inform the poem's rhetoric. In class students clearly felt able to talk about gender and other politically charged topics. Even so, I had noticed that several women who had avidly participated at the start of the quarter had begun disengaging.

These students did not fault exclusionary behavior or constraints on discussion topics or admissible interpretive approaches. Rather, they blamed *The Cantos* themselves, more specifically, the poem's rigid morality. Pound may include a bewildering variety of people and events, but he does not exhibit a nuanced sense of good and evil. Instead, in Manichaean fashion, he pits "the muddled forces of greed and materialism" "against those of natural process, intellectual clarity, and spiritual light," and characterizes this struggle as eternal and omnipresent, treating "everything occurring in time and space" as "interchangeable, recurrent, and best seen in its relationship to the same essential truth that governs both the seen and unseen worlds," the imperative to understand and venerate "universal beauty" (Kibler 26–27). As *The Cantos* insist over and over, the pursuit of truth and beauty can be difficult, can even fail spectacularly, but Pound never wobbles in his faith in the value of that pursuit.

How did the poem's moralizing produce a troublesome gender dynamic? Given our limited amount of face-to-face time—four hours a week—we had to move through individual cantos and passages at a fast clip. Initially, the text's cornucopia of dates, names, and quotations was a serious impediment. We appeared unable to cover more than a handful of lines in a discussion without also feeling that we were perhaps missing important information or claims. As the weeks went on, however, and as students became familiar with Pound's obsessions, it became increasingly easy to make snap judgments about particular instances in the text so that we could move quickly on. Daoists again? Bad. Andrew Jackson? Good. We ceased to allow time for ambiguity, hesitancy, or open-ended possibility.[3] While I had planned to allow the poem itself to instruct us how best to read it, I did not foresee this particular outcome. It had taken charge of how we, as a group, behaved.

In response, I tried to unsettle what had become rote patterns of analysis and debate. I brought in excerpts from poems such as Susan Howe's *Articulation of Sound Forms in Time* and Nathaniel Mackey's "Song of the Andoumboulou: 1–7" that, while they borrow certain Poundian compositional techniques such as paratactic juxtaposition, offer more progressive political viewpoints and, instead of prescribing a unified moral message, disport in indeterminacy. At this point, however, since we had already spent weeks reading nothing but Pound, these few excerpts registered as belated add-ons and ended up occluding rather than advancing the primary course goal, to reach the end of *The Cantos*.

I also brought up the fact that many of us, in an effort to speed up the reading process, had acquiesced to Pound's *mansplaining*, his talking at extraordinary length about every subject under the sun, from Homer to the Cold War, with total confidence in his rectitude and accuracy. I encouraged resistance to Pound's *directio voluntatis*, the direction of his will. While it is crucial to know that moneychangers are exemplars of evil in *The Cantos*, one should not fall into the trap of reducing each canto to a gallery of rogues and angels. I supplied Jackson Mac Low's and John Cage's writings-through of *The Cantos*—poems that rearrange words and phrases extracted from Pound's epic by chance and algorithmic procedures—as texts that highlight not *The Cantos*' moralizing but its multilingualism and its helter-skelter mix of Englishes from working-class to aristocratic Oxbridge, from Old English to newspaper-speak. The students liked the idea of reading against the grain, or reading entirely otherwise than for "content" as conventionally defined; but again, this intervention came too late in the quarter to reinflect our discussions to any appreciable degree.

If I taught this course once more, I would rethink the assignment structure. What if students, early in the quarter, engaged in their own writings-through of *The Cantos*? They might take more fully on board the fact that the poem could always be otherwise, that there are other ways to discover a work besides letting the work itself set the agenda. What if there were a short essay that required comparison of Pound's and Mackey's treatments of the city Wagadu in canto 74 and "Song of the Andoumboulou 5"? Students would see how readily Pound's particulars can be reimagined. In short, why fetishize one seminar work product, the proto-article, when a more diverse set of assignments might improve both classroom climate and student learning?

Effectiveness

One way to measure a seminar's effectiveness is to assess whether and to what extent its learning goals were met and to ask whether they should be modified or omitted in the future.

Gain a sense of The Cantos' *overall formal design.* Yes, students gained facility with comparing the different sections of *The Cantos*, and by quarter's end they could speak with confidence about how the "Dante plot" of hell-purgatory-heaven continues to inform the poem's unfolding up until its fragmentary conclusion.

Demonstrate a mastery of Pound's rhetoric and compositional strategies. Reading *The Cantos* "day after day" enabled the students to "naturalize" themselves in its "imagination," to echo Wallace Stevens (50). They learned how to follow Pound's quicksilver leaps, how to appreciate his movement between levels of diction and discourse, between prose and poetry, between invective and encomium.

Articulate what modernism means to Pound. We were unable to take what we had learned about *The Cantos* and use it as the basis for arguments about periodization and literary style. The poem, we discovered, resists generalization: it was written across too many decades, responds to too much socioeconomic history, and incorporates too much cultural history. The failure of this learning outcome may, in fact, be pedagogically significant. How does a critic respond when a paradigmatic work of high modernism proves impossible to fit neatly into scholarly debates about literary modernism?

Develop a critique of The Cantos. The seminar helped students appreciate the difference between "gotcha" criticism and critique. In prior courses, they had often been rewarded for their ability to reveal that a writer or text operates according to an underlying or covert ideological agenda. *The Cantos*, however, arrives in one's hands already, even proverbially, indicted and convicted of misogyny, racism, and so forth. By quarter's end, students had become aware that critique is not synonymous with calling somebody out. One elucidates how and why a text takes the form it does and how that text functions, produces meaning, and solicits uptake.

Synthesize what they have learned by writing a seminar paper. If I taught this class again, I would drop the seminar paper as a final assignment. The reading material was too difficult and covered at too fast a pace to give students sufficient time and critical distance to formulate and carry out a research project culminating in a long-form essay. Much more useful would be a series of assignments—such as annotation exercises, *Notes and Queries*-style elucidations of allusions, conference-style oral presentations, and faux book prospectuses—that could potentially serve as scaffolding for future seminar papers or dissertation chapters.

Reading *The Cantos* in tandem with *A Companion to the* Cantos *of Ezra Pound* can be the basis for a successful graduate seminar, when measured by the conventional standards applied to graduate-level instruction. That is, such a class can provide "content coverage" for "future professionals in training" (Khost et al. 19). One student in my class, for example, went on to write a dissertation chapter about *Drafts and Fragments*, which, retooled as a stand-alone article, appeared in a peer-reviewed journal in 2016.

A course that covers *The Cantos* in a quarter, however, puts a strain on that traditional model because merely reading the primary text requires an unusual amount of time, discipline, focus, and emotional labor. There will always be exceptional students who through nothing but "repeated exposure and osmosis" are able to master difficult texts and write model seminar papers (Micciche and Carr 484). To make such a class valuable for a larger circle of students, an instructor must think carefully about what assignments will lead to desired learning outcomes. A teacher will fail most students if the plan is simply to "let them read *The Cantos*, talk about it, and then write a research paper."

If I taught another seminar on *The Cantos*, I would adopt several of the recommendations that Peter H. Khost, Debra Rudder Lohe, and Chuck Sweetman have proposed: include short writing assignments that variously increase "intimacy" with a literary work; introduce periodic "strategic pauses" to allow for collective reflection on and possible readjustment of the seminar's progress and underlying design (so as to help avoid traps such as the tilt toward a masculinist discussion climate); and articulate "more explicit goals for specific seminar meetings" so that students can better perceive the reasons why one might undertake a sequential, "completist" reading of *The Cantos* in the first place (24–25). I would reimagine the course, too, as bringing students to the point of pursuing many possible next steps. Some might later draw on *The Cantos* in dissertation chapters and articles, certainly, but all would have practiced skills transferable to other professional settings. As E. Shelley Reid has said, one should not let ossified expectations about graduate-level pedagogy foreclose opportunities for "discovery" (199). *The Cantos* can launch myriad new journeys.

NOTES

I would like to thank my colleague Anis Bawarshi for his help in writing this essay.

[1] Some professors have, however, persevered. Gelpi recalls seminars at Harvard and at Stanford during the late 1960s and 1970s in which he assigned the complete *Cantos*. (Two of his students, Michael Palmer and Robert Grenier, later became founding members of the language school of poetry movement, and a third, Nathaniel Mackey, is one of the most honored living American poets, a winner of the National Book Award and the Bollingen Prize.) Another Poundian, Guy Davenport, told me about comparably ambitious *Cantos*-based classes at the University of Kentucky.

[2] See Micciche and Carr for a history of efforts to think through alternatives to the default mode of humanities graduate instruction in the United States, which for more than a century has consisted of "reading closely, critically, and voluminously" followed by a "final project" that requires students to engage in a mode of writing that they are expected to master through "repeated exposure" in an "osmosis-like process" (481–85).

[3] I am not claiming that ambiguity, hesitancy, and an embrace of open-ended possibility are somehow essentially or universally characteristic of women. These female students affectively rebelled against what they perceived as a masculinist discursive situation, and their gendered resistance took the form of a positive valorization of these characteristics. Under other circumstances and at different points in time, ambiguity and open-endedness can, of course, be mobilized in support of patriarchal authority.

Using Electronic Resources and Information Technologies to Teach Pound's *Guide to Kulchur* and Canto 45

Anderson D. Araujo

A little over a century ago, Ezra Pound wrote in "I Gather the Limbs of Osiris" that a life worth living is "made up in great part of things indefinite, impalpable" (33). It is not too much to say that he would have embraced the World Wide Web, that most impalpable, indefinite, and ever so inescapable of mediums. For the Web too, like the arts Pound had in mind, gives us access to the "indefinite poems" suggested by a painting and the "gallery of paintings" encoded in a line of verse. Perhaps even more evocative is his definition of the poetic image as "a radiant node or cluster," a pre-echo of the "radiant textuality" Jerome McGann locates in digital media. And what is the Web if not a hypervortex, to extend Pound's famous vorticist concept, "from which, and through which, and into which, ideas are constantly rushing" (*Gaudier-Brzeska* 92)? In keeping with this, hypermedia archives offer a stunning range of primary and ancillary materials to the enterprising teacher of Pound's work. We must proceed with caution, however, as we navigate an ever-increasing and often critically anarchic learning cyberspace. The findings of large-scale surveys in the past decade moreover indicate that the radical changes in learning and teaching expected from the widespread adoption of information and communication technologies in post-secondary education have not materialized. Rather, old and new technologies have formed a kind of "synergetic relationship" (Kirkup and Kirkwood 193). Hyper- and social media platforms and digital tools, including *Artstor*, *YouTube*, *Twitter*, *Facebook*, *Prezi*, *WordPress*, *The Rossetti Archive*, wikis, podcasts, and course blogs thus still tend to supplement, rather than supplant, analog tools and classroom-specific activities, such as close-reading exercises, group work, collaborative annotation, live peer review, on-site library instruction, class discussion, and even the traditional lecture-seminar model. This digital-to-analog ratio will likely alter dramatically in the future. In employing online resources in the smart classroom we must be mindful, to play on Pound's point at the outset, of the indefinite contingencies of live learning environments and communities. With these caveats in mind, I have experimented with multifaceted strategies aimed at optimizing the ways students interface with information technologies and hypermedia systems in critical and comparative approaches to Pound's poetry and prose.

I have found it especially worthwhile to enlist as a teaching reference Pound's last lengthy prose venture, *Guide to Kulchur*. The book constitutes his most methodical and condensed summary of the same 2,500-year history of "ideas going into action" that we find in *The Cantos*. Hence, *Guide* is an ideal companion to

Pound's epic poem (*Guide* 44). More broadly, this primer can altogether enhance the study of Pound's poetry and poetics. Written in 1937, it brings together, in its fifty-eight loosely arranged sections, the entire range of Pound's ideas and definitions of *kulchur*, his irreverent, disruptive alternative and challenge to mainstream culture. Pound argues that culture is an expressed consequence of, and reflects, the economic conditions under which it was produced, most especially the presence or absence of usury. Canto 45, his most trenchant indictment of usury, aptly illustrates the advantages of engaging *Guide* as a complement to *The Cantos*. It is not surprising that the urgent concerns of canto 45 were uppermost in Pound's mind as he wrote *Guide*—the poem appeared in the collection *The Fifth Decad of the Cantos (XLII–LI)* published by Faber and Faber in the late spring of 1937, just as Pound had completed the typescript of his prose opus.

Guide's polyphonic interplay makes up Pound's "new synthesis," but it also betrays a nagging structural anxiety with which students can easily identify as they themselves synthesize newly acquired knowledge and competencies to find their own critical voices (*Guide* 95). It is in this sense that *Guide*, more so than any other of Pound's prose works, structurally anticipates the Web's parataxis (Handa 45–46). The book comprises "a heteroclite set of impressions" (*Guide* 208). There is method nonetheless in Pound's stereoscopic tour de force. He wants us to join him in "mousing around for a significance in the chaos" (8). The unwitting pun could hardly be more fitting for our digital culture. In "mousing" around the unruly domains of cyberspace to enhance the teaching of Pound, we would do well to remember that new technologies not only shape but also condition the ways in which hypermedia-savvy students typically engage with his often cryptic and always allusive writings. The rhizomatic reach of Pound's work as a whole lends itself exceptionally well to a growing hypertextual ecology.

As suggested by its title, *Guide* is—in terms of content, intent, and tone—didactic and pedagogical. Here too, as he does in *The Cantos*, Pound presents "luminous" details paratactically (*Guide* 317). Electronic media arguably utilize Web links in ways similar to the epiphanies, the bursts of insight, Pound and other modernists believed could be ignited in their readers' minds. The rise of MOOCs, *iTunes U*, and other free online educational platforms has broadened the scope of learning far beyond the underprivileged "young men" for whom Pound wrote the book (6). Harnessing a range of hypermedia, technology-infused pedagogical strategies—such as Tom Creed's McLuhanite ur-manifesto for cyberspace lauding the advantages of the smart classroom over traditional methods because it is "*asynchronous* (time-independent) and *asyntopic* (place independent)"—can facilitate students' engagement with Pound's (and other modernists') difficult, referential, paratactic, and polyvocal rhetoric and content (7). Yet at the same time I interrogate such approaches. The smart classroom makes it possible for students to experiment with finding online sources independently, but specific resources and tools, listed below, are also prescribed:

Selected Literary and Multimedia Resources	
Academy of American Poets	poets.org/poetsorg/poet/ezra-pound
Artstor	artstor.org
The Cantos Project	thecantosproject.ed.ac.uk
"Ezra Pound" (*PennSound*)	writing.upenn.edu/pennsound/x/Pound.php
Literature Online	literature.proquest.com
Modern American Poetry	modernamericanpoetry.org
Modernism Lab	modernism.research.yale.edu
Modernist Journals Project	modjourn.org
Perseus Digital Library	perseus.tufts.edu
Rossetti Archive	rossettiarchive.org
"Vorticism" (*Tate*)	tate.org.uk/art/art-terms/v/vorticism

Selected Learning Management Systems and Presentation Software	
Blackboard	blackboard.com
Canvas	canvaslms.com
Discourse	discourse.org
Moodle	moodle.org
phpBB	phpbb.com
Prezi	prezi.com
ProBoards	proboards.com
WordPress	wordpress.com

The Web site *Modernist Journals Project* (*MJP*) recognizes the inherently collaborative nature of these hyperarchives. Its section on teaching defines the *MJP* itself as a "hybrid," offering a journal archive as well as a "new instructional wiki, where users can help us build up the teaching site by posting ideas and tools themselves" ("New Teaching"). The emerging Pound wiki on the *MJP* already contains a few of his critical writings, reviews, and essays ("Ezra Pound Teaching and Research"). I shall begin exploring the pedagogical potential of these and other electronic resources in the smart classroom by relating my recent experiments with teaching canto 45 alongside *Guide*.

Canto 45, the usura canto, defies facile interpretations. For a start, *usury* itself is a mystifying term. Pound thought as much, since he felt the need to define it at the close of the canto. The gloss hardly helps much, however: "A charge for the use of purchasing power, levied without regard to production; often without regard to the possibilities of production" (*Cantos* 230). At the end of a first reading of the canto in class, usury is likely to remain for students as alien a concept as the esoteric fragments scattered across the poem. Stranger still it is to listen for the first time to Pound's incantatory live reading of the canto. *PennSound* features the audio recording Pound made at Harvard in the spring of 1939 ("Harvard"). When consulted for this essay, quite a few students in an upper-level undergraduate course I taught on modernist poetics remarked that hearing Pound's quavering, burred singsong was like listening to a priest or prophet in the throes of a mystic revelation. Others found it difficult to get past his eccentric style of declamation. Others still found it mesmerizing, if unnerving. The thudding beat of a drum with which the poet marks his tirade against usury toward the end of the canto casts a rueful mood over the performance (cf. Moody, *The Epic Years* 304). The audio file thus opened up at a stroke an extra-textual dimension to our consideration of the poem. Crucially, too, it took students to the roots of poetry as an oral tradition. Other *PennSound* audio files allowed students to hear Pound's pronunciation of Chinese ideograms and the transliterated sounds of the Greek in *The Cantos*; H.D.'s carefully constructed cadences in her 1955 reading from *Helen in Egypt*; William Carlos Williams's mid-Atlantic staccato in a 1942 reading of "Classic Scene"; and W. B. Yeats's entrancing recitation of "The Lake Isle of Innisfree" in 1937. Unfettered virtual access to such previously restricted or inaccessible resources offers enormous learning and research potential, both in and outside of the classroom.

Along these lines, my first reference to *Guide* in the course had little to do with canto 45 itself. Rather, I singled out a passage in a chapter largely devoted to classical music and opera. Pound laments the struggle "to raise an audience to listen to the singing of better poetry" (155). His fusion of singing and poetry led to a self-reflexive moment for students still processing his bravura act in the recording of canto 45. Suddenly, we were no longer simply amusing ourselves with sound bites of arcane Poundiana. We had become a community, an audience—from the classical Latin *audentia*, "act of listening," "body of listeners"—immersed in a performance, "performance" likewise in the now rare sense of a "ceremony, rite, or ritual" ("Audience").

In this spirit, I invoked another high priest of modernism, Yeats. Pound's stint as the elder poet's personal secretary at Stone Cottage in Sussex in three consecutive winters from 1913 to 1915 probably also led to his picking up Yeats's "parsonic elocution," as Richard Aldington describes it in "The British Academy," a piece that students and others can now read in digital facsimile (248). I also drew on Pound's interview with D. G. Bridson in 1961 to connect our shared experience of listening to Pound with the poet's own memory of reading for Yeats in the ancient Greek theater in Syracuse in southeastern Sicily in January 1925. At Yeats's insistence that he "recite something," Pound "found that the only thing one could do in the open like that—the only thing I remember that you could speak clear enough to get across was Sappho's poem *Poikilothron*," the "Hymn to Aphrodite" (qtd. in Bridson 165). Pound thus re-created an ancient rite—Sappho's hymn was embedded in cult and ritual and was most likely performed in her time in a religious festival honoring the goddess (Breitenberger 46). More importantly, for the purposes of our course, Pound recovered for Yeats, as Dolores O'Higgins asserts (apropos of Sappho), "an ancient lyric tradition which sees and describes itself as essentially performative, and communicated, if not created, with the voice" (71). For my students, Pound's own voice piping phantasmally from the classroom speakers might have seemed at first as remote as Sappho's world. Yet the aural immediacy of the recording proved vital in bringing blood to Pound's (and Yeats's) ghost. The class was now primed to turn to the text of what Alec Marsh has aptly called the "great *chant* against USURA" (*Money* 117; my emphasis).

Since nearly every historical and cultural reference or allusion in canto 45 is also present in *Guide*, time and again the book has proven instrumental as a prose crib to the poem. Following a hypertextual logic in our exploration of the poem, we also shuttled back and forth in the digital edition of *The Cantos* hosted on *Literature Online*. We began at the end of canto 45, unpacking both the meaning of *usura* and its antidote, "the Medici bank" (*Cantos* 230).[1] The allusion to the Banca Monte dei Paschi of Siena, Pound's archetype of a virtuous bank, led us to a key chapter in *Guide*, suitably titled "Canti." It is here that he famously spells out his great poetic experiment, *The Cantos*, as "the tale of the tribe" (194). It is also here that he praises the Monte's foundation of "the true bases of credit, to wit the abundance of nature and the responsibility of the whole people." Students found it striking that the beginning of canto 52 reiterates the clause almost verbatim: "And of the true base of credit, that is / the abundance of nature / with the whole folk behind it" (*Cantos* 257). The class was also fascinated by the fact that the Monte's revenue came directly from the grazing rights to the *paschi*, or pastures, near Siena, "and the profits derived from the natural increase of the sheep that reproduced there" (Marsh, *Money* 119; cf. Surette, *Pound in Purgatory* 223).

Teaching canto 45, which espouses Italian Renaissance painting and sacred architecture as its chief arts, with the aid of complementary images can uncover visual narratives otherwise occluded in the text. I would even go so far as to contend that the visual economy of the canto can only be made legible to most students by means of a semiotic intervention. Once again, selections from *Guide* brought the welter of cultural signifiers into sharp focus. "You have two millennia of history wherein we see usury opposed to the arts," Pound writes, "usury at the antipodes of melody, of melodic invention, of design" (282). Earlier, he connects the *motz el son*, "the union of word and music," of Provençal troubadours to the fine demarcations of nonusurious architecture (60). Crossing aesthetic boundaries, these intertexts shed light on the "painted paradise" and the *harpes et luz* ("harps and lutes") of canto 45. The Old French phrase is found in *Le Testament* (*The Testament*), the poem composed in 1461 by the French medieval poet François Villon, which we study using a PDF facsimile of a 1913 version, hosted on the Warburg Institute's server. "Paradis painet, où sont harpes et luz" speaks to the joy and faith the troubadour's mother finds in the paintings of paradise on the walls of her parish church (Villon 265). A live audio rendition of Pound's opera *Le Testament de Villon*, performed by the ASKO Ensemble and recorded at the Holland Festival in 1980, is available on *YouTube* ("Ezra Pound—*Le Testament*"). Playing even a brief sample of the recording will bring Pound's musical extravaganza alive to the class. I also linked the subtext of "painted paradise" to the two French cathedrals explicitly cited in this canto and in canto 51—St. Trophime in Arles and St. Hilaire in Poitiers—as well as the Italian church to which canto 45 only alludes—San Zeno Maggiore in Verona (*Cantos* 230, 250). The last church in particular stands as a bulwark against usury. Pound synecdochically calls up an entire tradition of nonpareil craftsmanship by singling out the pillar in canto 45's "church of cut stone signed: *Adamo me fecit*" ("Adam made me") (230). I set up a brief virtual tour of all three churches using images available from *Artstor*. The photographs set in motion a vigorous debate on the contrast between the emblematic permanence Pound fetishizes in these medieval and early modern cathedrals and the mass production industry that made possible the cast iron and steel architecture of the nineteenth century, the "age of usury," as he labels it in *Guide* (26).

Formative assessments can also be quite productive in fostering meaningful and active student engagement with overdetermined concepts in Pound's poetry and prose, usury being no exception. With Pound's sweeping dismissal of the "age of usury" as a focal point, I assigned small groups of students to produce short speculative paragraphs on usury as a driving force in Victorian society. Students searched through the sixty instances of "usur-" (i.e., *usury*, *usura*, *usurer*, etc.) in the digital facsimile of *Guide*, freely available on the nonprofit digital library *Internet Archive* (archive.org/details/in.ernet.dli.2015.148695/page/n6/mode/2up), to locate Pound's range of perspectives on this "power of hell" (*Guide* 156). A lively class discussion ensued whereby students pondered each group's interpretation of Poundian usury, some linking it with the rise of laissez-faire capitalism, others connecting it with British imperialism and mercantilism. In another version of this activity (best suited for smaller classes), I ask that each group write a cogent synopsis of its findings on a laptop or tablet and e-mail it to me during the class. I then project each contribution on an overhead screen and critically revise it in consultation with the students. This feedback-intensive tactic considerably heightens overall participation and allows for deeper interconnections to emerge in the study of Pound's oeuvre. It also promotes an interdisciplinary heuristic, as students bring history, politics, economics, and aesthetics to bear on prosody.

Supporting the pedagogy I have outlined is recent evidence-based research on Assessment for Learning in higher education. As Kay Sambell and colleagues have uncovered, "peer feedback may be deemed more potent, because the recipient of the feedback believes it is coming from someone who is more authentically in touch with the subject from the point of view of a student" (89). In turn, purposefully moderated class discussions avoid the pitfalls Margaret Price and colleagues identify in "written feedback without dialogue," a frequent source of "frustration and disengagement" for students (284). To preserve otherwise ephemeral group activities and allow off-campus access, I post on *Canvas* all materials digitally created and edited in class.

I have learned to avoid the easy assumption that students will take to any digital platform. After spending much time setting up a *Facebook* account created exclusively for my undergraduate and graduate courses on modernism, I observed that most students were balking at posting content on the discussion threads. Even after I assured my classes that these were closed, invitation-only groups set up solely for each course, students expressed privacy concerns and aversion to being bombarded with ads, among other reasons for being wary of *Facebook*. They were right, of course. When a student alluded to the scandal surrounding a massive, weeklong "emotional contagion" experiment conducted on *Facebook*, unbeknownst to users (Kramer et al. 87–89), I decided to close the account. The subsequent exposé of a political data firm that harvested private information from more than fifty million *Facebook* profiles further dissuaded me from in-class use of this social networking Web site (Granville 2018). As Reynol Junco and colleagues have discovered, classroom time spent using *Facebook* also relates negatively to student engagement (275). The same study did find improvement in both student engagement and academic achievement when teachers integrate *Twitter* in the classroom (278). Even so, most of the students I consulted about this prospect said they would still prefer the comparatively clunky yet more secure and localized university-sponsored learning software. The lesson is obvious, but often only in hindsight: in experimenting with digital tools we must be mindful first and foremost of our students as end users. Far less peer-interactive than social media, digital archives can make less daunting the labyrinthine depths students must plumb to begin to grasp Pound's encyclopedic concerns. A case in point is usury, the inescapable bête noire of canto 45.

Illustrating the flourishing of the arts in an era not yet ravaged by usury are the several frescoes, paintings, artists, and architects cited or hinted at in canto 45 and fleshed out in *Guide*. Pound's charge that "with usura / seeth no man Gonzaga his heirs and his concubines" tends to ring hollow for most students, at least until it sinks in that "seeth" nods to the visual arts (*Cantos* 229). Without actually seeing at least one of the artworks named or suggested in the poem, however, readers will find it difficult to fathom the aesthetic and civilizational magnitude they convey for Pound. The litany of usura's negations of beauty masks the canto's praise of Andrea Mantegna, the virtuoso painter of the exquisite portraits of his patron, Francesco Gonzaga, the Marquess of Mantua from 1484 to 1519, and his family. Pound once again compels us to read between the lines: Mantegna is the real star here, not the Gonzagas. The hypertextual epiphanies that come from viewing Mantegna's frescoes in Gonzaga's Palazzo Ducale typify Pound's ideogrammic method, which he sums up memorably in *Guide* as "presenting one facet and then another until at some point one gets off the dead and desensitized surface of the reader's mind, onto a part that will register" (*Guide* 51). Images of Mantegna's frescoes are powerful registers for students of the nonusurious permanence of great art, perhaps all the more so because, unlike paintings hanging on a wall, the frescoes always stay put. The "fact of their force remains," Pound reminds us (94). An even more poignant token of permanence is Dante's mausoleum, designed by the architect-sculptor Pietro Lombardo for the Basilica of San Francesco in Ravenna. Lombardo too, canto 45 tells us, "came not by usura" (*Cantos* 229).

Guide is especially useful in illuminating "Pier della Francesca" and "Zuan Bellin'," canto 45's slangy monikers for Piero della Francesca and Giovanni Bellini (*Cantos* 230). These painters are among the chief avatars of *kulchur* and high civilization eulogized in the preface. They are but two in a constellation of artists and intellectuals that Sigismondo Malatesta, the Italian Renaissance condottiere, sponsored in Rimini. *Guide* can open a window through which students may peer into the nonusurious splendor of the Malatesta epoch, a window that canto 45 merely points at. Pound's associative indexing in *The Cantos* makes the visual immediacy of digital archives particularly instructive in the classroom.

Canto 45's "Ambrogio Praedis," the Milanese painter and book illuminator Giovanni Ambrogio de Predis, can also spark connective insights when twinned with *Guide*. Pound claims to "have a certain real knowledge which wd. enable me to tell a Goya from a Velasquez, a Velasquez from an Ambrogio Praedis, a Praedis from an Ingres or a Moreau" (*Guide* 28). One need not get sidetracked in covering all the painters listed here to hazard what kind of epistemology Pound might have in mind. Still, it may be worthwhile to project Predis's portrait of, say, Bianca Maria Sforza side by side with Velázquez's portrait of the Infanta Maria Teresa. Students have often remarked on the more "austere" style of Predis in contrast to the more "exuberant" technique of Velázquez. It is in steering discussion back to usury, however, that the engine behind Pound's "real knowledge" springs into view. He wagers that "finer and future critics of art will be able to tell from the quality of a painting the degree of tolerance or intolerance of usury extant in the age and milieu that produced it" (*Guide* 27). This is precisely the ethos of canto 45. The interweave of connections and "interrelations of causes" between canto 45 and *Guide*—from the secular portraiture of Hans Memling to the Eleusinian Mysteries—allows for technology-mediated moments of discovery that might otherwise be lost to the nonspecialist student (100).

The Eleusis coda to canto 45 signals the transhistorical span of pre-usurious epochs. Usury's profanation of Eleusis entails a moral and ethical perversion: "They have brought whores for Eleusis" (*Cantos* 230). The cryptic plural pronoun ("they") itself presents a source of much speculation for students. In *Guide*, Pound calls these shadowy figures "[f]ools" (145). Far from breaking with the canto's artcentric jeremiad against usury, Eleusis belongs to the same continuum. The mysteries were also intensely visual. Situated at the crossroads of a trade route linking Attica and the Peloponnese, Eleusis hosted secret rites to worship and honor Demeter, the Greek goddess of grain, and her daughter Korê ("maiden"), or Persephone, as told in the Homeric *Hymn to Demeter*. The two stages of initiation at Eleusis—*myêsis* and *epopteia*—entailed a progression for the initiant from being a *mystês* (one with closed eyes, closed mouth, or both) to becoming an *epoptês* (one who sees) (Foley 65–66, 79–80). Usury's debauchery (the "whores" of canto 45) perverts the path to vision. "[H]yper-usura," to borrow Pound's term, tantalizes the senses, but its pleasures are tawdry, its bounty illusory (*Guide* 136). "Corpses are set to banquet / at behest of usura," ends the canto grimly (*Cantos* 230). Like the gradual unveiling of the Eleusinian mysteries to the *epoptês*, an ekphrastic exploration of canto 45 can trigger profoundly epiphanic moments for the diligent student. As Demetres Tryphonopoulos suggests, the purpose of *The Cantos* is to bring about a "palingenesis" (or rebirth) "achieved through participation in the 'mystery' contained in the text" (*Celestial Tradition* 8). The multimedia and comparative approach that I have set forth simulates, as it were, a ritual of collective initiation into the poem's mythopoeic architecture, its *mysterium*.

I would argue moreover that in employing digital resources as heuristic tools to engage his poetry we respond directly to Pound's own frustration at the limits of knowledge. "I have howled in vain for odd bits of supplementary knowledge," he blurts out in exasperation (*Guide* 54). From the relative isolation of Rapallo, the town on the Ligurian coast of Italy where he wrote *Guide*, Pound felt keenly the need to extend the reach of his research and connect to a knowledge community. At the time, however, "no communication system worthy the name" (55) had yet come about. It is tempting to see the Web as just such a system, even if it can be just as irregular as the predigital networks Pound complained about in the 1930s. With laptops, tablets, and smartphones as ubiquitous on our campuses as spiral notebooks once were, students can enjoy access to extratextual material with a freedom Pound could hardly have dreamed of. This interactive learning is a far cry from the passive learning that a purely lecture-based style of teaching tends to produce (Cohen et al. 175). Duly utilized in the smart classroom, digital technologies can spark the "active discovery" Pound envisions in *Guide* (345).

Using *Guide* to teach Pound's poetry also entails teaching the book itself. My recently published *A Companion to Ezra Pound's* Guide to Kulchur may be a useful pedagogical tool, as it provides in-depth annotations mapped onto the widely available New Directions edition of Pound's text, allowing both books to be read side by side. While it might be unfeasible to cover all of *Guide* in one semester, it is possible to zoom in on chapters that telescope Pound's essential aesthetic principles, theories, and techniques. Accordingly, I assign chapters 6 ("Vortex") and 7 ("Great Bass: Part One") to one of my regular graduate courses, Imagism: Sculptural Poetics. The course is premised on Pound's idea that imagists wanted to create a style of poetry "as much like granite as it can be" ("How to Read" 12). I impress upon students that this entailed chiseling poetry down to its "hard light, clear edges," as Pound wrote to Amy Lowell in 1914 (*Selected Letters* 38). Imagist vers libre would be "austere, direct, free from emotional slither" ("How to Read" 12). To this end, imagism experimented with a mythopoeic aesthetic that incorporated into free verse the economy of Japanese haiku and the pathos of the Greek lyric while privileging "feelings of painting and sculpture" ("Marianne Moore" 424). The movement paved the way for a syncretic reinvention of avant-garde arts and culture. Read thus, *Guide* is a seamless fit: like Malatesta's Tempio, the book pulls off a "daring synthesis" (Pound, Review of *Stones of Rimini* 496).

Chapters 6 and 7 in themselves amount to just such a synthesis. Henri Gaudier-Brzeska's impressionistic historiography of sculpture in the sixth chapter is a verbatim reprint of the original publication in *Blast*, the literary magazine of vorticism. The essay is the last contribution in the first of only two issues and arguably constitutes the journal's core manifesto. "Vortex" embeds "Gaudier's real knowledge" (*Guide* 70). In turn, the sculptor's works reify the modernist vortex of "[w]ill and consciousness," subsuming cubist multiplicity and expressionist abstraction (68). It was Gaudier-Brzeska who carved in marble the famous *Hieratic Head of Ezra Pound*, a photograph of which can be shown to students on the Tate's Web site (Benington). Chapter 6 thus offers students a dazzling (if dizzying) entry into vorticism. Probing Pound's own vorticist manifesto in *Blast* can also be fruitful. It is here that Pound's cross-disciplinary projects intersect most forcefully—"All experience rushes into this vortex. All the energized past, all the past that is living and worthy to live" ("Vortex" 153).

Pound's "Vortex" in *Blast* suggests, as students are quick to point out, that imagism and vorticism have formed a continuum in his aesthetics. In the section titled "Ancestry," Pound defines an image as "that which presents an intellectual and emotional complex in an instant of time" (154). First published in 1913 in Harriet Monroe's *Poetry* magazine, which is now accessible in its entirety on the *MJP*, the maxim can be grafted interchangeably onto vorticism and imagism. This integrated approach to the two movements also informs my teaching of the eight poems Pound published in the second and final issue of *Blast*. In a similar vein, I approach his theory of the "Great Bass" in chapter 7 of *Guide* in class by cribbing his definition of music in *Antheil and the Treatise on Harmony* as "a composition of frequencies" (24). My in-class survey of chapters 6 and 7 also includes *YouTube* vignettes on the sculptors and sculptures and virtual tours of the cave paintings Gaudier-Brzeska mentions: Epstein, Brancusi, Archipenko, Dunikowski, Modigliani, Bernini's *Apollo and Daphne*, and the paleolithic paintings in the network of caves in the Dordogne region of southwestern France.

To keep students engaged with course material on and off campus, I organize a weekly discussion forum on *Canvas*. Alternative platforms include *Moodle*, *Proboards*, *WordPress*, *Discourse*, and *phpBB*, to name a few of the more intuitive open-source learning software brands. I assign topics that organically reflect the week's readings, live exercises, and the unforeseen directions opened up by classroom discussions. Once I post a topic online, each student composes a substantive paragraph directly concerning the subject matter. I also require that students post a cogent reply to at least one of their peers' posts. This dialogic activity ensures that even the less vocal students participate meaningfully.

However the opinions of my students diverge on how best to exploit technology to unravel the difficulties of Pound's poetry, no one contests that the Web is as promising as it is rife with perils. Hazards range from error-ridden electronic versions of poems to amateurish and plagiaristic interpretations. Also flagged is the common misperception that the mere decipherment of esoterica and myth (e.g., "triune azures" in "Blandula, Tenulla, Vagula" or Orcus in "Doria") automatically unlocks a poem's meaning (*Personae* 38, 64). A student recently cautioned in a discussion post that in mining "*Wikipedia* and *Google* without a proper knowledge and foundation" one will likely end up with unsound explanatory guesswork rooted in shoddy methodology. His responder echoed Pound's epistemic bellwether: "Knowledge is or may be necessary to understanding, but it weighs as nothing against understanding" (*Guide* 53). She put forth along the same lines that Googling Pound's opaque references without paying heed to their implications may create "a disconnect or dissonance of meaning." This disconnect, I suggested, is akin to gaining a profound understanding of Walt Whitman while studying Pound's "A Pact," but never realizing Whitman's function in the poem—or, for that matter, understanding why Pound dubs him a Romantic in *Guide* (181). Another student responder called upon the imagist writ "to compose in the sequence of the musical phrase" ("A Retrospect" 3). The injunction does not "nullify dissonance," he posited, "but rather makes sustaining dissonance a pleasant experience—a pleasant discomfort, something like Keats's 'negative capability,' a capacity for 'being in uncertainties, Mysteries, doubts, without any irritable reaching after fact and reason.'" His astute comment intersects Pound's seminal statement on the primacy of "things indefinite, impalpable," with which I began this essay. Digital technologies present us with precisely such an indefinite spectrum of possibilities. As I hope these snapshots into my pedagogical praxis show, electronic resources can be immensely productive in empowering students to engage synergistically with Pound's poetry and prose. The challenge, now and even more so in the years ahead, is to provide "a few tools for dealing with the heteroclite mass of undigested information" across cyberspace and hypertext environments (*Guide* 23).

NOTE

[1] This digital edition uses the same page numbers as the paperback.

Usury, Poetry, and Art: Canto 45

Peter Nicholls

"There they are, you will have to go a long way round / if you want to avoid them." So Basil Bunting in his poem "On the Fly-Leaf of Pound's Cantos" acknowledges at once the centrality and sheer difficulty of this epic poem. As we grapple with Pound's habit of allusion and his extensive, often idiosyncratic, range of reference, however, canto 45, the so-called usura canto, may seem something of a special case, for here Pound sought for once to be absolutely clear, even providing at the end of the canto a lucid prose definition of what he took *usury* to mean. The allusions to various Renaissance artists and their works are not obscure, and those who have worked their way through earlier cantos will appreciate the emphasis reaffirmed here on the production of pure food (bread, especially, will provide a major focus in later cantos 74 and 80), on the decadence of art that ensues from an unjust economic system, and on the obstacles placed in the way of all productive labor by the drive for profit. Instructors will find, too, that this canto can strike an immediate chord with contemporary student readers, a cohort acutely aware of the lasting burden of debt that will be the likely cost of their few short years of university education. Indeed, Pound's invective against the banking interests and their manipulation of indebtedness sounds, in the wake of movements such as Occupy, remarkably modern.[1] For once, perhaps, the poet seems to be preaching to the converted, and it is accordingly the medium of canto 45 rather than its message that will demand our special attention in the classroom. Why, for example, does Pound employ a self-consciously archaic diction here if the problem of usury is an immediate and pressing one? And why should poetry be a privileged medium in which to denounce the usurer when the prose statement at the end of the canto seems to do the job with such admirable concision?

To answer these questions, some historical context is necessary. Drafted in early 1935, canto 45 was published the following year in *Prosperity*, a journal of the "new economics" edited by Robert Scrutton and Jeffrey Mark. The so-called usura canto marked an abrupt shift in style and perspective. While the opening sequence of *The Fifth Decad of Cantos, XLII–LI* had explored the founding of the Monte dei Paschi bank in Siena, an institution notable in Pound's view for its provision of credit and its practice of charging only "moderate and legitimate interest" (canto 42 [*Cantos* 210]), canto 45 would take its distance from the vortex, so to speak, of historical detail so as to illuminate the root cause of economic injustice. By 1933, Pound was ready to acknowledge, "My Cantos XXXI–XLI are practically pure econ/propaganda," and this would also be the mode of the *Fifth Decad*'s opening.[2] Canto 45 presents a major interruption of this "propaganda" or documentary voice, not, as in earlier parts of the poem, to evoke a visionary landscape, but rather, as we shall see, to demonstrate its unavailability "with usura."

The "house of good stone" in the first line thus recalls Circe's "house of smooth stone" in canto 39; but erotic desire is absent here, and the background "'thkk, thgk' of the loom" is stilled (*Cantos* 229, 193). "[T]he sharp sound of a song" from canto 39 (193) yields now to what Peter Makin has called "the grand prophetic style," though the canto's emphatic ascending rhythms infect this prophecy with anger and frustration (*Ezra Pound's Cantos* 205). As if to emphasize the importance of the shift in register, Pound gives this canto alone a title, "With *Usura*," the italics naming the practice of making money from money as though it were some kind of monstrous *thing*. In his reprise of the canto, in canto 51, he names it again, this time as the foul creature of Dante's *Inferno*, Geryone.[3]

Like this brief nod to allegory, the reference to "usury" in 1935 may seem anachronistic, but the term was in fact regularly used at the time by those contesting conventional modes of economic thinking.[4] In Mark's *The Modern Idolatry: An Analysis of Usury and the Pathology of Debt*, for example, a work Pound regarded as "a rather good outline,"[5] the phrase "under usury" is repeated with a rhetorical insistence that may have suggested the mantric "with usura" of canto 45.[6] The reclaiming of the traditional term also signaled that modern capitalism was afflicted with a disease that was age-old and for that reason also relatively easy to recognize and to treat. In line with earlier theological condemnations of usury, Pound emphasized that the antisocial practice of excessive profit-making—in the canto, he described it as a "murrain" and a "canker"[7]—permeated all levels of society and could be exorcised only by treating it as an ethical problem rather than a purely economic one.[8] Some readers have been uneasy with the archaic style employed here, but it arguably signifies not so much a retreat from contemporary problems as an insistent reminder of society's remoteness from any properly ethical understanding of the economic. In periods of crisis like the one to which this canto responds, Adam Smith's "hand" that shapes the market seems far from invisible in its tireless promotion of the interests of the few against the many. Indeed, the fiscal crisis of our own time has provoked a similarly emphatic ethical challenge to the complacencies of neoliberal economic theory.

Pound's use of archaism in canto 45 is closely linked, then, to a traditional denunciation of usury that he derives from Aristotle, Dante, and the canon law theorists of the Middle Ages: usury is "CONTRA NATURAM" (*Cantos* 230), an obstruction of the generative forces of nature and a perversion that, following the *Commedia*, Pound likens to bestiality and sodomy—the usurer, says Dante, "takes another way [and] despises nature both in herself and in her follower" (*Divine Comedy* 12.109–10). As the translator of those lines, John Sinclair, observes, "It is by a very curious piece of medieval thinking that sins so different as blasphemy, sodomy, and usury are grouped together as forms of violence against God, directed respectively against God Himself, against nature, God's 'art', and against human art or industry, which springs from nature and follows it" (152–53). Sinclair's commentary succinctly defines the mental and moral landscape of canto 45; indeed, the historian Jacques Le Goff has observed of Pound that "no one expressed better than he what usury and the usurer were historically" (70). In the early Renaissance world, the Catholic Church's stand against the practice of usury had allowed "the craft and the craftsman" to flourish. Art—notably the art of the fresco—remained a property of the community, such that everyone might share in the "painted paradise" on a church wall; it was not easily available as wealth to be banked or exchanged for profit (canto 74 [*Cantos* 456]). With the rise of Protestantism, so Pound's argument runs, "[t]he Church slumped into a toleration of usury. Protestantism as factive and organised, may have sprung from nothing but pro-usury politics" ("The Individual in His Milieu" 243). The age of Luther and Calvin saw the demise of Deuteronomy's ban on usury and the modern market was born.[9]

The narrative sketched here may seem to indicate Pound's distance from the realities of the modern marketplace, though we may note that it was common practice among the "new economists" to write approvingly of the canon law's restrictions on usury (see, for example, Mark 191). We should also acknowledge that the plight of the spinners and weavers in canto 45 was real enough in Pound's adopted Liguria and was mirrored on a more dramatic scale in proposals in the early thirties for the so-called rationalization of Britain's textile industry.[10] The problem, of course, was to convey the human cost that was largely occluded by what Mark called "the fixed incantations of economic theory" (274). Canto 19 had acknowledged that you "[c]an't move 'em with a cold thing, like economics" mainly because the "dismal science," as Thomas Carlyle called it, takes no account of aesthetic or ethical values (*Cantos* 85; Carlyle 531). Pound's usura canto memorializes what is lost in this economy when art becomes merely a commodity "to sell and sell quickly," and where works such as Mantegna's great fresco of the Gonzaga family (with "his heirs and his concubines") and Botticelli's "La Calunnia" no longer come into being (*Cantos* 229). Like the Victorian critic John Ruskin, Pound conceives a direct connection between economic practice (or malpractice) and the formal achievements of the visual arts of the time. Soon after, he will "suggest that finer and future critics of art will be able to tell from the quality of a painting the degree of tolerance or intolerance of usury extant in the age and milieu that produced it" (*Guide* 27). In canto 45, we are told that "with usura the line grows thick / with usura is no clear demarcation," allegations that relate as much to painterly design as to the mode of thinking itself (*Cantos* 229). The "line" both separates and joins discrete masses of color, a work of "demarcation" or differentiation that usury seeks to undo in its drive toward chiaroscuro and indeterminacy.[11]

Usury—"[a] charge for the use of purchasing power, levied without regard to production; often without regard to the possibilities of production"[12]—interposes itself between producer and consumer, prizing money itself above the creative increase it should enable. As Richard Sieburth notes, "Much of Pound's monetary theory can be understood as an attempt to eliminate or severely regulate this third substance (money or gold) or third party (banker or usurer) in the free and direct circulation of goods" ("In Pound We Trust" 152–53). Usury is in this sense a force of erosion; like the thickening line, it destroys qualitative difference in the name of the universal equivalent that is money. We may hear this in the verbal inspissation of canto 45, in the reiterated "th" sounds that contrast with canto 39's "sharp sound of a song" and refer us instead to Pound's binding phrase, "with usura." The "with" suggests submission to an abstract force, not the sensuous relation between the individual and the picture that is made to "live with" (*Cantos* 229). And while the emphatic rhythms of the canto create a thunderous denunciation of the financiers, they also, as Christine Brooke-Rose suggests, evoke through repetition the frozen temporality of a world inimical to qualitative change. By manipulating debt, the usurer becomes the very thief of time, robbing the community of its future and its sense of creative possibility: "What indeed does he [the usurer] sell, if not the time that elapses between the moment he lends the money and the moment he is repaid, with interest?" (Le Goff 39)—or, as Sieburth writes in "In Pound We Trust," "[Usury] involves the selling of time (the profiting from the 'time-lag' separating loan from repayment)" (150). It is this twisted temporality—the tithe demanded before the harvest[13]—that has transformed debt from being just a sum of money to be repaid into a controlling condition of guilt and social obligation. Many commentators on the current economy would agree with Pound that perpetual indebtedness—individual and collective—is the primary instrument of subjection in the modern world. (See, for example, Graeber; Lazzarato.)

Understanding debt as the theft of time also helps explain the connection between this canto and canto 30, whose archaisms and parallelisms it deliberately echoes ("Pity slayeth my nymphs, / . . . / Pity befouleth April" [*Cantos* 147]). Canto 45 will allude again to the blocking of youthful desire by a "palsied" lover who "lyeth / between the young bride and her bridegroom" (230), as in canto 30 the "doddering" Vulcan intervenes between Venus and "young Mars" (147);[14] and both cantos allude to the murder of Inez de Castro and the exhumation of her body by her lover, King Pedro ("Corpses are set to banquet" [230]).[15] On the face of it, pity and usury are an unlikely couple, though Pound suggests that in different ways each impedes decisive action. In canto 30, Diana laments that pity has prevented the seasonal hunt from taking place—"Nothing is now clean slayne / But rotteth away"—and counsels that "none may seek purity / Having for foulness pity / And things growne awry," a state of affairs mirrored here in Pound's inverted syntax (147). The "foulness" returns in canto 45, where bread has become "dry as paper" and tastes of "stale rags" (229), and the echoing of canto 30's rhythm and idiom warns us to have no pity for those responsible (Pound in *The Spirit of Romance* had already noted Virgil's rebuke to Dante when he wept for the plight of the sorcerers and diviners: "Art thou, too, like the other fools? Here liveth pity when it is well dead. Who is more impious than he who sorrows at divine judgment?" [134–35]).[16] King Pedro's attempt in canto 30 to make the dead masquerade as the living ("Dead hair under the crown" [148]) is reversed in canto 45, where the dead hand of usury "slayeth the child in the womb" (230).

As early drafts of this canto indicate, Pound originally made that reversal more emphatic:

> . . . for this have they built vaults and cellars
> to make a tomb for the living
> and set corpses at their banquet,
> to set cadavers for banquet
> the corpses are met for feasting
> and the young lords made ready for funeral
> at behest of usura. (Draft of canto 45)

The usura canto powerfully evokes such a "tomb for the living," a vaulted space that is at once the grave of the young and the repository of financial wealth.[17] In canto 30, the tale of Inez is prefaced by the statement that "[t]ime is the evil. Evil," and this is the time stolen from the living—concrete time, we might say, the time of events and sensuous experience—now transformed by usury into abstract or commodified time (*Cantos* 147).[18] This empty and homogenous time is the medium of compulsion and necessity that stifles craft and invention: "Usura rusteth the chisel / It rusteth the craft and the craftsman" (canto 45 [*Cantos* 230]). In a masterful countermovement, however, the style and diction of the canto seem to reclaim the values of craftsmanship even as they lament their disappearance. The keynote here is one of conscious artifice. As Brooke-Rose observes, the rhythm is "heavily spondaic" and the mode one of declaration rather than of argument (61, 67).[19] Structurally, the canto seems to fall into two balanced halves, each of twenty-five lines, the second half beginning with the line, "Usura is a murrain, usura" (*Cantos* 229); and this underlying formal symmetry is reinforced by the syntactical parallelisms that gather around the key phrases "with usura" and "by usura."[20] The rhythm here articulates a resistance to the pattern of negation the canto condemns, asserting recurrence against the destructive momentum of usury.[21] At the same time, though, the archaism of Pound's language and its use of syntactic inversion ("Came not," "Not by") acknowledge with frustration the sheer difficulty of such resistance (229–30). Indeed, in the opening lines of the next canto, Pound buttonholes the reader who would dismiss this canto as a retreat into archaism, who would think that

> the Reverend Eliot
> has found a more natural language...you who think
> you will
> get through hell in a hurry... (231; ellipses in original)

In contrast to T. S. Eliot's ironic play with modern idioms, the "unnatural" rhythms of canto 45, with their weighty stressing and reiterated phrases, produce a self-retarding movement that leaves little doubt that this is a hell from which we shall not easily escape.[22]

With canto 46, "the first part, draws to a conclusion, / of the first phase of this opus" (*Cantos* 233) and we are still trapped in "a tomb for the living": "Aurum est commune sepulchrum. Usura, commune sepulchrum" (234). Canto 47 announces once again that, like Odysseus, we must "go the road / to hell"; but here the weaving together of fertility myths also signals the possibility of a world without usury (236). In contrast to the dry bread of canto 45, "[w]heat shoots rise new by the altar, / flower from the swift seed" (237), and we are en route to the fine imagistic discriminations of canto 49, "[w]here wine flag catches the sunset / Sparse chimneys smoke in the cross light" (244). But is this a world *without* usury or a world Pound believes to be *before* usury? "State by creating riches shd. thereby get into debt? / This is infamy; this is Geryon" (245). But the world of canto 49 is not that of Geryon; it is a world of simple agrarian rhythms ("Sun up; work / sundown; to rest") that absorb the lives of the peasantry so completely that they are unconscious of the remote imperial power ruling over them: "Imperial power is? and to us what is it?" (245). As if aware of the false seductiveness of this "dimension of stillness" (245), Pound in canto 50 plunges us into the "hell's bog" (247) of nineteenth-century Vienna and then in canto 51 proceeds to reprise the themes of canto 45. This, however, is repetition with a difference, the earlier canto rewritten in a more "natural language": "Wool does not come into market / the peasant does not eat his own grain / the girl's needle goes blunt in her hand" (250).

The effect of this rewriting is hard to specify, and readers will respond to it in different ways. The rhythmic shape of canto 45 certainly remains, though now it works in tension with a preponderance of intransitive constructions ("the girl's needle goes blunt in her hand" instead of "blunteth the needle in the maid's hand"). The modern vocabulary that now shadows our recollection of canto 45—"girl" rather than "maid," "cancer" rather than "canker," for example—and the seemingly deliberate flatness of some of the new lines—"It destroys the craftsman, destroying craft" in place of "It rusteth the craft and the craftsman"—these reformulations suggest that in canto 51 we are actors without agency, trapped in a "stage set" (*Cantos* 252).[23] Yet the canto has begun by alluding to the Neoplatonic light imagery of Guido Guinizelli's "Al cor gentil repara sempre amore" ("Shines / in the mind of heaven" [250]), and Pound now moves from the frozen time of usury to the arcane but practical knowledge of the fly-fisherman "[t]hat hath the light of the doer" (251). The touch of archaism in that phrase deftly recalls the idiom of canto 45 while signaling a way beyond the grisly tableau that provided its conclusion.

NOTES

[1] See, for example, David Graeber, *Debt: The First 5,000 Years*. Graeber was a leading figure in the Occupy Wall Street Movement of 2011.

[2] Letter to Hans Cohrssen, 24 December 1933, in Preda, *Ezra Pound's Economic Correspondence* (84). In a letter of 9 December 1933, Pound reflects on his early days, noting that "I was in them days a lyric writer" (80).

[3] See canto 12 of Dante's *Inferno*. Although Pound associated Calvin and Luther with the Church's capitulation to usury, the latter inveighed in similar terms against the practice: "Usury is a great huge monster, like a were-wolf, who lays waste all, more than any Cacus, Gerion or Antaeus" (qtd. in Marx, *Capital*, 740n22).

[4] Preda notes that Pound and his "fellow reformers" regularly referred to finance capital as "usury" (*Ezra Pound's Economic Correspondence* 44, 118). Marx characterizes the usurer as "that old-fashioned but ever-renewed specimen of the capitalist" (*Capital* 740n22).

[5] In a letter of 26 September 1934 to Hugo Fack, Pound writes, "Jeff Mark has just done a rather good outline / at any rate one that will do to go on with" (Preda, *Ezra Pound's Economic Correspondence* 118). Pound's reading of Mark's book thus predates the drafting of canto 45 and clearly had a formative effect on this part of the poem.

[6] For a representative use of the phrase, see Mark: "Under usury, interest is paid *in money* or debt claims, and this . . . is the root cause for all interruptions in the flow of the medium of exchange and therefore in the distribution of commodities to consumers" (191). Mark also presents usury as monstrous, alluding to Moloch and the golden calf (276). Christopher Hollis in his *The Two Nations*, a work Pound regularly cites, concludes that "the ultimate punishment then which usury exacts is a spiritual punishment—the destruction of joy" (252).

[7] "Murrain" refers to cattle plague and generally to pestilence. Then, much later, in "Addendum for C," Pound speaks of usury as "[t]he canker corrupting all things" (*Cantos* 818).

[8] See, for example, Pound's "The Individual in His Milieu": "No economic system can neglect these fundamental dissociations, and no monetary system can rise above the status of gadget if it be not in accord with some *order of thought*, with some system of moral criteria" (244).

[9] See also Benjamin Nelson: "The Age of Luther and Calvin is the time of Deuteronomy's crisis and demise" (29–30). As Lewis Hyde observes, the ban on usury in Deuteronomy 23:20 ("Unto a stranger though mayest lend upon usury; but unto thy brother thou shall not lend on usury") was in fact "a double law, both a prohibition and a permission" (142).

[10] Mark notes that "production is now being deliberately inhibited or actually destroyed, and distribution interfered with" (162). In a passage that might have caught Pound's eye, he also writes sarcastically of a 1932 proposal "to dismantle or immobilize 10,000,000 spindles and 100,000 looms as a 'means of *restoring prosperity* to the British textile industry!'" (30). Cf. Pound in canto 51: "The looms are hushed one after another / ten thousand after ten thousand" (*Cantos* 250).

[11] See Pound's letter to Carlo Izzo, 8 January 1938: "'Demarcation' is intellectual. It is also boundary of field if you like, but demarcation is universal. The bastid Cromwell and - - - - Anglican bishops and bankers obscure every hierarchy of values" (*Selected Letters* 304).

[12] Qtd. from the endnote to canto 45 (*Cantos* 230); incorporated in all editions of *The Cantos* after 1970.

[13] Pound, letter to Jencks, 9 May 1940: "no tithes before harvest" (Preda, *Ezra Pound's Economic Correspondence* 235).

[14] Cf. Marx: "Money is the *pimp* between need and object, between life and means of life" (*Economic and Philosophical Manuscripts*, 375).

[15] "When Pedro succeeded to the throne, he had her body exhumed, and the court did homage, the grandees of Portugal passing before the double throne of the dead queen and her king, kissing that hand which had been hers" (Pound, *Spirit* 218).

[16] The possible relation of this passage to canto 30 was first noted by Clark Emery in *Ideas into Action* (121).

[17] Compare Pound, *ABC of Economics*: "[T]he place of control is a dark room back of a bank, hung with deep purple curtains. No one must see what happens" (207).

[18] The phrase "Time is the evil" may echo *Ephesians* 5:16: "Redeeming the time, because the days are evil" (*King James Bible*).

[19] Brooke-Rose also notes that the verse of the canto contains few of the end spondees that are usually associated with Pound's visionary mode.

[20] I follow Brooke-Rose in including the canto's "title" in the line-count.

[21] Cf. Mutlu Konuk Blasing: "Distinct from meter, which belongs to the formal order, rhythm makes for the perceptibility of time. For rhythm is not simply the fact of temporal repetition or periodicity; it requires a perception of periodicity *as* rhythmic" (56).

[22] Brooke-Rose notes similarly the "curiously non-temporal effect" of the canto (28).

[23] Cf. Mark: "[M]an has been completely perverted by usury, and is, indeed, not responsible for his actions under it" (276).

Pound as Noh Student: The Lessons of *Hagoromo*

Carrie J. Preston

My students are often delighted to learn that Ezra Pound, usually familiar to them as the founder of the imagist movement, was quite dismissive of universities, or "beaneries," as he called them. He lasted just five months in his first teaching position, at Wabash College in Indiana, where he capped a series of eccentric behaviors, such as skipping chapel, with the transgression of allowing a burlesque dancer he found shivering on the street to spend the night in his room (he claimed to have generously given her the bed while he slept on the floor).[1] If the Wabash College affair prompted his departure for Europe, where he launched his writing career, it did not end his didactic aspirations, as evident in titles such as *How to Read*, *ABC of Economics*, and *ABC of Reading*. In the latter tome, Pound wrote:

> [A] Japanese emperor whose name I have forgotten and whose name you needn't remember, found that there were TOO MANY NOH PLAYS, he picked out 450 and the Noh stage LASTED from 1400 or whenever right down till the day the American navy intruded, and that didn't stop it. Umewaka Minoru started again as soon as the revolution wore off.
>
> (*ABC of Reading* 92)

To teach the aesthetic value of a limited canon, carefully selected for future audiences by an aristocratic authority, Pound turned to the Japanese Noh theater, a poetic dance-drama with masks and elaborate costumes that is still cited as one of the world's oldest continuous theater forms. This lesson begins by omitting the name of the emperor who selected the best plays and ensured the survival of Noh from an uncertain date ("1400 or whenever") until an invasion that failed to "stop it" and a revolution that also "wore off." From failed revolutions to discarded plays (the Noh canon actually consists of about 250 plays), Pound emphasizes failure and reveals the challenge of transmitting art and knowledge through time and across cultures. This is a useful reminder that diversity and global studies are more complex and fraught than Fiesta night and Mongolian BBQ in the cafeteria or the carefully curated study abroad experience.

To help my students examine the role of translation, cultural transmission, and exoticism in modernism, I develop a lesson plan around Pound's translation of the Noh play *Hagoromo* (羽衣; *The Feather Mantle*). Although the focus of the lesson is on Pound's aesthetics and transnational modernism, my students also gain an introduction to Noh as an important dramatic form, one that influenced such poets and playwrights as W. B. Yeats, Bertolt Brecht, Eugene O'Neill, and Samuel Beckett. Many students are productively uncomfortable with the ways Pound took, taught, and translated Noh. My own lessons in Noh performance technique have taught me that transnational teaching and learning should rarely be comfortable. I emphasize that aspect of the lesson by asking students to chant some of the lines of *Hagoromo* and try movements from one of the dances. For this purpose, teachers and students are welcome to use the clips I have posted at sites.bu.edu/learningtokneel.

My syllabus for two weeks of a course on transnational modernism includes Pound's translation of *Hagoromo*, based on Ernest Fenollosa's draft—published in *Certain Noble Plays of Japan* with an introduction by Yeats (which I add to the syllabus for graduate students) but more accessible in the expanded volume *The Classic Noh Theatre of Japan*—along with clips 1 and 2 at sites.bu.edu/learningtokneel/news; Royall Tyler's more authoritative translation of *Hagoromo* in *Japanese Nō Dramas* (and, for graduate students, Tyler's introduction to the volume); and Pound's *The Pisan Cantos*. I direct students to the *Japanese Text Initiative* for further translations of *Hagoromo* (jti.lib.virginia.edu/japanese/noh/hagoindex.html) and to *The Cantos Project* (thecantosproject.ed.ac.uk/index.php/homepage) and *PennSound* (writing.upenn.edu/pennsound/x/Pound.php) for multimedia resources related to *The Cantos*.

Pound's Hagoromo *as a Lesson on Imagism*

Hagoromo, by an unknown playwright, is perhaps the most famous play in the Noh repertory and a favorite of Pound's and Yeats's. Pound used it to teach imagism, particularly his developing notion of a long imagist poem. Scholars of modernism often consider Pound's Noh translations to be examples of modernist Orientalism and cultural appropriation or else categorize them as creative contributions to English literature but too full of errors to be called translations. I ask students to hold off on such judgments until after we produce a close reading of *Hagoromo*. The play introduces a fisherman named Hakuryō who discovers the feathered mantle of a Tennin, or celestial moon maiden, hanging on a pine bough. Hakuryō and his companion Fisherman enter the stage singing of the beauties of spring, frequently expressed through typically modernist synesthesia or sensory mixing and linkage: "the breath-colour of spring," whose "colour-smell is mysterious" (*Classic Noh Theatre* 98, 99). The Fisherman claims of the well-ordered layers of waves, mist, and moon "delaying above," "Here is beauty to set the mind above itself" (98). He appears to be correct that "we've no skill to grasp it," for what Hakuryō grasps instead is the feathered mantle of the Tennin, whose presence in the lower world is a manifestation of the "delaying" moon (98). Hakuryō initially claims that he is taking the mantle to his house to comfort "the aged" (99); then, when he learns the true nature of the robe from the Tennin, he nationalistically wants to keep it as "a treasure in the country" (100). He insists on his power to "take and keep hid the feather-robe" after the Tennin's "high words" lead him to assume she thinks he is "too stupid to recognize" the value and beauty of the feathered mantle (100). He relents after seeing her "sorrow" and watching her begin to die the death of a celestial being but says he will only return the garment if she will perform "the dance of the Tennin" (101). She will "gladly" help him "learn" the "dance that can turn the palace of the moon," but she needs her mantle to perform (101). He refuses to return it, fearing that she will fly off before dancing; but she shames him, saying, "Doubt is of mortals; with us there is no deceit" (102).

Pound's Tennin teaches sympathy, trust, and a dance but also imagist aesthetics. Pound offered Noh as the answer to a question he had been asked: "Could one do a long Imagiste poem, or even a long poem in vers libre?" (*Classic Noh Theatre* 27). Yes, if the long poem adheres to Noh's "Unity of Image"; "the better plays are all built into the intensification of a single Image: . . . the mantle of feathers in the play of that name, Hagoromo" (27). Pound never directly stated how this "Unity" was to be achieved; however, his translation of *Hagoromo* used the feathered mantle to establish related clusters of images. Pound's Tennin appears as a vernal spirit whose flowers begin "drooping and fading" after Hakuryō steals her mantle (100). Depictions of her celebratory dance unite her flowing robe with the season's blossoms and storms: "The sleeves of flowers are being wet with the rain" (102). "The rustling of the flowers, the putting on of the feathery sleeve; they bend in the air with the dancing" (104). The chorus sings of the "plumage of heaven," "feathery skirt of the stars," and "robe of mist" (103–04). These related images create a structural unity for the play; Hakuryō realizes that nature, humanity, and the spirit world "are doing one step," and he learns to dance in "unity" (102).

The "Unity of Image" Pound celebrated in Noh matches *Hagoromo*'s theme of connecting heaven and earth or the divine being and the fisherman. Hakuryō learns to be in "step" with the ephemeral spirit of nature without the desire to possess her or to take her magical garment for his nation. Pound learned how to organize an imagist long poem or play by related images. When I teach Yeats's introduction to *Certain Noble Plays of Japan*, I discuss how Pound's "Unity of Image" also influenced Yeats's poetics and dramaturgy. Yeats worked with Pound on Noh translations and was particularly interested in *Hagoromo* as a transnational folk play similar to an Irish story about the theft of a fairy's "red cap" (*Classic Noh Theatre* 159). He also claimed the feather mantle produces "its rhythm of metaphor" and quoted images such as "the plumage of heaven" and "feathery skirt of the stars" as part of that trope (161). The year he wrote this introduction, Yeats produced a play about a magical bird-woman, *At the Hawk's Well*, the first and most famous of his Noh-inspired "dance plays."

Tyler's Hagoromo: *Reconsidering Translation and Cultural Exchange*

Hakuryō's theft of the feathered robe as a treasure for his nation mirrors one of the major complaints launched against Pound and Yeats for their work on Noh: They were both engaged in cultural theft and Orientalist mystification. This is a complaint my students tend to embrace, as they have been taught long before they arrive at college to respect cultural difference and question cultural stereotypes. I ask students to read Royall Tyler's celebrated translation of *Hagoromo* alongside Pound's version, and they enthusiastically pick out discrepancies in the translations, noticing, for example, that Pound excised most of the references to Buddhism, the philosophical center of Noh. Comparing translations also helps them see how Pound's desires to make the play into a lesson on imagism encouraged him to mistranslate or creatively translate passages into examples of his "Unity of Image" and thereby turn *Hagoromo* into a template for a long imagist poem or play. For a graduate seminar including translation theory, Pound's *Hagoromo* provides a useful example of what Lawrence Venuti described as a "foreignizing" rather than "domesticating" translation (17). Pound made the English sound foreign with unusual syntax, unfamiliar names, and stereotypical images of Japan: "Windy road of the waves by Miwo, / Swift with ships, loud over steersmen's voices. / Hakuryō taker of fish, head of his house, dwells upon the barren pine-waste of Miwo" (*Classic Noh Theatre* 98). The relation between subjects and adjectives is ambiguous: Is the road "windy," or are the waves following a metaphorical "windy road"? Are the ships "swift," or do the waves or road seem swift because of the ships sailing there? "Taker of fish" sounds more exotic than "fisherman."

My students like comparing translations and realizing that Pound took liberties with the source text; but I work to complicate some of their assumptions about cultural appropriation. *Hagoromo* itself prompts one possible approach as the play turns the theft of a robe into a dance lesson. Hakuryō will never perfectly execute "the dance of the rainbow-feathered garment." He does, however, pass on the Tennin's dance to future Noh performers, following myths of Noh's origins in a divine dance lesson. To punctuate this insight, I perform *Hagoromo*'s celebratory dance and chant, acknowledging that I am an amateur student of Noh and inviting my own students to join me. As we awkwardly explore Noh movement and chant, usually feeling nothing like a graceful Tennin, we become aware of the challenges of cross-cultural learning and teaching and how these challenges complicate notions of authentic cultural representation. I offer examples of my own struggles to learn the Japanese language and seemingly simple Noh dances. See clip 2 at sites.bu.edu/learningtokneel/news for a particularly humiliating example of my attempt to learn a chant from *Hagoromo* and my many mistakes.

Any cross-cultural lesson involves collaborations between teachers and students that can be productive even when they are riddled with misunderstanding. Students seem both shocked and relieved when I acknowledge I do not assume they understand everything I say and admit to having taught Noh in ways I would now consider erroneous. Opening with a theft and misunderstanding and ending in a dance lesson, *Hagoromo* inspires a shift in focus from cultural appropriation to collaborative pedagogical transmission. In fact, Noh translations such as the one we call for convenience "Pound's" *Hagoromo* were the product of a series of transnational lessons and partnerships. Pound received Ernest Fenollosa's draft translation of Noh plays and other materials from Fenollosa's widow, Mary, in 1913. Mary Fenollosa's letters to Pound indicate that she sent the "Nō stuff" first because she viewed it as the most significant, as "a complete book in itself" (Kodama, *Ezra Pound* 6). These drafts were the result of a pedagogical scenario and international collaboration that Pound partially romanticized and partially suppressed in *The Classic Noh Theatre of Japan*. Fenollosa had studied Noh *utai* (謡), or chanting, with Umewaka Minoru, who had worked to revive Noh after the collapse of the Tokugawa shogunate in 1868. Pound embellished Fenollosa's role in preserving Japan's traditional artworks (and exporting many to American museums) during the rampant westernization of the Meiji period when he claimed in the book's biographical note that after Fenollosa died in London in 1908, "the Japanese government sent a warship for his ashes." In fact, a friend transported the ashes by rail for interment in Japan.

While Pound exaggerated Fenollosa's influence in Japan against "the apeing of Europe," he suppressed another pedagogical relationship crucial to the transmission of Noh (*Classic Noh Theatre* 3). Mary Fenollosa wrote to Pound about "little Mr. Hirata, a pupil of my husband's" who "did" the translations, although she did not "think much of his literary style" (Kodama, *Ezra Pound* 7). Hirata Kiichi, Fenollosa's colleague at the Higher Normal School, was neither a student of Fenollosa nor a student of Noh, but he became a renowned scholar of English literature under the pen name Tokuboku. He accompanied Fenollosa to lessons and produced literal translations of Noh plays as preparation for attending performances, including the production of *Hagoromo* the two attended together on 15 January 1899 (Miyake et al. 171). Hirata is mentioned twice without explanation in the publication of what should be called the Fenollosa-Hirata-Pound translations (*Classic Noh Theatre* 115).

While Pound positioned himself as the student of a dead man, his Noh work was dramatically shaped by a series of live collaborations focused on the Tokyo-born dancer Ito Michio. Because Ito is even more invisible in Pound's text than Hirata, I share his life and work with students through a minilecture, photographs, and dance clips (available at sites.bu.edu/learningtokneel). Pound met Ito in May 1915 and asked for his assistance in editing the Fenollosa-Hirata draft translations. Ito explains in his autobiography that he told Pound he had seen Noh as a child, but "as far as I'm concerned there's nothing more boring" (Carruthers 39). Pound persisted, and Ito eventually contacted Kori Torahiko and the painter Kumé Tamijūrō to help him give a demonstration for Pound and Yeats in June or July 1915; Kori and Kumé probably chanted *utai* while Ito danced an impression of Noh *shimai* (仕舞) not based on detailed study. Kumé had, however, taken lessons with Fenollosa's teacher, Umewaka, and Pound claimed in a 1939 article for *The Japan Times and Mail*, "Study of Noh Continues in the West," that Kumé performed *Hagoromo* at the recital: "Tami Koumé had danced the *Hagoromo* before the Emperor, taking the tennin part when he was, as I remember, six years old. At twenty he still remembered the part and movements of the tennin's wings, which as she returns to the upper heavens, are the most beautiful movements I have seen on or off any stage" (Kodama, *Ezra Pound* 156).

A child actor would never play the Tennin for the emperor, but Kumé is likely to have studied *Hagoromo* with Umewaka. Almost twenty-five years later, Pound's retelling of the anecdote indicates the significance of *Hagoromo* in his thinking about Noh, stage movement, and collaborators. Pound's textual collaboration with Fenollosa and Hirata and actual work with Ito and Kumé can help students consider the relationships, collaborations, and events that underlie cultural transmission and textual production.

Ito's continued work on adaptations of Noh reminds us that Orientalism is not exclusively the purview of Westerners. When Ito is known to modernist studies at all, it is for his choreography and performance as the Guardian in Yeats's *At the Hawk's Well*, a role he won during his Noh recital with Kori and Kumé. The war soon drove him to the United States, where he first staged *At the Hawk's Well* with new music by the Japanese composer Yamada Kosçak in New York in 1918, followed by a brief East Coast tour. In 1929, he staged the play at the Argus Bowl in California, teaching the Guardian role to the dancer Lester Horton. Ito directed and played the role of the Old Man in a Tokyo performance in 1939. Ito's tours with *At the Hawk's Well* influenced the Japanese modern theater, or *shingeki* (新劇); Noh; and late-twentieth-century developments in English Noh and fusion theater, all of which continue to perform versions of Yeats's play. Ito presented the Fenollosa-Hirata-Pound translation of *Hagoromo* for the Thursday Evening Club in January 1923, a production that was billed as "Japanese Noh Drama, GIVEN FOR THE FIRST TIME OUTSIDE OF JAPAN." This billing is not accurate given the fact that Ito had previously participated in a production of the Fenollosa-Hirata-Pound *Tamura* at the Neighborhood Playhouse in 1918, with a revival in 1921. These productions departed significantly from Noh traditions in Japan and appealed to audience desires for performances of the "exotic Orient," but they also influenced the modernist little theater movement and launched Ito's important career as a modern dancer and choreographer.

The Pisan Hagoromo

Hagoromo has a dramatic presence in *The Cantos*, and I use the play to help students find a foothold in the infamously difficult, allusive, and transnational work. A fisherman associated with *Hagoromo* is the first poetic persona in Pound's initial drafts of *The Cantos* published in *Poetry* in 1917, just after his most intense work on Noh: "Say that I dump my catch, shiny and silvery / As fresh sardines flapping and slipping on the marginal cobbles?" ("Three Cantos" 113). This Hakuryō has stolen and donned the mantle of artistic inspiration, but he doesn't know what to do with it: "Whom shall I hang my shimmering garment on; / Who wear my feathery mantle, *hagoromo*; / Whom set to dazzle the serious future ages?" (117). Pound was searching for a new form and speaker for the massive poem he would write for the rest of his life, and he turned to the "Unity" he discovered and invented in Noh.

The week immediately following our *Hagoromo* classes, we discuss *The Pisan Cantos*, which Pound composed in 1945 during his imprisonment in the United States Army's Disciplinary Training Center north of Pisa. While in solitary confinement, he was visited by the angel of *Hagoromo*, other Noh characters, and the spirits of Yeats, Ito, and Kumé. *The Pisan Cantos* presents anti-Semitic and pro-Fascist ideas along with allusions to Japanese, Chinese, Greek, and Roman literature. The poem is both difficult and disturbing to students, and I help them see that they can follow a strand, like the *Hagoromo* allusions, to analyze some elements of the text and reserve others for another reading. Tracking *Hagoromo* through *The Pisan Cantos* reveals that repeated moon images function as an organizing poetic trope.[2] In the first reference to Noh in the opening canto of *The Pisan Cantos*, the speaker is visited by the "nymph of Hagoromo . . . / as a corona of angels" (74.180). Pound echoes the question he posed in 1917 just as he was beginning his cantos: "Whom shall I hang my shimmering garment on; / Who wear my feathery mantle, *hagoromo*." If that version of Hakuryō was searching for a new poetic form, this fisherman has lost the magic robe of inspiration and needs the moon maiden to return with a coterie of angels, including the Greek and Roman moon goddesses, Artemis and Diana (74.226); the Sino-Japanese spirit of mercy, Kuanon (74.131); and the love goddesses Aphrodite, Venus, and "Cythera, in the moon's barge" (74.190, 80.596). Pound links the Hakuryō of *The Pisan Cantos* to Odysseus, renders the Greek hero's Cyclops-evading name as "OΎ TIΣ" or "noman," and lists it as the caption for the Chinese character *mo* 莫 ("no" or "not") in the *Hagoromo* allusion. Pound's ideogrammic reading of *mo* 莫 found the character for person 人 (see the two "legs" of the character) below the radical for sun 日 and read the character as "a man on whom the sun has gone down" (74.178). Moon images unify the speaking subject as Pound-Hakuryō-Odysseus-OΎ TIΣ- 莫 and illuminate his dream of redemptive goddesses. If the sun has gone down on him, this composite, even ideogrammic, speaker looks to the moon.

Students appreciate the Chinese characters in *The Pisan Cantos* once I suggest that they can enjoy associative reading practices like those that Pound used. The Pound-Hakuryō-Odysseus-OΎ TIΣ-莫 speaker takes on a material, visual presence in the text and can quickly add another facet or persona to the list. The speaker becomes the soldier and art patron Sigismondo Malatesta in a moonlit visionary encounter. While standing at a crossing of three paths, or *triedro*, Malatesta sees the ghosts of three women, including the compassionate lover of the troubadour Sordello, Cunizza da Romano, and "la scalza," a barefoot country woman fleeing the war's bombs. The latter is linked to *Hagoromo*'s moon nymph, who speaks one of *The Pisan Cantos*' prominent lyrical refrains: "Io la luna"

("I am the moon"). Just as the Hakuryō-speaker claims, "[T]he nymph of Hagoromo came to me," the Sigismondo-speaker insists, "[T]hey suddenly stand in my room here" (74.180, 76.11). "La scalza" and "the corona of angels" return with each repetition of the phrase, "Io la luna." Such refrains take on the quality of a choral song, and Pound's Hakuryō-Odysseus-ΟΥ̓ ΤΙΣ-莫 speaker wears many masks.

The poem's second reference to *Hagoromo* contrasts Pound's Japanese and Greek literary sources, distinguishing Hakuryō's return of the feathered mantle from the "Greek rascality" of Odysseus's opportunistic attack on Ismarus as he was leaving Troy. This didactic stance persists in the third reference to the moon maiden of *Hagoromo.* Her return is prompted by the darkest of the lunar references, when the barefoot woman, "la scalza," recounts an image left out of the previous visions: her dead son nailed to the ground with arms outstretched in the shape of a cross (80. 247–50). This leads to a parody of pretty, romantic moon imagery in an overblown personification: "the moon's arse been chewed off by this time" (80.258). *Hagoromo* returns with the line that shamed Hakuryō: "'With us there is no deceit' / said the moon nymph immacolata / Give back my cloak, *hagoromo*" (80. 260–62).

Did Pound learn Hakuryō's lesson? Did he echo the response, "I am ashamed. I give you your mantle" (*Classic Noh Theatre* 102)? The question of whether or not Pound felt shame and apologized for his pro-Fascist propaganda has been put to *The Pisan Cantos* since the book's early readers argued over whether the controversial author, having been determined mentally unfit for trial and confined in St. Elizabeths Hospital for the Criminally Insane, should have received the Bollingen Prize. Much of the debate about the sequence hinges on whether or not Pound is the speaker of the famous "Pull down thy vanity" chant (*Pisan Cantos* 81.117–74). Pound's ideogrammic, "noman" subjectivity renders this question one of the least answerable of the many invoked by *The Pisan Cantos.* The speaker of the poem is the humbled Hakuryō, who has stolen the magical mantle and must return it; and Odysseus, who will attack yet another city on his way home from Troy; and the one on whom the sun has gone down; and Pound himself—turning his incarceration into a gripping story.

In spite of Pound's own bleak position on education ("Teach? at Harvard? / Teach? It cannot be done" [*Pisan Cantos* 74.302–03]), I find that teaching Pound's Noh translations with *The Pisan Cantos* provides a challenging and rewarding lesson. *Hagoromo* creates one track through Pound's collage of Chinese ideograms, literary allusions, and personal anecdotes while helping students confront one of the most difficult and important lessons of the twentieth century: the atrocities produced by fascist political movements and militarization in Europe and Asia. As for the common complaint that Pound is guilty of Orientalism and misrepresentation of cultures, I agree. But I believe that is all the more reason to study his work. To discard it for its inaccuracy is to imagine that accurate cultural transmission is possible and to vainly presume we could accomplish it in our teaching.

NOTES

[1] Recounted in Nadel, *Ezra Pound: A Literary Life*, pp. 29–30. According to David Moody, there are two slightly different versions. In one, Pound slept on his sofa; in the other, he slept on the floor. In the morning, the two sisters who ran the rooming house found the young woman in Pound's bed. Pound himself had left for class (*Young Genius* 60–61).

[2] The discussion of moon imagery connecting *Hagoromo* with *The Pisan Cantos* is based upon Preston, p. 52.

Pound and Periodicals: Editing Modernism

Craig Monk

Teaching Ezra Pound effectively involves teaching his engagement with readers through periodicals. Many of his texts appeared first in literary magazines, and Donald Gallup's *Ezra Pound: A Bibliography* lists nearly two thousand individual works from periodicals. *Ezra Pound's Poetry and Prose: Contributions to Periodicals*, edited by Lee Baechler and colleagues, runs to eleven thick volumes. While Pound's anthologized works are often drawn from his published collections, the list below demonstrates that many of his most-taught pieces from his earliest years abroad appeared in magazines. For example, *Personae: The Shorter Poems*, that classroom staple revised for New Directions, was culled from other publishers' volumes, yet many of its works also had a magazine pedigree. Seventy percent of the pieces reprinted in *Selected Prose, 1909–1965*, the standard collection of Pound's essays, first appeared in periodicals.

Personae	*Selected Prose*
"Sestina: Altaforte" (*English Review*, 1909)	"I Gather the Limbs of Osiris" (*The New Age*, 1911–12)
"The Seafarer" (*The New Age*, 1911)	"The Wisdom of Poetry" (*Forum*, 1912)
"To Whistler, American" (*Poetry*, 1912)	*Patria Mia* (*The New Age*, 1912–13)
"In a Station of the Metro" (*Poetry*, 1913)	"Remy de Gourmont" (*Fortnightly Review*, 1915)
"Salutation the Third" (*Blast*, 1914)	"Affirmations—As for Imagisme" (*The New Age*, 1915)
"Provincia Deserta" (*Poetry*, 1915)	"Beddoes and Chronology" (*Future*, 1917)
"The Tea Shop" (*Others*, 1915)	"Provincialism the Enemy" (*The New Age*, 1917)
Homage to Sextus Propertius (*The New Age*, 1919)	"Economic Democracy" (*The Little Review*, 1920)
Hugh Selwyn Mauberley (*Dial*, 1920)	"Axiomata" (The New Age, 1921)

From these contributions, students should get some sense of Pound's shifting preoccupations over a decade, as well as his changing poetic techniques and critical strategies. In some cases, an examination of these works in the classroom will demonstrate the overlap between his poetry and prose.

In *Modernism in the Magazines: An Introduction*, a text indispensable for teaching modern periodicals, Robert Scholes and Clifford Wulfman outline several considerations relevant for instructors who wish to emphasize how Pound's work may be understood as something more than anthologized bits and pieces. While it is necessary to view contributions first as individual fragments from a magazine's contents, students should be encouraged to follow Pound's lead, as

Scholes and Wulfman understand it, and seek an understanding of the contents of a single number "from advertising to fiction to editorials" as well as "the culture represented" across "a whole set of magazines," whether that is one title over time or several titles produced at a given moment or in a given place (144).[1]

Context is essential. Was Pound successful in reaching a wide audience in publications like *Munsey's Magazine* and the *Saturday Review*? Was he attempting to foster a specialized readership in a venue like the *British-Italian Bulletin* or the *New English Weekly*? Was Pound a frequent contributor to the source being studied, as he was to the *Dial*, or did he place only a small amount of material there, as in a fleeting venue like *Blues*? Were his ideas incongruous to his surroundings, as they were in the *New Masses*, or were they framed by those of like-minded contemporaries, as they were in the *transatlantic review*? As successful as Pound was in preparing and placing his own works in these periodicals, he was known equally for his ability to place the works of others. Students should be encouraged to see the extent to which Pound can thus be understood to have curated several different magazines, extending the scope of his influence. By the late 1920s, he had edited four numbers of his own periodical and thus illustrated through his own labor many of the salient features of modern literary magazines. Scholes and Wulfman call Pound the founder of modern periodical studies, and it is through the essay that earned him this reputation that classroom treatments of his editorial experiences best begin.

"Small Magazines," Ezra Pound's prose contribution to the *English Journal* for November 1930, is a worthy and remarkably durable text for classroom examination. Widely available electronically and through library reference packages, the six-thousand-word essay is appropriate for detailed study in a senior-level or graduate class on Pound, periodical modernism, or publication history.[2] The text seeks to provide a survey of modern literary magazines in the United States, and of a number of similar publications abroad with which American writers were involved. Pound acknowledges that his attempt is not comprehensive, though he worked to make it so, adding further titles in endnotes just before publication ("Small Magazines" 704). Sixteen years later, Frederick J. Hoffman and colleagues published what is still the standard single-volume text relevant to this topic, *The Little Magazine: A History and a Bibliography*; Edward E. Chielens's *American Literary Magazines: The Twentieth Century* provides a valuable complement. Of course, a good place to start a more comprehensive study of the magazines in which Pound was interested is the multivolume *Oxford Critical and Cultural History of Modernist Magazines*, established at Oxford University Press by Peter Brooker and Andrew Thacker in 2009.

Pound begins his essay with the observation that "the significance of the small magazine has, obviously, nothing to do with format," touching with prescience on the fundamental debate in magazine studies, one essential for the classroom ("Small Magazines" 689). Literary magazines in the modern period, the so-called "littles," were small in terms of circulation but disproportionately influential in connecting writers with one another and with their evolving audience, and in building reputations that still stand. Pound was particularly interested in the economics of modern magazines. "The significance of any work of art or literature is a root significance that goes down into its original motivation," he writes. "When this motivation is merely a desire for money or publicity, or when this motivation is in great part such a desire for money directly or for publicity as a means indirectly of getting money, there occurs a pervasive monotony in the product corresponding to the underlying monotony in the motivation" (689). For this reason, Pound does not endorse the commercial magazines that defined the American marketplace throughout the modern period (he names as examples *The Atlantic*, *Century*, *Harper's*, and *Scribner's*) as venues where modern writers could place their most challenging works, or where readers might find "serious and consecutive criticism of literature." Indeed, he laments, "They leave a need for intellectual communication unconditioned by considerations as to whether a given idea or given trend in art will 'git ads' from the leading corset company" (690). Yet these periodicals did publish some modernist texts in exchange for a paycheck and may even have been challenged and changed by those texts. Every modernist introduction would benefit from even a cursory comparison between what are now called glossy (advertising-driven) publications and modern little magazines. "Small Magazines" raises issues of modernism and the publishing industry central to studies of modern literature and the marketplace, examined in greatest detail in texts like John X. Cooper's *Modernism and the Culture of Market Society*, Lawrence Rainey's *Institutions of Modernism*, Rod Rosenquist's *Modernism, the Market and the Institution of the New*, and Catherine Turner's *Marketing Modernism Between the Two World Wars*.

"Small Magazines" offers the student of Pound some further guidance through his work with periodicals in the second and third decades of the twentieth century.[3] He begins his history of "the active phase of the small magazine in America" (689) with *Poetry* and the work in Chicago of its editor, Harriet Monroe: "In 1911 Miss Monroe and her backers recognized that verse, to be of any intellectual value, could not be selected merely on the basis of its immediate earning capacity" (691). Monroe had sought him out, and he admired what she was trying to do, eventually becoming her foreign correspondent. He pushed upon her his contemporaries, an act that showed his willingness to make use of the symbolic capital available to him. "She meant to provide a place where unknown poets could be printed; she has done so," he confirms. "Where new ideas and forms could be tried, she has done so. She has provided a meal ticket when the meal ticket was badly needed" (692). He credited Monroe with publishing Richard Aldington, H.D., and Vachel Lindsay and praised "the purity of her intentions" while lamenting the conservatism of her taste (691–92).

Consulting the *Poetry* archive at poetryfoundation.org will help students judge the tenor of the magazine during the war years. The earliest poems about the conflict, like Rupert Brooke's "The Soldier" and Isaac Rosenberg's "Marching," are largely descriptive, and only on occasion do more discursive works like Aldington's "War Yawp" appear in *Poetry*. The archive makes it possible to examine

Pound's more specific complaint that Monroe "mutilated my 'Homage to Sextus Propertius' at a time when I had to take what I could get" ("Small Magazines" 692). Monroe doubted the fidelity of what she understood to be translations, though Pound's use of source material from antiquity is a more complex topic that deserves careful treatment in the classroom.[4] In fact, *Poetry* printed only four of the work's twelve sections, as "Poems from the Propertius Series," and instructors might compare these with the version reprinted in *Personae* (203–04) in order to demonstrate the compromise between modern writers and the magazines that published their work. The vision pursued by a magazine's editor, reflected even in specific changes made to individual works, is itself an authorial impulse that rivals that of a submitting author. An interesting assignment for students is to position the sections from *Poetry*, and pieces later printed in *The New Age*, within the longer poem. What might be the significance in Monroe choosing the first, second, third, and sixth sections? Pound complains, more generally, "Miss Monroe has occasionally mutilated a work by excisions and has occasionally failed to see the unity of a longer work and given it in fragments" (691–92). Most students today experience all manner of work in fragments meant to be understood as representative of something larger. The classroom is an excellent place to compare the impact of fragments with the essence of a completed piece: an opportunity to achieve a far more active learning environment.

Interestingly, Pound attributes his "A Few Don'ts by an Imagiste," widely available online through platforms like *Open Culture* and useful as a framing manifesto, to his editorial work with *Poetry*. "Irritated by the faults of work published in the opening numbers, I compiled a list of the more glaring," he explains. "This was intended to be used as part of the magazine's rejection slip" ("Small Magazines" 691). To understand and to teach this oft-quoted document not simply as a cri de coeur but as some reflection of a publication's editorial approach provides a contrast with the manifestos in Wyndham Lewis's *Blast*, a provocative magazine launched in response to what Pound calls the "disturbed condition" of wartime Europe (695). All editorial manifestos, whether bombastic or modest, should be approached in the classroom as essential to the critical function of modern periodicals. Students should be encouraged to see editorial selections as acts of criticism, of course, but also to consider them in the light of the principles editors claimed to follow. For example, they can be guided to perceive how formal works of critical prose, such as those Pound believed defined the "sober and authoritative" *Dial*, provided the means for modern art to develop a "thorough and less sloppy" mien (697). The classroom is a place where manifestos should be measured for consistency against the creative works that accompanied them.

Beyond Pound's work with *Poetry*, "Small Magazines" concerns itself primarily with his involvement with *The Egoist* and *The Little Review*. The Modernist Journals Project's hundreds of records of Pound's contributions to these titles allow students to assess a range of ideas that animated these magazines during

Pound's involvement (modjourn.org). There is enough material on the site for a class devoted to Pound's writing during World War I, or any unit on what preoccupied the poet while he was at work in London. His work with *The Egoist* (originally called *The New Freewoman*) began with a dedicated page. Soon he placed, for pay, the work of his contemporaries in the rebranded venue that, as he describes it, "took on" those works that other magazines "would not print" (693). It was *The Egoist* that printed sections of Lewis's *Tarr* and James Joyce's *A Portrait of the Artist as a Young Man*. Though periodicals had always serialized longer works, scholars of modern literature point out how the serial form now mirrored the fragmentary and disjointed nature of the urban experience.

Pound also placed longer, challenging pieces in *The Little Review* as foreign editor. "From 1917 to 1919 *The Little Review* printed all that Mr. Wyndham Lewis produced; it printed nearly all that either Mr. Eliot or I produced," Pound explains. "It wrote itself almost immediately into the history of European letters by publishing the opening chapters of *Ulysses*" (695). As even the casual student of Joyce likely knows, the novel's serialization led to the suppression of the magazine after a draft of the "Nausicaa" chapter was printed in 1920. It is likely that the magazine's willingness to flout American obscenity laws made it the object of government attention, and so students might well consider the effect on a reader of any single number. One could look, for example, at the March 1918 issue, which featured, in addition to the "Telemachus" episode from *Ulysses*, a prophetic discussion of state censorship from Pound himself. Might students find in these pages any evidence of an artistic sensibility so provocative as to move the American government to strike against some of its own citizens?

What "Small Magazines" does not capture is the importance of *The New Age* to Pound's work in periodicals. He dismisses this experience, since he sees *The New Age* not as a literary magazine but as a publication "devoted to social and economic causes" (703). Instructors must, of course, make similar distinctions in constructing reading lists; however, what may most clearly disqualify the periodical from consideration as a "little" was its large circulation, such that for a time its commercial success allowed it to pay its contributors. Pound was tireless in seeking to convince editors to compensate everyone who appeared in their pages, and instructors might use his editorial experience as a curator to discuss both the practical and symbolic value of paid contributions in modern literature. As modern writers were keen to have recognized their achievement as professionals, figures that almost always began as outsiders in the publishing industry leveraged their acceptance in magazines to seek publication elsewhere. The financial backers who underwrote some of the periodicals of the age also extended Pound's conception of patronage, just as contributing writers reinforced his appreciation of the customs of the troubadour. While *The New Age* set a standard to which "littles" could only aspire, the proficiency with which it was run influenced Pound over the following two decades.

A fundamental tension in Pound's poetry, the tension between the burnished image that should not, that could not, be altered and those intricate lines that defined his translations and his epics, can also be seen in his work as an editor. He sought talent for the magazines he curated, and he fought for the integrity of contributors' works. But, most famously, in seeking an iteration of *The Waste Land* that was "much improved" from T. S. Eliot's original manuscript, he demonstrated his faith that art could be painstakingly wrought through revision, and this fashioning and refashioning of the artistic work represents the essence of editorial acumen (*Selected Letters* 169). Students can see Pound exploring, fully, each element of the editorial function through his labor on his own short-lived magazine, *Exile*. Reprints of the four numbers are widely available, and the magazine is discussed in articles, chapters, and standard biographies.[5] In "Small Magazines," Pound makes passing reference to *Exile* in the context of a discussion of the *transatlantic review* and *This Quarter*, two journals that were not, or had ceased to be, useful outlets for his work by the mid-1920s. "The first issue of *Exile* was already in the press before I heard of the plans for *transition*," he writes of the most influential expatriate American magazine of the time ("Small Magazines" 701). The truth was that, having long sought a place to publish his work and the work of his friends, he had concluded that he might need to create that place for himself. In this sense, Pound's experience as a literary magazine editor was typical, but it is worth examining with students how one of the most recognized figures in a burgeoning modern literature was still challenged in reaching an audience. He described *Exile* to Joyce at the time as a magazine "designed to deal with various matters not adequately handled elsewhere," one that would "circulate freely to such as will pay for it" (*Selected Letters* 206–07). Pound never imagined distributing more than a thousand copies, and he counts *Exile* among the "fugitive periodicals," journals "of small circulation," "free reviews," "small periodicals," and even "little magazines," employing at the end of the 1920s the words we know to have come to define the field of modern literary publications ("Small Magazines" 701–03).

The difficulties that Pound had in importing his magazine to the United States demonstrate some of the practicalities facing an editor abroad. He discovered, initially, that he could print five hundred copies in Europe for between seventy-five and one hundred dollars. No one in the United States could print *Exile* for less than its cover price of fifty cents a copy. Here, of course, Pound encountered the same financial reality that shaped the editorial policies of the glossy magazines that he so abhorred. The strength of the American dollar abroad presented Pound with an opportunity, but it also brought him into conflict with an American "bureaucratic mindersatz" against which he railed. The essence of the story is told in "Interaction," printed at the back of *Exile* 3, an anecdote that helps instructors bring the story to the classroom. "The Port of New York saw *Exile*," he explains, "found that it was dated 'Spring 1927' instead of 'April 1927' and proclaimed that *Exile* was not a magazine but a 'book.'" Any printed matter not published at least four times a year with a month and frequency of publication displayed on its cover would be subject to a twenty-five-percent tariff. "The tax imposed on 'books' at the American frontier," Pound complains, is "a result of our governing powers, ever desirous of maintaining the present state of national stupidity" (109).

Pound takes the position that "any scrap of creative work" should be published before a "lengthy discussion of what might be but is not" ("The Exile" [vol. 3] 102), yet his creative output for *Exile* was restricted to fragments from cantos 20 and 23. He did, however, print more than seventy pages of his own critical prose, and some of this material has a place in the classroom when discussing Pound's view of the United States. As early as the first number, he asserts that his "editorial program" will be an examination of whether the state can recapture its essence as "convenience" or whether it will persist as "an infernal nuisance" ("The Exile" [vol.1] 89–90). Art maintained an important role in redeeming the United States. "The artist, the maker is always too far ahead of any revolution, or reaction, or counter-revolution or counter-re-action for his vote to have any immediate result," he claims, "and no party program ever contains enough of his program to give him the least satisfaction." In fact, in this moderate view, successful political thinkers follow creative minds that are, largely, dispassionate. "Blessed are they who pick the right artists and makers," Pound concludes. But students are unlikely to judge as dispassionate Pound's view that "America is *the* most colossal monkey house and prize exhibit that the astonished world has yet seen" (91–92). Essays from Pound's magazine at the end of the 1920s can be contrasted for effect with the heightened bluster of similar work through the 1930s, however. "Prolegomena," in *Exile* 2, provides a single-page assessment of an American "tendency to mess into other peoples' affairs before establishing order in one's own affairs, and in one's thought" (35). Pieces like "The Exile" and "Desideria," in *Exile* 3, proceed from the idea that, as modern art provides "the basis for a new poetry, and for a new music," there is hope for "a new civilization." Pound sets out a nineteen-point polemic on the topic ("Desideria" 108). Five shorter pieces at the beginning of *Exile* 4 discuss bureaucracy, conflict between nations, and the future of urban spaces; but the most interesting material may be on ethics, where Pound again makes specific reference to the United States Criminal Code, Section 211, on obscenity, as he had done in *The Little Review* a decade before ("Simplicities," "Bureaucracy," "Peace," "The City," "Article 11").

Pound recognizes that all these projects of "impractical publication" will, in the end, be "measured by the work they have brought to press." He explains that he had hoped *Exile* could serve as a "means of showing publishers where material was to be found." In his assessment, commercial enterprises "have been content and are still more than content to take derivative products ten or twenty years after the germ has appeared in the free magazines" ("Small Magazines" 701–02). Pound places "works of art" and "classics" with "scientific discoveries" as "permanent goods," and literary magazines had for him the responsibility in the modern period to pursue art in the absence of a profit motive ("The Exile" [vol. 1] 90–91). It is hard to argue that *Exile* raised from obscurity unknown writers or brought forward the most challenging works of writers who had found a tentative audience, but students can judge whether Pound created in his four numbers the "interesting line-up" he promised readers ("The Exile" [vol. 1] 88). To accomplish this task, all four numbers should be read as stand-alone texts and then considered together. There are significant pieces from Robert McAlmon, William Carlos Williams, and W. B. Yeats. Pound promotes Ralph Cheever Dunning and Howard Weeks, largely forgotten today. There is a story from the Canadian author Morley Callaghan, at the very beginning of his career, as well as early contributions from Carl Rakosi and Louis Zukofsky. But Pound shows an unwillingness to compromise in his search for ideal submissions. "Anybody attempting to contribute to this periodical ought to know at least two languages," he proclaims in a "Notice to Contributors" in the second number. "If intending collaborators do not already know French, I suggest that they learn it first and submit manuscript after they have" (121). The longest piece, by John Rodker, is judged "a definite contribution to letters" by the editor ("The Exile" [vol. 1] 88). Ultimately, these pieces speak to the heterogeneity of modernism as much as to any editorial program that defines *Exile*.

Pound concludes "Small Magazines" by acknowledging these publications' place in the emerging history of modern literature, reflecting on an evolving canon in a manner still relevant to a discussion of modernism today. "There are plenty of people over forty who are willing to acknowledge that Mr. Joyce, Mr. Eliot, and the rest [of their contemporaries] appeared (past tense) ten or fifteen years ago in small and allegedly eccentric magazines," he asserts. But he chides those same readers for refusing to entertain the possibility that there are "writers who will, in ten or fifteen years, hold analogous positions in the world of letters" and who were at that time "appearing in magazines as apparently tawdry and freakish" (704). That Pound's *Exile* was a commercial catastrophe is obvious; the American publisher Pascal Covici abandoned their collaboration, and the magazine failed even to pay its contributors. But Pound's experience in promoting his work and the works of others in marginal venues through the end of the 1920s provides for the classroom a context that brings alive the best scholarly treatments of little magazines: Suzanne W. Churchill and Adam McKible's *Little Magazines and Modernism*, Mark Morrisson's *The Public Face of Modernism*, and Eric B. White's *Transatlantic Avant-Gardes*. Pound's story is central to them all, and while it is true that one cannot teach Pound without teaching magazines, it is also true that Pound is the modern figure whose experience best illustrates periodical culture in the twentieth century.

NOTES

[1] Ezra Pound is central to *Modernism in the Magazines*. Besides developing from Pound a methodology for the scholarly reading of magazines, outlined in the eight-thousand-word chapter titled "Ezra Pound, Founder of Modern Periodical Studies" (1–25) Scholes and Wulfman make frequent reference to him throughout the text. Its appendix, "Studies in Contemporary Mentality, Ezra Pound" (223–326), reprints twenty articles

Pound printed in *The New Age* in 1917 and 1918. It is an obvious textbook choice for anyone teaching methodology in a senior-level or graduate class on modern literary magazines.

[2] Launched in 1995 at Brown University, the Modernist Journals Project, which provides access to this essay, has at the time of writing digitized complete runs of more than two dozen periodicals. Its instructional wiki, including "How to Read a Magazine," complements the primary material housed at modjourn.org.

[3] Among the most relevant collections is *Pound* / The Little Review*: The Letters of Ezra Pound to Margaret Anderson*, edited by Thomas L. Scott and colleagues. Many other volumes of Pound's correspondence include letters relevant to his work with magazines. Instructors should check indexes for periodical titles and for the names of many well-known magazine editors from the period.

[4] See essays by Ryan-Bryant, Qian, and Preston in this volume.

[5] Pound's accounts in "Small Magazines" must be supplemented with readings of his correspondence with various editors, reprinted in the many letters collections in wide circulation. See essays by Barry S. Alpert, Andrzej Gaşiorek, and Craig Monk for fair-use excerpts from relevant letters and other documents that provide details as to how Pound established the journal, including the financial considerations, and the principles by which he sought to edit it. Most noteworthy may be his steadfast determination not to publish women at a time when women editors and writers were animating literary magazines in Europe and the United States.

"Poundian Ambition on the Semester System": Pound, the Avant-Garde, and the Academy

Alan Golding

My title phrase comes from a recent essay by the contemporary poet Jennifer Moxley in which she lays out what she calls her poetic conversion narrative, leading from powerful readings in poetics that "justified" the literary and pedagogical ambition she defines "on a Poundian scale" to the realization that "Poundian-scale ambition is unrealistic on the semester system" (200). Within that system, then, she looks for ways to preserve and transmit "the spirit of Poundian ambition": "the quest and the independence of mind, with a slight touch of mentoring" (203). In what follows, I consider how various post–World War II experimental poets—and one unique college—have taken up exactly the challenge faced by Moxley, a challenge that Pound himself implicitly (and often explicitly) posed to the academy: how to extend the spirit of Poundian ambition in pedagogic contexts that Pound consistently both derided and sought to affect? Here is Peter Nicholls, in a useful statement of what I've taken as a basic premise of my own reading and teaching of Pound in the last few years:

> For Pound, . . . the genuine poet is by definition in advance of his weaker contemporaries and derives his pedagogical legitimacy directly from his avant-gardism. Yet it is this avant-gardism that also makes him inimitable, remote from that mimetic relation of social reciprocity and identification in which learning in modern societies finds its usual ground.
>
> ("'You'" 148)

This statement captures nicely a central contradiction within Pound's writing, where the rhetoric of avant-gardism is often complexly entangled with his vision of the university. In *ABC of Reading*, for instance, the outstanding student becomes an avant-garde artist in relation to the class, as the teacher is advised "to use the lively pupil for scout work, to exploit the quicker eye or subtler ear as look-out or listening post" (85).

In recent years, Pound scholars have paid renewed attention to the pedagogical impulse in Pound's work across a range of genres: poetry, criticism, cultural theory, letters.[1] One way to teach Pound—that, I propose, gets to the heart of his significance for later avant-garde poets—is to teach Pound as a kind of teacher, and certainly as a lifelong thinker about teaching and the academy. Therefore, I want to look at the impact of Pound's thinking about pedagogy and his modeling of a pedagogical poetics in three areas of post–World War II poetry and education: the poet-edited textbook-anthology; the work of some recent poet-critics who have explicitly engaged with Pound's didacticism and difficulty in their own thinking about the links between an avant-garde poetics and pedagogy;

and institutional models for enacting a Poundian pedagogy. Why is so-called avant-garde poetics specifically at issue? I am writing against the backdrop of longstanding historical assumptions that would set ideas of the avant-garde and the academy at odds. Against that background, Pound becomes a central figure for complicating this opposition—right around the time of F. T. Marinetti's famous call to "destroy the museums, libraries, academies of every kind" (50), Pound was proposing a college of avant-garde artists—and for thinking about how it has played out over the last hundred years.

Part of teaching Pound, as with most earlier authors, involves thinking about and teaching his place in, and influence on, the present, and that place is not likely to be uncontested. A dynamics of simultaneous appreciation, use, and critique will recur throughout my examples. First, I'll focus on the poet-editor Jerome Rothenberg's anthologies as pedagogical texts organized on Poundian principles, as gatherings that extend into a different context the polyvocality, range of cultural reference, and structural innovations of *The Cantos* that Pound's own more authoritarian pronouncements tend to undermine. Rothenberg's anthologies can be seen, in various ways, as Poundian poems in the form of textbooks that simultaneously honor and resist the implications of Pound's own example as a teacher. Of particular relevance here is Rothenberg and Pierre Joris's popular and widely adopted two-volume classroom anthology of international twentieth-century avant-garde poetries, *Poems for the Millennium*.[2] Second, I examine some poems by Bob Perelman and Rachel Blau DuPlessis, written from their positions as poet-critics and commentators on pedagogy who respond actively to Pound's ideas on teaching and learning in their poetry and criticism while—as with Rothenberg and his anthologies—deviating from those ideas. Deformation of a Poundian poetic and pedagogical model that cannot be unambivalently embraced or dismissed is central to these poets.[3] And third—moving from texts to institutions—I consider Black Mountain College as the embodiment of Pound's 1914 call for a college of arts made up of teacher-practitioners ("Preliminary Announcement"). The example of Black Mountain (where Pound was a central and revered figure among the writers) allows us to consider the risks, rewards, limitations, and challenges of a teaching institution dedicated both to making it new across the arts—an academy of the avant-garde—and to another central Poundian value, what Steven Yao and Michael Coyle call "education in the shape of conversations among people who come to know one another personally" (xii).

Marjorie Perloff commented some years ago on the Poundian poetics of the many anthologies that Jerome Rothenberg has produced in his career—in particular *America a Prophecy*—noting their organization as Poundian collages, as gatherings modeled on *The Cantos* (*Poetic License* 139–44). Charles Bernstein picks up on this connection in his own discussion of *America a Prophecy* and observes more generally of Rothenberg's anthologies how "the open form of 'collecting'—creating a music of contrasting parts—is clearly an outgrowth of Poundian compositional strategies" (162). I want to add to this discussion some consideration of the typical Rothenberg anthology in a teaching context. Regarded in that light, his method constitutes an intervention into pedagogy shaped by the principles both of *The Cantos* and of *ABC of Reading*, inviting us to teach Pound as a central influence not just on later avant-garde poetic practice but also on the forms of its cultural, including classroom, transmission.

Conceiving textbook organization as an act of poiesis, Rothenberg designs an anthology as a particular kind of poem—as "a composition & collage" (*Big Jewish Book* xl) or "a grand assemblage: a kind of art form in its own right" (*Poetics* 15). Along similar lines, Rothenberg describes *Poems for the Millennium* as less an anthology (though presumably he knew from the beginning that it would be received as one) and more an "*assemblage* or pulling together of poems and people and ideas about poetry (and much else) in the words of others and in our own words," like those cantos that are closer to an anthology than any other modernist long poem—the anthology, then, as "epic poem replete with histories and voices" (17). In remarks like these, Rothenberg provides some terms in which to think about his anthologies' construction. As forms in themselves, these anthologies are designed to counter any readings conducted in terms of canonizing judgments. Indeed, one telling contrast here would be with Pound's editorial practices: whereas Pound uses juxtaposition to make evaluative distinctions among texts, Rothenberg uses it to suggest previously unseen connections. Even though his anthologies follow a Poundian structural model, that model is used to non-Poundian ends as a way of broadening rather than narrowing the curriculum—a fruitful complication for students, who come to see that Pound's more authoritative assertions can be resisted while his forms and methods can be usefully adapted and adopted.

Both editors of *Poems for the Millennium* are acutely aware of the unavoidable central contradiction of the avant-garde anthology, which gathers anti-institutional cultural production in an institutional form and aspires to use one part of the literary academic system (the publishing of anthologies) against itself. At the same time, a gathering like *Poems for the Millennium* rests on the premise that the anthology in our own time can represent an institutional frame susceptible to useful intervention. It can be a medium of intellectual change as much as one of routinization, although to function as such the form itself needs to be challenged in some of the ways that Rothenberg and Joris indeed do. As Rothenberg says in a December 1995 forum on *Poems for the Millennium*, "[P]art of the pleasure of the book is for the first time being able to bring [previously excluded work] into the body of a purported University anthology, book of etc. etc." He goes on, "[T]here was a real excitement . . . in having captured that frame [of the institutionally sanctioned anthology] & then being able to use it towards the ends for which it should long ago have been used. But I had that feeling with anthologies from the start." Indeed, he describes the sections of commentary that occur mid-text in his anthologies going back to the 1968 *Technicians of the Sacred* as "typical paraphernalia of scholarly anthologies, which I could here bend to my uses" (*Pre-Faces* 4).

Rothenberg and Joris, then, "attempt to make visible the kind of anthology that poets of whatever stripe have always carried as part of their mental and spiritual equipment" rather than to produce "a textbook primarily for academic consumption" (*Poems* 2:19). Despite the claim not to have been created as a textbook, however, *Poems for the Millennium* is the anthology of Rothenberg's that most seems to announce itself—albeit tongue-in-cheek—as one, in its subtitle: *The University of California Book of Modern & Postmodern Poetry*. And due to the visibility, academic clout, and distributing power of its publisher, it has had the best chance of any of Rothenberg's anthologies to make an immediate canonical difference, counter to its own editors' stated resistance to canon-making. If the editors don't quite share Pound's ambition to reform literary education, they do aspire to remake one tool of that education. Rothenberg describes all his anthologies as "a *détournement* (a turning or a twist) on the structures and presumptions of those fixed anthologies that continue (like the darkness) to surround us," and continues in a more specific vein, "In *Poems for the Millennium* such détournements extend to the overblown subtitle . . . , the board of advisers (largely themselves experimental poets), the quasi-scholarly commentaries, and the various other accoutrements and paraphernalia of the *official* book" (*Poetics* 16). Even anthologies of linguistically innovative American or British poetry—gathering work that reassesses the boundaries and assumptions of genre in every way imaginable—commonly do not rethink the nature and form of the anthology itself. One signal part of Rothenberg and Joris's achievement is that, with Pound's collage poetics as a model, they do so.

Rothenberg's use of Poundian poetics to rethink the anthology genre represents one aspect of what Nicholls describes as "a third phase of [*The Cantos*'] reception . . . in which readers do indeed begin to occupy a position in relation to the work other than the one to which Pound wanted to assign them," a phase in which "readers suddenly felt less willing to be led by Pound" ("'You'" 151, 150). In a different form of dual honoring and resistance, Perelman and DuPlessis have persistently tested in their poetry the uneasy boundaries between avant-garde poetics, pedagogical forms and rhetorics, and academic convention, and in those testings Pound has been a constant presence. Perelman's "Homage to Pound's *Propertius*" is a more nimbly titled revision of his previously published "Guide to *Homage to Sextus Propertius*." The revision, while perhaps losing a layer of irony in editing out the idea of a guide on top of an homage, adds seventeen endnotes and a list of works cited, befitting publication in an academic volume.[4] Perelman begins, "[N]ow if ever it is time to translate modernism into a contemporary idiom" ("Homage" 225). He engages in what he calls (in a note) a "respectful detournment [sic]" of Pound's "now if ever it is time to cleanse Helicon" as he updates Poundian modernism while also treating it with appropriate skepticism (233). Placing Pound in dialogue with the very avant-garde project with which he himself has been associated, however, Perelman unironically states that he is "buying Pound's sense of a live tradition as a poetic proposition," "the usable, venerable good writing, the stuff that STAYS news" (233). Is Perelman embracing what he calls elsewhere the "great conservatism" encoded in Pound's definition of literature as "news that stays news" ("This Just In")? Hardly. He lays out his attitudes toward Pound quite explicitly ("I'm celebrating Pound the secular, civic love poet") while "saying no thanks to Pound's gods, both pagan and fascist" and to his "panoply of estranging *mots justes*" ("Homage" 233). Identifying with Pound's "assiduous courting / of cultural importance" (233–34), Perelman anticipates Moxley on the continuing appeal for the contemporary poet of "Poundian-scale ambition." The site of that ambition? "'Propertius' is his most extended stretch / of consecutively phrased poetry in [English]"—hardly the terms of praise one would expect from someone associated with the extreme disjunctiveness of much language writing (234). Meanwhile, all of the above is accomplished in the academic convention of the explanatory endnote. Perelman talks back to his predecessor in the institutional form and language that Pound's work seems to invite and that he would also have likely considered a pedantic excrescence.

Perelman's "My Pound Decoder Ring," on the other hand, is a deliberately disrespectful détournement of the "[p]aradis n'est pas artificiel" passage of canto 92 (*Cantos* 640), and one that again takes teaching institutions as part of the ground for its response to Pound. The poem rewrites that well-known passage by, in Perelman's explanation, "copy[ing] the movement of the lines and phrase rhythms closely while detourning the sad obnoxiousness of Pound's ridiculous certainties" ("This Just In"). This reworking replaces the imperial male (Pound's "that was in Caesar's time") with the lesbian avant-gardist ("that was in the Stein Era," pointedly *not* Hugh Kenner's "Pound Era"), and replaces Pound's phobic association of homosexuality and economic malfeasance ("who was buggar'd / and the coin ceased to be holy") with a celebratory association of lesbian sexuality and alternative meaning-making ("who had great sex / and new sense started making sense"). The valorizing of "new sense" partly inaugurated by Pound's characteristic sudden shifts (the poem repeats Pound's well-known nontransition "so that") nevertheless takes place in a world of "meter readers," "manuals," and "institutes" ("institutionalization" in an earlier draft of the poem). Furthermore, the momentary celebration of Stein, rather than Pound, as making it new is immediately modified by the assimilation of "new sense" into the educational bureaucracy: "but, of course, / they re-ordered the anthologies" (107). Stein's addition to the anthologies reorders them modestly; but the textbook's basic framework is preserved, and "new sense" will show up on the bookstore's shelves for next semester's courses. Working through these issues, students require little encouragement to understand the repackaging of the avant-garde tradition that Pound helped inaugurate in terms of what they already know, from their own experience, about the co-opting of independent music or outsider art. As the speaker of DuPlessis's "Draft 57: Workplace: Nekuia," the poet-theorist fully attuned to the academic jargon of recent decades, says in mock amazement, "And still no damage yet / to the symbolic order?" (*Drafts* 189).

Like Perelman's, DuPlessis's contestation with Pound's example in her recently completed serial poem *Drafts*—itself one of the most ambitious of contemporary writing projects, and one that "explicitly positions itself as not-*Cantos*"—takes place, among other sites, on the grounds of the institutional and the pedagogical (*Blue Studios* 278n9).[5] Thus in "Draft 57: Workplace: Nekuia," the instructive epic descent into the underworld does not reach the "fosse" of Pound's canto 1 (*Cantos* 3) and of DuPlessis's own "Draft XXX: Fosse"; rather, it is associated with that most mundane of sites, the poet-academic's office: "This is the place I work, / *This is the workspot, the office.*" If it is, punningly, "*a sacred office, scared and / or scarred*"—with the sometimes uneasy relation between poet and scholar perhaps reflected in that between the italics and Roman typeface—one still has to walk in every day and "turn on the work-processor" (*Drafts* 188). This is a poetry openly engaged with Pound, that asks (tongue in cheek) for Tiresias or Virgil or a *Guide to Kulchur*—"Was there a guide"—and that clearly echoes canto 45:

> With profit, with profit,
> even the babies
> cannot crawl or suck
> unscathed. The suture occurs
> on the level of cell, in interiority, so that: (189)

It is a poetry "that speaks in (and for) the convergence of quirks" via Poundian "statement, counter-statement, and huge sections / that don't settle anywhere" (194).[6]

Starting with its title, however, *Drafts* distances itself from the confident didacticism that can mark Pound's approach to knowing. Both more self-reflexive and more intellectually exploratory than *The Cantos*, in "Draft 57" "the project finding itself out / is itself," asking itself (and ventriloquizing the often baffled student-reader of the high modernist epic), "*why not simplify this / what will these intricate layers achieve*?" (188). Pound's intertextuality has fueled an academic industry, and *The Cantos* continue to generate scholarly annotation projects; as if to respect his complexity while tweaking the source-hunting that his range of reference invites, DuPlessis's intertexts appear in the scholarly format of the footnote.[7] If *The Cantos* aspire to the totalizing of the Wagnerian *Gesamtkunstwerk*, *Drafts* is its neologistic opposite, a "'*Gesamtnichtwerk*'" of "wavering overtones," "never whole," "imperfectly fluent" (193–94). In "Draft XXX: Fosse," another explicit "not-*Canto*," we are asked to "imagine a reader, who would resist / and not resist," "resist / and still articulate" (*Drafts 1–38, Toll* 189) a far less forceful pedagogy than that offered by the poet whom T. S. Eliot, in the dedication to *The Waste Land*, called *il miglior fabbro*, the better craftsman: "the instruction it offers / is delicate, maybe misplaced." The "it" here refers to a "little book" that is not the little book of Pound's "Envoi" but an Ann Hamilton artist's book "whose words are covered / one by one / with the smallest pebbles" (187)—metonyms for the shards out of which DuPlessis, honoring Pound, constructs her demystifying text, not in the spirit of following "foundational commandment" "but just in the course of things / casting oneself to the same winds" (192).

Both Perelman and DuPlessis enact in these examples the often fraught relationship between disruptive experimental formal commitments and the stability of institutional affiliation. If pedagogical or institutional forms (like the anthology), diction, and conventions are one site of contemporary experimental poetic engagement with Pound, and thus one site of teaching Pound's importance for that poetry, David Moody invokes a literal institution when he suggests that with his call for a college of arts Pound "might have been calling in general for the Black Mountain experiment" (*Young Genius* 132). To develop this view of Black Mountain College as an institution built on Poundian principles, I'll turn to the call to which Moody refers, Pound's 1912 proposal in *Patria Mia* for a "super-college" of artists: "a hundred men, in New York or Chicago, kept to work at painting, sculpture, architecture, musical composition and all branches of literature," who would be selected by other artists, funded out of an endowment, and who would constitute "a reasonable beginning" toward some kind of American cultural renaissance (139). In this super-college "there should be no sort of formal instruction" and thus "no danger of an academic standard being fostered by such a system" (139–40). Informal instruction would happen through the interaction of artists working in different media and would also involve "foreign artists, the important ones"—Poundian "discoverers"—being invited to "loaf about and converse with such of the younger men as should prove sufficiently intelligent to be conversed with." "This sort of college . . . would make some sort of a centre," Pound argued (139)—and while Black Mountain aspired less to the status of a center and more to the status of aggressively marginal opposition to such a notion, many of its basic teaching practices fit this earlier Poundian ideal.

A more fully articulated and institutionalized version of this utopian vision appears in Pound's "Preliminary Announcement of the College of Arts," published anonymously in *The Egoist* for 2 November 1914. (The term *utopian* is literally appropriate here, for an institution that did not and never would exist.) To "American students" seeking to study the arts abroad, "The College of Arts offers a temporary refuge and a permanent centre" (413). In particular, it offers an alternative to the pedagogical models of "instruction by private teachers," unpredictable in its quality, and "that of 'institutions' for the most part academic, sterile, professorial" (413). As Black Mountain and MFA programs would in different ways come to do, this alternative arts-centered academy would offer courses variously designed for aspiring artists "who desire practical and technical instruction" and for "serious art students and for the better sort of dilettanti." The source of this alternative pedagogy is to be the London avant-garde circa 1914: "Painting and sculpture are taught by the most advanced and brilliant men of our decade," Pound's code for Wyndham Lewis and Gaudier-Brzeska, while in the department of "Letters," "Comparative Poetry" would be offered by one "Ezra Pound, MA." This unaccredited institution with its arts-centered curriculum taught by cutting-edge contemporary practitioners, where "the cost of instruction will [vary] . . . depending on how much the student wishes to do himself and how much he wishes to have done for him," is a clear precursor of the Black Mountain experiment, not least in its ambition. If Charles Olson, Black Mountain's influential poet-rector in the 1950s, would not have used Pound's language, he shared his hardly modest goals: "We aim at an intellectual status no lower than that attained by the courts of the Italian Renaissance," Pound claimed (414). Pound idealizes "the individual city" of the Italian Renaissance as a cultural vortex ("Paris Letter" 192); Black Mountain might be thought of metaphorically as such a city, as, indeed, Olson obliquely presents it in his 1950 poem "The Praises."[8]

It would be hard to argue that Pound directly influenced the formation of an institution like Black Mountain, but in his thinking about education he can surely be said to have anticipated it, and his work was central to the literary instruction there. Gail McDonald comments on Black Mountain as a Poundian institution in her foundational study *Learning to Be Modern*, laying out a number of principles shared by Pound and by John Dewey, whose educational progressivism did demonstrably influence Black Mountain: the spirit of optimistic reform, education through the cultivation of each individual's intellectual appetites, education as nonvocational preparation for living or usable knowledge, an emphasis on "the forces of invention and concrete particulars" (130). On the question of the best kind of teaching, of course, Pound was hardly consistent. Sometimes he would privilege method over content, as in the famous example of Louis Agassiz and the fish.[9] Sometimes he would privilege content over method: "[P]edagogy has often fussed about how to get ideas to the student, long before it had anything substantial or useful to transmit" (*Letters to Ibbotson* 93). Sometimes he seems to hold the student as passive receptacle for teacherly wisdom (his own), while elsewhere he will offer an early counter to what Paulo Freire came to call the banking concept of education: "I always wonder . . . when the mind of the student is to be recognized as, at least potentially, dynamic, and not solely as a receptacle" (*Selected Letters* 61). This respect for the distinctive individual was central to Black Mountain pedagogy, even if it sometimes reached the point of overindulgence, and can be inspiring to students who walk into a classroom dulled by the routinization that marks most aspects of their educational experience.

The post-Poundian challenge that Black Mountain took on was to honor the claims both of radical individualism and of community. As Andrew John Miller puts it, Pound's utopian supercollege would be "a place of leisured neutrality in which artistic minds could meet without forming a community in any of the usual senses of the term"—a collection of individuals, then, pursuing their own work but not necessarily engaged in a shared project (89). With a student and faculty body as geographically isolated, small, and financially strapped as Black Mountain, however, commitment to the community—often fraught and ambivalent, admittedly—was a matter of survival. And yet, like Pound, most people at Black Mountain would have agreed, and had already learned, that—to quote *Patria*

Mia, written long before the proliferation of MFA programs—"universities [make] no provision whatever for the fostering of the creative energies" (132).

In thinking about Pound's relevance for our understanding of avant-garde poetics and pedagogy, it's salutary to recall that we still find poets openly turning away from Pound as a viable teacher, model, or influence. When Evie Shockley notes the often competing investments that creative writers and critics have in different poetic canons, Pound belongs with the scholars: "Distinct interests and priorities lead creative writers to embrace a poetic canon that at times prominently celebrates figures that scholars would deem 'minor' (Stanley Kunitz, for instance) while giving respect but little attention to poets whose work commands 'major' bodies of scholarship (say, Pound)." David Biespiel finds Pound's poetry increasingly archaic-sounding and irrelevant, to the point where he actually seems to consider Pound hardly a poet: "[T]here are influencers and there are poets. Pound is the former." Biespiel concludes his critique with what are, by the final paragraph, rhetorical questions: "Should today's poets be looking to Pound for their influence? Should our professional poetry teachers be using him to teach our emerging poets? Well, look where you must," he sniffs.

In both these examples, teaching and learning become the site for arguing over Pound's corpus, and corpse. And yet, thinking about the future of the humanities, as Pound was always doing, Jeffrey Nealon couches intellectual innovation in terms of Poundian parataxis: "Innovation these days consists of putting existing things together in stark and productive 'new' ways; and the humanities are (or should be) a key laboratory for such a transformed practice of innovation" (194). Nealon argues that theorists should scale back any grand delusions of social radicalism in favor of a more localized and material cultural diagnosis—what Pound called "the art of diagnosis and the art of cure" ("The Serious Artist" 45).

My argument here invites a classroom focus on the method and ambition of Pound's writing more than on content or theme: on how it works rather than what it means (a fictional binary, of course, theoretically untenable but pedagogically convenient). To think about *The Cantos* in relation to Rothenberg's anthologies, for instance, is to invite students to consider the form as well as the content of literary history—literary history as a set of provocatively instructive juxtapositions rather than as a narrative of established judgments, as a formal structure richly embodied in Rothenberg's texts in a way that it is not in the chronological organization of standard classroom anthologies and modeled by that quintessential anthology, *The Cantos*. This literary history is also *lived*, in the writing of later experimental poets who, at a later moment in that history, necessarily read Pound partly through institutional lenses and rhetorics that his work itself both provoked and still productively engages. In turn, this argument also involves a way of teaching Pound—one I've used often myself, in courses on avant-garde poetics and pedagogy and on Black Mountain—that foregrounds him not just as poet and critic but also as cultural and educational theorist: a role that he himself considered central to his literary project (his "ambition").

From Pound to Dewey to Black Mountain to the early years of the SUNY Buffalo Poetics Program, we can trace a lineage of thinking about avant-garde poetics and pedagogy that becomes a way of teaching Pound as teacher, or at least as thinker about education. Thus, teaching Pound includes teaching him as avant-garde pedagogue, as the poet of the twentieth century in whose work all the subsequent tensions and ironies of the relation between the academy and experimental writing are fully played out. Testifying to the force for a young poet of Pound's example and ambition in *Guide to Kulchur*, Perelman enlists a revealing institutional metaphor: "It offered a glimpse of the Ezuversity, where learning is anti-systematic and energizing and knowledge is instantaneous recognition. I enrolled immediately" (*Modernism* 92).

NOTES

[1]See McDonald, *Learning*; Yao and Coyle; Golding, "From Pound to Olson"; and Matthew Hofer, "Education."

[2]I refer here specifically to the first two volumes of *Poems for the Millennium*, those devoted to international modern and postmodern poetry (1995 and 1998).

[3]While direct poetic influence is not precisely my subject in this essay, I should acknowledge the major study of Pound's influence on post–World War II experimental poetry in the United States: Christopher Beach, *ABC of Influence: Ezra Pound and the Remaking of American Poetic Tradition*. See also Marjorie Perloff, "The Contemporary of our Grandchildren: Ezra Pound and the Question of Influence"; and, for an emphasis (not exclusive) on British poetry, *News from Afar: Ezra Pound and Some Contemporary British Poetries*, edited by Richard Parker.

[4]The poem also appears, in a somewhat different form, as chapter 5 of Perelman's *Modernism the Morning After* (pp. 47–52), where the title is printed as "Homage to Pound's 'Propertius,'" the (modified) endnotes (now framed as notes to chapter 5) do not appear until the end of the book, and the works cited are folded into the overall works-cited list for the volume.

[5]For a more extensive discussion of DuPlessis's relationship to Pound, see my "Drafts and Fragments: Rachel Blau DuPlessis's (Counter-) Poundian Project" and Perelman, *Modernism* (53–68).

[6]In DuPlessis's use of "quirks," I hear the "quirks and tweaks" that Pound claims for the modernist epic in his draft version of canto 1. See Pound, "Three Cantos" 113–21.

[7]*Drafts* features voluminous endnotes throughout, an aspect of the work's form and rhetoric too layered to discuss here. It is hardly accidental, however, that the "not-*Canto*" "Draft 57" is one of only two poems to feature footnotes.

[8]For a discussion of "The Praises" along these lines, see Golding, "From Pound to Olson," 199–200.

[9]Pound begins chapter 1 of *ABC of Reading* with an anecdote in which the biologist Louis Agassiz obliges a graduate student to produce ever-more-nuanced descriptions of a decomposing fish over a period of weeks. Pound's pedagogical point: "The proper METHOD for studying poetry and good letters is the method of contemporary biologists, that is careful first-hand examination of the matter" (17).

NOTES ON CONTRIBUTORS

Stephen J. Adams is emeritus professor of American and modernist literature at Western University. His research interests over his four-decade career have been related, in one way or another, to Ezra Pound and music. He is coeditor of *The Ezra Pound Encyclopedia*, has written extensively on prosody and metrical theory, including the guidebook *Poetic Designs* (1997), and is the author of *R. Murray Schafer*, a book on the Canadian composer (1983). His most recent publication is an extensive study of the American ode: *The Patriot Poets: American Odes, Progress Poems, and the State of the Union* (2018).

Anderson D. Araujo is associate professor of English at the University of British Columbia, Okanagan. In 2014, he received the Faculty of Creative and Critical Studies Teaching Innovation Award. His *A Companion to Ezra Pound's Guide to Kulchur* (2018) has appeared jointly with Clemson University Press and Liverpool University Press.

Rebecca Beasley is associate professor of English at the University of Oxford and tutorial fellow, The Queen's College. She is the author of *Ezra Pound and the Visual Culture of Modernism* (2007), *Theorists of Modernist Poetry: Ezra Pound, T. S. Eliot, and T. E. Hulme* (2007), and *Russomania: Russian Culture and the Creation of British Modernism, 1881–1922* (2020). She has coedited *Russia in Britain: From Melodrama to Modernism* (2013).

Leonard Diepeveen is the George Munro Professor of Literature and Rhetoric at Dalhousie University. He is the author of *The Difficulties of Modernism* (2003), *Mock Modernism: An Anthology of Parodies, Travesties, Frauds, 1910–1935* (2014), and *Modernist Fraud: Hoax, Parody, Deception* (2019). As well, he is coauthor of *Artworld Prestige: Arguing Cultural Value* (2013). His edition of *Tender Buttons* (with a host of contextual materials) was published by Broadview Press in 2017.

Sara Dunton received her PhD in 2016 from the University of New Brunswick, where she serves as an honorary research associate in the Department of English and Creative Writing. Her doctoral dissertation, *H.D.'s Ways of Seeing: Encountering Artworks and Practising Ekphrasis in Pursuit of the "Art-Dimension,"* focuses on H.D.'s prose works. She has published articles in *Paideuma* (2013), *H.D. and Modernity* (2014), and in *Make It New* (2017 and 2018).

John Gery is research professor of English at the University of New Orleans and director of the Ezra Pound Center for Literature (EPCL), Brunnenburg, Italy. Since 2005 he has served as secretary of the Ezra Pound International Conference. He is also series editor for the EPCL Book Series at Clemson University Press. The author of twenty essays on Pound's work, he has coedited two collections of criticism and published seven collections of poetry, most recently *Have at You Now!* (2014).

Alan Golding teaches poetry and poetics at the University of Louisville and has directed the Louisville Conference on Literature and Culture since 1990. He is the author of *From Outlaw to Classic: Canons in American Poetry* (1995) and of numerous essays on modernist and contemporary poetry and literary institutions. With Lynn Keller and Dee Morris, he coedits the University of Iowa Contemporary North American Poetry Series.

J. Matthew Huculak is digital scholarship librarian at the University of Victoria Libraries. He holds a PhD in English Language and Literature and an MLIS with a concentration on archives and preservation. He is the director of the Modernist Versions Project and managing editor of *Modernism/Modernity*'s open access Print Plus platform. He served as project manager for the Modernist Journals Project at the University of Tulsa (2004–2006). You can follow his work at orcid.org.

Alec Marsh is professor of English at Muhlenberg College. He is the author of *Money and Modernity: Pound, Williams, and the Spirit of Jefferson* (1999) as well as *Ezra Pound: A Critical Life* (2011) and *John Kasper and Ezra Pound: Saving the Republic* (2015).

Susan McCabe is professor of literature and creative writing at the University of Southern California. Her books include *Elizabeth Bishop: Her Poetics of Loss* (1994), *Swirl* (2003), *Cinematic Modernism* (2005), and *Descartes' Nightmare* (2008). She is currently finishing a book on H.D. and Bryher, *A Modernist Love Story*, for Oxford University Press.

Craig Monk is provost and vice-president, academic, at MacEwan University in Edmonton, Alberta. He is the author of *Writing the Lost Generation: Expatriate Autobiography and American Modernism* (2008). His work on interwar print culture is supported by a grant from the Social Sciences and Humanities Research Council of Canada.

Jennifer Moxley is professor of poetry and poetics at the University of Maine. She is the author of six books of poetry, most recently *The Open Secret* (2014), winner of the Poetry Society of America's William Carlos Williams award, and a finalist for the Kingsley Tufts Poetry Prize. She has also published a book of essays, a memoir, and three translations from the French. In 2005 she was granted the Lynda Hull Poetry Award from *Denver Quarterly*. Robert Creeley included her poem "Behind the Orbits" in *The Best American Poetry 2002*.

Ira B. Nadel, professor of English at the University of British Columbia, has published biographies of Leonard Cohen, Tom Stoppard, Ezra Pound, David Mamet, and Leon Uris. He has also edited *The Cambridge Companion to Ezra Pound* (1999) and *Ezra Pound in Context* (2010). Two recent critical works are *Modernism's Second Act* (2013) and *Cathay, Ezra Pound's Orient* (2015). He is currently completing a critical life of Philip Roth.

Peter Nicholls is Henry James Professor of English and American Letters at New York University. His publications include *Ezra Pound: Politics, Economics and Writing* (1984); *Modernisms: A Literary Guide* (1995); *George Oppen and the Fate of Modernism* (2007)—as well as many articles and essays on literature and theory. He has coedited a number of volumes, including *The Cambridge History of Twentieth-Century English Literature* (2004), *Ruskin and Modernism* (2001), *On Bathos: Literature, Art, Music* (2012), and *How Abstract Is It? Thinking Capital Now* (2016). He is currently United States associate editor of *Textual Practice*.

Carrie J. Preston is the Arvind and Chandan Nandlal Kilachand Professor and director of Kilachand Honors College and associate professor in English and women's, gender, and sexuality studies at Boston University. Her most recent book, *Learning to Kneel: Noh, Modernism, and Journeys in Teaching* (2016), was a finalist for the Modernist Studies Association Book Prize.

Zhaoming Qian is the Qiantang Professor of Comparative Literature at Hangzhou Normal University and the Chancellor's Research Professor emeritus at the University of New Orleans. He is the author and editor of many books, including *The Modernist Response to Chinese Art: Pound, Moore, Stevens* (2003) and *East-West Exchange and Late Modernism: Williams, Moore, Pound* (2017). His research has been supported by fellowships from the National Endowment for the Humanities, the American Philosophical Society, and the Chinese Academy of Social Science.

Brian M. Reed is chair and professor of English at the University of Washington, Seattle. He is the author of three books, most recently *Nobody's Business: Twenty-First-Century Avant-Garde Poetics* (2013), as well as more than thirty essays and articles on modern and contemporary poetry and poetics. He is currently serving as president of the MLA Forum on Poetry and Poetics, and he is the poetry editor for the journal *Contemporary Literature.*

Jennifer Ryan-Bryant is associate professor of English at State University of New York, College at Buffalo. She is the author of *Post-Jazz Poetics: A Social History* (2010) and *BioPoetics: The Shared Artistry of Ted Hughes and Sylvia Plath* (2020). Her essays have appeared in *Modern Fiction Studies*, *Feminist Teacher*, *Women and Performance*, *College Literature*, *MELUS*, *African American Review*, *Radical Teacher*, and *Modern Language Studies*, as well as in several edited collections.

Trevor Sawler is associate professor of English at Saint Thomas University in Fredericton, New Brunswick. His work has appeared in many publications, including *Paideuma, Modern Fiction Studies, The Antigonish Review, and The Nashwaak Review.* He also owns and operates a small information technology consulting business that services clients across North America, Europe, and the Caribbean.

Demetres P. Tryphonopoulos is dean and executive officer, Augustana campus, University of Alberta. He is the author, editor, coeditor, or translator of fifteen volumes, including *The Celestial Tradition: A Study of Ezra Pound's* The Cantos (1992), *"I Cease Not to Yowl": Pound's Letters to Olivia Rossetti Agresti* (1998), *The Ezra Pound Encyclopedia* (2005), and an annotated edition of H.D.'s *Majic Ring* (2009). He is currently working on several book projects, including *Approaches to Teaching C. P. Cavafy's Poetry.*

SURVEY RESPONDENTS

Meryl Altman, *DePaul University*
Ronnie Apter, *Central Michigan University*
Anderson D. Araujo, *University of British Columbia*
Massimo Bacigalupo, *University of Genoa*
Michele Balze, *University of the Sciences in Philadelphia*
Greg Barnhisel, *Duquesne University*
Jonathan N. Barron, *University of Southern Mississippi*
Robert F. Barsky, *Vanderbilt University*
Richard L. Blevins, *University of Pittsburgh, Greensburg*
Bartholomew Brinkman, *University of Illinois, Urbana*
Edward Brunner, *Southern Illinois University, Carbondale*
Stephen Burt, *Harvard University*
Ellen C. Carillo, *University of Pittsburgh*
Randolph Chilton, *University of St. Francis*
Peter Cockelbergh, *Technische Universität Darmstad*
Ryan Cull, *New Mexico State University*
Phillip Dibble, *University of Missouri, Kansas City*
Maryann Pasda DiEdwardo, *Lehigh University*
Leonard Diepeveen, *Dalhousie University*
Tom Dolack, *University of Oregon*
James J. Donahue, *State University of New York, College at Potsdam*
Susan Donalson, *College of William and Mary*
Cathy Downs, *Texas A&M University, Kingsville*
Rachel Blau DuPlessis, *Temple University*
Lee Einhorn, *University of Washington, Seattle*
Varerio Ferme, *University of Colorado*
Susan Friedman, *University of Wisconsin, Madison*
John Gery, *University of New Orleans*
Alan Golding, *University of Louisville*
Tom Grieve, *Simon Fraser University*
Evelyn Haller, *Doane College*
Ron Harris, *University of Wisconsin, Madison*
Carl Herzig, *St. Ambrose University*
Miranda B. Hickman, *McGill University*
Matthew R. Hofer, *University of New Mexico*
Ann K. Hoff, *University of Alabama, Birmingham*
Jennifer Hoofard, *Mills College*
Heather Duerre Humann, *University of Alabama*
Daniel Katz, *University of Warwick*
Jacqueline Kay, *University of Essex*
Eric Keenaghan, *University at Albany, State University of New York*
James Keller, *Michigan State University*
Robert E. Kibler, *Minot State University*

Martina Kolb, *Penn State University*
Rajiv C. Krishnan, *English and Foreign Languages University, Hyderabad*
William Lawlor, *University of Wisconsin, Stevens Point*
John Lawson, *Robert Morris University*
Peter Th.M.G. Liebregts, *Leiden University*
Helene Littmann, *University College of the Fraser Valley*
Marc Malandra, *Biola University*
Douglas Mao, *Johns Hopkins University*
Henry Marchand, *Cedar Crest College*
Alec Marsh, *Muhlenberg College*
Reka Mihalka, *Eötvös Loránd University, Budapest*
Brett Millier, *Middlebury College*
Joe Moffett, *Kentucky Wesleyan College*
Craig Monk, *MacEwan University, Edmonton*
Susan Smith Nash, *Literature Institute, Norman, OK*
John Nichols, *Christopher Newport University*
Hank Nuwer, *Franklin College*
Mario Rene Padilla, *Santa Monica College*
Anita Patterson, *Boston University*
Catherine E. Paul, *Clemson University*
Bob Perelman, *University of Pennsylvania*
Roxana Preda, *Edinburgh University*
Kristin Prevallet, *St. John's University*
Jonathan Price, *California State University, Sacramento*
Zvonimir Radeljkovic, *Faculty of Philosophy, Sarajevo, Bosnia/Herzegovina*
Stephen Ratcliffe, *Mills College*
Tim Redman, *University of Texas, Dallas*
Brian M. Reed, *University of Washington, Seattle*
Matthias Regan, *University of Chicago*
Robert Reginio, *Frostburg State University*
Diane Reid, *University of New Brunswick*
John Paul Riquelme, *Boston University*
Matthew Roudan, *Georgia State University*
Jennifer Ryan-Bryant, *State University of New York, College at Buffalo*
Roxanne Schwab, *Saint Louis University*
Stephen Sicari, *Saint John's University, NY*
Ellen Keck Stauder, *Reed College*
Leon Surette, *Western University*
Tony Trigilio, *Columbia College, Illinois*
Lara Vetter, *University of North Carolina, Charlotte*
Eric Wagner, *Notre Dame High School, Riverside, CA*
Milton L. Welch, *North Carolina State University*
Sharon Wilson, *University of Northern Colorado*
Steven Yao, *Hamilton College*
Robert Lynn Zamsky, *New College of Florida*

WORKS CITED

Works by Pound

ABC of Economics. 1933. *Selected Prose* [Faber and Faber], pp. 203–34.

ABC of Reading. 1934. New Directions Publishing, 1960.

"Affirmations: As for Imagisme." *Selected Prose* [New Directions], pp. 374–77.

"Affirmations II: Vorticism." *The New Age*, vol. 16, no. 11, 14 Jan. 1915, pp. 277–78, modjourn.org/issue/bdr444106.

"Affirmations IV: As for Imagisme." *The New Age*, vol. 16, no. 13, 28 Jan. 1915, pp. 349–50.

Antheil and the Treatise on Harmony. P. Covici, 1927.

"Apparuit." *Personae* [rev. ed.], p. 68.

"Arnaut Daniel Poems." *Translations*, pp. 144–88, 416–25.

"Article 11." *Exile*, no. 4, 1928, pp. 20–23.

"Berlin." *Exile*, no. 4, Autumn 1928, pp. 113–17.

The Blue Spill: A Critical Manuscript Edition. With Olga Rudge, edited by Mark Byron and Sophia Barnes, Bloomsbury, 2019.

"Bureaucracy." *Exile*, no. 4, 1928, pp. 6–15.

The Cantos of Ezra Pound. New Directions Publishing, 1996.

Cathay: The Centennial Edition. Edited by Zhaoming Qian, foreword by Mary de Rachewiltz, New Directions Publishing, 2015.

Cavalcanti: A Perspective on the Music of Ezra Pound. Edited by Robert Hughes and Margaret Fisher, Second Evening Art, 2003.

The Chinese Written Character as a Medium for Poetry. With Ernest Fenollosa. *Early Writings, Poems and Prose*, pp. 304–29.

"The City." *Exile*, no. 4, 1928, pp. 24–29.

The Classic Noh Theatre of Japan. With Ernest Fenollosa. New Directions Publishing, 1959.

Collected Early Poems of Ezra Pound. Edited by Michael John King, New Directions Publishing, 1976.

"The Condolence." *Personae* (rev. ed.), pp. 83–84.

The Confucian Odes: The Classic Anthology Defined by Confucius. New Directions, 1954.

"Desideria." *Exile*, no. 3, 1928, p. 108.

Draft of canto 45. Ezra Pound Papers, Beinecke Rare Book and Manuscript Library, YCAL MSS 43, Box 73, folders 3296, 3301.

A Draft of XXX Cantos. 1933. New Directions Publishing, 1990.

Early Writings: Poems and Prose. Edited by Ira B. Nadel, Penguin, 2005.

"Economic Democracy." *Selected Prose* [Faber and Faber], pp. 180–83.

Ego Scriptor Cantilenae: The Music of Ezra Pound. Various artists, conducted by Robert Hughes, Other Minds, 2012. CD and digital download.

"The Exile." *Exile*, no. 1, 1927, pp. 88–92.

"The Exile." *Exile*, no. 3, 1928, pp. 102–07.

Exultations. Elkin Matthews, 1909.

Ezra and Dorothy Pound: Letters in Captivity, 1945–1946. Edited by Omar Pound and Robert Spoo, Oxford UP, 1999.

"Ezra Pound." *Who's Who.* A. C. Black, 1915, p. 1741.

Ezra Pound and Dorothy Shakespear: Their Letters, 1909–1914. Edited by Omar Pound and A. Walton Litz, 1985.

Ezra Pound and Globe *Magazine: The Complete Correspondence*. Edited by Michael T. Davis and Cameron McWhirter, Bloomsbury, 2015.

Ezra Pound and James Laughlin, Selected Letters. Edited by David M. Gordon, W. W. Norton, 1994.

Ezra Pound and Music: The Complete Criticism. Edited by R. Murray Schafer, New Directions Publishing, 1977.

Ezra Pound and Senator Bronson Cutting: A Political Correspondence 1930–1935. Edited by E. P. Walkiewicz and Hugh Witemeyer, UP of New Mexico, 1995.

"Ezra Pound—*Le Testament de Villon*—Opera." *YouTube*, uploaded by atomkraft-teddy, 31 October 2013, https://www.youtube.com/watch?v=h87wzHikkwc.

"Ezra Pound: On 'Gender.'" *Modern American Poetry*, www.modernamericanpoetry.org/content/ezra-pound-gender.

"Ezra Pound Speaking": Radio Speeches of World War II. Edited by Leonard W. Doob, Greenwood Press, 1978.

Ezra Pound's Poetry and Prose: Contributions to Periodicals. Edited by Lee Baechler et al., Garland, 1991. 11 vols.

Ezra Pound to His Parents: Letters 1895–1929. Edited by Mary de Rachewiltz et al., Oxford UP, 2010.

"A Few Don'ts by an Imagiste." *Poetry*, Mar. 1913, pp. 200–06. *Poetry Foundation*, www.poetryfoundation.org/poetrymagazine/articles/58900/a-few-donts-by-an-imagiste.

"The Garden." *Personae*, p. 83.

Gaudier-Brzeska: A Memoir. 1916. New Directions Publishing, 1970.

"A Girl." *New Selected Poems*, p. 28.

"Gold and Work 1944." *Selected Prose* [New Directions], pp. 336–51.

Guide to Kulchur. 1938. New Directions Publishing, 1970.

Hagoromo. Classic Noh Theatre, pp. 98–104.

"Harold Monro." *Criterion*, vol. 11, 1932, pp. 581–92.

"The Harvard Vocarium Readings, Recorded in Cambridge, Mass., May 17, 1939: Canto XLV." *PennSound*, writing.upenn.edu/pennsound/x/Pound.php.

"*Hilda's Book* by Ezra Pound." H.D., *End to Torment: A Memoir of Ezra Pound*, pp. 67–84.

"Histrion." *Early Writings*, p. 12.

"How I Began." *Early Writings*, p. 211.

"How I Began." *T.P.'s Weekly*, vol. 21, 1913, p. 707.

"How to Read." *Literary Essays*, pp. 15–40.

Hugh Selwyn Mauberley. *Early Writings*, pp. 127–42.

Hugh Selwyn Mauberley. *New Selected Poems*, pp. 109–23.

Hugh Selwyn Mauberley. *Personae* [rev. ed.], pp. 183–202.

"I Cease Not to Yowl": Ezra Pound's Letters to Olivia Rossetti Agresti. Edited by Demetres P. Tryphonopoulos and Leon Surette, U of Illinois P, 1998.

"I Gather the Limbs of Osiris." *Selected Prose* [New Directions], pp. 19–43.

"In a Station of the Metro." *Poetry*, vol. 2, no. 1, Apr. 1913, p. 12.

"The Individual in His Milieu." *Selected Prose* [Faber and Faber], pp. 242–52.

"Interaction." *Exile*, no. 3, 1928, p. 109.

"Irony, Laforgue, and Some Satire." *Literary Essays*, pp. 280–84.

"The Jefferson-Adams Letters as a Shrine and a Monument." *Selected Prose* [New Directions], pp. 147–58.

Jefferson and/or Mussolini. 1935. Liveright, 1970.

Letter to Bryher. February 1925. Bryher Papers, Beinecke Rare Book and Manuscript Library, Yale U, box 50, folder 1841.

Letter to Jerry Voorhis. 13 September 1939. Ezra Pound Papers, Beinecke Rare Book and Manuscript Library, Yale U, YCAL MSS 43, box 54, folder 2467.

Letters to Ibbotson, 1935–1952. Edited by Vittoria I. Mandolfo and Margaret Hurley, National Poetry Foundation, 1979.

"Letters to Viola Baxter Jordan." Edited by Donald Gallup. *Paideuma: Modern and Contemporary Poetry and Poetics*, vol. 1, no. 1, 1972, pp. 107–11.

"Lingua Toscana." *Spirit of Romance*, pp. 101–17.

"Lionel Johnson." Preface to *The Poetical Works of Lionel Johnson*. 1915. *Literary Essays*, pp. 361–70.

Literary Essays of Ezra Pound. 1954. Edited by T. S. Eliot, New Directions Publishing, 1968.

"Machine Art." *"Machine Art" and Other Writings: The Lost Thought of the Italian Years*, edited by Maria Luisa Ardizzone, Duke UP, 1996.

"Mang Tze." *Selected Prose* [Faber and Faber], pp. 95–111.

"Manifesto 1." *Blast*, no. 1, June 1914, pp. 11–29.

"Manifesto 2." *Blast*, no. 1, June 1914, pp. 30–43.

"Marianne Moore and Mina Loy." *Selected Prose* [New Directions], pp. 424–25.

"The Natural Philosophy of Love." Sieburth, *Instigations*, pp. 19–58.

New Selected Poems and Translations. Edited by Richard Sieburth, New Directions Publishing, 2010.

"Notice to Contributors." *Exile*, no. 2, 1927, p. 121.

"Paris Letter." *The Dial*, vol. 72, no. 2, Feb. 1922, pp. 187–92.

Patria Mia. *Selected Prose* [New Directions], pp. 99–142.

Pavannes and Divisions. Alfred Knopf, 1918.

"Peace." *Exile*, no. 4, 1928, pp. 15–20.

Personae: The Collected Shorter Poems of Ezra Pound. 1926. New Directions Publishing, 1971.

Personae: The Shorter Poems. Revised edition. Edited by Lea Baechler and A. Walton Litz, New Directions Publishing, 1990.

"Piccadilly." *Collected Early Poems*, p. 98.

"The Picture." *Collected Early Poems*, p. 197.

The Pisan Cantos. 1948. Edited by Richard Sieburth, New Directions Publishing, 2003.

Poems and Translations. Edited by Richard Sieburth, Library of America, 2003.

"Poems from the Propertius Series." *Poetry*, vol. 13, no. 6, March 1919, pp. 291–99.

"Portrait d'une Femme." *New Selected Poems*, p. 28.

Posthumous Cantos. Edited by Massimo Bacigalupo, Carcanet Press, 2015.

Pound/Cummings: The Correspondence of Era Pound and E. E. Cummings. Edited by Barry Ahearn, U of Michigan P, 1996.

Pound/Joyce: The Letters of Ezra Pound to James Joyce, with Pound's Essays on Joyce. Edited by Forrest Read, New Directions Publishing, 1967.

Pound, Thayer, Watson, and The Dial*: A Story in Letters*. Edited by Walter Sutton, UP of Florida, 1994.

Pound / The Little Review*: The Letters of Ezra Pound to Margaret Anderson*: The Little Review *Correspondence*. Edited by Thomas L. Scott and Melvin J. Friedman, with the assistance of Jackson R. Bryer, New Directions Publishing, 1988.

Pound/Williams: Selected Letters of Ezra Pound and William Carlos Williams. Edited by Hugh Witemeyer, New Directions, 1996.

"Preliminary Announcement of the College of Arts." *The Egoist*, vol. 21, no. 1, Nov. 2, 1914, pp. 413–14.

"Probari Ratio." *Selected Prose* [Faber and Faber], pp. 177–79.

"Prolegomena." *Exile*, no. 2, 1927, p. 35.

"Psychology and Troubadours." *Spirit of Romance*, pp. 87–100.

"The Quality of Lope de Vega." *Spirit of Romance*, pp. 179–213.

"A Retrospect." *Literary Essays*, pp. 3–14.

Review of *Credit Power and Democracy*, by Maj. C. H. Douglas and A. R. Orage. *Contact*, vol. 4, 1921 p. 1.

Review of *Poesies*, by Jean Cocteau. *The Dial*, Jan. 1921, p. 110.

Review of *Stones of Rimini*, by Adrian Stokes. *Criterion*, vol. 13, 1934, pp. 495–97.

The Selected Letters of Ezra Pound, 1907–1941. Edited by D. D. Paige, 1950. New Directions Publishing, 1971.

The Selected Letters of Ezra Pound to John Quinn, 1915–1924. Edited by Timothy Materer. Duke UP, 1991.

Selected Poems. 1928. Edited by T. S. Eliot, New Directions Publishing, 1957; Faber and Faber, 1971.

Selected Poems of Ezra Pound. New Directions Publishing, 1949.

Selected Prose, 1909–1965. Edited by William Cookson, Faber and Faber, 1973.

Selected Prose, 1909–1965. Edited by William Cookson, New Directions, 1973.

"The Serious Artist." *Literary Essays*, pp. 41–57.

"Sestina: Altaforte." *Collected Early Poems*, pp. 108–09.

"Shop Girl." *New Selected Poems*, p. 51.

"Simplicities." *Exile*, no. 4, 1928, pp. 1–6.

"Small Magazines." *English Journal*, vol. 19, no. 9, 1930, pp. 689–704, www.modjourn.org/render.php?view=mjp_object&id=mjp.2005.00.091.

Social Credit: An Impact. Peter Russell, 1951.

The Spirit of Romance. New Directions Publishing, 1968.

"The Teacher's Mission." *Literary Essays*, pp. 58–63.

"The Tea Shop." *New Selected Poems*, p. 51.

Le Testament. 1923 facsimile edition. Edited by Robert Hughes and Margaret Fisher, Second Evening Art, 2011.

Le Testament: Paroles de Villon, 1926 and 1933 Performance Editions. Edited by Robert Hughes and Margaret Fisher, Second Evening Art, 2008.

"Three Cantos." *Poetry*, vol. 10, nos. 3–5, June-August 1917, pp. 113–21, 180–88, 248–54.

The Translations of Ezra Pound. Introduction by Hugh Kenner, New Directions Publishing, 1953.

"Translators of Greek: Early Translators of Homer." *Literary Essays*, pp. 249–275.

"The Tree." *Collected Early Poems*, p. 35.

"T. S. Eliot." *Literary Essays*, pp. 418–22.

"A Visiting Card." *Selected Prose* [New Directions], pp. 306–35.

"Vortex." *Blast*, no. 1, 1914, pp. 153–54.

"Vorticism." *The Fortnightly Review*, vol. 96, 1 Sept. 1914, pp. 461–71, fortnightlyreview.co.uk/vorticism.

"What Is Money For?" *Selected Prose*, pp. 290–302.

"Xenia." *Collected Early Poems*, p. 82.

Critical Works

Abercrombie, Lascelles. "The Sale of Saint Thomas." *Georgian Poetry, 1911–1912*, London Poetry Bookshop, 1913, pp. 3–21. *Internet Archive*, archive.org/details/georgianpoetry1900unknuoft.

Adams, Stephen J. "A Case for Pound's 'Seafarer.'" *Mosaic*, vol. 9, Winter 1976, pp. 127–46.

———. "The Metrical Contract of *The Cantos*." *Journal of Modern Literature*, vol. 15, Summer 1988, pp. 55–72.

———. *Poetic Designs: An Introduction to Meters, Verse Forms, and Figures of Speech*. Broadview Press, 1997.

Ahearn, Barry. "*Cathay*: What Sort of Translation?" Qian, *Ezra Pound and China*, pp. 31–48.

Aldington, Richard. "The British Academy." *The New Freewoman*, vol. 1, no. 13, 1913, pp. 248–50, modjourn.org/render.php?id=1303310644562627&view=mjp_object.

———. "War Yawp." *Poetry*, vol. 5, no. 2, November 1914, pp. 78–81.

Alexander, Michael. *The Poetic Achievement of Ezra Pound*. Faber and Faber, 1979.

Alpert, Barry S. "Ezra Pound, John Price, and the *Exile*." *Paideuma: Modern and Contemporary Poetry and Poetics*, vol. 2, no. 3, 1973, pp. 427–48.

Antliff, Mark, and Scott Klein. *Vorticism: New Perspectives*. Oxford UP, 2013.

Araujo, Anderson. *A Companion to Ezra Pound's* Guide to Kulchur. Clemson UP / Liverpool UP, 2018.

"Audience, *N*." *Oxford English Dictionary*, Oxford UP, 2019, www.oed.com/view/Entry/13022.

Babich, Babette E. "Nietzsche's 'Gay' Science." *A Companion to Nietzsche*, edited by Keith Ansell-Pearson, Blackwell, 2006, pp. 97–114.

Bacigalupo, Massimo. "Ezra Pound's Tigullio." *Paideuma: Modern and Contemporary Poetry and Poetics*, vol. 14, nos. 2–3, Fall-Winter 1985, pp. 179–209.

———. *The Formèd Trace: The Later Poetry of Ezra Pound*. Columbia UP, 1980.

Barbarese, J. T. "Ezra Pound's Imagist Aesthetics: *Lustra* to *Mauberley*." *The Columbia History of American Poetry*, edited by Jay Parini and Brett C. Millier, Columbia UP, 1993, pp. 284–318.

Barnhisel, Gregory. *James Laughlin, New Directions, and the Remaking of Ezra Pound*. U of Massachusetts P, 2005.

———. Review of *Ezra Pound's Fascist Propaganda, 1935–1945*, by Matthew Feldman. *Make It New*, vol. 1, no. 2, 2014, pp. 13–14, makeitnew.ezrapoundsociety.org/volume-i/vol-i-no-2/controversy-feldman?start=3.

Baym, Nina, et al. *The Norton Anthology of American Literature, Volume D: 1914–1945*. 8th ed., W. W. Norton, 2012.

Beach, Christopher. *ABC of Influence: Ezra Pound and the Remaking of American Poetic Traditions*. U of California P., 1992.

Beasley, Rebecca. *Ezra Pound and the Visual Culture of Modernism*. Cambridge UP, 2007.

Bell, Ian F. A. *Critic as Scientist: The Modernist Poetics of Ezra Pound*. Methuen, 1981.

———, editor. *Ezra Pound: Tactics for Reading*. Vision Press, 1982.

———. "Middle Cantos XLII–LXXI." *The Cambridge Companion to Ezra Pound*, edited by Ira B. Nadel, pp. 92–108.

Benington, Walter. Henri Gaudier-Brzeska carving *Hieratic Head of Ezra Pound*. c. 1914. "Drawing the Vortex: The Vorticists II," by Mark Antliff, *Tate Etc.*, 1 May 2011, www.tate.org.uk/tate-etc/issue-22-summer-2011/drawing-vortex.

Benstock, Shari. *Women of the Left Bank: Paris, 1900–1940*. U of Texas P, 1986.

Bernstein, Charles. *My Way: Speeches and Poems*. U of Chicago P, 1999.

Bernstein, Michael André. "Image, Word, and Sign." *Critical Inquiry* 12, 1986, pp. 347–64.

———. *The Tale of the Tribe: Ezra Pound and the Modern Verse Epic*. Princeton UP, 1980.

The Bible. Authorized King James Version, Oxford UP, 1998.

Biespiel, David. "David Biespiel's Poetry Wire: Why I'm Quitting Ezra Pound." *The Rumpus*, 24 Oct. 2012, therumpus.net/2012/10/david-biespiels-poetry-wire-why-im-quitting-ezra-pound.

Bion. "The Lament for Adonis." *The Greek Bucolic Poets*, translated by J. M. Edmonds, Harvard UP, 1977.

Bischoff, Volker. *Ezra Pound Criticism, 1905–1985: A Chronological Listing of Publications in English*. Schriften der Universitätsbibliothek Marburg, 1991.

Bishop, John Peale. "The Intelligence of Poets." Homberger, pp. 207–08. Originally published in *Vanity Fair*, Jan. 1922, pp. 13–14.

Blasing, Mutlu Konuk. *Lyric Poetry: The Pain and Pleasure of Words*. Princeton UP, 2006.

Boccioni, Umberto. *States of Mind, I: The Farewells*. 1911. Museum of Modern Art, www.moma.org/collection/works/78648.

———. *Unique Forms of Continuity of Space*. 1913. Museum of Modern Art, www.moma.org/collection/works/81179.

Bodenheim, Maxwell. "The Isolation of Carved Metal." Homberger, pp. 203–06. Originally published in *Dial*, vol. 72, 1922, pp. 87–91.

Breitenberger, Barbara. *Aphrodite and Eros: The Development of Greek Erotic Mythology in Early Greek Poetry and Cult*. Routledge, 2007.

Bridson, D. G. "An Interview with Ezra Pound." *New Directions in Prose and Poetry, 17*, edited by James Laughlin, New Directions Publishing, 1961, pp. 159–84.

Brooke, Rupert. "The Soldier." *Poetry*, vol. 6, no. 1, April 1915, p. 19.

Brooker, Peter. *A Student's Guide to the Selected Poems of Ezra Pound*. Faber and Faber, 1979.

Brooker, Peter, and Andrew Thacker, editors. *Oxford Critical and Cultural History of Modernist Magazines*. Oxford UP, 2009–2013. 3 vols.

Brooke-Rose, Christine. *A Structural Analysis of Pound's Usura Canto: Jakobson's Method Extended and Applied to Free Verse*. Mouton, 1976.

Bryant, Marsha. "Counter-Intuitive Innovation." *Modernism/Modernity*, vol. 16, no. 3, 2009, pp. 482–84.

Bullen, J. B., editor. *Post-Impressionists in England*. Routledge, 1988.

Bunting, Basil. "On the Fly-Leaf of Pound's Cantos." *Complete Poems*, edited by Richard Caddel, Bloodaxe Books / New Directions Publishing, 2000, p. 130.

Burke, Carolyn. *Becoming Modern. The Life of Mina Loy*. U of California P, 1997.

Bush, Ronald, and David Ten Eyck. "A Critical Edition of Ezra Pound's Pisan Cantos: Problems and Solutions." *Textual Cultures*, vol. 8, no. 2, 2013, pp. 121–41.

Bush, Ronald L. *The Genesis of Ezra Pound's Cantos*. Princeton UP, 1976.

Byron, Mark. *Ezra Pound's Eriugena*. Bloomsbury, 2014.

Cage, John. "Writing through the *Cantos*." *X: Writings '79–'82*, Wesleyan UP, 1983, pp. 109–15.

Carlyle, Thomas. "Occasional Discourse on the Negro Question." *Fraser's Magazine for Town and Country*, 1 Feb. 1849, pp. 527–38.

Carpenter, Humphrey. *A Serious Character: The Life of Ezra Pound*. Houghton Mifflin, 1988.

Carr, Helen. *The Verse Revolutionaries: Ezra Pound, H.D., and the Imagists*. Jonathan Cape, 2009.

Carruthers, Ian. "A Translation of Fifteen Pages of Ito Michio's Autobiography, *Utsukushiku Naru Kyoshitsu*." *The Canadian Journal of Irish Studies*, vol. 2, no. 1, 1976, pp. 32–43, 39.

Casillo, Robert. *The Genealogy of Demons: Anti-Semitism, Fascism, and the Myths of Ezra Pound*. Northwestern UP, 1988.

Cather, Willa Sibert. *Early Novels and Stories*. Library Classics of the United States, Inc. 1987.

———. "Paul's Case: A Study in Temperament." *McClure's Magazine*, vol. 25, May 1905, pp. 74–83, cather.unl.edu/ss006.html.

Chielens, Edward E., editor. *American Literary Magazines: The Twentieth Century*. Greenwood, 1992.

Child, Harold. Review of *Ripostes*, by Ezra Pound. Homberger, pp. 94–95. Originally published in *The Times Literary Supplement*, 12 December 1912, no. 570, 568.

Childs, John Steven. *Modernist Form: Pound's Style in the Early Cantos*. Susquehanna UP, 1986.

Churchill, Suzanne W. "Modernism in Black and White." *Modernism/Modernity*, vol. 16, no. 3, 2009, pp. 489–92.

Churchill, Suzanne W., and Adam McKible, editors. *Little Magazines and Modernism: New Approaches*. Ashgate, 2007.

Cohen, Louis, et al. *A Guide to Teaching Practice*. Routledge, 2004.

Cole, William. "Critical Reception: 1945–1980." Tryphonopoulos and Adams, p. 71.

Coleridge, Samuel Taylor. *Biographia Literari*. G. Bell and Sons, 1905.

Conover, Anne. *Olga Rudge and Ezra Pound: "What Thou Lovest Well . . ."* Yale UP, 2012.

Cookson, William. *A Guide to* The Cantos *of Ezra Pound*. Persea, 1985.

Cooper, John X. *Modernism and the Culture of Market Society*. Cambridge UP, 2004.

Cork, Richard. *Vorticism and Abstract Art in the First Machine Age*. Gordon Fraser, 1976. 2 vols.

Cornell, Julien. *The Trial of Ezra Pound: A Documented Account of the Treason Case by the Defendant's Lawyer*. The John Day Co., 1966.

Coyle, Michael. *Ezra Pound, Popular Genres, and the Discourse of Culture*. Pennsylvania State UP, 1995.

Creed, Tom. "PowerPoint, No! Cyberspace, Yes." *The National Teaching and Learning Forum* 6.3 (1997): 5–7.

Cuddon, J. A., editor. *The Penguin Dictionary of Literary Terms and Literary Theory*. Rev. ed., Penguin, 1998.

Culler, Jonathan. *Structuralist Poetics: Structuralism, Linguistics, and the Study of Literature*. Cornell UP, 1975.

Cushman, Stephen. *Fictions of Form in American Poetry*. Princeton UP, 1993.

Dante Alighieri. *The Divine Comedy: 1. Inferno*. Translated by John D. Sinclair, The Bodley Head, 1958.

Dasenbrock, Reed Way. *Imitating the Italians: Wyatt, Spenser, Synge, Pound, Joyce*. Johns Hopkins UP, 1991.

———. *The Literary Vorticism of Ezra Pound and Wyndham Lewis: Towards the Condition of Painting*. Johns Hopkins UP, 1985.

Davenport, Guy. *Cities on Hills. A Study of I–XXX of Ezra Pound's* Cantos. UMI Research P, 1983.

Davie, Donald. *Ezra Pound*. U of Chicago P, 1975.

———. *Ezra Pound: Poet as Sculptor*. Oxford UP, 1964.

Del Mar, Alexander. *The History of Monetary Systems,* 1896. National Poetry Foundation, 1983.

Dickinson, Emily. *The Poems of Emily Dickinson*. Edited by R. W. Franklin, Harvard UP, 1999.

Diepeveen, Leonard. *Changing Voices: The Modern Quoting Poem*. U of Michigan P, 1993.

Dirda, Michael. Introduction. *ABC of Reading*, by Pound, pp. 1–8.

Douglas, C. H. *Social Credit*. Cecil Palmer, 1924.

Duchamp, Marcel. "The Richard Mutt Case." *The Blind Man*, vol. 2, 1917, p. 5.

Duncan, Robert. *The H.D. Book*. U of California P, 2011.

DuPlessis, Rachel Blau. *Blue Studios: Poetry and its Cultural Work*. U of Alabama P, 2006.

———. *Drafts: Drafts 39–57, Pledge, with Draft, Unnumbered: Précis*. Salt, 2004.

———. *Drafts 1–38, Toll*. Wesleyan UP, 2001.

———. *The Pink Guitar: Writing as Feminist Practice*. Routledge, 1990.

———. *Writing beyond the Ending: Narrative Strategies of Twentieth-Century Women Writers*. Indiana UP, 1985.

Eastman, Barbara C. *Ezra Pound's* Cantos: *The Story of the Text, 1948–1975*. National Poetry Foundation, 1979.

Edwards, John Hamilton, and William W. Vasse. *Annotated Index to the* Cantos *of Ezra Pound: Cantos I–LXXXIV*. U of California P, 1957.

Edwards, Paul. *Wyndham Lewis: Painter and Writer*. Yale UP, 2000.

Eliot, T. S. *Ezra Pound: His Metric and Poetry*. Alfred A. Knopf, 1917, www.gutenberg.org/files/7275/7275.txt.

———. Introduction. *Literary Essays of Ezra Pound*, pp. ix–xv.

———. Introduction. *Selected Prose of T. S. Eliot*, pp. 11–30.

———. "The Metaphysical Poets. *Times Literary Supplement*, 20 Oct. 1921, pp. 669–70.

———. "Professional, or . . ." *The Egoist*, vol. 5, no. 4, 1918, p. 61.

———. "Reflections on 'Vers Libre.'" *Selected Prose of T. S. Eliot*, pp. 31–36.

———. *Selected Prose of T. S. Eliot.* Edited by Frank Kermode, Faber and Faber, 1975.

———. "Tradition and the Individual Talent." *The Sacred Wood: Essays on Poetry and Criticism.* Knopf, 1921, pp. 42–53.

———. *The Waste Land: A Facsimile and Transcript of the Original Drafts Including the Annotations of Ezra Pound.* Mariner Books, 2001.

Emery, Clark. *Ideas into Action: A Study of Ezra Pound's* Cantos. U of Miami P, 1958.

English, Daylanne. *Unnatural Selections: Eugenics in American Modernism and the Harlem Renaissance.* U of North Carolina P, 2004.

Epstein, Jacob. *Sun God.* 1910. Metropolitan Museum of Art, www.metmuseum.org/art/collection/search/480810.

Espey, John J. *Ezra Pound's* Mauberley*: A Study in Composition.* U of California P, 1955.

Ezra Pound's Justice Department Criminal Division File. Internet Archive, uploaded by The Memory Hole 2, June 21, 2016, ia800401.us.archive.org/10/items/ezra-pound_DOJ-CD/pound_ezra_DOJ-CD.pdf.

"Ezra Pound Teaching and Research Page." modjourn.pbworks.com/w/page/27064013/Pound%2C%20Ezra.

Feldman, Matthew. *Ezra Pound's Fascist Propaganda, 1935–45.* Palgrave Pivot, 2013.

Fenollosa, Ernest. *The Chinese Written Character as a Medium for Poetry.* Edited by Ezra Pound, City Lights, 1968.

Ferrero de Luca, Maria Costanza, editor. *Ezra Pound e il canto dei sette laghi.* Diabasis, 2004.

Finch, Annie. *The Ghost of Meter: Culture and Prosody in American Free Verse.* U of Michigan P, 1993.

Fisher, Margaret. *Ezra Pound's Radio Operas: The BBC Experiments, 1931–1933.* MIT P, 2002.

Fitts, Dudley. "'Music Fit for the Odes.'" *Hound and Horn*, vol. 4, no. 2, Winter 1931, pp. 278–89. Homberger, pp. 246–55.

Flory, Wendy Stallard. *The American Ezra Pound.* Yale UP, 1989.

———. *Ezra Pound and* The Cantos*: A Record of Struggle.* Yale UP, 1980.

Fogelman, Bruce. *Shapes of Power: The Development of Ezra Pound's Poetic Sequences.* UMI Research P, 1988.

Foley, Helene P., editor. *The Homeric Hymn to Demeter: Translation, Commentary, and Interpretive Essays.* Princeton UP, 1993.

Forrest-Thomson, Veronica. *Poetic Artifice: A Theory of Twentieth-Century Poetry.* Manchester UP, 1978.

Foucault, Michel. *The History of Sexuality, Volume 1: An Introduction.* Vintage, 1990.

Frank, Joseph. "Spatial Form in Modern Literature: An Essay in Two Parts." *Sewanee Review*, vol. 53, 1945, pp. 221–40, 433–56, 643–53.

"Frequently Requested Records: Ezra Pound." *United States Department of Justice*, updated 15 June 2015, www.justice.gov/criminal/frequently-requested-records-0.

Friedlander, Benjamin. "Radio Broadcasts." Nadel, *Ezra Pound in Context*, pp. 115–24.

Friedman, Susan Stanford. *Psyche Reborn: The Emergence of H.D.* Indiana UP, 1987.

Froula, Christine. *A Guide to Ezra Pound's Selected Poems*. New Directions Publishing, 1982.

———. *To Write Paradise: Style and Error in Pound's* Cantos. Yale UP, 1984.

Gallup, Donald C. *Ezra Pound: A Bibliography*. 1969. UP of Virginia, 1983.

Gallup, Donald C., and Archie Henderson. "Additions and Corrections to the Revised Edition of the Ezra Pound Bibliography." *Paideuma: Modern and Contemporary Poetry and Poetics*, vol. 12, no. 1, Spring 1983, pp. 117–130.

Gaşiorek, Andrzej. "Exiles: The *transatlantic review* (1924) and the *Exile* (1927–8)." *The Oxford Critical and Cultural History of Modernist Magazines: Volume II, North America, 1894–1960*, edited by Peter Brooker and Andrew Thacker, Oxford UP, 2012, pp. 697–717.

Gay, Peter. *The Enlightenment: An Interpretation: Vol. II. The Science of Freedom*. W. W. Norton, 1977.

Gibson, Mary Ellis. *Epic Reinvented: Ezra Pound and the Victorians*. Cornell UP, 1995.

Gildersleeve, D. Britton. "The Poem as Cartographer: A Survey of Scholarship on Ezra Pound's Chinese Cultural/Poetic Translations." *Bulletin of Bibliography*, vol. 55, no. 4, 1988, pp. 223–41.

Golding, Alan. "Drafts and Fragments: Rachel Blau DuPlessis's (Counter-) Poundian Project." *Jacket2*, Dec. 2011, jacket2.org/article/drafts-and-fragments.

———. "Faking It New" *Modernism/Modernity*, vol. 16, no. 3, 2009, pp. 474–77.

———. "From Pound to Olson: The Avant Garde as Pedagogue." Yao and Coyle, pp. 183–210. Originally published in *Journal of Modern Literature*, vol. 34, no. 1, 2010, pp. 86–106.

Graeber, David. *Debt: The First 5,000 Years*. Melville House, 2011.

Graff, Gerald. *Beyond the Culture Wars: How Teaching the Conflicts Can Revitalize American Education*. W. W. Norton, 1992.

———. *Professing Literature: An Institutional History*. U of Chicago P, 1989.

Granville, Kevin. "Facebook and Cambridge Analytica: What You Need to Know as Fallout Widens." *The New York Times*, 19 Mar. 2018, www.nytimes.com/2018/03/19/technology/facebook-cambridge-analytica-explained.html.

Grieve, Thomas F. *Ezra Pound's Early Poetry and Poetics*. U of Missouri P, 1997.

Gruetzner Robins, Anna. *Modern Art in Britain, 1910–14*. Merrell Holberton, 1997.

Guest, Barbara. *Herself Defined: The Poet H.D. and Her World*. Doubleday, 1984.

Hamilton, Scott. *Ezra Pound and the Symbolist Inheritance*. Princeton UP, 1992.

Handa, Carolyn. *The Multimediated Rhetoric of the Internet: Digital Fusion*. Routledge, 2014.

Hartman, Charles O. *Free Verse: An Essay on Prosody*. Princeton UP, 1980.

Harvey, David. *Seventeen Contradictions and the End of Capitalism*. Oxford UP, 2014.

Hauck, Christina. "Abortion and the Individual Talent." *ELH*, vol. 70, no. 1, 2003, pp. 223–66.

Hayot, Eric. "Critical Dreams: Orientalism, Modernism, and the Meaning of Pound's China." *Twentieth-Century Literature*, vol. 45, no. 4, 1999, pp. 511–33.

H.D. *End to Torment: A Memoir of Ezra Pound.* Edited by Norman Holmes Pearson and Michael King, New Directions Publishing, 1979.

———. "Garden." *Selected Poems*, by H.D., p. 7.

———. "Heat." *Collected Poems 1912–1944*, by H.D., edited by Louis L. Martz, New Directions, 1986, p. 25.

———. "Helen." *Selected Poems*, by H.D., p. 48.

———. "Hermes of the Ways." *Selected Poems*, by H.D., pp. 13–14.

———. *Notes on Thought and Vision.* City Lights Books, 1982.

———. "Oread." *Selected Poems*, by H.D., p. 17.

———. *Paint It Today.* New York UP, 1992.

———. "Sea Rose." *Selected Poems*, by H.D., p. 3.

———. *Selected Poems.* New Directions Publishing, 1957.

———. *Tribute to Freud.* 1956. New Directions Publishing, 1984.

Hemingway, Ernest. *A Moveable Feast.* Jonathan Cape, 1964.

Henderson, Archie. "Updating the Pound Bibliography." *Ezra Pound, Language and Persona*, special issue of *Quaderni di Palazzo Serra*, vol. 15, 2008, pp. 315–32.

Henderson, Archie, and Roxana Preda. "Bibliography of English Language Scholarship on Ezra Pound." *The Ezra Pound Society*, 2019, ezrapoundsociety.org/index.php/2019.

Hewitt, Andrew. *Political Inversions: Homosexuality, Fascism, and the Modernist Imaginary.* U of Chicago P, 1996.

Heymann, C. David. *Ezra Pound: The Last Rower. A Political Profile.* Viking Press, 1976.

Hickman, Miranda B. *The Geometry of Modernism: The Vorticist Idiom in Lewis, Pound, H.D., and Yeats.* U of Texas P, 2005.

Hofer, Matthew. "Education." Nadel, *Ezra Pound in Context*, pp. 75–84.

Hoffman, Frederick J., et al. *The Little Magazine: A History and a Bibliography.* 1946. Cambridge UP, 2009.

Hollander, John. "Blake and the Metrical Contract." *From Sensibility to Romanticism*, edited by Frederick W. Hilles and Harold Bloom, Oxford UP, 1965, pp. 293–310.

———. *Vision and Resonance: Two Senses of Poetic Form.* Oxford UP, 1975.

Hollis, Christopher. *The Two Nations: A Financial Study of English History.* George Routledge and Sons, 1935.

Homberger, Eric, editor. *Ezra Pound: The Critical Heritage.* Routledge and Kegan Paul, 1972.

Howe, Susan. *Articulation of Sound Forms in Time.* Awede, 1987.

Hughes, Robert, and Margaret Fisher. *Cavalcanti: A Perspective on the Music of Ezra Pound.* Second Evening Art, 2003.

Humphreys, Richard, and Allen Bowness. *Pound's Artists: Ezra Pound and The Visual Arts in London, Paris and Italy.* Tate Gallery Publications, 1985.

Hutchins, Patricia. *Ezra Pound's Kensington: An Exploration, 1885–1913*. Faber and Faber, 1965.

Hyde, Lewis. *The Gift: Creativity and the Artist in the Modern World*. 2nd ed. Vintage Books, 2007.

"Intérieur de l'atelier Brancusi reconstitué par Renzo Piano, 1997." "Brancusi's Studio," *Centre Pompidou*, www.centrepompidou.fr/en/Collections/Brancusi-s-Studio.

Jones, Peter, editor. *Imagist Poetry*. Penguin, 1972.

Jonson, Ben. "Poets and Poetry." *Ben Jonson and the Cavalier Poets*, edited by Hugh Maclean, W. W. Norton, 1974, pp. 413–17.

Joseph, Nancy. "Metacognition in the Classroom: Examining Theory and Practice." *Pedagogy*, vol. 3, no. 1, Winter 2003, pp. 109–14.

Junco, Reynol, et al. "Putting Twitter to the Test: Assessing Outcomes for Student Collaboration, Engagement and Success." *British Journal of Educational Technology*, vol. 44, no. 2, 2013, pp. 273–87.

Kadlec, David. *Mosaic Modernism: Anarchism, Pragmatism, Culture*. Johns Hopkins UP, 2000.

Kandinsky, Wassily. *The Art of Spiritual Harmony*. Translated by M. T. H. Sadler, Constable, 1914. Translation of *Über das Geistige in der Kunst*, R. Piper, 1912.

———. *Improvisation No. 29 (The Swan)*. 1912. *Philadelphia Museum of Art*, www.philamuseum.org/collections/permanent/51017.html.

———. *Small Pleasures* (*Kleine Freuden*). 1913. *Guggenheim*, The Solomon R. Guggenheim Foundation, www.guggenheim.org/artwork/1868.

Kearns, George. *Guide to Ezra Pound's Selected Cantos*. Rutgers UP, 1980.

———. *Pound:* The Cantos. Cambridge UP, 1989.

Kenner, Hugh. *The Poetry of Ezra Pound*. 1951. U of Nebraska P, 1985.

———. *The Pound Era*. U of California P, 1971.

Kern, Robert. *Orientalism, Modernism, and the American Poem*. Cambridge UP, 1996.

Khost, Peter H., et al. "Rethinking and Unthinking the Graduate Seminar." *Pedagogy*, vol. 15, no. 1, Jan. 2015, pp. 19–30.

Kibler, Robert E. "*Draft of XXX Cantos*." Tryphonopoulos and Adams, pp. 26–30.

Kindellan, Michael, and Joshua I. Kotin. "*The Cantos* and Pedagogy." *Modernist Cultures*, vol. 12, no. 3, 2017, pp. 345–63.

Kirk, Russell. "Personality and Medium in Eliot and Pound." *Sewanee Review*, vol. 82, no. 4, 1974, pp. 698–705.

Kirkup, Gill, and Adrian Kirkwood. "Information and Communications Technologies (ICT) in Higher Education Teaching—a Tale of Gradualism rather than Revolution." *Learning, Media and Technology*, vol. 30, no. 2, 2005, pp. 185–99.

Kleitz, Dorsey. "Ezra Pound and the Limits of Exile." 22nd Ezra Pound International Conference, June 2007, Venice, Italy.

Kodama, Sanehide. "The Eight Scenes of Sho-Sho." *Paideuma: Modern and Contemporary Poetry and Poetics*, vol. 2, 1977, pp. 131–45.

———, editor. *Ezra Pound and Japan: Letters and Essays*. Black Swan, 1987.

Koestenbaum, Wayne. "*The Waste Land*: T. S. Eliot's and Ezra Pound's Collaboration on Hysteria." *Double Talk: The Erotics of Male Literary Collaboration*, by Koestenbaum, Routledge, 1989.

Korn, Marianne, editor. *Ezra Pound and History*. National Poetry Foundation, 1985.

Kramer, Adam D. I., et al. "Experimental Evidence of Massive-Scale Emotional Contagion through Social Networks." *Proceedings of the National Academy of Sciences*, vol. 111, no. 24, 2014, pp. 8788–90.

Kristeva, Julia. "Women's Time." *The Kristeva Reader*, edited by Toril Moi, Columbia UP, 1986, pp. 187–213.

Kuberski, Philip. *A Calculus of Ezra Pound: Vocations of the American Sign*. UP of Florida, 1992.

Lan, Feng. *Ezra Pound and Confucianism: Remaking Humanism in the Face of Modernity*. U of Toronto P, 2005.

Langer, Susanne. *Philosophy in a New Key*. New American Library, 1951.

Laughlin, James, *Pound as Wuz: Essays and Lectures on Ezra Pound*. Graywolf Press, 1987.

Lazzarato, Maurizio. *The Making of Indebted Man: An Essay*. Semiotext(e), 2011.

Leavis, F. R. *New Bearings in English Poetry: A Study of the Contemporary Situation*. 1932. U of Michigan P, 1960.

Le Goff, Jacques. *Your Money or Your Life: Economy and Religion in the Middle Ages*. Zone Books, 1990.

Lewis, Wyndham. "To Suffragettes." 1914. *Blast 1*, edited by Lewis, Black Sparrow Press, 1989, pp. 151–52.

Liapis, Vayos. "Prayer to Aphrodite." *The Greek Poets: Homer to the Present*, edited by Peter Constantine et al., W. W. Norton, 2010, pp. 88–89.

Liebregts, Peter. "The Classics." Nadel, *Ezra Pound in Context*, pp. 171–80.

———. *Ezra Pound and Neoplatonism*. Fairleigh Dickinson UP, 2004.

Longenbach, James. *Modernist Poetics of History: Pound, Eliot, and the Sense of the Past*. Princeton UP, 1987.

———. *Stone Cottage: Pound, Yeats, and Modernism*. Oxford UP, 1988.

Lyon, Janet. *Manifestoes: Provocations of the Modern*. Cornell UP, 1999.

Machacek, Gregory. "Allusion." *PMLA*, vol. 122, no. 2, 2007, pp. 522–36.

Mackey, Nathaniel. "Song of the Andoumboulou: 1–7." *Eroding Witness*, U of Illinois P, 1985, pp. 8–15.

Mac Low, Jackson. *Words nd ends from Ez*. Avenue B, 1989.

MacNiven, Ian S. *"Literchoor Is My Beat": A Life of James Laughlin, Publisher of New Directions*. Farrar, Straus and Giroux, 2014.

Makin, Peter, editor. *Ezra Pound's* Cantos*: A Casebook*. Oxford UP, 2006.

———. *Pound's* Cantos. George Allen and Unwin, 1985.

Marcus, Jane. *Virginia Woolf and the Languages of Patriarchy*. Indiana UP, 1987.

Marinetti, F. T. *Let's Murder the Moonshine: Selected Writings*. Edited by R. W. Flint, translated by R. W. Flint and Arthur A. Coppotelli, Sun and Moon, 1991.

Mark, Jeffrey. *The Modern Idolatry: An Analysis of Usury and the Pathology of Debt.* Chatto and Windus, 1934.

Marsh, Alec. *Ezra Pound.* Reaktion Books, 2011.

———. *John Kasper and Ezra Pound: Saving the Republic.* Bloomsbury, 2015.

———. *Money and Modernity: Pound, Williams, and the Spirit of Jefferson.* U of Alabama P, 1998.

———. Review of *Ezra Pound's Fascist Propaganda, 1935–1945*, by Matthew Feldman. *Make It New*, vol. 1, no. 2, 2014, pp. 11–12, makeitnew.ezrapoundsociety.org/volume-i/vol-i-no-2/controversy-feldman?start=2.

———. "Social Credit: An Impact." Tryphonopoulos and Adams, pp. 275–76.

Marsh, Nicky, and Peter Middleton, editors. *Teaching Modernist Poetry.* Palgrave Macmillan, 2010.

Marx, Karl. *Capital.* Vol. 1, translated by Ben Fowkes, Penguin Books, 1990.

———. *Economic and Philosophical Manuscripts of 1844. Early Writings*, translated by Rodney Livingstone and Gregor Benton, Penguin Books, 1977.

Materer, Timothy. *Vortex: Pound, Eliot, and Lewis.* Cornell UP, 1979.

McAlpine, Lynn, and Cynthia Weston. "Reflection: Issues Related to Improving Professors' Teaching and Students' Learning." *Instructional Science*, vol. 28, nos. 5–6, 2000, pp. 363–85.

McDonald, Gail. "Hypertext and the Teaching of Modernist Difficulty." *Pedagogy: Critical Approaches to Teaching Literature, Language, Composition, and Culture*, vol. 2, no. 1, 2002, pp. 17–30.

———. *Learning to Be Modern: Pound, Eliot, and the American University.* Oxford UP, 1993.

McGann, Jerome. *Black Riders: The Visible Language of Modernism.* Princeton UP, 1993.

———. *Radiant Textuality: Literature after the World Wide Web.* Palgrave Macmillan, 2001.

Menand, Louis. "The Pound Error." *The New Yorker*, 9 June 2006, www.newyorker.com/magazine/2008/06/09/the-pound-error.

Micciche, Laura R., and Allison D. Carr. "Toward Graduate-Level Writing Instruction." *College Composition and Communication*, vol. 62, no. 3, Feb. 2011, pp. 477–501.

Miller, Andrew John. "Dreaming the Super College: Ezra Pound, Lionel Trilling, and the Arnoldian Ideal." Yao and Coyle, pp. 67–93.

Miller, J. Hillis. *Illustration.* Harvard UP, 1992.

Mitchell, W. J. T. *Iconology: Image, Text, Ideology.* U of Chicago P, 1986.

Miyake, Akiko. *Ezra Pound and the Mysteries of Love. A Plan for* The Cantos. Duke UP, 1991.

Miyake, Akiko, et al. *A Guide to Ezra Pound and Ernest Fenollosa's* Classic Noh Theatre of Japan. The National Poetry Foundation and The Ezra Pound Society of Japan, 1994.

Monet, Claude. *Stacks of Wheat (End of Summer)*. 1890/91. *Art Institute of Chicago*, www.artic.edu/artworks/64818/stacks-of-wheat-end-of-summer.

Monk, Craig. "The Price of Publishing Modernism: Ezra Pound and the *Exile* in America." *Canadian Review of American Studies*, vol. 31, no. 1, 2001, pp. 429–46.

Monroe, Harriet. "What Next?" *Gender of Modernism*, edited by Bonnie Kime Scott, U of Illinois P, 2007.

Moody, A. David. *The Epic Years, 1921–1939*. 2014. *Ezra Pound: Poet: A Portrait of the Man and His Work*, vol. 2, Oxford UP, 2007–15.

———. "On Matthew Feldman's *Ezra Pound's Fascist Propaganda, 1935–1945*: Some Notes Further to Leon Surette's Review in *MIN* 1.2." *Make It New*, vol. 1, no. 3, 2014, pp. 44–51, makeitnew.ezrapoundsociety.org/volume-i/vol-i-no-2/controversy-feldman?start=1.

———. *The Tragic Years, 1939–1972*. 2015. *Ezra Pound: Poet: A Portrait of the Man and His Work*, vol. 3, Oxford UP, 2007–15.

———. *The Young Genius, 1885–1920*. 2007. *Ezra Pound: Poet: A Portrait of the Man and His Work*, vol. 1, Oxford UP, 2007–15.

Moore, Marianne. *The Selected Letters of Marianne Moore*. Edited by Bonnie Costello, et al., Knopf, 1997.

Morrison, Mark. *The Public Face of Modernism: Little Magazines, Audiences, and Reception, 1905–1920*. U of Wisconsin P, 2001.

Morrison, Paul. *The Poetics of Fascism: Ezra Pound, T. S. Eliot, Paul de Man*. Oxford UP, 1996.

Moxley, Jennifer. "Poundian Poetic Ambition on the Semester System." *Poets on Teaching: A Sourcebook*, edited by Joshua Marie Wilkinson, U of Iowa P, 2010, pp. 198–203.

Mullins, Eustace. *The Secrets of the Federal Reserve*. 1952. Rpt. John McLaughlin, 1993.

———. *This Difficult Individual, Ezra Pound*. Fleet Publishing, 1961.

Munson, Gorham. *Aladdin's Lamp: The Wealth of the American People*. Creative Age Press, 1945.

Nadel, Ira B. *The Cambridge Introduction to Ezra Pound*. Cambridge UP, 2007.

———. *Cathay: Ezra Pound's Orient*. Penguin, 2015.

———. *Ezra Pound: A Literary Life*. Palgrave MacMillan, 2004.

———, editor. *Ezra Pound in Context*. Cambridge UP, 2010.

———. "Introduction: Understanding Pound." *The Cambridge Companion to Ezra Pound*, edited by Nadel, Cambridge UP, 1999, pp. 1–21.

Nänny, Max. *Ezra Pound: Poetics for an Electric Age*. Francke Verlag, 1973.

Nealon, Jeffrey. *Post-Postmodernism; or, the Cultural Logic of Just-in-Time Capitalism*. Stanford UP, 2012.

Nelson, Benjamin. *The Idea of Usury: From Tribal Brotherhood to Universal Otherhood*. 2nd ed., U of Chicago P, 1969.

Nicholls, Peter. "An Experiment with Time: Ezra Pound and the Example of Japanese Noh." *The Modern Language Review*, vol. 90, no.1, Jan. 1995, pp. 1–13.

———. *Modernism: A Literary Guide*. U of California P, 1995.

———. "The Poetics of Modernism." *The Cambridge Companion to Modernist Poetry*, edited by Alex Davis and Lee M. Jenkins, Cambridge UP, 2007, pp. 51–67.

———. "'You in the Dinghy Astern There': Learning from Ezra Pound." Yao and Coyle, pp. 137–61.

Nietzsche, Friedrich. The Birth of Tragedy *and* The Case of Wagner. Translated by Walter Kaufman, Vintage, 1967.

———. *The Use and Abuse of History*. 1873. Cosimo, 2005.

Nordau, Max. *Degeneration*. D. Appleton, 1895.

Norman, Charles. *Ezra Pound*. 1960. Rev. ed., Minerva Press, 1969.

North, Michael. *The Final Sculpture: Public Monuments and Modern Poets*. Cornell UP, 1985.

Oderman, Kevin. *Ezra Pound and the Erotic Medium*. Duke UP, 1986.

O'Higgins, Dolores. "Sappho's Splintered Tongue: Silence in Sappho 31 and Catullus 51." *Re-reading Sappho: Reception and Transmission*, edited by Ellen Greene, U of California P, 1996, pp. 68–78.

"Other Translations of 'A River-Merchant's Wife.'" *Modern American Poetry*, maps -legacy.org/poets/m_r/pound/othertranslations.htm.

Palmer, Herbert. *Post-Victorian Poetry*. J. M. Dent and Sons, 1938.

Parisi, Joseph, and Stephen Young. *Dear Editor: A History of Poetry in Letters*. W. W. Norton, 2002.

Parker, Richard, editor. *News from Afar: Ezra Pound and Contemporary British Poetries*. Shearsman, 2014.

———, editor. *Readings in the* Cantos. Vol. 1, Clemson UP / Liverpool UP, 2018.

Pearlman, Daniel D. *The Barb of Time: On the Unity of Ezra Pound's* Cantos. Oxford UP, 1969.

Perelman, Bob. "A Guide to *Homage to Sextus Propertius*." *Iflife*, by Perelman, pp. 82–90.

———. "Homage to Pound's *Propertius*." Yao and Coyle, pp. 225–36.

———. *Iflife*. Roof, 2006.

———. *Modernism the Morning After*. U of Alabama P, 2017.

———. "My Pound Decoder Ring." *Iflife*, by Perelman, pp. 106–07.

———. "This Just In: Past Haunts *Lip Service*." *Jacket*, vol. 22, May 2003, jacketmagazine.com/22/and-perel.html.

"Performance, *N*." *Oxford English Dictionary*, Oxford UP, 2019, www.oed.com/view/Entry/140783.

"Periodical Database: 1890–1922." *Modernist Journals Project*, Brown University / University of Tulsa, modjourn.org/periodical-database.

Perloff, Marjorie. "The Contemporary of Our Grandchildren: Ezra Pound and the Question of Influence." *Poetic License: Essays on Modernist and Postmodernist Lyric*. Northwestern UP, 1990, pp. 119–44.

———. *The Dance of the Intellect: Studies in the Poetry of the Pound Tradition*. Northwestern UP, 1996.

———. *The Futurist Moment: Avant-Garde, Avant Guerre, and the Language of Rupture*. U of Chicago P, 1986.

———. *The Poetics of Indeterminacy: Rimbaud to Cage*. Princeton UP, 1981.

———. "Re: Pound and Fascism." Listserv.buffalo.edu, Poetics List Info, University of Buffalo, 19 March 1996. Accessed 2 July 2017.

———. "The Search for 'Prime Words': Pound, Duchamp, and the Nominalist Ethos." *Differentials: Poetry, Poetics, Pedagogy*. U of Alabama P, 2004, pp. 39–59.

Pitkethly, Lawrence, director. *Ezra Pound: American Odyssey*. New York Center for Visual History, 1988, www.learner.org/catalog/extras/vvspot/Pound.html. Voices and Visions 10.

Plato. *The Collected Dialogues of Plato*. Princeton UP, 1989.

Poggioli, Renato. *The Spirit of the Letter*. Harvard UP, 1965.

Powell, James A. "The Light of *Vers Libre*." *Paideuma: Modern and Contemporary Poetry and Poetics*, vol. 8, Spring 1979, pp. 3–34.

Preda, Roxana, editor. *The Edinburgh Companion to Ezra Pound and the Arts*. Edinburgh UP, 2019.

———, editor. *Ezra Pound's Economic Correspondence, 1933–1940*. UP of Florida, 2007.

Preston, Carrie J. *Learning to Kneel: Noh, Modernism, and Journeys in Teaching*. Columbia UP, 2017.

Price, Margaret, et al. "Feedback: All That Effort, but What Is the Effect?" *Assessment and Evaluation in Higher Education*, vol. 35, no. 3, 2010, pp. 277–89. doi:10.1080/02602930903541007.

Proposed Indictments for Treason of the Following American Citizens Broadcasting Enemy Propaganda from Axis Countries to the United States April 24, 1942. United States Department of Justice, www.justice.gov/sites/default/files/criminal/legacy/2010/04/11/ezra-pound-p1.pdf.

Pryor, Sean. *W. B. Yeats, Ezra Pound, and the Poetry of Paradise*. Ashgate, 2011.

Qian, Zhaoming, editor. *Ezra Pound and China*. U of Michigan P, 2003.

———, editor. *Ezra Pound's Chinese Friends: Stories in Letters*. Oxford UP, 2008.

———. *The Modernist Response to Chinese Art: Pound, Moore, Stevens*. U of Virginia P, 2003.

———. *Orientalism and Modernism: The Legacy of China in Pound and Williams*. Duke UP, 1995.

———. "Pound's Seven Lakes Canto." *The Modernist Response to Chinese Art*, by Qian, pp. 123–140.

Rabaté, Jean-Michel. *Language, Sexuality and Ideology in Ezra Pound's* Cantos. State U of New York P, 1986.

Rachewiltz, Mary de. *Discretions*. Little, Brown, 1971.

Rainey, Lawrence S., editor. "The Creation of the Avant-Garde: F. T. Marinetti and Ezra Pound." *Modernism/Modernity*, vol. 1, no. 3, 1994, pp. 195–220.

———. *Ezra Pound and the Monument of Culture: Text, History, and the Malatesta Cantos*. U of Chicago P, 1991.

———. *Institutions of Modernism: Literary Elites and Public Culture.* Yale UP, 1999.

———. *A Poem Containing History: Textual Studies in* The Cantos. U of Michigan P, 1997.

Ramazani, Jahan, et al. *The Norton Anthology of Modern and Contemporary Poetry, Volume 1: Modern Poetry.* 3rd ed., W. W. Norton, 2003.

Read, Forrest. *'76, One World, and the* Cantos *of Ezra Pound.* U of North Carolina P, 1981.

Read, Herbert. "Ezra Pound." *The Tenth Muse: Essays in Criticism,* by Read, Routledge and Kegan Paul, 1957, pp. 260–75.

———. "Obscurity in Poetry." *Collected Essays in Literary Criticism.* Faber and Faber, 1938, pp. 89–100.

Redman, Tim. *Ezra Pound and Italian Fascism.* Cambridge UP, 1991.

Reid, E. Shelley. "Teaching Writing Teachers Writing: Difficulty, Exploration, and Critical Reflection." *College Composition and Communication,* vol. 61, no. 2, Dec. 2009, pp. 197–221.

Retallack, Joan, and Juliana Spahr, editors. *Poetry and Pedagogy: The Challenge of the Contemporary.* Palgrave Macmillan, 2006.

Review of *A Lume Spento. Book News Monthly,* vol. 27, May 1909, p. 719. Homberger, p. 42.

Rodman, Selden. Introduction. *A New Anthology of Modern Poetry,* edited by Rodman, Random House, 1938, pp. 21–46.

Rosenberg, Issac. "Marching." *Poetry,* vol. 9, no. 3, December 1916, p. 128.

Rosenquist, Rod. *Modernism, the Market and the Institution of the New.* Cambridge UP, 2009.

Rossa, Jesse, "Prolegomenon." *Ezra Pound in His Time and Beyond: The Influence of Ezra Pound on Twentieth-Century Poetry: A Catalog of an Exhibition,* by David P. Roselle et al., U of Delaware Library, 2006,www.lib.udel.edu/ud/spec/exhibits/pound/prolegomenon.htm.

Rothenberg, Jerome, editor. *A Big Jewish Book: Poems and Other Visions of the Jews from Tribal Times to the Present.* Doubleday, 1978.

———. *Poetics and Polemics, 1980–2005.* U of Alabama P, 2008.

———. *Pre-Faces and Other Writings.* New Directions Publishing, 1981.

Rothenberg, Jerome, and Pierre Joris, editors. *Poems for the Millennium: The University of California Book of Modern and Postmodern Poetry.* U of California P, 1995, 1998. 2 vols.

Ruskin, John. *Munera Pulveris.* John Wiley and Son, 1872.

Ruthven, K. K. *Ezra Pound as Literary Critic.* Routledge, 1990.

———. *A Guide to Ezra Pound's* Personae *(1926).* U of California P, 1969.

Sambell, Kay, et al. *Assessment for Learning in Higher Education.* Routledge, 2013.

Saussy, Haun, et al., editors. *The Chinese Written Character as a Medium for Poetry: A Critical Edition.* Fordham UP, 2008.

———. "Fenollosa Compounded: A Discrimination." Saussy et al., pp. 1–40.

Sawler, Trevor. "Hypertexting High Modernism: Ezra Pound's *Pisan Cantos* as Hypertext." 2012. U of New Brunswick, PhD dissertation.

Say, Jean Baptiste. *Treatise on Political Economy; or, Production, Distribution and Consumption of Wealth*. Edited by Clement C. Biddle, translated by C. R. Prinsep, Lippincott, Grambo, 1855, oll.libertyfund.org/ titles/274.

Schneidau, Herbert. *Ezra Pound: The Image and the Real*. Louisiana State UP, 1969.

Scholes, Robert, and Clifford Wulfman. *Modernism in the Magazines: An Introduction*. Yale UP, 2010.

Scott, Bonnie Kime, editor. *The Gender of Modernism: A Critical Anthology*. Indiana UP, 1990.

Sedgwick, Eve Kosofsky. *Between Men: English Literature and Male Homosocial Literature*. Columbia UP, 1985.

Sherry, Vincent. *Ezra Pound, Wyndham Lewis, and Radical Modernism*. Oxford UP, 1993.

———. *The Great War and the Language of Modernism*. Oxford UP, 2004.

Shockley, Evie. "Shifting the (Im)balance: Race and the Poetry Canon." *Boston Review*, 6 June 2013.

Sieburth, Richard. "In Pound We Trust: The Economy of Poetry / the Poetry of Economics." *Critical Inquiry*, vol. 14, no. 1, Autumn 1987, pp. 142–72.

———. *Instigations: Ezra Pound and Remy de Gourmont*. Harvard UP, 1978.

Sinclair, May. "The Reputation of Ezra Pound." Homberger, pp. 177–85.

Smith, Adam. *The Theory of Moral Sentiments. The Glasgow Edition of the Works and Correspondence of Adam Smith*, vol. 1, Oxford UP, 1976, p. 184.

Smith, Paul. *Pound Revised*. Croom Helm, 1983.

Smith, Stan. *The Origins of Modernism: Eliot, Pound, Yeats and the Rhetorics of Renewal*. Harvester Wheatsheaf, 1994.

Stark, Robert. *Ezra Pound's Early Verse and Lyric Tradition: A Jargoner's Apprenticeship*. Edinburgh UP, 2012.

Stasi, Paul, and Josephine Park, editors. *Ezra Pound in the Present: Essays on Pound's Contemporaneity*. Bloomsbury, 2016.

Stauder, Ellen Keck. "Poetics." Nadel, *Ezra Pound in Context*, pp. 23–32.

Stein, Gertrude. *Three Lives*. Penguin, 1990.

Stevens, Wallace. *The Necessary Angel: Essays on Reality and the Imagination*. Vintage, 1951.

Stock, Noel. *The Life of Ezra Pound*. 1970. Expanded edition, North Point Press, 1982.

———. *Reading* The Cantos*: A Study of Meaning in Ezra Pound*. Routledge and Kegan Paul, 1967.

Stoicheff, Peter. *The Hall of Mirrors:* Drafts and Fragments *and the End of Pound's* Cantos. U of Michigan P, 1995.

"The Story of the Armory Show." *Smithsonian*, www.si.edu/spotlight/armory-show.

Sun, Hong. "Pound's Quest for Confucian Ideals: The Chinese History Cantos." Qian, *Ezra Pound and China*, pp. 96–119.

Surette, Leon. *The Birth of Modernism. Ezra Pound, T. S. Eliot, W. B. Yeats, and the Occult.* McGill-Queen's UP, 1993.

———. *Dreams of a Totalitarian Utopia: Literary Modernism and Politics*. McGill-Queen's UP, 2011.

———. *A Light from Eleusis: A Study of Ezra Pound's* Cantos. Oxford UP, 1979.

———. *Pound in Purgatory: From Economic Radicalism to Anti-Semitism*. U of Illinois P, 1999.

———. Review of *Ezra Pound's Fascist Propaganda, 1935–1945*, by Matthew Feldman. *Make It New*, vol. 1, no. 2, 2014, pp. 8–10, makeitnew .ezrapoundsociety.org/volume-i/vol-i-no-2.

Swift, Daniel. *The Bughouse: The Poetry, Politics, and Madness of Ezra Pound*. Farrar, Straus and Giroux, 2017.

Sword, Helen. "Making It New: Innovative Approaches to Teaching Modernism." *Modernism/Modernity*, vol. 16, no. 3, 2009, pp. 471–73.

Taylor, Richard. *Variorum Edition of "Three Cantos" by Ezra Pound: A Prototype*. Boomerang P / Norbert AAS, 1991.

Ten Eyck, David. *Ezra Pound's Adams Cantos*. Bloomsbury, 2012.

Terrell, Carroll F. *A Companion to the* Cantos *of Ezra Pound*. 2 vols. 1980; 1984. U of California P, 1993.

Torrey, E. Fuller. *The Roots of Treason. Ezra Pound and the Secret of St. Elizabeths*. McGraw-Hill, 1984.

Tremblay, Tony. "Douglas, Major Clifford Hugh (1879–1952)." Tryphonopoulos and Adams, pp. 83–85.

Tryphonopoulos, Demetres P. *The Celestial Tradition: A Study of Ezra Pound's* The Cantos. Wilfrid Laurier UP, 1992.

Tryphonopoulos, Demetres P., and Stephen J. Adams, editors. *The Ezra Pound Encyclopedia*. Greenwood Press, 2005.

Turner, Catherine. *Marketing Modernism between the Two World Wars*. University of Massachusetts P, 2003.

Tyler, Royall, translator. *Hagoromo. Japanese Nō Dramas*, edited and translated by Tyler, Penguin, 1992, pp. 1–19.

———. Introduction. *Japanese Nō Dramas*, edited and translated by Tyler, Penguin, 1992, pp. 1–19.

Tytell, John. *Ezra Pound: The Solitary Volcano*. Anchor Press, 1987.

Venuti, Lawrence. *The Translator's Invisibility: A History of Translation*. Routledge, 1995.

Villon, François. *The Poems of François Villon*. Translated by H. De Vere Stacpoole, Hutchinson, 1913, warburg.sas.ac.uk/pdf/ebh450b2626373.pdf.

"Vorticism." *Tate*, tate.org.uk/art/art-terms/v/vorticism. 18 May 2017.

Wang, Guiming. *A Study of Ezra Pound's Translation: An Interpretation of* Cathay. Foreign Languages Press, 2012.

"Wealth." *Merriam-Webster Unabridged*. Britannica Digital Learning, 2019, unabridged.merriam-webster.com/unabridged/wealth.

Whistler, James Abbot McNeill. *Nocturne in Grey and Gold—Piccadilly*. 1881–1883. National Gallery of Ireland, onlinecollection.nationalgallery.ie/objects/11817.

White, Eric B. *Transatlantic Avant-Gardes: Little Magazines and Localist Modernism*. Edinburgh UP, 2013.

Wilde, Oscar. *The Artist as Critic: Critical Writings of Oscar Wilde*. Edited by Richard Ellman, U of Chicago P, 1969.

Wilhelm, James J. *Dante and Pound: The Epic of Judgment*. U of Maine P, 1974.

———. *Ezra Pound in London and Paris, 1908–1925*. Pennsylvania State UP, 1990.

———. *Ezra Pound, the Tragic Years, 1925–1972*. Pennsylvania State UP, 1990.

Wilkinson, Marguerite. *New Voices: An Introduction to Contemporary Poetry*. Macmillan, 1929.

Williams, William Carlos. *Paterson*. New Directions Publishing, 1963.

Wilson, Peter. *A Preface to Ezra Pound*. Routledge, 1996.

Witemeyer, Hugh. *The Poetry of Ezra Pound: Forms and Renewal, 1908–1920*. U of California P, 1969.

———. "*Selected Poems* (1949)." Tryphonopoulos and Adams, p. 267.

Xie, Ming. *Ezra Pound and the Appropriation of Chinese Poetry*. Routledge, 1999.

Yao, Steven G. "Toward a Prehistory of Asian American Verse: Pound, *Cathay*, and the Poetics of Chineseness." *Representations*, vol. 99, no. 1, Summer 2007, pp. 130–58.

———. *Translation and the Languages of Modernism Gender, Politics, Language*. Palgrave Macmillan, 2002.

Yao, Steven G., and Michael Coyle, editors. *Ezra Pound and Education*. National Poetry Foundation, 2012.

Yeats, W. B. Introduction. *Certain Noble Plays of Japan*, by Ezra Pound and Ernest Fenollosa, Cuala Press, 1916, pp. i–xiv.

Yip, Wai-lim. *Pound and the Eight Views of Xiao Xiang*. National U of Taiwan Publishing Center, 2008.

Zeng Baosun. *Zeng Baosun Huiyilu*. Longwen, 1989.

Zinnes, Harriet, editor. *Ezra Pound and the Visual Arts*. New Directions Publishing, 1980.